WATERLOO
BETRAYED

Stephen M. Beckett II

Waterloo Betrayed

Copyright © 2015 by Stephen M. Beckett II

Cover Photo by Miroslav Pejic

All brand names and product names used in this book are trademarks, registered trademarks, or trade names of their respective holders. I am not associated with any product or vendor in this book.

ISBN: 978-0-9863757-5-0

Published By Mapleflower House, LLC
130 Prominence Point Parkway
Suite 130 #106
Canton, GA 30114
www.mapleflowerhouse.com

Contents

Foreword i
Preface v
Acknowledgements vii
Notes to the Reader ix
Introduction 1
    The conventional history of Napoleon's return
    and the Waterloo Campaign 1
    A history of Betrayal 7

CHAPTER 1	The Bourbon Restoration 17
	Minister of War 20
	Louis-Philippe 21
CHAPTER 2	Napoleon's Return 25
	Soult's Proclamation 26
	Marshal Ney, The King's Last Hope 28
	Departures 29
CHAPTER 3	Empire! 31
	Soult Works hard for post of Major-Général 34
	Preparing for War 38
CHAPTER 4	June 1st - June 9th 43
CHAPTER 5	June 10th 51
CHAPTER 6	June 11th 57
CHAPTER 7	June 12th 61
CHAPTER 8	June 13th 69
CHAPTER 9	June 14th 77
	Strategic Surprise 79
	Surprise Spoiled 80
CHAPTER 10	June 15th 83
	Right Column 83
	Center Column 103
	Left Column 112

CHAPTER 11	June 15th, Evening	119
CHAPTER 12	June 16th	131
	Morning on the Left Wing	131
	Morning on the Right Wing	141
	Battle of Ligny	142
	Battle of Quatre Bras	150
	Opportunity Lost	152
CHAPTER 13	June 17th	157
	Pursuit	157
	Castiglione, Italy 1796	162
	Orders to Grouchy during the night of the 17th/18th	164
CHAPTER 14	June 18th	175
	Morning	175
	Afternoon	183
CHAPTER 15	Aftermath	189
CHAPTER 16	Closing Arguments	207
CHAPTER 17	Conclusion	213
APPENDIX 1	Instead of Soult	235
APPENDIX 2	Account of Exelmans Affair	241
APPENDIX 3	Questions of Treason	243
	Traitors of 1815	246
	Mauduit's suggestions of Treason	249
	On Traitors	262
APPENDIX 4	Traitors and Royalists	265
	Treasonous Correspondence with Ghent	267
	François Guizot's Troubles	273
APPENDIX 5	Lettow-Vorbeck	277
	Lettow-Vorbeck	277
APPENDIX 6	Gourgaud's Diaries	299
APPENDIX 7	On Censorship	305
APPENDIX 8	Traitors & Prisoners in German Sources	309
	Seconde-Lieutenant Johann von Wussow	309
	Major Zach	314
APPENDIX 9	Evidence Relating To Grouchy's Recall	317
	Baudus	317
	Marbot's Letter on June 26, 1815	319

Dupuy's Account of Waterloo	321
On Zenowicz and his Account	321
Colonel von Sachsen-Weimar Account	329

APPENDIX 10   Essay on Grouchy, the Recall, and the Prussians 331
- Evening and night of the 17th 332
- Morning and Afternoon of the 18th 332
- The Orders Sent to Grouchy 347

APPENDIX 11   Select Correspondence 355
- May 9, 1815 356
- June 1, 1815 357
- June 3, 1815 358
- June 5, 1815 362
- June 7, 1815 362
- June 10, 1815 364
- June 11, 1815 365
- June 12, 1815 366
- June 13, 1815 370
- June 14, 1815 375
- June 15, 1815 384
- June 16, 1815 401
- June 17, 1815 420
- June 18, 1815 427

APPENDIX 12   Translated Select Correspondence 435
- May 9, 1815 435
- June 1, 1815 435
- June 3, 1815 437
- June 7, 1815 440
- June 10, 1815 442
- June 11, 1815 443
- June 12, 1815 444
- June 13, 1815 447
- June 14, 1815 451
- June 15, 1815 460
- June 16, 1815 475
- June 17, 1815 492
- June 18, 1815 499

Bibliography 507
- Archives, Eyewitness Accounts, and Histories written by Combattants .. 507
- Military and Political History 511

About The Author 517

About The Translator 519

FOREWORD

Waterloo is consecrated ground to many Anglo-Saxons. While the Russians, Austrians, and even the Germans and Spaniards may be considered apathetic, the world's English-speaking visitors to the battlefield, Waterloo, *the last battle of the Napoleonic era*, behold it with the utmost significance. The victory, the ingression of British preponderance, the era of peace thereafter—these, and more, have since become endlessly drawn over topics. The French, au contraire, view the battle as being simultaneously an end and a beginning, for it was the end of an extraordinary epic, a fantastic adventure with Napoleon, and one that spanned fifteen years and stretched sensationally across Europe. But it was also a beginning. It is this concept, the battle as a *beginning*, that is the more important, thus its comprehension is essential.[1]

Though subsequent centuries have lost interest in Napoleon and the Battle of Waterloo, the 19th century French saw the battle as a new point de depart. For them, as for many contemporaneous Europeans (including the Italians, Polish, a number of Germans, etc.) with an aversion to the new European map and the objectives of the very "Ancien Regime" Sainte Alliance, the defeat of Napoleon at Waterloo was a pivotal event, the induction of a new era. This new era was marked by the expansion, albeit slow, of the ideas of the French Revolution; in particular, the principle of national sovereignty, embodied in the fight for liberal transformations of the European countries, though also in the principle of the right to self-determination.

But is this it? Is this the answer to the endless fascination with Waterloo, the cause of the inexhaustible vitality it holds? Of course not! What, then, holds the constant and concentrated celebration of this battle? It is a big battle, a drama, a tragedy (and for some a tragedy of fatalistic, metaphysical proportion, as in the beliefs of the Ancient Greeks, whose gods choose outcomes in the theatre of the world). It is also the most well known battle

---

[1] See Victor Hugo's chapter on Waterloo in *Les Miserables* which sums up the thoughts of the French Republicans about the battle seen as a beginning.

of all time. For what is now two hundred years, countless lines have been written about the epic struggle of the 18th of June 1815.

To better understand, it must be put in both a political and a military context. In regards the political[2], there is the strange and dramatic predicament of *The Hundred Days*. Here a considerable portion of the French nation hastened to again follow this man, Napoleon, in what he felt was his indissoluble duty, his life's mission; and, so, for a short time, the Revolution was resurrected. This French faction applauded the return of Napoleon from Elba Island in March 1815; it is doubtless they had strong hostility toward the Restoration, which was viewed as a return of the Ancien Régime.

So, during the Hundred days, France was still a nation divided, and more so than ever before. The Revolution and Ancien Régime were once again face to face. Bourbon legitimists, networks, and spies were working undercover. And even the French who supported Napoleon were divided: Bonapartists, Liberals, and Republicans did not agree on many things, except, of course, French independence… Moreover, the French people felt ambivalent; for, although many of them may not have liked the Bourbons, they were tired of war, fatigued from its many long years (1792-1814).

In terms of the military, there are several key points. Napoleon had to reorganize and rebuild an entire army. He was ultimately successful in doing so, but not without encountering great difficulties. For instance, the units had been reformed three times in one year. Many officers did not even know their men when they marched toward the enemy! Also, Napoleon did not dare use the Conscription of 1816 (young men aged 19); instead, he recalled only the 40,000 conscripts of 1815, who had been put under arms in 1814 (though they had not yet served), and he did this very late (the 9th of June). One must keep in mind that the Armée du Nord was *not* equivalent to the well-trained army of 1805; though it was certainly full of enthusiasts, it was hastily raised, which resulted in a lack of discipline and cohesiveness. Some officers and generals viewed themselves as: "Crusaders who follow the same adventures but without the duties towards each other," as one such man pointed out.

Regardless of these internal military obstacles, Napoleon decided to take the offensive in June of 1815, and, the Battle of Waterloo is the end of the advance of Napoleon in Belgium. But what was Napoleon's intended outcome? Some British writers, in sheer enthusiasm, have stated that Napoleon was trying to reclaim the Empire lost in the 1813-1814 campaigns against

---

2 Steven Englund, *Napoleon, a political life*, Harvard University Press, 2005.

the Russians, Austrians, Prussians, and Swedes. This is not serious. What Napoleon had hoped for was a victory, and to the outcome of disrupting the Coalition and forcing the Allies to renegotiate. It is uncertain, of course, whether the Allied Powers would have accepted Napoleon's conditions; not only had they declared Napoleon an outlaw, but they were also in a very powerful position, with a million soldiers at their disposal. Who would have thought that they would wait, arms at the ready?

Whatever his hopes were, Napoleon entered his last campaign with a fragile, though enthusiastic, army, with a divided nation behind him, and with the majority of the Liberal Deputies in the Chamber determined to keep his powers limited. To understand the history of this last campaign (and so far the Bicentenary as proven hopeless), it is absolutely essential that the following receive thorough attention: Firstly, *all* of the documents published; secondly, *all* of the remaining manuscripts; and thirdly, *all* of the historiography in French, English, German, and Dutch. But this has yet to be written. As it stands, *there is no definitive account of Waterloo and the campaign of 1815*.

And so enters Stephen Beckett. At a time when the Internet provides the opportunity to read many books and discover many sources online, and when the "Big Data" is seen as the (near) future in Science, and even History, Beckett set out to investigate and to test his ideas on Napoleon's 1815 campaign. I have been particularly interested in how he deployed his efforts, and in which directions, since we discussed French Napoleonic/1815 military problems and France's internal politics.

Beckett is well aware that the campaign and battles of 1815 have been widely scrutinized. Indeed, many episodes have been discussed *ad nauseam*: the question of Quatre-Bras and the orders given to Ney on 16th of June, what happened to d'Erlon's 1st corps on the 16th of June, the pursuit of Grouchy on the 17th-18th of June, the concentration of Wellington's army—and this only names a few. It is well known to Historians and readers alike that one of the most fascinating elements in historical enquiry is not to establish the sequence of events, but to discover the reason why they fell into a particular pattern! But precisely, it seems that a number of elements have been overlooked in the campaign, and this because the events BEFORE the 15th of June have been overlooked. By concentrating his work on the opening stages of the campaign, Beckett raises a number of questions, all of which deserved more effort long before his own work. For example, in his study of the staff work, he makes a very good point about the campaign, which he does by carefully using what remains of the orders given by Napoleon and his generals and their staffs to the Armée du Nord. And the English speaking readers will note with interest that some of these orders have never been translated before.

As the title suggests, themes central to the book are treachery, treason, and how Napoleon was betrayed. Quite frankly, for anyone familiar with, say, the *Wellington Dispatches*, where the evidence lies, this is not a new idea. Nor is the notion that a portion of the French army felt that they were betrayed *the very evening* of the 18th of June. However, the way Beckett handles the question is entirely new. He knows that all that can be done is to re-use the remaining original documents and old books/studies to re-examine actions in the light of what the generals knew (or did not know) at the time. And, at the same time, he accepts that this is to rely on circumstantial evidence. But he doesn't stop at this point, because he realizes that in detective literature as well as in History, the crime is not always committed by the obvious suspect, nor can the circumstantial evidence always reveal motive, and, furthermore, a decision may have been made for completely different reasons. He does as effective a job of finding the 'real' groups of traitors behind the hundred of pages of mainly mainstream history as we've seen thus far. Which is why, focusing on the various kinds of traitors, legitimists, cautious or incompetent commanders, and curious solidarities amongst generals and high-ranking officers, he presents Marshal Soult as the main traitor of the campaign.

With some bold ideas, we are enticed to better understand which obstacles led to the key events which, more than anything, destroyed Napoleon's plans. Though we must recall that, ultimately, Napoleon was responsible for choosing most of his men, and for this he was held accountable, as he is for having underestimated his enemies. Some readers will find that there are grey areas, that some points simply cannot be proven. However, it is well worth putting forth a hypothesis that challenges the conventional narrative of the 1815 campaign. We will probably never know with absolute certainty if what Soult did was indeed treason, or just incompetence, though regardless of the true cause, Stephen Beckett's work delineates in fine detail how Napoleon's brilliance was undermined.

Jean-Marc Largeaud (Université de Tours)
Author of *Napoléon et Waterloo: la défaite glorieuse de 1815 à nos jours.*

Preface

Why should one be interested in another book on the Waterloo campaign?

This particular work has no new research, an unoriginal thesis, and cannot be compared to literature. Yet despite these weaknesses, this work contains an original narrative that won't be found in other books. I know this because after having read many books on the events of 1815, I found this story by chance. This story has been hinted at by others, but it has never been told.

In the late 1980s, I worked on two Napoleonic computer wargames. Since that time, I have worked in the enterprise software field, but I have always wanted to get back to using the power of computing to simulate this time period. I decided that by building a database of correspondence between Napoleon's headquarters and the various corps during a campaign, I could find a data model and analytics which would help me build a simulation of operational command and control.

I thought the Waterloo campaign would be a great choice due to its small theater of operations and short duration. I soon found that the French defeat, the sudden end of the empire, and the Bourbon restoration had scattered the correspondence. It would take decades for archivists to restore the historical record, while much was lost forever. The early memoirs and histories had the advantage of eye witness testimony from surviving veterans, but also lacked a full and accurate record.

The challenge led to countless hours browsing online book archives, and slowly putting a record together. As I was starting at the moment Napoleon first decided on concentrating on the frontier, my research began more than two weeks before June 15th, 1815, the day the French crossed the frontier. I learned a lot of interesting things that I had never found in any of the books I had read, and was disappointed to learn that some prominent authors had even held back major details. Why?

An answer started to emerge while reading Gaspard Gourgaud's diaries. Gourgaud served on Napoleon's staff during the Waterloo campaign and after Waterloo became one of his closest aides, choosing to follow Napoleon into exile. Gourgaud wrote an account of the campaign that was published in 1818, and in 1899 his diaries, which were never meant to be seen, were finally published. In these works, Gourgaud reveals that neither he nor Napoleon knew very basic facts about the troop dispositions of the army on the evening of June 15th. In fact, not only did Napoleon not know the truth, but he had apparently been given an explanation for why a corps was out of position, and that explanation was also false.

Napoleon had been lied to during the campaign. But who would have lied to Napoleon during a campaign? A traitor. And one thing I had also discovered in this recent research was that there were many traitors in France and the French army during 1815… far more than I had ever realized.

Armed with the knowledge that Napoleon was being betrayed during the Waterloo campaign, I reevaluated every event from the moment he landed through his defeat on June 18th. Not surprisingly, numerous events made a lot more sense. In fact, all the mysteries of this campaign that have gnawed at me for years were now explained.

I hope that even if the reader is not convinced that treason was the motivation behind the events described, that value will still be found in the details provided in this work.

Stephen M. Beckett II, 2015

Acknowledgements

The answer is quite simple: the Registre d'ordres du major Général is lost. I'm quite certain Jean-Marc Largeaud did not expect when he gave me such a simple and definitive answer, that it would lead to the hundreds of emails I have sent him since! Without his patient and thorough responses, this project would not exist. I have tried, but failed, to find where his mastery of 19th Century France and the Waterloo campaign ends.

Jean-Marc also provided much welcomed assistance with the more difficult areas of the French translations when dealing with contemporary rhetoric, idioms, the old French, and military terms.

As the various ideas in this work came to life, my wife Lorrie provided an ear for hours of speculation and simulation which led me to the inescapable conclusion that the many mysteries of the Waterloo campaign were beyond the simple answer of the incompetence of Soult. It was very much a decision we made together to create this work, and she has provided enumerable hours since on every related element.

My father, the first Stephen M. Beckett, who sparked my love of military history with his vast library of books, and who provided enumerable challenges, critiques, and insight. My mother, for all the times she helped me so I could focus on this work. Thanks to Alissa and Spencer for putting up with my prolonged absence while pursuing this work.

John W. Kerns provided great assistance with the maps, and I hope some of the more complex maps he worked on will find a home on a website.

Thanks to the many test readers and their feedback, in no particular order: Chris Clarke, Spencer Beckett, Robnet Kerns, Duane Schell, Robert Bastian.

Special thanks to Oliver Schmidt, who challenged many elements, provided keen insights, and found numerous errors.

Jack Gill for his numerous comments, criticisms, and error finding that went far beyond my expectations, but for which I am very appreciative.

Kevin Kiley, for his pointed feedback which prevented me from becoming too comfortable or attached to my thoughts, leading me to return to numerous conclusions.

John Lee, for his feedback and encouragement, which was a real morale booster when it was needed the most!

Chris Rollet, whose message postings on the Napoleon1er.org forums are worthy of publication, and are, in themselves, a wonderful source that rival most of the books I have on my shelf. Chris also provided numerous sources as well as pointed out the unreliability of others. Finally, the essay he contributed (In the appendices) is an important contribution to the work.

Finally, without a doubt the single best source I found on the events and historical sources for the 1815 campaign in Belgium was Pierre de Wit's website: http://www.waterloo-campaign.nl/ This has to be considered the most definitive study of the campaign to date.

Notes to the Reader

This work is not a history of Napoleon's return in 1815 nor the Waterloo campaign. I realized very quickly that I could do nothing more but repeat the work of others, and in a mediocre fashion. Instead, this work is a study of specific individuals, their actions, and their correspondence. If you are unfamiliar with the campaign, you may need additional background to fully understand this work.

For a few minute primer on the campaign: http://napoleonistyka.atspace.com. About two-thirds down the page, there are 3 links for 1815; they cover Napoleon's landing through the battle of Waterloo.

For a detailed military treatment, the English translation of Henry Houssaye's book which focuses on the creation of Napoleon's army as well as offering a campaign analysis which draws from the French archives is freely available here: https://books.google.com/books?id=lVguAAAAMAAJ

William Siborne's book, which was written with the aide of numerous eye witness accounts on the Allied side, is freely available here: https://books.google.com/books?id=-8hCAAAAYAAJ

Many other free sources are listed in the bibliography.

The maps used in this book are based on a template that has largely been inspired by a map included in Siborne's history of the campaign. It can be found here: http://commons.wikimedia.org/wiki/File:Part_of_Belgium_engraved_by_J._Kirkwood.jpg

See www.mapleflowerhouse.com for resources from the book, such as maps.

In the Appendices, Select Correspondence, in both the original French and English, is given in chronological order along with their sources. Thus, when correspondence is used during the narrative, it will refer to the original French entry in the Select Correspondence Appendix where one will find the sourcing as well.

Introduction

The conventional history of Napoleon's return and the Waterloo Campaign

For the last 100 years, the conventional history of the Waterloo campaign has largely been unchanged.

Napoleon's genius was on full display as brilliant staff work concentrated the French army on the Belgian frontier in June of 1815; but Soult's inexperience and Napoleon's arrogance led to the French defeat at Waterloo.

In the afternoon of March 1, 1815, a fleet consisting of one warship and six smaller vessels dropped anchor off Golfe-Juan on the southeastern coast of France, in view of what are today the most luxurious vacation spots on the Côte d'Azur but where then miserable fishing villages clinging to the edge of an inhospitable landscape. As soon as they were anchored, the ships lowered their small boats. Shortly thereafter squads of soldiers began to disembark on the shore, despite the protests of the flabbergasted customs official who had rushed to the scene to contest this highly irregular landing. The first troops to reach solid ground went to knock on the gates of the nearby French fort at Antibes and were immediately placed under arrest; but the small boats kept bringing ashore other soldiers, and soon more than a thousand grenadiers had been disembarked, along with two cannon and an entire squadron of lancers who spoke Polish among themselves. Finally, toward evening, the leader of this host came ashore in person, walking over an improvised gangway, which his men, standing in water to their waists, held up for him; and an officer was sent to notify the commandant of the fort that the emperor Napoleon, after *ten months of exile on the island of Elba, had returned to France to reclaim his throne.*³

ALESSANDRO BARBERO, *The Battle*

*News that Napoleon had escaped from Elba first reached Vienna on the evening of 7 March 1815. Three days later, the Congress heard he had landed on the southern coast of France. From there Napoleon began a triumphant march to Paris while the King Louis and his supporters fled into exile once again.*⁴

PETER HOFSCHRÖER, *1815, The Waterloo Campaign*

In the general confusion the King and Soult were among the few people in Paris who kept calm. Against the advice of Soult, Blacas and some others, who thought that action rather than deliberation was needed, the Chambers were reconvened and were addressed in dignified terms by the old King, while, inevitably in the circumstances, Soult produced in the Moniteur a proclamation in suitably vitriolic terms against the returned Emperor, to the effect that "Napoleon had no right to see France again! So let us rally around our King, the father of his people... the worthy descendant of Henry of Navarre!" He also dealt vigorously and competently with the incipient mutiny in the north. His old friend, Mortier, was sent northward with orders to shoot the leaders of the revolt if necessary. Mortier succeeded in having the ringleaders arrested and the revolt collapsed.

However, despite all his energetic if last minute activities, Soult's days as Minister of War were numbered. The disastrous events in the south, with regiment after regiment going over to Napoleon, with Ney following suit and the royal princes fleeing in panic, were in no way Soult's fault but an immediate scapegoat was needed. Had the Minister sent an army to Lyons that would welcome the returning Emperor? Was his opposition to the summoning of the Chambers another example of his treachery? Had his 'agents' sabotaged the Chappe semaphore system? In fact there was no question of Soult betraying the King and each suggestion to this effect was

---

3 Barbero, Alessandro (2009-05-26). The Battle (Kindle Locations 71-72). Bloomsbury Publishing Plc. Kindle Edition.
4 Hofschröer, Peter, *1815, The Waterloo Campaign*, Greenhill Books, 1998, p. 39

more absurd than the last. The best evidence for Soult's loyalty was given by Napoleon himself. Long afterwards he talked frankly to Dr O'Meara in St Helena. "Appearances may have been against Soult but he did not betray the King. He was no way privy to my return: indeed he thought I was quite mad when he first heard that I had landed." Wellington, too, no doubt based on the knowledge he had acquired as British ambassador in Paris, strongly defended, in discussion later, Soult's decision to send troops to Lyons which were there as a potential threat to Murat and for no other reason.

But most of the King's ministers, let by the Abbé Montesquieu, came to quite a different conclusion at the time and they demanded Soult's resignation. The King, while still maintaining confidence in him, felt that he would have to resign in order to appease the indignant and highly embarrassed royal advisers after almost the whole regular army had gone over to the Emperor. When Soult handed the king his sword, the King returned it saying he was sure it would only be drawn in his service – an ironic moment! At the end of his last ministerial meeting Soult was escorted out of the Tuileries by two of the men who had now become his admirers, Blacas and Vitrolles. At the gate outside, Soult raised his plumed hat in salute to the considerable crowd gathered on the pavement. He then made a dignified departure with his family to his country estate at Villeneuve L'Etang. His short but hectic three months as Minister of War was at an end. He was succeeded by his old enemy, Clarke, the crafty Duke of Feltre.[5]

Sir Peter Hayman, *Soult*

On 13 March the Congress declared Napoleon an Outlaw. On 25 March, the four Great Powers – Austria, Russia, Britain and Prussia, – formed a new coalition, reviving the terms of the Treaty of Chaumont of 1 March 1814. According to this Treaty, if the balance of power in Europe were disturbed, each of the Great Powers would be required to raise or fund an army of 150,000 men to restore it.[6]

Peter Hofschröer, *1815, The Waterloo Campaign*

---

5 Hayman, Peter, *Soult*, 1990, pp. 219-220
6 Hofschröer, Peter, *1815, The Waterloo Campaign*, Greenhill Books, 1998, p. 39

Soult, who had had no experience of such an important post, and although he had been Louis XVIII's Minister of War, was appointed chief of staff in Berthier's place. It was an unfortunate choice. But there seemed so few alternatives. Napoleon felt that Davout could not be spared from his duties as Minister of War in Paris; Murat, who had rashly moved north with an untrustworthy Neapolitan army in April, had been routed at Tolentino and was now in disgrace; Junot's mind had given way as a result of the Russian campaign; Suchet, it was felt, should not leave his command in the Alps. There was Ney and there was Grouchy; but although both of these men were brave officers neither was to be fully trusted in independent command.

Yet, with or without trustworthy generals, the war would have to be fought. The allied sovereigns had still been in Vienna when it was learned that Napoleon had returned from Elba, and it had only taken a fortnight to draw up the terms of a military alliance against the man who was condemned as an outlaw. A plan had been formed for six armies to cross the French frontier simultaneously – an Anglo-Dutch-Belgian army of 93,000 under Wellington, a Prussian army of 117,000 under Blücher, a 200,000-strong army of Austrians and Bavarians, 150,000 Russians, and two Austrian-Piedmontese armies, which would cross the Alps and march on Lyons and Provence; more than half a million men in all.

    This threat had to be met, and would be met in Belgium. A campaign there offered the best chance of rallying the people of France behind him.[7]

Christopher Hibbert, Waterloo

The French concentration for the offensive had commenced on June 6 and was practically complete by the time the Emperor reached his forward headquarters at Beaumont on the 14th. Brilliant staff work resulted in the secret concentration of five corps, the Imperial Guard and the reserve cavalry into a zone of thirty kilometers square from a dispersal area of more than two hundred miles.[8]

David Chandler, The Campaigns of Napoleon

---

7 Hibbert, Christopher, *Waterloo*, 2003, pp. 98-99
8 Chandler, David, *The Campaigns of Napoleon*, 1966, p. 1020.

Introduction

Napoleon struck on June 15. Nobody expected him.

He had massed l'Armée du Nord around the small city of Beaumont in an area some six hours' marching time in width and three in depth. On June 7 the French frontiers had been closed; no travelers could pass, no ships might sail. Several misleading rumors had been leaked as to Napoleon's plans. (Allied agents swallowed them.) While the troops along the frontier carried on their routine activities and Napoleon and the Guard remained highly visible in Paris, the rest of Nord had shifted into this concentration area swiftly and secretly, bivouacking under the cover of its hills and woods. Some regiments had to complete their organization as they came. Soult had managed to forget the Cavalry Reserve's four corps; Grouchy pulled them in, but it was late and some of them like the 9th Cuirassiers, shifting from Colmar on the Rhine frontier—had to force their marches, getting only two or three hours' sleep a night. Brigadier Pilloy marveled that their horses stood such treatment. Some didn't; many others were sadly jaded and hardly in condition to charge British squares.

Napoleon's offensive on June 15 had been scrupulously planned. Nord would advance in three columns behind a cavalry screen, with engineers and pontonniers right behind the light infantry advance guards. Reconnaissance would be pushed to the front and flanks, and intelligence reports made to Napoleon at every opportunity.

Pajol's cavalry corps would lead the center column with Vandamme's III Corps following it. Pajol moved out on schedule, Vandamme was four hours late. Soult had sent a single staff officer with Vandamme's orders, and Vandamme couldn't be found. (Speculations are various, but he apparently had left his headquarters to sleep in a comfortable farmhouse, which possibly is putting it politely.) Berthier's hellions would have found him and had him out of bed; Soult's amateur got lost, had a bad fall, and broke his leg (possibly the origin of that old nursery rhyme, 'For want of a nail...'). The orders were not delivered, and Soult never checked to learn if they had been.

The campaign proceeded in that same thwarted fashion. At Ligny the next day, with only 67,000 soldiers, Napoleon fought one of his finest battles, routing Blücher's 83,000 Prussians out of a strong position, inflicting 34,000 casualties to his own 11,500. But his planned complete destruction of Blücher's army was bollixed by another staff foul-up that kept D'Erlon's I Corps wandering uselessly between Ligny and Ney's mismanaged fight against Wellington at Quatre Bras.

After Ligny, Napoleon detached Grouchy with 33,000 men to follow up the Prussians and keep them from interfering while he dealt with Wellington. That left his cavalry without a commander, who might have kept Ney from committing it prematurely at Waterloo. And Soult did not bother to establish a courier line to keep Grouchy in constant communication with Napoleon's headquarters.[9]

JOHN R. ELTING, *Swords Around a Throne*

Napoleon, with the reserves, made a late start on 17 June and joined Ney at Quatre Bras at 13:00 to attack Wellington's army but found the position empty. The French pursued Wellington but the result was only a brief cavalry skirmish in Genappe just as torrential rain set in for the night. Before leaving Ligny, Napoleon ordered Grouchy, commander of the right wing, to follow up the retreating Prussians with 33,000 men. A late start, uncertainty about the direction the Prussians had taken and the vagueness of the orders given to him meant that Grouchy was too late to prevent the Prussian army reaching Wavre, from where it could march to support Wellington. By the end of 17 June, Wellington's army had arrived at its position at Waterloo, with the main body of Napoleon's army following. Blücher's army was gathering in and around Wavre, around 8 miles (13 km) to the east of the city.

Although Napoleon ordered Ney to have the men properly fed and their equipment checked 'so that at nine o'clock precisely each of them is ready and there can be a battle', it was to be another two hours before the fighting started. By then Napoleon had held a breakfast conference of senior officers in the dining room next to his bedroom at Le Caillou. When several of the generals who had fought Wellington in Spain, such as Soult, Reille, and Foy, suggested that he should not rely on being able to break through the British infantry with

---

9 Elting, John R. (2009-06-16). *Swords Around A Throne* (pp. 656-657). Da Capo Press. Kindle Edition.

Introduction

> *ease, Napoleon replied, 'Because you've been beaten by Wellington, you consider him to be a good general. I say that he's a bad general and that the English are bad troops. It will be a lunchtime affair!' A clearly unconvinced Soult could only say, 'I hope so!' These seemingly hubristic remarks completely contradicted his real and oft-stated views about Wellington and the British, and must be ascribed to his need to encourage his lieutenants just hours away from a major battle.*[10]
>
> Andrew Roberts, *Napoleon a Life*

A history of Betrayal

When Napoleon escaped his first exile and returned to France in 1815, his longtime *Major-Général*, Berthier, did not join his cause. As Major General, Berthier was responsible for the writing and distribution of Napoleon's orders. Napoleon had Berthier at his side for all his greatest victories.

With Berthier unavailable, Napoleon appointed another of his Marshals, Jean-de-Dieu Soult, to the position of *Major-Général*. History tells us that Soult performed poorly during the Waterloo campaign. The opinion of Soult's performance as *Major-Général* in 1815 has so often been described as ineffective that it has reached factual status, usually stated without substantiation. In reality, he performed brilliantly. Soult betrayed Napoleon before French troops had even crossed the frontier. With unparalleled subtlety he undermined Napoleon's plans on each day of the campaign all the while enabling others to become targets of blame.[11]

The Waterloo disaster certainly didn't tarnish Soult. Within a few years after the defeat, Soult had reentered Paris with his wealth and titles intact, and would go on to have a political career that by any measure surpassed his accomplishments on the battlefield, even rising to the position of Prime Minister of France on three separate occasions.

Marshal Soult had a most successful career in all his pursuits… except, it seems, for two weeks in June, 1815.

Napoleon died in exile on a small island in the South Atlantic on May 5th, 1821. He is best remembered as the loser of the battle of Waterloo.

---

10 Roberts, Andrew, *Napoleon a Life*, Penguin, 2014, pp. 759-760
11 The families of Ney and Grouchy published numerous accounts of the campaign of 1815 in an attempt to restore their honor.

The bitter truth is that he was betrayed.[12]

The French soldiers knew, and they tried to tell us. The cry of "We are betrayed!" is a well-known anecdote from the close of the battle of Waterloo. This has often been linked to defections from I Corps on the 16th of June and earlier, and certainly the numerous traitors within the Army must have rattled the soldiers. But the fact is the army was complaining of treason long before the campaign had even begun. As Henry Houssaye[13] wrote:

> *Defeat was only possible in case of treachery, but then the soldiers imagined traitors to exist everywhere. "Do not employ the marshals during the campaign," somebody wrote to Napoleon. Complaints and denunciations poured into the War Office and to the officials at the Tuileries, concerning officers who had shown leanings towards the Bourbons or the Orleanists under the preceding reign, or who were merely guilty of having a handle to their name.*[14]

Houssaye then goes on to briefly touch upon several suspected conspiracies, including the remarkable distribution of "ball cartridges containing, not gun-powder, but bran, clay, and iron filings."

But did the soldiers really "imagine" traitors?

During the weeks leading up to the campaign, and during every day of the campaign, French soldiers went over to the Allies delivering valuable intelligence. In the months before the hostilities began, moles within the government were sending detailed reports on the composition and location of the army to the King's ministers at Ghent,[15] the city in Belgium that the

---

12 Napoleon's return to the throne in 1815 was a revolution, and the resulting conflict was very much a civil war with the European powers allied with the Bourbon cause. Can there be traitors in such a conflict? Certainly, those that served the Empire yet aided the Bourbons and their allies were traitors to their countrymen. Those that served the King in Ghent were enemies of France under Napoleon. The King felt the same way, and fixed the date as March 22nd. For the purpose of this work, a traitor will be defined as anyone who served the Empire on April 1st and later deserted or aided the Bourbons.

13 Houssaye's work on the Waterloo campaign was one of the most thorough examinations of the French operations that had been done to date with extensive use of the archives.

14 Houssaye, Henry, *1815, Waterloo*, Translated from the 31st edition, London, 1900, p. 43 http://books.google.com/books?id=xWBAAAAAYAAJ

15 Romberg et Malet, *Louis XVIII et les Cent-Jours a Gand*, Volume II, (Paris, 1902), pp. 242-243, 258-259

king fled to after Napoleon's return. The Ministry of Police was aware of groups of conspirators, including soldiers, meeting in Paris and in communication with the Allies.[16]

Was Napoleon fully aware of the extent of the conspiracies working against him? One can assume not, considering his Minister of Police, Joseph Fouché, was one of the ringleaders. Speaking to a King's aide prior to Napoleon's arrival in Paris, Fouché said:

> *Our position is quite logical. Resistance is useless. I will be even more frank with you. We shall join forces with the tyrant. I whom he detests, I who abhor him, I shall resume the Ministry of Police under him two days after his return. He cannot do without me. When he thinks himself strong enough he will try to destroy us; but we shall not give him enough time. Within three months from now we will bring him down.*[17]

After Waterloo, Fouché would provide the final nail in the coffin, organizing political dissent that would demand Napoleon's abdication and would eventually see Napoleon exiled to Saint Helena.

While Napoleon's admirers clearly see his defeat in 1815 as the result of betrayal or the incompetence of others, the consensus is not so forgiving. The expression *to meet one's Waterloo* is not generally believed to mean *to have performed brilliantly yet been let down or betrayed*. On the contrary, it has come to mean *suffering an ultimate and career ending defeat*. The cries of treason in 1815 have been explained away as nothing more than excuses and sour grapes. Worse are the claims the treason had minimal impact.

One reason the treason narrative has not received much attention is that it's difficult to link the accepted acts of treason with any one of the myriad of mistakes that doomed Napoleon in 1815. Marshal Ney's tardiness at Quatre

---

http://books.google.com/books?id=Facf9oBJHqYC
16 Stefane-Pol, *De Robespierre a Fouche, Notes de Police*, etc., Paris, s.d., In-12, Rapport anonyme a Fouche, Paris, June 21, 147-152. This was cited by Le Gallo, Emile in *Les Cent-Jours : essai sur l'histoire intérieure de la France depuis le retour de l'île d'Elbe jusqu'à la nouvelle de Waterloo*, Paris, 1923, p. 331
http://gallica.bnf.fr/ark:/12148/bpt6k5427468n
17 Castlereagh, Robert Stewart, Viscount, *Correspondence, Despatches, and other papers*, Volume 10, London, 1853, p. 339
http://books.google.com/books?id=OysMAAAAYAAJ

Bras or his slaughter of the cavalry at Waterloo led members of Napoleon's entourage to accuse him of treason before the campaign even ended, yet it was the Bourbons that executed Ney for treason against the King! Marshal Grouchy's lethargy pursuing the Prussians, his refusal to "march to the sound of the guns" and his absence at Waterloo left him defending his competence the rest of his life, but there have been few credible accusations of treason. A plethora of theories thrive on the internet mixing Grouchy with the Rothschild family, the masons, and UFOs.[18] Even the model of fidelity, Davout, who continued to occupy Hamburg on the Emperor's orders for more than a month after Napoleon's first abdication, has been the target of suspicion for how he turned on Napoleon after Waterloo and was a patsy to Fouché.

But few have analyzed Soult's performance from the perspective of treason. By doing this, what emerges are not mistakes, but willful acts by a mastermind who understood that in a theater of operations barely three days march wide or deep, the slightest delays would have fatal consequences. As will be outlined, Soult was able to defeat every plan of Napoleon without attracting any significant suspicion. At Saint Helena, Napoleon had his complaints of Soult's performance, but at the same time he vouched for his fidelity when O'Meara directly asked about Soult, and even described Soult as a good *Major-Général*:

> *I asked his opinion about Soult, and mentioned that I had heard some persons place him in the rank next to himself as a general. He replied, 'He is an excellent Minister for War, or Chief of the Staff: one who knows much better the arrangement of an army than how to command in chief.'*[19]

This does not mean that Soult was beyond suspicion. Hippolyte de Mauduit, a sergeant in the 1st Grenadiers of the Old Guard during the 1815 campaign, boldly challenged Soult to explain his conduct in his 2 volume

---

18 An internet search involving the Rothschild family and almost any significant historical event of the last few hundred years reveals a cornucopia of nonsense. For those inclined to take this journey, or who simply want a good laugh, see Maj. Gen., Count Cherep-Spiridovich's *The Secret World Government*.

19 O'Meara, Barry Edward, *Napoleon at St. Helena*, Volume 1, 1889, p. 107 http://books.google.com/books/download/Napoleon_at_St_Helena.pdf?id=sHAuAAAAMAAJ

history of the 1814 and 1815 campaigns[20], the first edition published while Soult was still living. In several of his footnotes, he either implied or outright suggested Soult was a traitor.

Mauduit's work makes extensive use of the existing published dispatches from the campaign as well as unpublished letters with fellow veterans, though conspicuously absent were materials from officers on Soult's staff. The lone exception was by Colonel Baudus, a royalist who was also Soult's ADC. Additionally, Mauduit was working with a severe disadvantage, one that was only partially remedied by the late 19th century: the military records for the 1815 campaign were missing. Thus Mauduit was forced, like all those who studied the campaign during the middle 19th century, to piece together the events of 1815 with scarce primary sources as a result of the chilling effect of the politics during the decades after Napoleon's defeat.

After the second restoration, the Bourbons persecuted Bonapartists in a period called the White Terror.[21] Even after the White Terror ended, publishing material that supported or was positive about Napoleon was limited.[22]

Bonapartism was a strong political force in France that both the Bourbon and, after the July revolution of 1830, Orleanist monarchies had to deal with. On March 1st, 1815, Napoleon landed on the south of France with less than a 1000 men and by March 20th, the King was fleeing to Ghent, and Napoleon, aided by foes of the Monarchy, was back on the throne. The fact that Napoleon's supporters felt he was betrayed in 1814, not defeated, greatly aided his cause. In 1848, *over thirty years later*, the July Monarchy fell and the Second Republic was established. Louis-Napoleon Bonaparte was elected its first President. When he was prevented constitutionally from running for president for a second term, he declared himself emperor and ruled for 18 years. This was the power of the name Napoleon, and proof that the threat of Bonapartism to the Bourbon and Orleanist's monarchies was real.

While many dispatches and artifacts from the campaign were distributed across private collections and the veterans from the campaign were excellent

---

20 Mauduit, Hippolyte, *Les Derniers Jours de La Grand Armee* (1847) 2 Volumes http://books.google.com/books?id=qdlBAAAAcAAJ
Second Edition (1854):
http://gallica.bnf.fr/Search?adva=1&adv=1&tri=&t_relation=%22cb30909342v%22&lang=en
21 Resnick, Daniel, *The White Terror and the Political Reaction after Waterloo*, Cambridge, 1966
22 Polowetzky, Michael, *A Bond never Broken : The Relations Between Napoleon and the Authors of France*, Fairleigh Dickinson Univ Press, 1993, p. 167
http://books.google.com/books?isbn=0838634826

sources that many 19th century histories were based on, key information was still held in the military archives. Under the Bourbons, this information was not available to anyone looking to defend the reputation of Napoleon. If he had been betrayed in 1814, he had been decisively defeated in 1815, and the Bourbons would not tolerate any explanation other than the fault was his alone.

The July Monarchy was friendlier to the legacy of the Empire, and even organized the return of Napoleon's remains. During this time, there were many books published on the First Empire, including Mauduit's. However, those seeking the truth on the Waterloo campaign had yet an even greater obstacle, for who did Louis Philippe appoint as Minister of War and in charge of the *Ministre de la Guerre* with oversight of the archives? Marshal Soult! Thus, the most incriminating documentation was lost to generations of historians, and we can assume that much was lost forever. This is not the first time Soult has been suspected of pruning the archives of incriminating evidence, as Jacques Garnier wrote in *Dictionnaire Napoléon*:

> He was a good general, composed, with a sharp eye, but his character seems not to have been at the height of military form. He was the "adulator" of all the powers, and was even accused of removing from the archives the documents that were likely to disserve him.[23]

The vast majority of books that focus on a military narrative of the Waterloo campaign have a fatal flaw. They gloss over what is commonly believed to be the masterful concentration of the French army on the frontier below Charleroi, and then start the detailed discussions with the **15th of June**. By doing so, one has already lost the initial clues to Soult's treason which had completely sabotaged Napoleon's masterful plan.

Likewise, the detailed studies of the concentration[24] have either hidden Soult's questionable actions, or have questioned some of Soult's actions, but

---

23   Tulard, Jean, "Soult", *Dictionnaire Napoléon*, 1989, p. 1586
24   Jean-Charles-Louis Regnault, *La Campagne de 1815 : mobilization et concentration*, Paris, 1935 and J. T. Oosterman, "Opmarsch en concentratie van het Fransche leger in Juni 1815", *Militaire Spectator* in 1912 and 1913
http://www.kvbk-cultureelerfgoed.nl/MS_PDF/1913/1913-0001-01-0003.PDF
http://www.kvbk-cultureelerfgoed.nl/MS_PDF/1912/1912-0769-01-0141.PDF
Much of Lettow-Vorbeck's analysis of the French concentration is included in this work, "Lettow-Vorbeck" on page 277.

without the full narrative of the entire 100 days and the detailed analysis of the rest of the campaign. The net effect of these disparate analyses in their respective vacuums is that Soult's willful culpability is lost.

In some ways this does a disservice to Soult. My thesis is that far from being ineffective in June of 1815, Soult was brilliant. Each of his actions was part of a well-choreographed design that misled Napoleon into thinking his plans were being realized when in fact they were not. Each opportunity was painfully missed by mere hours, and from Napoleon's point of view, always due to the fault of others or simply the fate of war.

In fact, Soult should be considered one of history's most brilliant masterminds who engineered the final defeat of one of the world's great captains. Soult went on to take his place as his country's supreme military personality while historians have been left debating the actions of his peers.

In this work the daily correspondence of the campaign shall be reviewed from the very beginning of the concentration on the frontier. It is a study of correspondence, not battles, and will lack the thrilling accounts of heroism that dominates the Waterloo literature. In its stead will be the plain and simple account of orders being rewritten and information being withheld that directly led to the defeat of history's greatest General.

PART I
RETURN OF THE EAGLE

CHAPTER I
THE BOURBON RESTORATION

Soldiers of my Old Guard: I bid you farewell. For twenty years I have constantly accompanied you on the road to honor and glory. In these latter times, as in the days of our prosperity, you have invariably been models of courage and fidelity. With men such as you our cause could not be lost; but the war would have been interminable; it would have been civil war, and that would have entailed deeper misfortunes on France.

I have sacrificed all of my interests to those of the country.

I go, but you, my friends, will continue to serve France. Her happiness was my only thought. It will still be the object of my wishes. Do not regret my fate; if I have consented to survive, it is to serve your glory. I intend to write the history of the great achievements we have performed together. Adieu, my friends. Would I could press you all to my heart

NAPOLEON'S FAREWELL ADDRESS TO HIS OLD GUARD,
April 20th, 1814

IN APRIL, 1814, AFTER A brilliant campaign, Napoleon abdicated the French throne and was exiled to Elba. He had been rushing to the defense of Paris when he was notified that Marshal Marmont, *Duc de Raguse*, had marched his troops over to the enemy.

Paris was lost.

Raguser, "to betray," entered the French language.

The Allies restored the Bourbons to the throne, but on the condition that a constitution be adopted. The Charter of 1814 was bicameral and established an elected Chamber of Deputies, and a hereditary Chamber of Peers appointed by the King. While many Imperial Senators were included in the Chamber of Peers, the King chose to exclude certain individuals for prior bad acts or opinions. Among these was Marshal Soult, "…the most consummate of Napoleon's lieutenants, *suspected of a personal ambition, reaching even to the throne* [emphasis added], and who had prolonged the struggle at Toulouse, by a battle fought, it was said, more for his own popularity than for the country."[25]

Soult's qualities as a general have been debated, but few would describe him as lacking in ambition. "On the establishment of the Consulate, Soult, *whose politics rested solely on personal ambition, and not on principle* [emphasis added], at once divined the aims of Bonaparte,"[26] writes one biographer. In John Cam Hobhouse's diaries of his stay in Paris during 1815, he writes in the April 18th entry of the rumor that Soult desired to "… embroil the military and civilians as to create a disturbance and *offer himself for the crown.* [Emphasis added]"[27]

Furthermore, Soult had earned the nick-name "King Nicolas" for a suspected attempt to gain the throne of Portugal. Amazingly, or maybe because Soult's ambition was so widely known, the name "Nicolas" has stuck with Soult to this day. A fawning biographer, Sir Peter Hayman, writes:

> *There was, too, the* canard *about 'Roi Nicolas', initiated as Professor Tulard, the historian, suggests by his arch-enemy, Ney, when Soult had tried desperately to find a solution for France's Portuguese problem. The derisory name 'Nicolas' has stuck to him quite undeservedly ever since.*
>
> *The name 'Nicholas', which became attached to him over the years, appears nowhere in his baptismal, marriage or death*

---

25 Lamartine, Alphonse, *The History of the Restoration of Monarchy in France*, Volume 1 ,France, 1854, p. 458
http://books.google.com/books?id=GXEuAAAAMAAJ
26 Dunn-Pattison, R. P., *Napoleon's Marshals*, 1909, p. 80
http://www.gutenberg.org/files/34400/34400-h/34400-h.htm
27 John Cam Hobhouse was a Whig and vocal detractor of the Bourbons. His diaries were accessed from http://petercochran.wordpress.com/hobhouses-diary/

certificates, nor in his patents of appointment as a marshal of the Empire or as a peer of France.[28]

Decades later while serving in Louis-Philippe's government, Soult continued to make a spectacle of himself with his unrestrained ambition:

> *It is well known that, in their familiar communications, the king and the Duke of Orleans professed, at that time, the most sovereign contempt for Marshal Soult, and often amused themselves with laughing at the gasconading efforts of that minister to get himself appointed president of the council.*[29]

For a man with such ambition, his career under Napoleon must have been one of frustration. While his peers were gaining titles based on legendary military triumphs, Soult had to settle for praise. On December 2nd, 1805, Napoleon won his greatest victory at Austerlitz over the combined forces of Austria and Russia. There, it was Soult's IV Corps that shattered the allied center. After the battle, Napoleon would declare Soult to be the best tactician in Europe. There would be no *Duc d'Austerlitz*, however, as Napoleon kept the accolades for Austerlitz for himself. Soult eventually was made the *Duc de Dalmatie*, a title for a place he had never been, simply because it was available.[30]

On April 10th, 1814, Soult defeated Wellington at Toulouse[31], and only heard of Napoleon's abdication after the battle. Shortly thereafter, relieved of command, Soult returned to his residence in Paris, anxious to reconcile with the new regime. A couple of months later, and with the assistance of a former aide-de-camp[32], Soult was given command of the very royalist 13th

---

28 Hayman, Peter, *Napoleon's Maligned Marshal*, London, 1990, pp. 13, 17
29 Sarrans, Bernard, *Lafayette, Louis-Philippe, and the revolution of 1830; or, History of the events and men of July*, Volume 2 , London, 1832, p. 38
http://books.google.com/books?id=4ibWlqU_N4EC
30 Hayman, Peter, *Napoleon's Maligned Marshal*, London, 1990, p. 81
31 While both sides claim victory, Soult inflicted a significantly higher percentage of casualties while denying Wellington's goals. If the reader disagrees, just bear in mind that what is important for this narrative is what Soult believed.
32 An aide-de-camp was a military officer who provided assistance to a superior officer, and might serve on the superior's staff for many years and could take many roles including secretary, orderly, and leading units in combat.

military division headquartered at Rennes in Brittany.[33] This command, in time, would prove to be most opportune.

Minister of War

France may have been relieved for the end of war, but it did not take long for the nobility and returning *émigrés* to remind the people why there had been a revolution. As Vincent Cronin wrote:

> *The whole family were set on putting the clock back. The tricolor was replaced by the white flag, Napoleon's image removed from the Legion of Honour, the old Household Corps revived, thousands of regular officers discharged on half pay, while plum jobs were given to returned émigrés in powdered wigs.*[34]

The discontent of the Army, and especially that of the half-pay officers that congregated in the cafés of Paris, breeding discontent, was clearly the greatest threat to the monarchy. By December, 1814, the King decided that he needed a stronger Minister of War.

Soult had been busy integrating himself with the new regime. Within his military district, he supervised the construction of a memorial at Quiberon to royalists who invaded Republican France with the help of England. They had been defeated with many hundreds executed. According to Adolphe Thiers, "The astonishment of the army was as great as the satisfaction of the royalists."[35]

Once completing this project, Soult sought inclusion in the peerage that he had been previously excluded from. The favor he gained in the King's eyes was so great that on December 3rd, 1814, Soult was appointed Minister of War. Soult's ambition was paying off.

In his zeal to impress his new master, Soult further alienated his Imperial comrades. He instituted an internal exile of the half-pay officers ordering them to live at the towns or villages of their birth. Shortly after this decree,

---

33 Hayman, Peter, *Napoleon's Maligned Marshal*, London, 1990, p. 211
34 Cronin, Vincent, *Napoleon*, Harper Collins, London, 1996, p. 385
35 Thiers, Adolphe, *History of the Consolate and Empire of France under Napoleon*, Volume 5, 1863, p. 345

a letter from General Exelmans, then the Inspector-General of Cavalry, to Murat, then sitting on the throne of Naples, was intercepted. In the letter, the strongly Bonapartist Exelmans stated that if the European powers decided to remove Murat from the throne of Naples, "... a thousand French officers trained in Your Majesty's school would have flown to your assistance." Soult seized upon this to charge Exelmans with espionage, placed him on half-pay, and ordered him to leave Paris and reside in his home town despite his wife's inability to travel. Exelmans fought back, and in his trial was acquited on all counts.[36]

With these actions, Soult became both distrusted and disliked by Imperial soldiers and officers alike. For some, hate was not too strong a word.

General Drouet d'Erlon, commander of the garrison at Lille, presided over Exelmans' trial. Little did Soult and d'Erlon know that this was the first of many dramatic events they would share during 1815.

Louis-Philippe

During the course of 1814, the Bourbons were losing their grip on the country. Alexandre Dumas, writing about October 25th, said:

> *Although at this date I was still very young, I well remember the general consternation at the successive appearance of all the customs of the old régime, disallowed and forgotten for two-and-twenty years. There were the Sundays, the holidays and half-holidays which closed all shops and stopped all business; there was the ceremony of the Vow of Louis XIII, then the Expiatory Mass of January 21st, and, worse than all these, some impudent remarks had been dropped on the subject of the sale of emigrants' estates, hinting that such sales might be invalidated.*[37]

---

36 See "Account of Exelmans Affair" on page 241
37 Dumas, Alexandre, *The Last King; or The New France*, Vol. 1, Stanley Paul & Co, London, 1915, pp. 195 and 196

With the anxiety about the state of France growing within the courts of Europe, Metternich, the Austrian Chancellor, wrote to Joseph Fouché, Napoleon's former Minister of Police who still possessed a firm grasp on the state of the country, in January of 1815 with three questions:

> *(1) What would happen if Napoleon were to return to France? (2) If the King of Rome were to appear on the frontier supported by an Austrian army corps? (3) If neither of these contingencies were to take place, but were a revolution to break out of itself? To these questions Fouché replied that everything would depend on the behavior of the first regiment; should it go over to Bonaparte, the whole army would follow its example. In the second case, that France would declare for the King of Rome; and in the third, that the Revolution would be made in favour of the Duc d'Orleans.*[38]

During the fall of 1814 and spring of 1815, Fouché was both aware and involved with conspiracies to overthrow the Bourbons. As Lamartine wrote, "… he courted the Bourbons, he spared Napoleon, he stirred up the Orleans party, he flattered the republic; he knit and unraveled at the same time beginnings of plots with all parties."[39]

Fouché had no interest in facilitating the return of Napoleon where his role would be at will of and subservient to the Emperor. He had a "preference for a regency in which he hoped to play a leading part,"[40] but there was little chance of the King of Rome escaping the custody of the Austrians.

The Duc d'Orleans was an entirely different matter.

Louis-Philippe was the king's cousin and son of Philippe Egalité. Egalité had supported the revolution, and even voted for the King's death, though he eventually would be condemned himself. Louis-Philippe had inherited some of his father's politics, and held a unique spot amongst the émigrés, as described by Munro Price:

---

38 Hall, John, *The Bourbon Restoration*, Alston Rivers, London, 1909, p. 55
39 Lamartine, Alphonse, *History of the Restoration of Monarchy in France*, Volume 2, George Bell & Sons, 1882, p. 59
40 Cole, H. *Fouché: the Unprincipled Patriot*, McCall, 1971, p. 236

> *Ever since his return to France, Louis-Philippe had enjoyed several political advantages over his relatives. He had supported the Revolution, without being associated with its excesses; he had fought for France rather than against her, with some glory, in 1792 and 1793; and he was now known to be firmly in favour of a liberal constitution. He was certainly not above advertising these facts, and had done so with most effect on 29 May 1814, when he had gone to mass at the Tuileries in his old lieutenant-general's uniform of the post-1789 army, which his cousins had pointedly refused to wear. Immediately a gaggle of Napoleonic marshals rushed up to him, exclaiming with joy and 'making delighted bows'. Over the next few weeks, they vied with each other to pay their court at the Palais-royal. Most prominent were those who had fought with Louis-Philippe in those first revolutionary campaigns – Mortier, Macdonald, Berthier, Ney.*[41]

While Louis-Philippe never made an overt move for the throne, Munro Price, in *The Perilous Crown*, makes a fascinating case examining Louis-Philippe's words and actions, that he may have been involved in the 'Conspiracy of the North,' a cabal of Generals that Fouché would unleash upon hearing of Napoleon's landing.[42] Twice in April, Wellington would inform Castlereagh of a military conspiracy on behalf of Louis-Philippe, probably informed by Fouché.[43]

Regardless of Louis-Philippe's ambition or role, it is a fact that he was considered by many to be a compromise between the ideals sought during the revolution, and the Allied powers' demand for a monarchy.

---

41 Price, Munro, *The Perilous Crown*, pp. 71 and 72
42 For details on the The Conspiracy of the North, see Houssaye's *1815*, Chapter 3; Lamartine, Alphonse, *The History of the Restoration of Monarchy in France*, Harper & Brothers, New York, 1852, Volume 2, pp. 59-64; Hall, John, *The Bourbon Restoration*, Alston Rivers, London, 1909, pp. 60-62
43 Price, Munro, *The Perilous Crown*, p. 84

CHAPTER 2
Napoleon's Return

On March 5th, 1815, Louis XVIII would learn of Napoleon's return. Just a few days earlier, on March 1st, Napoleon had landed at Antibes on the southern coast of France with his personal guard. A nation of over 30 million souls had been invaded by 1,000 men.

Soult was confident. To deal with trouble in Italy, Austria and France had previously agreed to a military operation. Numerous regiments were already being deployed in the south, and would soon interdict Napoleon.

This was not considered enough by the King's aides. A Prince must go, and rally the army and the people against this usurper. The King's brother, the Comte d'Artois, left immediately for Lyons. A day later, the Duc d'Orleans followed him.

Upon hearing the news, Fouché launched his 'Conspiracy of the North' by sending General Lallemand off to Lille to signal his fellow conspirators. Possibly tipped off, or possibly in response to Napoleon's landing, Soult sent Marshal Mortier to Lille, of which he was Governor. Mortier was one of the few who had remained close to Soult and had served with him since the republic. On the way there, Mortier ran into General d'Erlon and his column of troops marching without orders, and had d'Erlon arrested. Without d'Erlon's troops, the other conspirators lost their nerve and scattered.

On March 7th, Napoleon met a battalion of the 5th Line blocking the road to Grenoble. "Soldiers of the 5th... if you want to kill your Emperor, here I am." With cries of *"Vive l'Empereur!"* they joined his ranks. The 7th Line, under Colonel Labedoyere, followed, along with the town of Grenoble.

Napoleon's army swelled to over 7,000.

Soult's Proclamation

On March 8th, Soult had the following proclamation printed in the *Moniteur*:

Ministry of War
Order of the Day

Soldiers!

That man who recently abdicated, in the sight of all Europe, the power he had usurped, which he had used so fatefully, has landed on French soil which he should never have seen again.

What does he desire? Civil war: what does he seek? Traitors: where will he find them? Shall it be among those soldiers he has deceived and sacrificed so many times, wasting their bravery? Shall it be in the bosoms of those families whom his name alone fills with fear?

Buonaparte[44] *despises us enough to believe that we will desert our legitimate and beloved sovereign, to share the fate of a man who is no better than an adventurer. He believes it, the madman! And his last foolish act is to make it known.*

Soldiers, the French army is the bravest in Europe, it will also be the most loyal.

Let us rally to the banner of the fleur-de-lis, to the voice of the father of the nation, of that worthy heir to the virtues of the great Henry. He himself decreed for you the duties which you have to fulfill. He places at your head that prince, a model of French knighthood, whose happy return to our country has already driven out the usurper, and who now by his presence will destroy the usurper's sole and final hope.

Paris, March 8, 1815
The Minister of War,
Marshal, Duke of Dalmatia[45]

---

44 Buonaparte, specifically this spelling, was used by detractors of Napoleon to emphasize that he was foreign, not French.
45 *Le Moniteur Universel*, Issue 1, 1815
http://books.google.com/books?id=DTxHAAAAcAAJ
Translation from: http://www.poetryintranslation.com/PITBR/Chateaubriand/ChateaubriandMemoirsBookXXIII.htm. Compare to Soult's proclamation of June 1st.

On the same day, Soult sent an order to Mortier. D'Erlon was to be "court-martialed and shot within twenty-four hours."[46]

By March 10th, Fouché had learned of his conspiracy's failure. This was of no bother, for Fouché had become a royalist! He later declared, "I am more devoted to the King than most of those he brought back from exile."[47]

Napoleon triumphantly entered Lyons that evening. Artois and the duc d'Orleans had given up the fight and fled in the morning. The residents, and most importantly the garrison, had made their intentions clear; they joined with Napoleon. Napoleon's army swelled to over 14,000.

On March 11th, the King's advisors accused Soult of working with Napoleon. How else to explain the regiments joining the invader other than Soult having placed them in Napoleon's path in preparation for his return? Insulted, Soult resigned, and as he departed the Tuileries, he led a salute to the King. He was replaced by General Clarke, who would later follow the King to Ghent.

On March 13th, the Chamber of Deputies heard a report that every town and village on Napoleon's march to Paris wore the white cockade and cried *Vive Le Roi*, along with the news of d'Erlon's execution.[48]

> *He was immediately tried and condemned to death: he was led to the square of the citadel; his eyes were bandaged; a file of soldiers were drawn up before him; their pieces were presented, and the fatal word was momentarily expected; when the troops suddenly rose up against Mortier, and declared Erlon commander of the fortress. Erlon, however, speedily released the marshal, and sent him to Paris.*[49]

It seemed the Chamber's intelligence was flawed.

---

46 Austin, Paul Britten, *1815 The Return of Napoleon*, London, 2002, pp. 174-175
47 Cole, Hubert, *Fouché The Unprincipled Patriot*, McCall, 1971, p. 239
48 The European Magazine and London Review
http://books.google.com/books?id=sygoAAAAYAAJ
49 Encyclopaedia Londinensis, Vol. 18
http://books.google.com/books?id=oFoMAQAAMAAJ
This story is also told in Hobhouse's diaries, the entry for Wednesday, March 22nd, 1815.

Marshal Ney, The King's Last Hope

The King's cause was now up to Marshal Michel Ney, who Napoleon called the *Bravest of the Brave*. When Ney had met with the king upon hearing of Napoleon's landing, he had famously promised to bring Napoleon back in an iron cage. Since the 10th, he had been assembling the scattered forces of his district, maybe 6,000 in number. Now on the 13th, he learned that Napoleon had left Lyons with 14,000 men. Ney remained intent on opposing Napoleon.

Early the following morning, he received a letter and a soaring proclamation from Napoleon. That afternoon, Ney ordered General Louis-Auguste-Victor de Ghaisnes, Comte de Bourmont, his second in command, to assemble the troops. Bourmont was a loyal royalist who had once been arrested for involvement in a plot against Napoleon, but later rallied to the Empire. Bourmont quietly went along as Ney announced his allegiance to the Emperor. The soldiers responded, like all before them, with delirium and cries of *"Vive l'Empereur!"*

On the 15th, Ney ordered Bourmont to ready the troops for marching to join Napoleon's army. That night, Ney's former chief-of-staff, Colonel Clouet, arrived.

> *Violently anti-Bonapartist, Clouet has been travelling day and night to rejoin his marshal and heard about his defection en route. Now, rushing in, he demands to see Ney; and Levavasseur, introducing him into a room apart, hears the two men having a loud altercation. Rushing out again, Clouet seizes a scrap of paper, and scribbles on it the words: "My ADC Clouet is ordered to proceed to Paris at once with my cook and a servant. By order of the Marshal, signed...". Seals it with Ney's seal. And leaves.*[50]

While Bourmont had passively stood by during Ney's actions before finally departing, Clouet instantly and decisively expressed his loyalty to the King. Clouet would meet up with Bourmont on the way to Paris where they would inform the King of Ney's defection. They would be inextricably linked for the rest of their lives.

---

50 Austin, Paul Britten, *1815 The Return of Napoleon*, London, 2002, p. 214

Late that evening in Paris, Fouché met with Artois. He explained that there was nothing they could do to stop Napoleon. Fouché claims in his memoirs that as they parted, he told Artois, "Take measures to save the king, and I take upon me to save the monarchy."[51]

Departures

On March 17th, Ney's defection had been confirmed. Napoleon would soon be on the throne without a shot fired.

By March 19th, gloom had settled over the Tuileries. After some indecision, the Royal aides formulated a plan… the King would depart at night! Later that evening, the House of Bourbon would sneak out of Paris.

Fouché would say to Bourmont, "Napoleon is mad. We shall not let him throw France into the abyss again."[52] For some, the planning had long since begun.

At Fontainebleau, an arrest warrant was issued for Bourmont, Clouet, and others who had refused to follow Ney. At some point before March 22nd, Bourmont gave Napoleon his resignation. Napoleon accepted, and ordered Bourmont to inform Davout of his residence. On March 22nd, Davout wrote to Bourmont at Besançon and gave him six days to leave the territory.[53]

As the King left France, the duc d'Orleans wrote to Marshal Mortier:

> *LILLE,*
> *March 23rd, 1815.*
>
> *MY DEAR MARSHAL,*
>
> *I leave in your hands the entire command of the northern departments. Most gladly would I have shared it with you, but I am too true a Frenchman to be willing to sacrifice my country's interests when fresh misfortunes compel me to leave it. I go to seek exile and oblivion. The king having left France I cannot give you any orders*

---

[51] Fouché, Joseph, *Memoirs of Josept Fouché*, London, 1894, p. 424
[52] Pingaud, Leonce, *Bourmont et Fouché*, 1912, p. 866
[53] Gautherot, Gustave, "Bourmont à Waterloo", *Revue des Questions Historiques*, Volume 92, pp. 94 - 129.

in his name, and I can only cancel those already given, and advise you to do whatever your excellent judgment and stainless patriotism may suggest as being best for the interests of our country, and most in conformity with the various duties you will have to undertake.

Adieu, my dear marshal; it is with a sorrow-laden heart that I write thus, but whatever changes Fortune may have in store, I hope to retain your friendship, even as you may always count upon mine. I shall never forget what I have seen of you during the short time we have been together. I admire your character and your loyalty as much as I admire and love you personally, and with all my heart I wish you all the good fortune you deserve, and which I trust you may enjoy.

L. P. D'ORLÉANS[54]

Louis-Philippe would be served well by Napoleon's Marshals. It was only a question of when.

---

54 Dumas, Alexandre, *The Last King or The New France*, Volume 1, London, 1915, pp. 210-211

CHAPTER 3
Empire!

On March 20th, 1815, Napoleon entered the Tuileries and once again was Emperor of the French. He immediately began to form his government. Marshal Davout, the most faithful and feared of his Marshals, was appointed Minister of War while Fouché, even sooner than he predicted, received Ministry of Police. Napoleon wished to keep Fouché close, and once his power was secure, dismiss him once and for all against some wall. These bitter enemies knew exactly what the other was doing.

According to Napoleon, he met with Soult for the first time after his return on March 26th.[55] In Charles d'Agoult's memoirs, he cites a recollection of General Evain made in 1830:

> *(...) on the return from the Isle of Elba, having been summoned to Tuileries, he waited some time. The Emperor spoke intently with Marshal Soult, and while leaving, the Marshal said emphatically to the Emperor: "You broke the treaties, you come to bring to France civil and foreign war."*
>
> *General Evain was a serious and truthful man. But how to explain these words of Marshal Soult who, a few days after, at Waterloo, was the Emperor's major general?*[56]

The above encounter was possibly from the March 26th visit. Soon after, Soult underwent a remarkable change of heart from his proclamation and

---

55 Gourgaud, Gaspard, *Sainte-Hélène Journal Inédit de 1815 à 1818*, Volume 1, p. 490
56 Cited at http://www.1789-1815.com/soult.htm

personal confrontation. Soult began writing to Marshal Davout imploring for assistance in getting back in Napoleon's good graces.[57]

At the same time, General Bourmont also was having a change of heart. While many royalist officers and soldiers followed the King, sometime in March, someone[58] figured out that a few more officers in Ghent were useless. Where Royalists could do the most damage were in positions of command in Napoleon's army. Bourmont went to the Tuileries and met with Bertrand and Gérard. Gérard expressed his desire for Bourmont to lead one of the divisions of the *Armée de la Moselle* which Gérard had been given command, and said he would take the issue up with Napoleon.

Was this a coordinated effort?

> *Concerning the change of the cockade of Bourmont, General Berthezène said: "Baron Von Eckstein, chief of police in Ghent during the stay of Louis XVIII, assured me that d'André, nephew of the chief of the French police force, officer in a regiment of light cavalry stationed around Valenciennes, and who deserted a few days before the opening of the campaign, had served as intermediary between Fouché and Ghent; he added that the reports of Fouché with General de Bourmont were frequent."*[59]

Not surprisingly, Davout had little patience for the royalists. On March 27th, Bourmont visited Davout seeking his orders. Davout steadfastly refused to employ Bourmont and expressed great displeasure with Bourmont's earlier abandoning of Ney. Gérard intervened, and confidently told Bourmont to select generals for two brigades and to put together his staff.

---

57 Houssaye, Henry, *1815, Waterloo*, Translated from the 31st edition, London, 1900, p. 33, footnotes 217, 219, and 220 on page 318 delineates the correspondence between Soult and Davout
http://books.google.com/books?id=xWBAAAAAYAAJ

58 In his memoirs, Saint-Chamans said that when Napoleon was approaching Paris after his landing, the Duc de Berry ordered him to stay with his regiment and wait for his orders, even if it defected.
Mémoires du général Cte de Saint-Chamans
http://books.google.com/books?id=ZVVBAAAAIAAJ

59 Blockqueville, Adelaide Louise Eckmuhl, *Le Marechal Davout, Prince D'Eckmuhl, Un Dernier Commandement*, Volume 4, p. 156

On April 1st, General Bourmont was put in command of the 14th Infantry Division of Gérard's IV Corps. Time would reveal many royalists that would rally to the tricolor only to betray France both before and during the upcoming hostilities.

Not all traitors or defectors were motivated by love of king. For some, Bourbon gold earned their oath. Soldiers on the frontier were offered 20 francs to defect, 80 if they were mounted. Members of Davout's War Ministry were successfully bribed and delivered incredibly detailed information of the dispositions and strengths of the French Army.[60]

For those with a noble background, future positions were promised. For example, the *Moniteur* and *La Gazette de France* published the identities of defectors, such as Battalion Commander Bois-David of the 17th Line, Adjutant Doisonville of the 7th Hussars, Capitaine Naylies and Sous-Lieutenant Buisseret. Naylies and Buisseret would see their actions rewarded with appointments to the cavalry of the Garde Royale after the second restoration.

Capitaine d'André, who had helped Bourmont and Fouché communicate, defected on May 13th. The son of Chancellor Dambray, Capitaine Dambray of the 1st Lancers, deserted on May 15th. The name d'Andre is also listed in the *Maison du Roi* after the second restoration.[61]

On April 30th, Napoleon organized the forces of France.[62] The army that Napoleon would personally command was the *Armée du Nord*.

---

60 Bonnal, Edmond, *Les royalistes contre l'armée les archives due Ministére de la guerre : 1815-1820*, Volume 1.
61 The *Ordonnance du Roi* of December 25th, 1815 lists the following: M. le Comte de Bourmont, M. D'Andigne, M. Blouquier de Trelan, Du Barail, D'André, Naylies, and De Buisseret. The *Maison Militaire du Roi* for 1817 lists the following: Le Baron de Bois-David, Du Barail, and M. Le Cte. De Villoutreys.
Some of the above could just be common names, while others are clearly deserters or traitors during 1815 that have been rewarded by the king. It would be interesting to cross reference all the names that could be found on any rosters of the Garde Royale after the 2nd restoration with all the orderlies and headquarters staffs for the *Armée du Nord* to see if there are more or definitive matches. How wide and deep the royalist infiltration of Napoleon's army is not known.
62 *Correspondance*, Tome 28, no. 21855

Soult Works hard for post of Major-Général

Meanwhile, Soult, who in his post-Waterloo justification of his conduct made it clear he was employed reluctantly after great resistance and only due to his loyalty to France, continued to hound Davout for Napoleon's decision on how he would be used. In response to these overtures, Davout wrote on April 10th:

> M. Marshal, I received your letter of April 9: I will show it to the Emperor this evening.
>
> You will find a note and the copy of the oath attached, which was addressed to you: I suppose that it will have reached you. If this is not the case, you could sign another one using the copy I'm sending to you.
>
> You can expect, M. Marshal, that I will do with the Emperor all that could be agreeable for you. I will do this in friendship for you, by recognition of what you did for me under the last government, and because I am convinced that my efforts will be in the interest of the service of the Emperor.[63]

Davout would eventually deliver a written oath that Soult was required to sign, and set up an appointment for when Soult would present the oath

---

63 Davout, Louis-Nicholas, *Correspondance du Marechal Davout*, Paris, 1885, p. 423, No. 1567. http://books.google.com/books?id=sik3AQAAMAAJ
Additional of interest:
1597 :
April 15, 1815.
M. Marshal, I am charged by the Emperor to warn you that His Majesty will receive your oath tomorrow before the mass.
It will be necessary that you return to the apartments of the Tuileries around eleven o'clock in the morning.
1598:
M. Marshal, I receive your letter of this day, at half past ten o'clock in the morning, where you say to me that the letter that I wrote to you yesterday evening just reaches you.
Yesterday, at half past ten o'clock in the evening, I received from Duke de Bassano the invitation to notify you to return today to Chateau Tuileries, at eleven o'clock in the morning, to give your oath there.
At ten forty-five, my letter was written and sent so that you have notice. You will find enclosed a receipt signed by a man at your place, who proves that at eleven o'clock in the evening, one of your men received this dispatch.

to Napoleon in person. To some, this might seem like an overbearing indignity that only a person highly motivated to regain the good graces of their former leader would bear. Certainly Soult, with all his reluctance and expressed disdain for *Buonaparte*, would not both sign an oath and deliver it in person just to take a job he didn't want.

The Paris newspapers in April reported that Marshal Soult would certainly have an important position in the event of war. "It is known that for a long time the ambition of Marshal Soult was to succeed Berthier as Major General."[64]

Louis-Alexandre Berthier had been at Napoleon's side since 1796 and was the *Major-Général* of the *Grande Armée* through 1814. The *Major-Général* was effectively second in command of the army answerable only to Napoleon.[65] Berthier has often been described as Napoleon's Chief of Staff in order to relate to modern organizations. The Imperial Headquarters, the *Grand Quartier-Général*, served all of Napoleon's needs during campaign allowing him to be Chief of State as well as direct the army. The army staff, *Grand État Major-Général*, had detailed procedures for the management of correspondence between the headquarters and all the various formations of the army regardless of size. It was largely a creation of Berthier, though its roots pre-dated the Revolution.[66]

Elting, in his classic work *Swords Around a Throne*, provides a succinct insight into Berthier's methods:

> *Berthier's operational instructions were simple and should be engraved inside every modern staff officer's skull. The chief of staff is the headquarters pivot. He must see everything that comes in and sign (or at least approve) everything that goes out. The assistant chiefs of staff must keep abreast of the general situation in addition to running their own sections. Speed and accuracy are the most important factors in staff work. The staff exists only for the good of*

---

64 *Le Moniteur Universel* http://books.google.com/books?id=DTxHAAAAcAAJ page 16.
65 This was not always technically accurate, as Murat at times was named as Napoleon's second, and even took over the army when Napoleon left Russia. However, all obeyed the orders that Berthier sent with the assumption that he was executing the will of Napoleon. In 1815, Soult was the second in command, and would lead the army for a period of time when Napoleon returned to Paris.
66 See Chapter V of John R. Elting's *Swords Around a Throne* for a detailed study of the history and function of Napoleon's Imperial headquarters.

the army and so has no regular office hours. It works as long as may be necessary, rests when it has nothing left to do, takes care of the troops before consulting its own comfort, and is always ready to move out, regardless of the hour or "pain" involved. Up-to-the-minute intelligence on enemy forces and actions must always be available; therefore reconnaissance must be continuous to the front and flanks, and its results reported promptly. (In broken country, where infiltration is easy, reconnoiter to your rear also.) Finally, the commander-in-chief must always be told the truth, the whole truth, and nothing else – no matter how unpleasant the results may be.[67]

Berthier spent much of a campaign at Napoleon's side, and was responsible for taking Napoleon's orders and having them delivered. Napoleon's intentions would be translated by Berthier into detailed orders transcribed by numerous secretaries. There would typically, but not always, be multiple copies of each order, including one archived into the *Registre du Major-Général*. Because these were hand-copies, and possibly made by different individuals, it wasn't uncommon for there to be minor differences between copies of the same order.

Orderlies, mounted officers, would then take and deliver the order to its destination, typically a named individual at a known location, or on some line of march. Berthier was meticulous in detail recording the time an order was sent and its courier. When the situation demanded it, such as in hostile territory or in the midst of enemy cavalry such as swarms of Cossacks, Berthier would send multiple orderlies. A common practice was for each corps to send to the General Headquarters a staff officer at the end of the day with reports. This office would then rest during the night at headquarters and then return to the corps during the pre-dawn hours with new orders.

While Berthier oversaw the Army's general staff, Napoleon had his own staff as well. As head of state, he managed the country as well as the army during campaigns and produced correspondence daily. This staff included secretaries, orderlies, and Aides de Camp, and as supreme commander, he could dispatch an order at any time to any formation. Typically, the ADCs were reserved for battlefield missions at climatic moments, but as will be

---

67 Elting, John, *Swords Around a Throne*, Da Capo Press, New York, 1997, p. 83.

seen during 1815, he carried out his own intelligence, reconnaissance, and dispatching of orders.

There is no doubt that Napoleon and Berthier made for a dynamic coupling of genius and execution. Unfortunately for Napoleon, Berthier had remained loyal to the King in 1815, and would die mysteriously on June 1st, 1815. Napoleon thus needed someone with both organizational skill and seniority. As Berthier was a Marshal, Napoleon may have felt uneasy promoting one of Berthier's subordinates to the role of *Major-Général*. For a campaign so close to Paris, Davout was a logical choice as Berthier had fulfilled both the roles of *Major-Général* and Minister of War until 1807. However, Napoleon's fixation with the security of Paris, possibly due to the events of 1814, seemed to rule this out.

Another choice frequently suggested was Bailly de Monthion, who had served as Berthier's Chief of Staff for several years. It has even been suggested he could have been made a Marshal. There is very little one can find on Monthion, but Davout might give insight for his lack of appointment in the following letter written to Bertrand on May 8th:

> *It is my duty to the Emperor to make observations about the choice of M. General Monthyon as chief of staff, that I consider as very poor. This general is despised in the army; he is inept; his campaigns of 1812, 1813, 1814, unfortunately gave proof of this. I consider him less than sure; this could be kept in the realm of imagination, but what is not kept there, is his conduct in the armies. I ask you, M. Count, to place my observations under the eyes of His Majesty; I will add that if the choice of the staff officers has been made by General Monthyon, it is desired that you take informations about them before sending letters of employment.*[68]

One can only wonder what Davout finds "less than sure." It isn't his competence, as Davout makes it clear that whatever his doubts are, Monthion's military competence is without a doubt poor. Is Davout questioning Monthion's loyalty? And is this why he wants the officers appointed by Monthion to be scrutinized? Could Monthion have been a traitor during the campaign? And would this explain his membership in the cult of silence?

Monthion would not be the first officer Davout had doubts about.

---

68 Saint Chamant, Henri, *Napoléon, ses dernières armées*, 1902, p. 203

In 1813, Soult had served as an understudy of Berthier before being sent back to Spain. While this was far from Monthion's experience, Soult was also a Marshal, and at the very least had Napoleon's respect.

At some point in the middle of April, Soult gave the oaths of loyalty Napoleon demanded from him. On May 9th, Marshal Soult was, according to Soult's later *justification*, surprised and disappointed to be appointed *Major-Général* of the *Armée du Nord*, yet immediately accepted the position.

Preparing for War

During these months, the Allies were busy exchanging and ratifying the treaties which would once again put their armies in the field against France. Upon Napoleon's return, France was weak. Yet, ostensibly to preserve peace, Europe once again declared war against Napoleon and declared him an outlaw.

As part of these exchanges, Britain added a stipulation that it was, "... *not to be understood as binding his Britannic Majesty to prosecute the War with a view of imposing upon France any particular Government.*"[69]

If Napoleon was the problem, then any replacement government, regardless of form or monarch, should have been acceptable to the Allies as long as France abided by the treaties of 1814. However, if the problem was that the senior branch of a royal family was replaced by the people, then the only result of the war would be restoring King Louis XVIII, no matter that the country had deposed of the Bourbons twice.

Time would demonstrate the true motivations of the Allied monarchs.

With the Allies intentions clear, Napoleon and Davout immediately went to work mobilizing France for war. Everything was in short supply. Horses were collected or bought from across France. Thousands of muskets were repaired. It was an amazing effort that produced a formidable army.

Marshal Macdonald, who had not only served the Royalists, but had tried even at risk to himself to rally forces against Napoleon during his return,

---

69 http://en.wikisource.org/wiki/Treaty_of_Vienna_(Seventh_Coalition)

was still actively recruited to serve. Even Davout made strong recruitment overtures. Macdonald declined, and Napoleon granted his request to retire to his estates. Had Soult not wished to serve in Napoleon's army, he clearly could have refused.

Considering the successes Napoleon had in 1814 with less than 100,000 men, a defensive campaign with an army of more than 200,000, and Davout with an army at Paris, the chances for military success were great.[70] Often the total numbers of Allied forces are thrown about as an unbeatable foe. However, as Napoleon had demonstrated his entire career, he was well capable of achieving superior numbers on the battlefield. This would be especially true facing invading armies each with a separate command. With Davout in the field, inevitable defeat was not a certainty.

However, the political situation was less stable. Napoleon felt he needed a dramatic military victory to cement popular support behind his return and contain the various factions working against him throughout the country. Waiting for the Allied invasion meant necessarily fighting a battle within the borders of France, and while the prospects of achieving a victory against one or two of the invading allied armies was great, the impact Napoleon desired could have been offset by the damage of the other allied armies descending on Paris.

An opportunity available to Napoleon was to strike first and try to overwhelm one or more of the Allied armies before their invasion. The closest Allied armies were the Anglo-Dutch under Wellington and head quartered at Brusssels, and the Prussian under Blücher headquartered at Namur. Though Napoleon could not match the combined strength of these

---

[70] It has become popular to declare Napoleon's cause helpless with a guaranteed inevitable defeat. This analysis is shallow based on nothing but resource calculations and declarations that the Allies had suddenly become masters of warfare whereas Napoleon was stuck with antiquated ideas. If this analysis is true, then what does this say of Davout and the many others that rallied to Napoleon? Were they just idiots? Or consider Wellington – why did he give battle before Brussels? Did he not know that all that was required is simply running out the clock? In fact, the contemporaries of the time knew that they that had certain material advantages, yet they also knew quite well that had Napoleon achieved successes, he could have been ultimately victorious. As this work demonstrates, Napoleon's plans were brilliant, and the Allies were only spared a decisive defeat due to treason. Indeed, the mere fact that the allies planned to concentrate so close to the frontier upon a Napoleon advance via Charleroi shows that they were still easily out maneuvered and ripe for destruction. Seen in this light, Wellington's caution at the beginning of the campaign is commendable.

two armies, which was over 200,000 men, Napoleon could concentrate a far superior army with better troops, cavalry and artillery.

Additionally, the King was held up in Belgium protected by the Anglo-Dutch army. There were several attractive elements to engaging the Anglo-Dutch army in Belgium. This army was a collection of different nationalities, much of dubious quality. Britain had a significant political contingent that did not support a war to impose a government on France. Belgium had also once been part of the French domain with its army having fought for Napoleon. Napoleon's thinking was that a lightning strike with a decisive victory in Belgium could severely impact Royalists efforts, reduce the size of the frontier to defend, add a source of soldiers, and possibly even knock Britain out of the war. It was exactly the type of bold stroke Napoleon needed as he began the defense of his empire.

François Pierre Guillaume Guizot (1787-1874), Secretary-General of the Ministry of the Interior for Louis the XVIII, had resigned his post shortly after the return of Napoleon on March 25th. On May 23rd, he left Paris to join the King in Ghent, forever earning the insulting moniker "The Man of Ghent." His opponents considered it unpatriotic for him to go over to the King while the country was under attack. However, it appears they were also not aware that he was betraying the nation. Guizot delivered information provided by a mole in Davout's war ministry to Clarke, Louis XVIII's Minister of War.[71]

Insurrections in the Royalist Vendee, and one led by the duc d'Angoulême in the south, had to be dealt with. General Grouchy decisively dealt with Angoulême, and in doing so earned his Marshal's Baton. He would be put in command of the reserve Cavalry Corps.

The Vendée was a more difficult affair. Almost a corps' worth of strength was dispatched and was not available for the campaign in Belgium.

On May 25th, possibly due to dispatching forces to deal with the Vendee insurrection, Napoleon ordered *Armée de la Moselle*, stationed around Metz, to be ready to move to the Belgium frontier.[72] This is a clear sign that Napoleon had settled on a Belgium offensive.

---

71 Malet, M. Albert, *Louis XVIII et Les Cent-Jours à Gand,* Paris, 1902
72 Chuquet, Arthur, *Inédits Napoléoniens*, Paris, 1919, Volume 2, 3332. This entry, titled *Notes et lettres de Soult dictées par l'Empereur* and dated the end of May delineates many

Figure 1, the approximate dispositions of the *Armée du Nord* is shown for the end of May. There were detachments from various corps that were not with their parent body that would be recalled during the concentration on the frontier. The Cavalry formations are indicated as it would be reorganized in early June. The 14th Cavalry division was actually farther east, but would end up marching behind IV Corps once it began its movement to join the *Armée du Nord*.

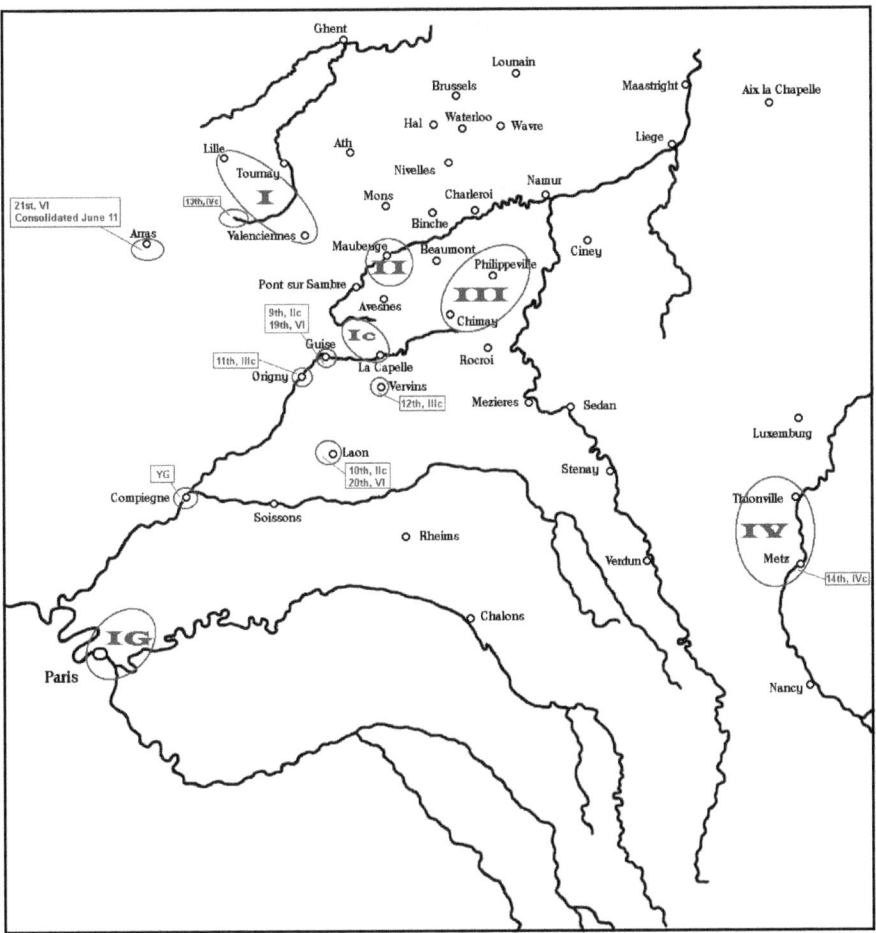

Figure 1 – Disposition of the *Armée du Nord* at the end of May

---

prefatory maneuvers. It has not been reproduced.

CHAPTER 4
JUNE 1ST - JUNE 9TH

ON JUNE 1ST, HAVING PREVIOUSLY denounced the usurper *Buonaparte*, Soult proudly announced his love for Napoleon.

Order of the Day

Paris, 1 June 1815.

> *A most impressive ceremony has just sanctified our institutions. The Emperor received from representatives of the people and deputations of all army corps, the expression of the wishes of the whole nation on the Additional Act to the Constitutions of the Empire, which had been sent for its acceptance; and a new oath united France and the Emperor; so destinies are fulfilled, and all the efforts of an impious league can no longer separate the interests of a great people from the hero whose most brilliant triumphs are universally admired.*
>
> *It is when the national will shows itself with as much energy, that war cries are heard; it is when France is at peace with all Europe, that foreign armies are advancing on our borders: What is the hope of this new coalition? Does it want to remove France from the existing nations? Does it want to put into servitude twenty-eight million French! How could it have forgotten that the first league which was formed against our independence served our independence and our glory! Hundred brilliant victories, that momentary setbacks and unfortunate circumstances could not erase, remind it that a free nation, led by a great man is invincible.*

Everyone is a soldier in France when it comes to national honor and freedom: a common interest today unites all French. The commitments forced upon us by violence are destroyed by the flight of the Bourbons outside the French territory, by the call they made to foreign armies to restore them to the throne they have abandoned, and by the unanimous wish of the nation which, by taking again the free exercise of its rights, solemnly repudiated everything that was done without its participation.

The French cannot receive laws from abroad, even those who went there to beg parricidal help will discover again without delay and will experience, as did their predecessors, that contempt and infamy follow their steps, and that they can erase the shame which they cover themselves only by going back into our ranks.

But a new path of glory opens before the army; history will consecrate the memory of military events that the defenders of the homeland and of national honor will have illustrated! The enemies are many, they say, it doesn't matter! It will be more glorious to prevail, and their defeat will be all the more sensational: the fight which is about to begin is not above the genius of Napoleon, nor above our strength; don't you see how all departments are competing in enthusiasm and devotion, having raised, as if by magic, five hundred superb battalions of national guards, who already came to double our ranks, defend our fortresses and join the glory of the Army? It is the impulse of a generous people that no power can overcome and that posterity will admire. To arms!

Soon they will give the signal; everyman shall do his duty, our victorious phalanxes will shine in new splendour against our enemies. Soldiers! Napoleon will guide us, we will fight for the independence of our beautiful country; we are invincible!

Marshal of the Empire, Major-General,
Duke of Dalmatia.[73]

With the above, Soult wished to gain the trust of the army.

---

73 See "Soult's Order of the Day" on page 357

Having reascended the throne, Napoleon attempted to demonstrate a commitment to a more liberal reign by adopting amendments, the *Acte additionnel aux constitutions de l'Empire*, to previous imperial constitutions that granted the people more rights. June 1st was the day of a national plebiscite, and the Army was presented with the ability to sign their support or rejection. Bourmont and his staff were among the 320 who rejected the act. Speaking about Bourmont, Clouet, who having joined Bourmont in abandoning Ney during Napoleon's march on Paris and was now serving as one of his aides, recalled:

> *From this moment, he must be considered as having lost his command. He wanted to go to find General Gérard to inform him of the resolution where he was to withdraw; I made all my efforts to dissuade him. "I like you," I told him, "have the highest esteem for the character of M. General Gérard; I am convinced that he is worthy of your frankness, and that acting with full liberty, nothing will be held against you that is unworthy of him; but he is surrounded by people who are unlike him; you will cause him to be easily filled with grief, he will be compromised and he will be forced to put you under arrest." I pleaded with M. Bourmont for a long while for a change of resolution; he ultimately gave way to my requests, but he wanted to see the General one last time. I have no knowledge of what occurred in this interview; but, on his return, M. de Bourmont appeared to me firmly disposed to leave the army, and to join the King as soon as possible. He knew that I would share his fate, whatever it might be, despite the revulsion that I experienced to cross over to a foreign army.*[74]

While remaining one of the King's staunchest supporters, Bourmont was still acting in a passive manner reminiscent of when he seemingly acquiesced to Ney's actions when leading over their men to Napoleon during Napoleon's march on Paris. His request for leave from the army starting on June 1st is documented,[75] but Clouet would have us believe he talked

---

74 Clouet, Anne-Louis-Antoine, *Quelques notes sur la conduit de M. le Cte de Bourmont en 1815* http://gallica.bnf.fr/ark:/12148/bpt6k850545n/f7.image
75 Gautherot, Gustave, "Bourmont à Waterloo", *Revue des Questions Historiques*, Volume 92, Pages 94 - 129. Details in section titled « L'ACTE ADDITIONNEL ET LE DESSEIN

Bourmont out of leaving the army. One reason given is that they feared arrest if they retired from the army. However, if their goal was to defect to the allies, this could have just as easily, if not arguably more easily, taken place from Fontoy – the frontier was only a couple hours north.

On June 2nd, Karl Friedrich Heinrich von der Goltz, a Prussian general serving as ambassador to Louis XVIII, wrote to the Prussian Chancellor Prince Hardenberg with the military details Guizot had just delivered[76], "… who got them directly by an employee in the office of Marshal Davout." Guizot would later play a large role in the governments of Louis-Philippe alongside Soult, but always denied having been a traitor.

On June 3rd Napoleon asked Soult for the initial plan for concentration of the army on the Belgium frontier targeting a completion date of June 13th. The order began:

> *Give me a plan of movement for the Corps of Général Gérard or Corps of the Moselle, concealing it as much as possible from the enemy, because this corps is to march on Philippeville. It should arrive there on the 12th, marching as quickly as possible. Inform me about who will then command at Metz and Nancy. You will give the order at once to suspend the communications, and all of the posts, Thionville, Longwy, Metz, etc. must be strengthened.*

June 14, the anniversary of Marengo, was Napoleon's target date for the commencement of the campaign.[77]

On June 3rd, Napoleon wrote to Drouot, then the chief of staff of the Imperial Guard, with the precise marching orders for the guard to advance to the Belgium frontier starting not later than June 5th. This day, Napoleon also ordered the reorganization of the cavalry such that each infantry corps

---

DE BOURMONT »
https://books.google.com/books?id=WpojAQAAIAAJ
76 See "Treasonous Correspondence with Ghent" on page 267
77 See De Wit's analysis http://waterloo-campaign.nl/bestanden/files/preambles/adn.1.pdf pg. 14-15.

had a division of light cavalry while the rest of the cavalry was organized into four cavalry corps.

On June 4th, according to Lettow-Vorbeck, Soult wrote to Napoleon and suggested an advance on the Sambre in two columns where the III Corps and IV Corps would form the right column.[78] Napoleon did not respond to this suggestion. It should be noted that Lettow-Vorbeck says he received this information from Baron Stoffel, whose uncle was on Soult's staff. Unfortunately, almost nothing is known about this correspondence and it has never been seen.

On June 5th, Soult sent an order to Gérard to have the *Armée de la Moselle* march to Rocroi and to arrive by June 13th in seven stages.[79] The Army of the Moselle was comprised of IV Corps and was headquartered at Metz with divisions at Fontoy and Thionville. As we saw on June 3rd, Napoleon had asked Soult for a plan to deliver IV Corps to Philippeville by June 12th marching *as quickly as possible*. Instead, Soult's order directed IV Corps to Rocroi which was a day's march south of Philipeville, and worse, to arrive a day later than Napoleon's original order. Had Soult and Napoleon discussed this change, presumably after having reviewed a plan Soult may have presented? Or was Soult operating on his own?[80]

Napoleon had a rough idea of how the Anglo-Dutch and Prussian forces were deployed. Their junction was approximately centered on Charleroi and defended by one Prussian Corps that was deployed over a wide area. Napoleon was presented a golden opportunity. By advancing with overwhelming strength upon Charleroi, he could put his army between the Anglo-Dutch and Prussian armies. With this accomplished, if either Wellington or Blücher chose to fight, they would risk their destruction. If they retreated, Napoleon could seize Brussels without significant losses.

With the mobilization of the guard and the orders sent to Gérard, **June 5th can be thought of as the beginning of the military operations of the Waterloo campaign**; the day the *Armée du Nord* was set into motion.

---

78 See "Lettow-Vorbeck" on page 277, "pages 219-224"
79 See "Lettow-Vorbeck" on page 277, "page 222"
80 Oliver Schmidt suggests that Soult could have been aware of details such as road conditions, provisioning, or the desire for secrecy in making these adjustments.

Napoleon was aware of royalist spies and the existence of leaks from within the Army and War Ministry. Knowing this, he created a story of a false attack on Charleroi with the main thrust going towards Mons.[81] This false plan, as well as amazingly accurate information on the dispositions and strengths of the French army reached the Allies. While the ruse of the attack on Mons may have led to Wellington's slow response at the onset of the campaign, there was really no useful information. The only actionable intelligence would be where Napoleon and his guard was at an exact moment, as that would indicate the center of operations for any French offensive. As long as this was uncertain and unclear, the allies were compelled to remain deployed in such a manner as to defend all approaches Napoleon could make. Furthermore, they could not easily concentrate and supply an army for any length of time. These basic realities worked to Napoleon's advantage. As long as he could finalize the concentration of his army and strike in a few days, he would achieve a local numerical advantage over the Allied forces, and have an opportunity to dictate the initial events of the campaign. The concept of surprise must be viewed in this manner – of achieving a local numerical advantage against a strategically more numerous enemy.

One can also wonder if the number of deserters and traitors was somewhat numbing to Wellington as he was slow to respond to the increasing reports of French troop concentration.

On June 7th Gérard received Soult's order to concentrate on the Belgium frontier joining the *Armée du Nord*. Lettow-Vorbeck describes it thusly where 3 German miles was roughly equivalent to 7.5 kilometers:

> *The work the Emperor had assigned to the chief of staff was a tremendous one, and one can hardly blame the latter that only on June 5th, he issued the order to the 4th corps to start marching on the 7th and to reach Rocroi on the 13th, in seven stages of 3 miles each, via Stenay, Mézières. The commander of the corps, General Gérard, nevertheless was to remain in Metz until the 10th, in order to give the necessary instructions concerning the surveillance of the border*

---

81 Philippe de Callatay, 'La concentration de l'armée francaise pour la campagne de juin 1815', *Bulletin de la Société Royale Belge d'Etudes Napoleoniennes*, Tome 51, 2007, translation by John Hussey, *First Empire*, #102, p. 24, citing *Wellington's Supplementary Dispatches* Volume X, pp. 423-425.

> *between Metz and Thionville to General Rouyer who was to march out of Nancy on the 7th, with the 2nd division of the national guard. Probably Soult had used the term of "relieve" (relever), such as in the simultaneous notification to Vandamme, and this would explain why, on the 7th, Gérard had only one of his divisions march off, and had the other two follow on the 8th and the 9th. The cavalry and artillery of the corps were also assigned to the last squadron.* [82]

The text of this order is not available today. However, it seems clear that Soult did not properly convey Napoleon's wishes. The speedy march Napoleon originally asked for was now further delayed by the staggering of the departure times of the infantry divisions and attached cavalry. Based on the time-table above, the IV Corps could not be fully assembled in Rocroi until the evening of June 15th, while Napoleon had given every indication of targeting June 14th for the commencement of hostilities. Did Soult change Napoleon's original order? Or was it simply unclear leading to a misunderstanding by Gérard? Or was it some combination of both?

While Lettow-Vorbeck gives the departure of the infantry divisions as June 7th, 8th, and 9th, Jean Charles Louis Regnault, in his book *La Campagne de 1815 mobilisation et concentration*, gives it as the 8th, 9th, and 10th, as well as the bivouacs for each day of their march. Regnault's version is further substantiated on account of a letter written by Bourmont to his wife and dated on June 8th from Fontoy, the 14th division's cantonment prior to receiving the movement orders.[83]

Additionally, on June 7th Soult was ordered to inspect the northern fortresses, and to leave from Paris on the evening of 8 June for Lille. This decision has been highly criticized as it removed the *Major-Général* from the headquarters during the concentration and on the eve of the campaign.

Oosterman theorized that Soult was to gather spies or those that knew the roads of Belgium, as well as to be seen by the Allies such that they would not think an offensive was imminent. While Soult was ordered to

---

82 See "Lettow-Vorbeck" on page 277, "pages 219-224"
83 Gautherot, Gustave, "Bourmont à Waterloo", *Revue des Questions Historiques*, Volume 92, pp. 94 - 129. Details in section titled « L'ACTE ADDITIONNEL ET LE DESSEIN DE BOURMONT »
https://books.google.com/books?id=WpojAQAAIAAJ

travel incognito, it is almost a certainty that Soult's presence was noticed in this very royalist region, and thus this could very well have been a ruse. With Lille's strong royalist sympathies, if Soult had a desire to gain any insight from those sympathetic to the King, this trip would have afforded a great opportunity.

On June 9th, the march of IV Corps to the Belgium frontier was well under way. The 14th Infantry division, commanded by Bourmont, ended the day at Sivry-sur-Meuse; the 12th division bivouacked at Etain; the 13th division stopped at Conflans. Bourmont had covered about 29 kilometers.

CHAPTER 5
JUNE 10ᵀᴴ

On June 10ᵀᴴ, Napoleon sent the following orders for the final concentration of the Army before commencing hostilities:

Paris, June 10, 1815.

Position of the army on the 13th.

> *Imperial Headquarters and the Imperial Guard at Avesnes.*
> *Artillery parks and bridge supplies on the banks before Avesnes.*
> *Of the Reserve Cavalry 1ˢᵗ and 2ⁿᵈ Corps at Beaumont.*
> *3ʳᵈ and 4ᵗʰ Corps between Avesnes and Beaumont.*
> *6ᵗʰ Corps at Beaumont. The headquarters to the rear. If the 6ᵗʰ Corps finds it troublesome to arrive at Beaumont, they could arrive halfway.*
> *1ˢᵗ Corps at Pont sur Sambre. This Corps will move without passing by Bavay. They will pass by Le Quesnoy, in order to avoid the enemy. They will reveal their movement as late as possible. As we do not suppose that it is necessary to spend more than one day in Valenciennes, it will be just the 13th that they will prepare their movement to arrive on the Sambre.*
> *The 2ⁿᵈ Corps behind Maubeuge in columns on the Thuin road, without passing the border, and moving as unnoticed as possible.*
> *The 3ʳᵈ Corps at Philippeville.*
> *Armée de la Moselle at Mariembourg.*
> *All of the communications on the border will be intercepted.*

The soldiers will have four days of bread on their backs, half-pound of rice, fifty cartridges.

The batteries will be with the divisions: reserve batteries with their army corps.

The light cavalry of each army corps will be in front of the corps.

Each ambulance with its division

Each division will have on the auxiliary or military wagons eight days of bread, biscuits, and a cattle pen for eight days.

We will make no change on the border, we will not cross it at any point. We will fire no cannons. We will do nothing that could wake the enemy.

This order will remain secret.[84]

As with several of the crucial orders leading up to the commencement of the campaign, this order is absent from *Correspondance de Napoléon Ier* and *Correspondance Militaire De Napoleon* published by the *Ministre de la Guerre* in 1877. Houssaye references this order in his footnotes[85] in 1899, but gives no detail. Callatay states that this order was first published by Lettow-Vorbeck in 1904.[86]

Presumably, Soult would have turned Napoleon's order into a series of orders for each Corps commander and recorded a copy of them in the *Registre du Major-Général*, along with all other orders emanating from the *Grand État-Major Général*.

The book may have been bound in "long-grain red morocco," a tanned goatskin, and may have been gilded on its edges with embossed gilded lettering on its cover announcing the *Major-Général*.[87] Colonel Vachée, quoting liberally from Foucart's *La Campagne de Prusse*, and with the reference to Marshal Soult simply a coincidence, tells us:

---

84 See "Napoleon's Order of the Day" on page 364
85 Houssaye, *1815*, p. 330, footnote #47
86 Philippe de Callatay, 'La concentration de l'armee francaise pour la campagne de juin 1815', *Bulletin de la Société Royale Belge d'Etudes Napoleoniennes*, tome 51, 2007, translation by John Hussey, *First Empire*, #102 footnote #30.
87 On Sunday, December 4th, 2011, an order book of Berthier's sold at auction. A picture of hit can be seen here:
h t t p : / / w w w . o s e n a t . f r / h t m l / f i c h e . jsp?id=2179479&np=1&lng=fr&npp=1000&ordre=&aff=&r=&sold=

June 10th

The dictations and minutes, which replaced the rough draughts, were written down the right-hand side of a piece of double elephant paper divided into two. They were headed by the address: "To the Chief of the Staff, Marshal Soult." Within the margin, the secretary indicated the place, date, hour, and often a summary of the subjects contained in the despatch. He added the name of the officer or courier who carried the despatch and the hour of his departure.

Despatches, which were copied the first, in order to be sent off without delay, were on vellum-post with gilt edge, little elephant size, written without a margin and presented to the Emperor for his signature.

The archivist kept daily a numbered work-sheet, containing a summary of the despatches sent out during the day by the Emperor. These work-sheets bore, at the top, for example, "Feuille de travail number 13," and the date below, "Auma, October 12th, 1806," was written on one half of the paper, and constituted a repertory of the Emperor's work. The archivist inscribed on the sheet the names of the officers or couriers entrusted with the despatches, and the hour of their departure. And when the Emperor changed his residence and worked twice on the same day, the same sheet of paper, with an indication of the new residence and hour, served the whole of the day.[88]

The Register, also called *Correspondance du Major-Général* or often simply the order book[89], is one of the key characters of the campaign. As we'll see, it has provided as much mystery as it has answers.

Napoleon's order intended to produce the following disposition:

Imperial Guard at Avesnes
I and II Reserve Cavalry at Beaumont
VI Corps at Beaumont
III and IV Reserve Cavalry between Avesnes and Beaumont

---

88 Vachée, Colonel, *Napoleon at Work*, translated by G. Frederic Lees, London, 1914, pp. 104-105.
Double Elephant paper is 101.6 x 67.8 cms, or 40 x 26.75 inches.
Little Elephant paper is 71.1 x 58.4 cms, or 28 x 23 inches.
89 See *Registre d'ordres du maréchal Berthier pendant la campagne de 1813* for a collection of Berthier's orders during 1813, at http://gallica.bnf.fr/ark:/12148/bpt6k67976m

I Corps at Pont sur Sambre
II Corps behind Maubeuge on road to Thuin
III Corps at Philippeville
IV Corps at Mariembourg

As one can see from the Figure 2, Napoleon planned for 3 columns that would converge on Charleroi.

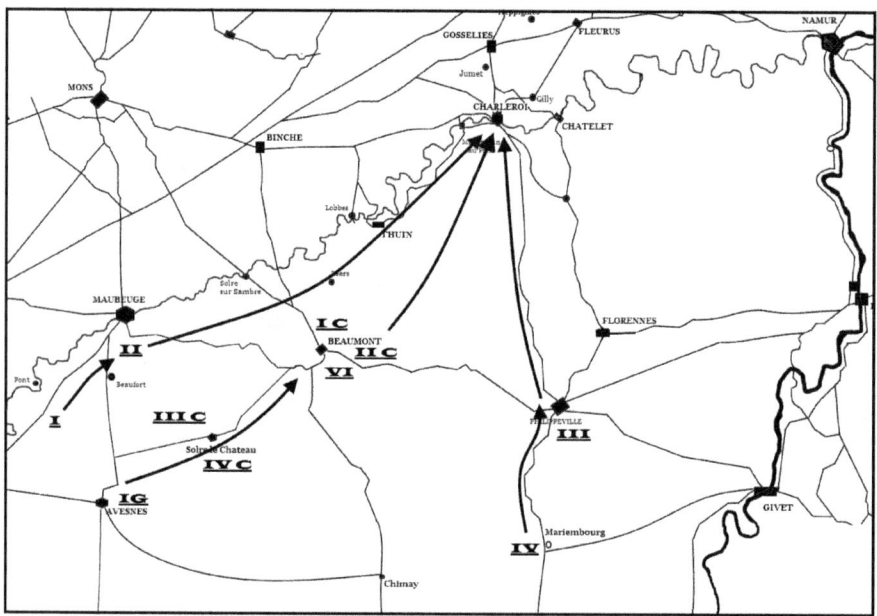

Figure 2 - Intentions of Napoleon's order of June 10th

One thing that is immediately clear is that Napoleon desired IV Corps to assemble at Mariembourg on June 13th. Had IV Corps been ordered to Philippeville, then achieving Mariembourg by the 13th would have presented no problems. However, as Soult had ordered Gérard to Rocroi by the 13th, more than a half day's march south of Mariembourg, and worded the orders in such a way that Gérard had failed to understand the urgency, IV Corps was now executing its movement in a manner that would fail Napoleon's intentions. This makes it unlikely that Napoleon had prior knowledge or approved of the orders Soult sent to Gérard.

Was this simply a mistake? This would certainly be consistent with Soult's legacy as *Major-Général*. At this point, there was simply no reason to believe Soult would have willfully changed Napoleon's orders.

IV Corps' march continued. The 14th Infantry division ended the day at Mouzon; the 12th division bivouacked at Sivry-sur-Meuse; the 13th division stopped at Etain. Bourmont had covered about 32 kilometers.

CHAPTER 6
JUNE 11ᵀᴴ

On June 11ᵀᴴ, Clarke sent to Goltz the information that the royalist spies in the Ministry of war had delivered via an officer that had left Paris on June 4ᵗʰ.[90] The information about the Army was very accurate.

On this day, Napoleon made it clear when he planned to commence the campaign, pending any setbacks. Writing to Davout, he said:

> *My Cousin, you will inform Marshal Suchet, by courier and by telegraph, that hostilities will begin on the 14th, and that on that day he can seize Montmélian. If it is essential that he does so before this time, because of the movements of the enemy, then it is permitted. However it would be desirable that he did not do it before 15th.*

With everything going to plan, Napoleon wrote to Davout to summon Ney to the front if he wished to participate in the campaign:

> *My Cousin, call up Maréchal Ney; tell him, if he wishes to be present when the first battle takes place, then he must be at Avesnes on June 14th, there he will find my headquarters.*

While this book makes a case that Napoleon was massively betrayed in 1815, one should not interpret this to mean that Napoleon was otherwise flawless. Napoleon's use of Ney, such as his late call to the army and the

---

90 Malet, M. A., *Louis XVIII et Les Cent-Jours à Gand*, 1902, Volume 2, Clarke à Goltz of June 10, 1815 reproduced in "Treasonous Correspondence with Ghent" on page 267

responsibilities he would be later given despite his lack of staff or preparation, has often been criticized.

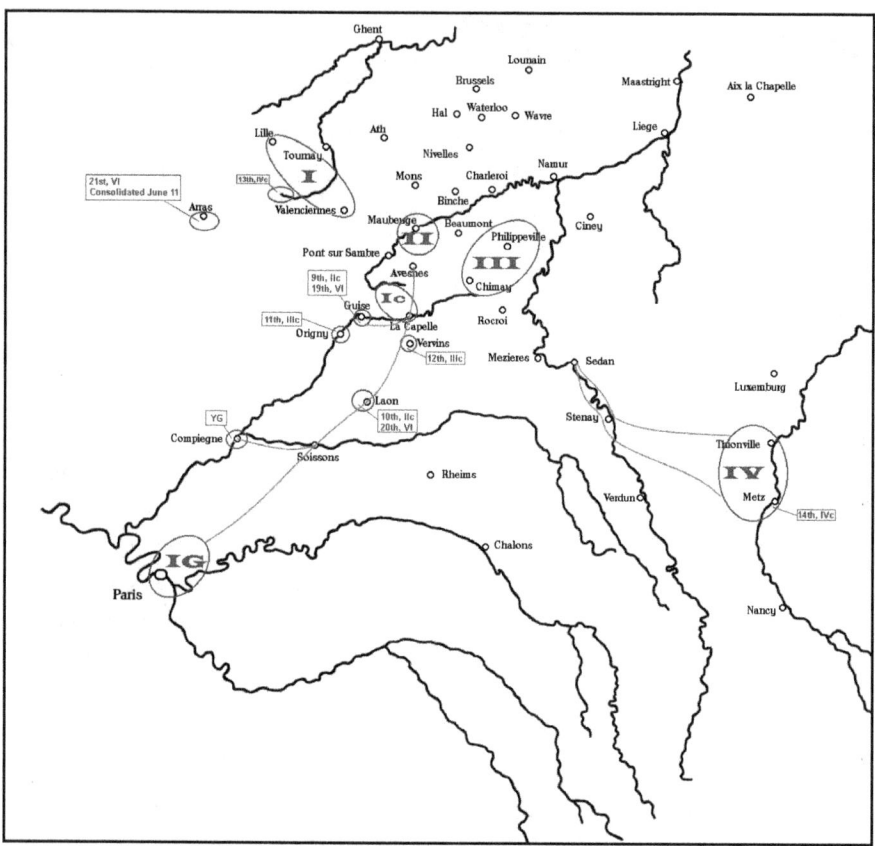

Figure 3 - *Armée du Nord* Concentration through June 11th

Figure 3 gives the progress of the *Armée du Nord* concentration as of June 11th. Other than the 14th Division of the IV Cavalry Corps (and a regiment of Dragoons from the 9th Division of the II Cavalry Corps), none of the reserve cavalry divisions had yet moved. The Imperial Guard, including the Young Guard that was at Compiegne, was ahead of schedule marching up from Soissons, probably due to Napoleon's personal oversight of their orders. The 19th and 20th Divisions of VI Corps united at La Capelle on the evening of the 11th while at the same time its 21st Division had formed

June 11th

up at Arras. I Corps, II Corps, and III Corps were all basically in theatre and would hold their positions until the last moment.

IV Corps had by far the most difficult assignment, and it was not going according to plan. The 14th Infantry division ended the day at Sedan; the 12th division bivouacked at Mouzon; the 13th division stopped at Damvillers. Bourmont had only covered about 14 kilometers.

Napoleon's plan was brilliant and decisive, yet also far from complex. Despite a few blemishes which are always expected in the controlled chaos of 19th century military operations, things were seemingly going smoothly.

This was all about to change.

CHAPTER 7
JUNE 12TH

On June 12th, Soult gave the following report to Napoleon on his efforts to carry out the orders of June 10th.

Avesnes, 12 June 1815

In executing the order that Your Majesty gave on the 10th of this month, I have issued the following dispositions regarding the sites that the various army corps must occupy on the 13th:

The 2nd Corps on the Sambre, from below Maubeuge to Solre-sur-Sambre, occupying the villages of Hantay, Montigny, Bousignies, Bersillies, Colleret, Cerfontaine, and Ferrière-la-Grande.

The 1st Corps between Pont-sur-Sambre and Maubeuge, staying ready to debouch on one or other bank of the Sambre, as your Majesty has ordered.

The 3rd Corps at Beaumont.

The 6th Corps at Beaufort where it will have its headquarters, Fontaine, Limont, Eclaibes, Dimont, Dimechaux, Wattignies, Choisies, Damousies, Obrechies, and Ferrière-la-Petite.

The 1st, 2nd, 3rd and 4th Cavalry Corps, under the command of Marshal Grouchy, at Solre-le-Château and in the villages of Sars, Lez-Fountain, Offies, L'Epine, Chamoul, Clairfayts, Epmoy, Beaurieux, Grandrieu, Hestrud, Leugmes, Cousolre, Aibes, Quiévelon, Solrimes, Eccles.

The artillery parks and bridging equipment will be placed in front of Avesnes; we have left some villages vacant so that they can stable their horses.

> *The town of Avesnes is left at the disposal of Your Majesty's Guard, as well as the villages behind and those in the Helpe valley on the right and left of Avesnes.*[91]

As with the order of June 10, this report had not been published until Lettow-Vorbeck offered it in his 1904 book *Napoleons Untergang* published in German, and Arthur Chuquet included the order of June 10th in *Ordres et Apostilles* and the report of June 12th in *Inédits Napoléoniens* both published after 1910. It is not known when this report became available in the archives, but it had certainly escaped attention during the initial waves of critical analysis of the campaign.

Additionally, Lettow-Vorbeck included the following in Soult's report:

> *According to a report received from Count Gérard, the first division of the Armee de la Moselle will reach Rocroi on the 13th, the second on the 14th, the third on the 15th, the cavalry division and the artillery park also on the 15th. I immediately wrote that Your Majesty had ordered that he should be fully assembled at Rocroi on the 13th and that I had given him an order to this effect. I repeated the order to him to accelerate the march of his troops to make up for the time lost, and to continue the march of his Army by directing it via Chimay on Beaumont, where it will form the second line behind the 3rd corps and follow it on its march towards the Sambre as soon as that begins.*
>
> *General Delort, commanding the 14th cavalry division, wrote to me from Metz on the 9th that his division would arrive at Mézières on the 13th and that he could not reach his destination at Hirson until the 15th. I sent him an order to march from Mézières via Rocroi and Chimay to Beaumont to reach there by the 15th and to place himself in line with the remainder of the cavalry. I have informed Marshal Grouchy of this.*[92]

---

91 "Soult's report to Napoleon" on page 366
92 Callatay, Philippe de, "La Concentration de l'armee francaise pour la campagne de juin 1815", *Bulletin de la Société Royale Belge d'Etudes Napoleoniennes*, Tome 51, 2007, English translation by John Hussey, *First Empire*, #102, p. 27

June 12th

Soult's orders fundamentally changed Napoleon's orders of June 10th.

As seen in Figure 4, Soult completely removed the right column. Instead, the left column was now comprised of I Corps, II Corps, and VI Corps, while the central column was now comprised by the III Corps, IV Corps, and Imperial Guard. All the reserve cavalry was concentrated in the center of the army.

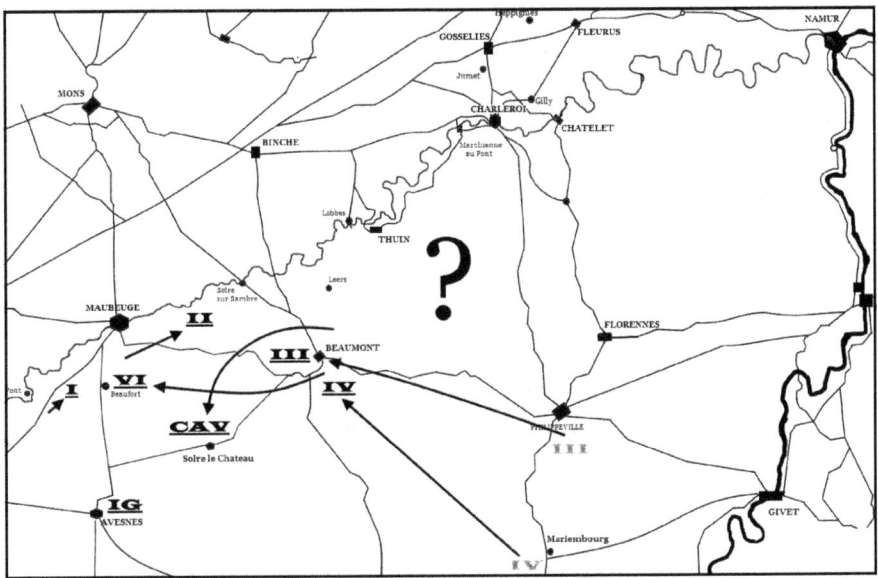

Figure 4 - Soult's Modifications to Napoleon's June 10th Order

Those historians who have commented on this have been unable to comprehend Soult's actions.

Pierre De Wit wrote:

> *What possible reason could Soult have had for his disregard for Napoleon's orders of the 10th?*
> *Why Soult issued the wrong orders for these units is simply an enigma. It would be too simple to assume that Soult would be mistaken at these very crucial orders, just at the crux of the concentration,*

placing the corps in their starting points for the advance into the Netherlands.[93]

Philippe de Callatay wrote:

Soult's behavior in this matter is incredible and incomprehensible. Although he is at pains to state that his instructions had been given to the different corps in accordance with the imperial order of 10 June, his report shows that, at least for the right wing, his orders were in total contradiction to those he had received.[94]

Was someone hiding something?

According to Philippe de Callatay, the answer is yes:

In the 19th Century, care was taken to conceal Soult's fault; neither the 10 June order nor the report of 12 June were published. Military solidarity was evident. For instance, among the documents he quoted in his own defence, Grouchy published in 1841 the contents of Soult's register of orders and correspondence - but only from the next day (13 June) onwards. The imperial order of 10 June was not published in the Correspondance de Napoleon Ier; *yet it was certainly known. Henry Houssaye stated that the order of 10 June was in the* Archives de la guerre, Armee du nord, *and that the report of 12th was in the national archives, AF. IV, 1938; but he did not disclose the contents of those documents. Again, in 1935, Commandant Jean Regnault, a qualified staff officer, repeatedly referred to the documents of 10 and 12 June, but cited nothing that could reveal the fault of Soult.*[95]

---

93 DeWit, Pierre, Page 17 http://www.waterloo-campaign.nl/bestanden/files/preambles/adn.1.pdf
94 Callatay, Philippe de, *La Concentration de l'armee francaise pour la champagne de juin 1815, Bulletin de la Société Royale Belge d'Etudes Napoleoniennes*, Tome 51, 2007, English translation by John Hussey, *First Empire*, #102, p. 27
95 Callatay, Philippe de, "La Concentration de l'armee francaise pour la campagne de juin 1815", *Bulletin de la Société Royale Belge d'Etudes Napoleoniennes*, Tome 51, 2007, English translation by John Hussey, *First Empire*, #102, footnote 36

June 12th

What could explain Soult's orders?

Had Napoleon's false intelligence of a ruse on Charleroi followed by an advance on Mons confused him? He does state that I Corps is positioned to advance on either side of the Sambre.

The change is too detailed and complex to be a simple mistake, and the original plan was too simple for Soult to have claimed it was not understood. Lettow-Vorbeck theorized that it was possible this change was related to Soult's suggestion of June 4th to advance in two columns, but considering this change was insubordination as well as the change did not match his June 4th recommendation, he did not find this explanation credible.[96]

As Soult *clearly* changed Napoleon's written order, his actions with Gérard and the orders of IV Corps sent on the 5th are now much more suspect. If one wondered if Soult was capable of willfully changing Napoleon's orders, his report of the 12th leaves no doubt. Soult was sabotaging the campaign.

Napoleon left Paris on June 12th in the early morning and arrived in Laon around noon, over 120 kms! When urgency demanded it, and with frequent changing of horses, great distances could be traveled in a short time.

Arriving at Laon, Napoleon found that the reserve cavalry of Grouchy had not moved towards the front. Soult and/or his staff had not sent them orders; most likely an oversight due to Soult's journey to Lille. Napoleon instructed Grouchy to get them moving towards the frontier, while on this same day, Soult simply forwarded Napoleon's order of the 10th which still had campaign's commencement scheduled for the 14th:

> *Marshal, I have the honor to address to you a copy from the Emperor dated the 10th, relating to the position of the army on the 13th. The Emperor orders that you prepare to march, the 1st, 2nd, 3rd and 4th Cavalry Corps and that you direct them on Avesnes, from where they will continue on their route to establish, the 1st*

---

[96] See "Lettow-Vorbeck" on page 277, "pages 219-224." Oosterman also discusses Soult possibly being motivated by his own plan, though concludes Soult's actions were inexecusable and very harmful in "Opmarsch en concentratie van het Fransche leger in Juni 1815", *Militaire Spectator*, 1913
http://www.kvbk-cultureelerfgoed.nl/MS_PDF/1912/1912-0769-01-0141.PDF.

and 2nd Corps in front of Solre-le-Château, occupying the villages of Coursolre, Leugnies, Grandrieu, Hestrud, Eccles, Solrinnes, Quierelont, and their dependences.

The 3rd and 4th Corps at Solre-le-Château, while occupying Borieu, Epinoy, Harnault Fountains, Sartz and Offies. You must, M. Maréchal, establish yourself at Solre and make all arrangements so that the movement of these four Cavalry Corps is finished by the evening of the 13th. I request, Marshal, that you realize the execution of this order. Receive etc.

This oversight of the cavalry has often been used as an example of Soult's shortcomings as *Major-Général*. Even Mauduit, so quick to accuse Soult of treason, can only ask, "What was the traitor or the culprit on this occasion?"[97] However, not all acts have ominous back-drops. In this case, it merely appears that Soult's mission to Lille created a breakdown, and it was repaired with forced marches with significant stress placed on those cavalry divisions farthest from the frontier.

The fatigue so many French horses gained during the concentration should not be discounted. It is possible that the French cavalry's performance during the campaign was significantly negatively impacted.

Napoleon and Soult had been in almost constant war for over 20 years. Mistakes were common. Moving so many parts, when communicating by horse, and dealing with orders written as neatly and as quickly as human hands were able, possessed a significant built-in limitation. Knowing this, Soult realized that as *Major-Général*, he could hide maleficence rather easily, as will be seen. However, the bungling of the orders of the 10th were something quite different, and whatever Soult said that satisfied Napoleon, it was not something he would be able to easily get away with again prior to Napoleon's defeat.

Whatever Soult gave as an explanation, it worked. In fact, while very little is known about Soult's activities during this campaign, they most likely were seemingly diligent and hard working as Napoleon was suitably impressed enough to praise Soult as an excellent Chief of Staff, as we have previously seen in his conversation with O'Meara while in exile.

---

97 Mauduit, Volume 2, p. 498

June 12th

On the evening of June 12th, the 14th and 12th divisions of IV Corps reached Mézières. The 13th division reached Sedan. Bourmont had only covered 18 kilometers. For a second straight day, Bourmont's division had made only a half-days march. Maybe he was allowing the rear divisions to close. Or, considering we know he had no intention of leading his division into battle, maybe Bourmont was purposely delaying the march. Having informed Soult of his corps' progress, Gérard was ordered to hurry the march.

While the French army concentrated, Blucher's Chief of Staff, Gneisenau, was just this day found writing to Hardenberg that "… the danger of an attack has almost completely disappeared."[98]

The surprise was well under way.

---

[98] See "Lettow-Vorbeck" on page 277, "page 192"

CHAPTER 8
JUNE 13TH

REGARDLESS OF WHEN NAPOLEON RECEIVED Soult's report, on the 13th corrective orders were issued. Responding to Soult's orders of the 12th, the III Corps bivouacked the night of the 13th outside of Beaumont. Napoleon countermanded the corrective order when it was clear III Corps had already made too much progress. From this point forward, IV Corps would alone constitute the right column, and Vandamme's III Corps was now the lead infantry corps of the center column.

Considering that the right and center were not expected to encounter much resistance, especially considering the surprise, this must not have been too alarming. The army was going to converge near Charleroi, and it would be easy enough to redress once across the Sambre.

The Cavalry reached their assigned positions by the evening of the 13th, though some had significant forced marches.

I Corps and II Corps moved to their appointed positions, but not without more defections.

The VI Corps bivouacked around Beaufort with the 21st division trailing below Avesnes.

The IV Corps, originally ordered for Mariembourg, had responded to Soult's orders and veered towards Beaumont. However, as Napoleon's intentions had not been followed, IV Corps was not consolidated around Philippeville nor ready for the start of the campaign. The 14th division was near Chimay on the evening of the 13th with the 12th division following closely behind. The 13th division reached Rimogne, south of Rocroi, which was south of Mariembourg. As a result of IV Corps' delay, as well as that of the Cavalry reserve, Napoleon postponed the start of the campaign until June 15th.

At this point, it is worth reviewing IV Corps' march to the campaign theatre, as it is very revealing. Focusing on Bourmont's 14th Division, we have surmised that it began its march on June 8th from Fontoy and bivouacked at Etain, or about 32 kilometers. It bivouacked on June 9th at Sivry-sur-Meuse for a march of about 29 kilometers. It bivouacked on June 10th at Mouzon for a march of about 32 kilometers. Bourmont was clearly pushing the division diligently. On June 11th, Bourmont's division bivouacked near Sedan having only made 14 kilometers. On June 12th, Bourmont's division bivouacked near Mouzon having only made 18 kilometers. Bourmont had dramatically slowed his division. Had he become aware that they were marching to war, something he clearly lacked the motivation for? Or was he simply allowing the rear divisions to close? Soult sent orders on the 12th to Gérard to hasten their march per his report to Napoleon. Bourmont certainly responded. On June 13th, Bourmont's 14th division made its farthest march of about 40 kilometers. While Bourmont was following orders, at this point he must have been plotting his defection. As he and his staff could have left on any day of the march and easily reached the frontier before anyone noticed their absence, there must have been some motivation to stay with the army.

Napoleon was known to keep his plans close to the vest. It is quite likely that at this point, Bourmont lacked any actionable intelligence. Even if he had access to Napoleon's orders of the 10th, there was nothing that indicated the direction of advance. As we saw previously, Clouet claimed that after he had talked Bourmont into remaining with army, Bourmont seemed strongly disposed to join the King *as soon as possible*. This was clearly false, for he could reach the King at a far greater pace than his infantry division could march – especially a division which had been slowed down for two days. Something else was clearly keeping Bourmont at his post, and his sympathizers have spent 200 years ignoring basic common sense. They would have us believe Bourmont had simply given notice on June 1st, and was committed to doing his duty until the last possible moment.[99]

---

[99] Gautherot, Gustave, "Bourmont à Waterloo", *Revue des Questions Historiques*, Volume 92, pp. 94 - 129.
https://books.google.com/books?id=WpojAQAAIAAJ
Gautherot promotes the case that Bourmont desired to retire on June 1st, per letters to his wife and Gérard. He quotes von Ollech's work as well to substantiate the Bourmont was entitled to leave the army. The whole premise is ridiculous. If Bourmont felt his first loyalty was to the King, so be it. This was war, it wasn't tennis. But Bourmont and his sympathisers wish to paint this as a man following his conscious, even to this day on various

June 13th

As we shall see, Bourmont was committed to doing his duty, and the moment he was waiting for was rapidly approaching.

The gathering French army had not gone unnoticed by the Allies. According to Siborne:

> *During the night of the 13th, however, the light reflected upon the sky by the fires of the French bivouacs, did not escape the vigilant observation of Zieten's outposts, whence it was communicated to the rear that these fires appeared to be in the direction of Walcourt and of Beaumont, and also in the vicinity of Solre-sur-Sambre; further, that all reports received through spies and deserters, concurred in representing that Napoleon was expected to join the French army on that evening; that the imperial guard and the 2nd corps had arrived at Avesnes and Maubeuge; also that, at one o'clock in the afternoon of that day, four French battalions had crossed the river at Solre-sur-Sambre, and occupied Merbes-le-Chateau; that late in the night the enemy had pushed forward a strong detachment as far as Sart-la-Bussiére; and lastly, that an attack by the French would certainly take place on the 14th or 15th.*[100]

Despite Siborne's strong statement, the Prussian's made no effort to concentrate their army to meet an attack that would "certainly" be taking place as early as the next day! Clausewitz delineates a timeline for the concentration of the Prussian army, where eight hours was "…necessary for notifying and turning out the troops."[101] Even without knowing Napoleon's intended advance, could not this time have been saved by having each Corps mobilize and be ready to march to meet this *certain* attack?

---

internet message boards. They go to great pains to suggest that very little harm came from the defection. Yet the timing and place of his action goes undiscussed as though they are irrelevant details instead of proof of a well planned act.
100 Siborne, Captain William, *History of the War in France and Belgium in 1815*, beginning of chapter IV.
101 Clausewitz, Carl von; Duke of Wellington, Arthur Wellesley, *On Waterloo: Clausewitz, Wellington, and the Campaign of 1815*, Kindle Edition, p. 85.

Despite a steady stream of deserters, such as a trooper of the 5th Lancers reported by General Collaert[102], the illumination of the sky by the campfires of the French army, and the detailed intelligence provided by spies, a significant response would not take place until something definitive was received by the Allied high-command. The uncertainty which clearly hung over the Prussian response appears to have only been removed by hindsight.

With the campaign's delay, Napoleon's Order of the Day for June 13th, reproduced in the Select Correspondence in the Appendix, made further adjustments that edged the army closer to the frontier. This order is less known than the famous Order of Movement issued on June 14th for the commencement of hostilities, but with this order, Napoleon identifies Charleroi as the initial target for the June 15th advance and identifies the departure time of 3 am

Here is an excerpt relating to the 2nd Corps:

> *The 2nd Corps will take a position at Leers, being as close as possible to the border, without crossing it. The four divisions of this army corps will be massed and will bivouac on two or four lines: the headquarters in the middle, the cavalry forward, scouting all of the debouches, but without crossing the border and protecting it from the enemy partisans who would wish to invade.*
>
> *The bivouacs will be placed so that the fires cannot be seen by the enemy; the Generals will prevent anyone from leaving the camp; they will assure that the troops are equipped with 50 cartridges per man, four days of bread and a half pound of meat; that the artillery and the ambulances are in good condition, and they will be placed in their order of battle. Thus the 2nd Corps will be arranged so that it can begin marching on the 15th, at 3:00 o'clock in the morning, if the order is given, to march on Charleroi and to arrive there before nine o'clock.*

---

102 De Bas, *Prins Frederik der Nederlanden en zijn tijd*, page 1157 http://babel.hathitrust.org/cgi/pt?id=wu.89097621346;view=1up;seq=713

JUNE 13TH

Thus, while up until this point Napoleon had kept his ultimate plan close to the vest, now, with a full day before the attack, he had finally revealed his designs.

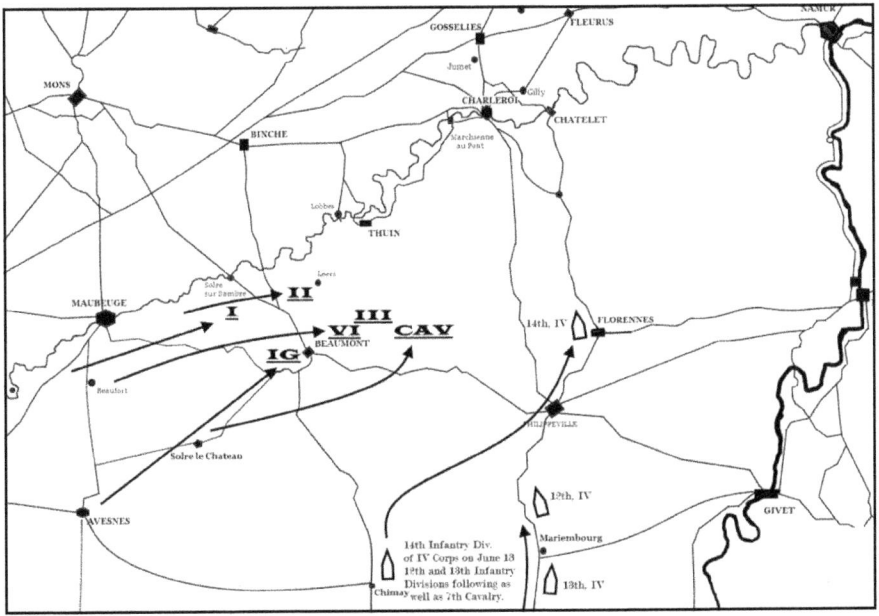

Figure 5 – Final Concentration Movements

PART II
Opening Moves: Armies and Traitors

CHAPTER 9
JUNE 14TH

From Avesnes, Napoleon wrote to his brother Joseph in the morning:

> *Avesnes, June 14, 1815, morning*
> *My brother, I move my Imperial Headquarter to Beaumont this evening. Tomorrow the 15th, I will march on Charleroi, where the Prussian army is; this will give way to a battle or the retreat of the enemy. The army is handsome and the weather fine enough; the country support us strongly.*
> *I will write this evening if we must have communications on the 16th. In the meantime, we must prepare.*
> *Farewell*[103]

The *Armée du Nord* assumed final positions per the Order of the Day given on the 13th.

The IV Corps advanced in the position originally intended for the III Corps, with Bourmont's division in the lead making at least a 30 kilometer march with Toussaint's brigade bivouacking at Walcourt and Hulot's brigade bivouacking at Florennes where Bourmont established his headquarters. Curiously, Bourmont's division was the only one to get north of Philippeville, despite being closely following by the 12th Division. Bourmont was only a few kilometers from the frontier and only 30 kilometers from Namur, where Blücher had the Prussian Army headquarters. Furthermore, the order of

---

103 *Correspondance*, Vol. 28, No. 22050 See "Napoleon to Joseph, Morning" on page 451

June 13th had firmly established that on the morning of June 15th, the French army would be advancing on Charleroi.

During the night, the final orders for the attack, the well known Order of Movement, reproduced in the Select Correspondence of the Appendix, was written and distributed. Figure 6 shows the intentions of the order.

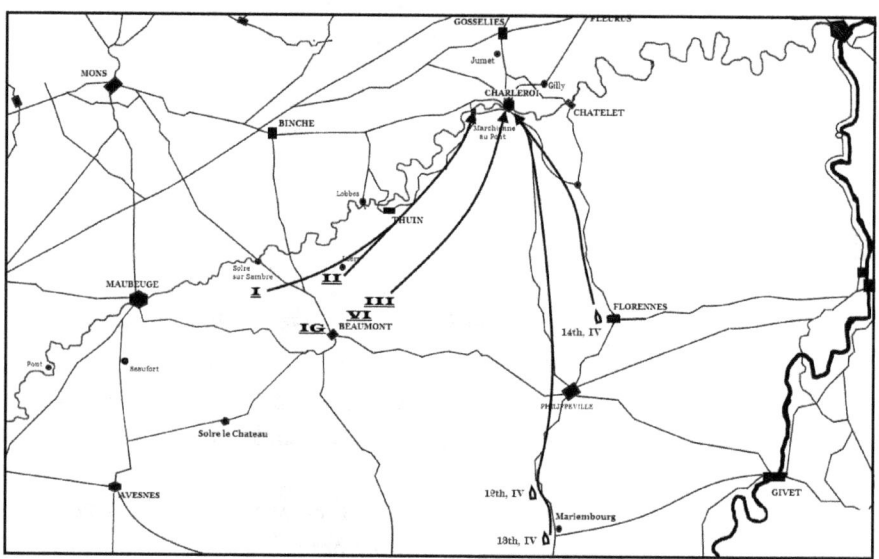

Figure 6 - June 14th Movement Orders

While the Order of the Day on the 13th had started with the HQs and the Guard, and then moved from left to right across the French columns of advance, the order of movement started with the central column with Vandamme receiving the first directive. Events would almost make this humorous.

An interesting observation about the Order of Movement was Napoleon's desire that Flemish speaking officers were to accompany the advanced guards of the columns. Flemish was found predominantly north of Brussels, and seems to indicate that Napoleon expected a rapid advance with minimal opposition until he occupied that city. With what he knew about the enemy dispositions, if he could seize the Nivelles-Namur road, he could separate the Prussian and Anglo-Dutch armies and dictate their only chance for cooperation to be north of Brussels.

June 14th

Strategic Surprise

In his book, *1815: The Waterloo Campaign*, Hofschröer provides a detailed narrative on the allied gathering of intelligence during the first two weeks of June. Between spies, observations, and the traitors, the Allies had a tremendous amount of information. So much so that Hofschröer refutes Napoleon's view that the Allies had been surprised:

> *Napoleon was clearly unaware of how good the Allied network of spies actually was, and how much the Allies knew of his movements. He based his view on the situation on reports from his spies in Brussels and Namur who reported that all there was quiet. This information was misleading. Although no significant troop movements had taken place, the various Allied headquarters were buzzing with reports coming in from all directions. Napoleon commenced his offensive in the firm belief that he had taken his enemies completely by surprise. This was his first error, and it would not be his only one in this campaign.*[104]

Napoleon had rapidly assembled a lethal fighting force just hours south of the frontier, even while a stream of traitors had kept the allies well informed of its composition and position. Yet as the sun set on June 14th, the eve of the commencement of hostilities, not to mention the day Napoleon had originally intended to start the campaign, only a few allied units on the frontier had prepared for the possibility of attack. While no one can argue that the attacked Prussian forces were literally surprised by the presence of the French, it is clear that Napoleon had achieved his objective. As Hofschröer himself admits, "*... no significant troop movements had taken place...*" Thus, though outnumbered considerably, Napoleon's army was able to invade the enemy's territory, including crossing a river, and overpower all resistance. If the Allies were not surprised, they should have been able to destroy much of the French army as it crossed the Sambre. Instead, they spent the 15th June retreating in the face of greatly superior numbers.

What other measure of success could there possibly be?

Napoleon's final campaign was proceeding splendidly.

---

104 Hofschröer, Peter, *1815 The Waterloo Campaign*, London, 1998, p. 160.

Surprise Spoiled

Unfortunately for Napoleon, the enemy he could not out maneuver were the traitors.

Late in the evening of June 14th a party of riders led by a Prussian staff officer appeared at the bridge over the Meuse at Namur demanding to see Blücher.[105] Initially denied, the party insisted claiming to have with them a French General! The sentry believed the claim of escorting a French general to be an exaggeration in order to gain an audience, but relented in letting them pass. As Blücher had already retired, Gneisenau met with the party.

Whoever these riders were, the intelligence they brought was explosive. By midnight, Gneisenau had dispatched orders for the concentration of the Prussian army. II Corps was to concentrate on Mazy, III Corps on Namur, and the IV Corps on Hannut. From these points, they would be further ordered to Sombreffe. Significant troop movements would now take place at least 12 hours earlier than they would have otherwise.

Zieten's I Corps was braced for the attack, and would fall back on Fleurus if necessary.

Writing about the Prussian concentration, General Oscar Lettow-Vorbeck, authoring the German General Staff's official history of the 1815 campaign, wrote:

> *Indeed, these orders made it possible to unite three Army Corps at Sombreffe, on the 16th, still before Napoleon's attack. The IV. Corps could also have arrived there on time, had the order it had received been executed. However, it must not be overlooked that this was only possible because of the special messages received in the night leading up to the 15th. If the orders had only been given on the 15th, at 9 AM, after receipt of Zieten's first message, a timely gathering so far frontwards would have been impossible and would have had to happen further behind.* ***Without this treason committed by members of the French army, the surprise intended by Napoleon would have been successful to an even stronger degree than was the case now.*** *[Emphasis added]*[106]

---

105 See "Lettow-Vorbeck" on page 277, "Pages 196 - 199"
106 Ibid.

June 14th

Zieten, who commanded I Corps headquartered at Charleroi, had received intelligence from a French drum-major who had defected on June 13th. The Prussians had also noticed a large number of campfires which were lighting up the sky. There was no doubt of the concentration of the French army, and this information was reported to Namur. As a result, on the 14th at noon Gneisenau had already sent orders to all the other Corps to be *ready* to concentrate. However, it was not until the late night intelligence of June 14th that definitive orders of concentration were issued.

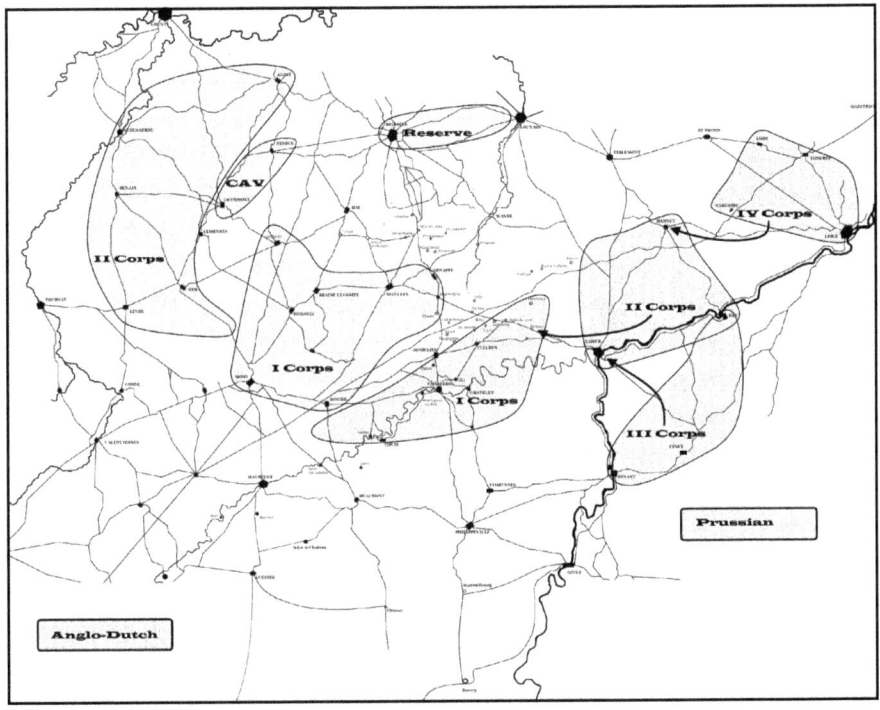

Figure 7 – Allied Dispositions of June 14th along with Prussian Concentration Orders for II, III, and IV Corps Shown

With all the traitors we've seen, just who was this mysterious "French General" who Lettow-Vorbeck believed to be the source of the intelligence compelling enough for Gneisenau to order the *very significant* movements of concentrating the entire Prussian army as prescribed by Wellington's and Blücher's plans in the event of an attack via Charleroi? Considering the vast amounts of intelligence the Prussians had to date, much of which was provided by French traitors, there is no doubt this material and individual must have been very significant indeed!

CHAPTER 10
JUNE 15TH

IN THE PRE-DAWN HOURS OF June 15th, 1815, three columns of Napoleon's army began their advance on Charleroi. If Napoleon's plans were executed, an isolated Prussian corps would be seriously mauled, and by the end of the day the French army would drive a wedge between Wellington and Blücher. Once separated, if either army decided to give battle, Napoleon would have a chance to destroy it. If the Allies tried to maneuver together, with their communications to each other compromised, Napoleon would have the type of advantage he had built his career on. If the Allies retreated on their bases, Napoleon had a chance to occupy Brussels without suffering significant loss.

The entire campaign was a race; time, the commodity Napoleon valued most, was of the essence.

RIGHT COLUMN

Bourmont's Defection

As a result of Soult's jumbling of Napoleon's plans, the vanguard of the right column was the 14th Division of IV Corps led by General Bourmont. Curiously, according to Houssaye, Soult requested that Bourmont should leave the Army of the North on May 22nd, while Napoleon, at that time, had not even ordered what was then the Army of the Moselle to join the *Armée du Nord*.[107] One must wonder what actions of Bourmont Soult found

---

[107] See Houssaye, Henry, *1815, Waterloo*, Translated from the 31st edition, London, 1900, p. 314 footnote 170

objectionable. Had Bourmont led a salute for the King at the Tuileries during Napoleon's return? Maybe Bourmont had published a proclamation condemning Napoleon? Did Soult despise those whose loyalties were so easily changed? Maybe Soult had learned something about Bourmont's plans, and had not yet decided on his own course. Whatever Soult's reasoning, Soult's orders in the week leading up to the commencement of hostilities had assured that Bourmont was now the tip of the spear of the right column of the Armée du Nord.

Rumigny, then a Colonel in the IV Corps staff, gives the following account in his memoirs:

> *In the evening of the 14th, orders to move came from the imperial quarter. I was charged to go to the Bourmont division that was stationed around Florennes and I left at 2 o'clock in the morning. I went at a full gallop, when two chasseurs on horseback, arriving from the direction of the outposts, beckoned me to stop:*
>
> *"General Bourmont has deserted," they shouted to me from a distance.*
>
> *"Shut your mouth, for heavens sake," I said to them, with sabre in hand, "it's impossible!"*
>
> *"We swear to you!"*
>
> *Stunned by this news, and because they gave all the details, I ordered them to go to the headquarters at Philippeville, to speak of this matter only to the chief of staff, Colonel Saint-Rémy, and advised that I would continue on my route to Florennes. I arrived at this place a few minutes later. Upon entering, I was surrounded by soldiers who shouted: "We are betrayed, down with the traitors!"*
>
> *These cries were directed against all of the officers, not excluding myself. I was aware of the danger of these threats, but I placed myself in the middle of them saying: "Bourmont has left you, because he is not worthy of your command. I bring the order to march, my children, take your arms."*

---

http://books.google.com/books?id=xWBAAAAAYAAJ for reference to Soult's request for Bourmont's removal.
See Chuquet, Arthur, *Ordres et Apostilles de Napoleon*, Paris, 1911, p. 485 No. 3332 for disposition of Army of Moselle at the end of May.
https://archive.org/details/ordresetapostillo2franuoft on 01/27/2014.

June 15th

> *I delivered the orders to General Vichery, I encouraged the men and managed to restore faith in their hearts. Here is what I learned about Bourmont and his companions. About midnight, he tore up all of the military papers that he did not want to carry. The scraps were scattered near the staff. At one o'clock, he got on horseback with all of his officers and the two orderly chaussers with him. He headed straight north, to the Prussian outposts, a distance of no more than two miles. Arriving there, he engaged the two orderlies to follow him. They refused, and in spite of promises of money, they returned. It was them that I encountered.*
>
> *The news of the desertion had spread, I'm not sure how; but, when arriving in Florennes, I heard the rumor. The division was ordered to cross the Sambre at 8 o'clock. We were in front of the bridge, when General Gérard joined us. He was stigmatizing Bourmont in an animated and passionate harangue and, in the midst of the soldier's cries of rage, he encouraged them to observe the strictest discipline.*
>
> *After a thousand oaths to follow him everywhere, Bourmont's former division began to march again, and we all crossed the Sambre to the sound of some fusillades that we heard from ahead.*
>
> *It appears that Bourmont, on arriving, declared that the army was on the march, of this the enemies were unaware. He or his officers said what they knew about our movements, and the alarm was given before we were in the vicinity of Châtelet. Fortunately, no effort, nor any measures, had been carried out to destroy the bridge, which was in no way defended. After having passed Châtelet, we encountered the other army corps who was forming their lines of battle. We advanced towards Fleurus.*[108]

Rumigny is the first witness of the events who left an account. In Hulot's report to Gérard, Bourmont and his staff are reported to have left later, sometime between 5:30 am and 6:00 am. What accounts for the difference in time?

Hulot also reports that Bourmont handed two letters addressed to Gérard to be carried back. One of the letters was his, and the other was

---

108 Rumigny, *Souvenirs de Général Comte De Rumigny* 4th Edition, Paris, 1921, pp. 93 – 95. https://archive.org/details/souvenirsdugnoorumi

from Clouet.[109] Besides for Colonel Clouet, who was serving as Bourmont's Chief of Staff, *Chef d'Escadron Adjudant* Villoutreys, *Capitaine* d'Andigné, *Lieutenant* de Trelan, and *Capitaine* Sourdat, all members of Bourmont's staff, were known to be absent after Bourmont crossed over to the Prussians. But neither Rumigny nor Hulot's account specifically identifies the individuals who accompanied Bourmont on that morning.

Impact of Defection on Right Column

General Hulot assumed command of Bourmont's division, and it performed well during the campaign. IV Corps soon headed north, where, at 3:30 pm, Napoleon ordered Gérard to cross the Sambre at Châtelet. By that time, Charleroi had been taken and the Prussians were retreating towards Gosselies and Fleurus.

Bourmont's defection is often cited for delaying IV Corps' arrival, but as the trailing divisions were positioned at Roly and Mariembourg at dawn on the 15th, they made very good progress to close around Châtelet by late evening, despite a delayed start. One could criticize Gérard for not having all the divisions pass the Sambre, as this would delay his march on the 16th; however, as no divisions marched farther on the 15th, let alone completed more than a week of forced marches, this seems unfair. Regardless, some believe the delay was instrumental in preventing the right wing from achieving Sombreffe.[110]

But *none* of IV Corps' delays can compare to the 12 hour head start the Prussians had received.

There is no evidence that Soult and Bourmont coordinated the defection. However, we know that Soult became extremely interested, and lobbied for the role of Major General, shortly after Bourmont gained his command. Had Soult, who had just served the King as Minister of War, and who undoubtedly had many former associates with the King at Ghent, become

---

109 See Etienne Hulot's report to Gérard in *La Spectateur Militaire*, January-March, Volume 24 from 1884, the article titled, "Un Chapitre Inédit dur Ligny-Waterloo-Paris." http://babel.hathitrust.org/cgi/pt?view=plaintext;size=100;id=hvd. hw27gs;page=root;seq=127;num=121

110 Hamilton-Williams, *Waterloo New Perspectives*, p. 164

aware of the conspiracy to place royalist officers into the French army? Had Soult during his tour of Lille (a hotbed of royalist activity) used that opportunity to become aware of royalist efforts to undermine Napoleon's war effort? Did Soult know that Bourmont was planning to betray the French army?

Whatever Soult knew, it's undeniable that it was Soult's "inexplicable" actions that facilitated Bourmont's treason on the eve of the campaign. This was not poor staff work or a mistake. We do not know what explanation Soult gave to Napoleon. We do know that Soult had moved III Corps completely out of the way, and at such a time that IV Corps was able to easily take its place. With Bourmont's division in the vanguard, and without the entire III Corps between him and the frontier, he was able to easily cross over to the enemy in the pre-dawn hours of June 15th. But this is just half the story.

We shall explore several theories.

Napoleon and Bourmont's Actions on the 14th of June

When Napoleon wrote about the Waterloo campaign, he said that Bourmont defected on the 14th of June. Napoleon's detractors, such as Charras[III], have seized upon this statement, both to discredit Napoleon's statements about the campaign and minimize the impact of the ongoing treason of 1815.

Sources agree with the basic facts of Bourmont's defection, though the time of the departure varies. In all cases, Bourmont and his staff defected after Gneissau's 11:30 pm June 14th orders for the Prussian army to consolidate; also, Bourmont defected prior to receiving Napoleon's June 15th Movement Orders. These two facts have generally been used to downplay the significance of Bourmont's treason. But there is much more.[112]

First, Bourmont was a General, and the rest of his staff were officers, some with strong noble backgrounds. Anyone who has seen *Downton Abbey* is aware that men of means in the early 20th century had their "man," a servant or valet, if not several. This was even truer in the early 19th century.

---

111 Charras, Jean Baptiste Adolphe, *Histoire de la campagne de 1815*, p. 99, footnote 1 http://books.google.com/books?id=oBUgAAAAMAAJ

112 It should be noted that Alberto Pollio, in his *Waterloo (1815) : avec de nouveaux documents* (1908), also presented a narrative of Bourmont or someone affiliated as playing a role in delivering intelligence to Gneissenau and the Prussians on June 14th, and also touched upon Bourmont's coordination with the King at Ghent as well as Bourmont and Clouet's strong roles during the period. This is not surprising, as many of the same sources are referenced.

Napoleon had servants. Marshal Ney had servants. Even Captain Coignet, the author of the popular memoirs, whose background was that of destitute peasant orphan, had a servant![113] It is certainly safe to assume that Bourmont and his staff were most likely accompanied by several servants, significant baggage, and possibly extra horses. None of the accounts of the defection mention anything about baggage or servants. And how could they? How could Bourmont and his staff explain their baggage and servants accompanying their ride towards the enemy at the commencement of hostilities? And considering Bourmont's actions were determined well in advance and coordinated with the King, couldn't we assume that he would have had plenty of time to plan the safety of his staff's servants and baggage?

The first theory is that Bourmont and his staff defected earlier. Royalist Frédéric-Jacques Louis Rilliet de Constant wrote an account of serving the King in 1815, which included meeting Bourmont and his staff after their defection.[114] Rilliet paints a rather unflattering picture of the group:

> *On June 14 I was strolling, as usual, by the Hotel Flanders windows where I was lodging, having for recreation, from time to time, the view of some Prussian officers or soldiers; suddenly I saw a French staff entering the court: a lieutenant-general, a staff colonel, a lieutenant-colonel, two aides-de-camp* **with horses and baggage following. [Emphasis added]** *All of these figures were unfamiliar to me, except one which I believe I recognize, I am not slow to make sure that it was my former military schoolmate, the same one that I had seen in Lons-le-Saulnier; I understood that the general was the one that said T*** was aide-de-camp, i.e. the Count de Bourmont. I hastened to go to find out the reasons for this strange arrival. T*** was very pleased to find among the Prussians someone who was an acquaintance. He was a good boy, but having little tact, nor spirit. "Ah!" he said, "what a funny adventure, when the orders of the general in chief arrive at the division staff, there will not be one*

---

113 Coignet, Jean-Roch, *The Narrative of Captain Coignet*, New York 1890, pp. 293-294 https://archive.org/details/narrativeofcaptaoocoig

114 De-Constant, Rilliet, *Les Cent Jours en Belgique (Bibliotheque universelle de Geneve, Volume 35)*, 1857, pp. 352-354
http://books.google.com/books?id=tZ9CAAAAcAAJ

June 15th

officer found to open the dispatches!" and by saying that he laughed with all his heart, as if it was a comic joke. Somewhat eager that I was to see the imperial army experiencing all possible failures, I must agree that this gaity of T*** appeared at least inopportune to me. I admit that, for my behalf, I did not regret having anticipated the 14th of June to come to join the King.

I hastened to go to share my discovery with M. de Castries; he appeared by this as surprised as me, and immediately went to the hero of the adventure, to try to collect some information on the French Army projects, and we were not long in going to join him.

The emotion of the trip had not effected the appetite of the travelers, they were all at the table when we were introduced to the general. General de Bourmont was small in stature, not a very remarkable figure, the tone and the sound of a very-soft voice, the small eyes, somewhat polished and gracious, which then appeared to be rather the effect of a natural benevolence than a consequence of a long practice of life in courts. His chief of staff, colonel Chouet (sic, Clouet) had a more pronounced aspect, but very pleasant, and the spirit of good company. I could see later that he lacked neither knowledge, nor activity. M. V***, commandant chief of staff, was a large dandy with blond hair, very occupied with his figure and a decoration of the order of Saint-Hubert of Bavaria, which he wore with ostentation, for services which were unknown to his close friends. In seeing this character more closely, I was convinced that it was difficult for the royal cause to acquire a more useless man in every respect. I spoke about my friend T***, who was better company than M. V***, but not very resourceful, neither for the service of the King, nor for humanity in general. To complete this collection, I will name Captain S***, the type of fool who appeared to be the joker of this staff. All of these characters honored the table of the Hôtel de France. They said to us that they believed for a long time that General Gérard's corps, of which they formed a part, and whose headquarters was in Metz, was to serve as an observation corps opposed to the Russian army which advanced by Mainz, when suddenly they received the order to carry out forced marches to form the right of the Grande Armée.

Trelan had "little tact, nor spirit." Clouet "lacked neither knowledge, nor activity." Villoutreys was: "a large dandy with blond hair, very occupied with his figure ... a useless man in every respect." Sourdat was simply a fool!

As Rilliet continues, he turns to Bourmont and he relates the deserter's plan. He paints a nice portrait of Bourmont as a brave man, but it is clear that he won't comment on Bourmont's actions, which he disapproves of despite appreciating that Bourmont has treated him well since.

> *This account described the reasons for the conduct of M. de Bourmont: it was easy to see, by correctly calculating, that the great attacks were to happen in Belgium, M. de Bourmont, placed far from the theatre of events, and armed with the royal orders which authorized him, he said, to remain with the imperial army, would have waited this way for the outcome ready to shout: "Vive l'Empereur," if he knocked down English and Prussians, no less disposed to put General Gérard at the door and to recover its white plume at the command of the Army of the Moselle, if the events did not favor Napoleon. But the reunion of the grand army destroyed the plan, and it appears that the royal orders did not say that soldiers had to charge in the name of the Emperor. It was necessary to decide, and M. de Bourmont came to Namur.*
>
> *This historical fact was the object of too many comments for me to come to mix mine with them. Besides, I am prevented by a peremptory reason, as M. de Bourmont always treated me, in the service reports that we have assembled since, with extreme benevolence. His memory is dear to me, I am neither his lawyer, nor his defender, I'll make only one observation: there is a suspicion which could never reach M. de Bourmont in the assessment that we can make of the act of June 14, 1815, he never has been wanting to be sheltered from personal dangers. Brave defender of Nogent, in February 1814, who, with 1200 men, had repulsed the attacks of 15,000 allies over two days, who was wounded during this glorious defense, and thus Napoleon wrote "for this, I am happy," cannot be suspected of lacking bravery. He was chivalrous and he was, with his friendly character, the cause of ascendancy that he always exerted on the troops in all the positions where he was placed.*

Rilliet de-Constant could be mistaken on the date, but he definitively states June 14th twice in his narrative. Was this simply a gross error? We don't know, though he does mention their baggage as well as the extra horses that as officers they most probably had. No account of Bourmont's defection ever mentions their baggage; which, for high ranking officers, would have been a significant amount. Servants are not mentioned, but this was not uncommon for writings from the time. Their presence was so routine that they blended into the background. It is not likely that royalist officers would have been able to easily function without their baggage or servants, even if they were committing treason.

Furthermore, Trelan is quoted as saying, "...what a funny adventure, when the orders of the general in chief arrive at the division staff, there will not be one officer found to open the dispatches!" If they were in Namur when this was said, and had left at 2 am or 5 am on June 15th, then the orders would have long since arrived... but this is spoken as though it was yet to happen.

This account also mentions the "royal orders," which authorized Bourmont and staff to remain in the Imperial army, but not to the point of engaging in combat. Note that Bourmont's goal was to take command from Gérard in the event of Napoleon's defeat, but this plan was interrupted when Gérard's corps was ordered to join the main army.

There is another, even more authoritative, source: Clouet, Bourmont's Chief of Staff, wrote, in his piece justifying Bourmont's actions, the following:

> *On June 14, at three o'clock in the morning, we separated from M. General Hulot; we were escorted by fifteen chasseurs: we soon arrived near the Prussian outposts. There, M. de Bourmont would not allow any of the chasseurs to follow; he had the escort return, and was accompanied only by four or five officers who, like him, had refused to sign the Acte Additionnel. We reached the first Prussian post, while promising the general absolute silence about everything concerning the French Army. I must believe that each one of us kept his word, because no one left M. de Bourmont. We were held more than twelve hours, taken from post to post as far as the headquarters of Marshal Blücher. The Prussians were surprised and thought we changed sides in order to fight in their ranks. This speculation and the horror, which I experienced in finding myself in the middle of*

an army that at one time treated me as an enemy, left me a memory that will never be erased. It was without a doubt the greatest sacrifice that I could make in accomplishing what I regarded then, and that I regard still today, as my duty.

Finally, we were allowed to go free, and we went to sleep in Namur. The following day the fighting began near Charleroi, and two days later on the 16th, the French were victorious in Fleurus, and the sound of this victory brought terror all the way to Brussels, where we had arrived. We know what followed the first success: the victorious French at Fleurus succumbed at Waterloo as a result of circumstances that nobody in the army had been able to foresee.[115]

The above account is flawed. It states that they left on the morning of the 14th and slept in Namur that night. On the 15th was the fighting near Charleroi, and on the 16th was the Battle of Ligny. That timeline works, except that everyone agrees that they crossed over to the enemy and sent the escort back on the morning of the 15th. It would be acceptable to say Clouet was considering the predawn hours of the 15th as a continuation of the night of the 14th, but this does not work with the timeline, as it would put the battle of Ligny on the 17th. There is clearly an error. Additionally, Clouet fails to remember the identities of his fellow conspirators, instead stating that there were four or five, and he claimed that the escort consisted of over a dozen chasseurs, which is far more than any other account.

In Hulot's account,[116] he left Bourmont and staff at 11 pm. Bourmont then wrote to Hulot at midnight with instructions based on his absence the following morning:

My Dear General,

You know the order that I gave in respect to the roads involved in the attached letter from the General in Chief, and, as I could well be gone tomorrow morning, I ask you to send an officer of your

---

115 Clouet, *Quelques notes sur la conduite De M. Le Comte De Bourmont en 1815*, p. 11
116 See Etienne Hulot's report to Gérard in *La Spectateur Militaire*, January-March, Volume 24 from 1884, the article titled, "Un Chapitre Inédit dur Ligny-Waterloo-Paris." http://babel.hathitrust.org/cgi/pt?view=plaintext;size=100;id=hvd.hw27gs;page=root;seq=127;num=121

brigade, at an early hour, to Huzinette and Hauzienne, passing by Mariasme, in order to make sure that we work on the repair of the Charleroi road.

If some incident happened on this matter, I wish that you wanted to give orders in the name of the General in Chief, as I could give them myself, in order to prevent the problems that could be encountered, and to give a report about them directly.

Be assured of my sincere and lasting dedication.

Lieutenant General
DE BOURMONT[117]

As Gustave Gautherot (a fawning biographer of Bourmont) makes clear, Hulot should have been aware of something happening, and he chose to do nothing. Further, the correspondence between Clouet, Bourmont, Hulot, and Gérard after the war was profuse, with all parties showing strong mutual admiration. Aside from the fact that this may have been sincere, there was certainly a symbiotic element at work. Hulot and Gérard desired Bourmont to put in a good word on their behalf with the King during the second restoration, minimizing potential damage to them or their families. Clouet and Bourmont desired Gérard and Hulot to support their argument that, despite defecting, they were not traitors in the worst sense – they had done their duty until they decided to serve the King, and they had not given damaging information to the Allies. For example, during the July Monarchy after 1830, when Imperial veterans played a greater role, Bourmont wrote Gérard reminding him that he had done his duty until the moment of defection.[118]

---

117 Gautherot, Gustave, "Bourmont à Waterloo", *Revue des Questions Historiques*, Volume 92, pp. 94 - 129.
https://books.google.com/books?id=WpojAQAAIAAJ
The footnote for the order is interesting: *Note du Spectateur Militaire, 1884 (mars) : « Cette lettre, fermée d'un cachet aux armes du général de Bourmont, est entièrement écrite, texte et signature, de sa main ; l'enveloppe porte, avec la suscription service militaire : à Monsieur le maréchal de camp Hulot, commandant la 1ʳᵉ Brigade de la 14ᵉ Division, à Florenne, - le Lieutenant-général de Bourmont ».*
If Clouet was his Chief of Staff and was present, then why did Bourmont write this letter himself?
118 Gautherot, Gustave, "Bourmont à Waterloo", *Revue des Questions Historiques*, Volume 92, pp. 94 - 129. The entire article is written to put Bourmont in the best possible light. It

This letter to Hulot can also dispel the oft repeated notion that when Bourmont went over to the Prussians, he did so lacking any knowledge of the impending advance upon Charleroi. From the letter's text, it seems quite clear that Gérard, having received the orders for June 13, had communicated to Bourmont the importance of Charleroi, and the need to assure that the roads leading to Charleroi were prepared for IV Corps' advance.

Knowing the background of these individuals' relationships and their point of view of the activities of June 14th and June 15th 1815, it is abundantly clear that their accounts are self-serving. Hulot claimed ignorance of any of Bourmont's plans. He had to, or else he would be admitting to being complicit. Had Bourmont and/or his staff done something greater, such as being absent for a long time on June 14th, or had sent the servants or baggage away, Hulot would only be exposing himself to comment on this. Bourmont and Clouet wished to downplay their acts, diminish the accusation of treason, which became especially true after 1830. Bourmont's other Brigade General, Toussaint, was, according to Hulot, at Walcourt on June 14th, and thus would not have been privy to any of the activities at Florennes. Altogether, understanding the relationships and interactions between Bourmont, Clouet, Hulot, and Gérard clarifies why the details of Bourmont's activities are terse.

Had Bourmont and his party rode ahead on June 14th, there would have been hard rides to Namur and back. Utilizing post-horses, the distance is more than manageable when one considers that Napoleon left Paris in the predawn hours and arrived at Laon by noon!¹¹⁹ On the 14th, Bourmont would not have needed to have Napoleon's marching orders to effectively tip off the Prussians. The order of the 13th clearly states the objective was Charleroi, and this may have been known by Bourmont, regardless. Confirmation of an

---

likewise demonstrates the strong relationships between Clouet, Bourmont, Gérard, and Hulot. One can also sense the struggle Bourmont had between his duty to the King and to the men he led, which of course, Gautherot's intention. Bourmont may have wished every soldier who followed Napoleon be eliminated, which would strengthen the monarchy upon restoration. If he did not, Clouet certainly did.

119 There is no way to know which route could have been taken, but its fair to estimate that the first stage, from Chimay to Namur, could have been 75 km and possibly taken 8 - 10 hours. The Order of the Day for June 13th could have been received early in the morning; therefore it's possible that they could have organized the Division's march on Florennes and left very early. The division's march would have been almost 40 km and taken most of the day.

imminent attack on Charleroi would have been sufficient for the Prussians to order the concentration on Sombreffe.

Despite all the intelligence the Prussians had received, and all the observations that they had made about the concentration of the French army, they still had not ordered a concentration by the time darkness fell on June 14th. Some believe that the observation of camp fires led to the Prussian concentration orders, though using fake campfires was a military ruse that goes back to Hannibal's victory over the Romans at the Battle of Lake Trasimene, and probably earlier. Would the presence of a glow in the night sky really have lead to the concentration of the Prussian army? Besides, all the reasons given for Gneisenau's actions had been true for days.

Let us return to Lettow-Vorbeck:

> *If a few hours later, Gneisenau found it necessary to order the gathering of the entire troops, very reliable news must have prompted him to do so. Ollech follows Nostitz's diary, which states that two defectors, brought to Namur during the night of the 15th, had stated with great firmness that Napoleon was about to attack the Prussian army the following morning. These cannot have been any ordinary defectors whose statements, according to their restricted horizon, would only have had some value regarding their specific part of the troops, and would otherwise have been restricted to mere rumors, later to be recognized as exaggerated or wrong. In the present case, these were persons knowledgeable of the orders that had been given concerning the advance of the French army on the morning of the 15th. From this point of view, Major retd. Ritz's memoires, which, however, were only put down on paper in 1861, become more important. In the respective night, he had stayed on guard at the Meuse bridge in Namur, as a cadet in the second Infantry Regiment. He states that a squad of 5 or 6 horsemen had arrived at his post at about 11 PM. Whilst being examined, one of them had replied that he was a Prussian field-grade officer and asked to be taken to the prince's lodgings, because he was accompanied by a French general who needed to speak to the latter in a very urgent matter. Ritz himself believes that the term "general" might have been used to make him leave his post which he had refused to do initially. Furthermore, it*

seems highly probable that these were indeed French officers, according to his statement.[120]

Bourmont must have realized that the best way to get the Prussian army to respond to the intelligence of Napoleon's imminent attack was to deliver it in person, or to have the officers serving him deliver correspondence sealed with a stamp bearing his arms. Had he done so in person, it would have been necessary to return to the army, so as Napoleon would be left unaware that the enemy had gained this intelligence. As Rumigny's account demonstrates, as soon as Bourmont's defection was known, it was going to spread through the army rapidly.

In the 17 years since the event, had long rides to and from Namur, then the defection, and an equally long and stressful period, blurred Clouet's memory? Or was it a simple matter of editing in order to continue to keep the true extent of the treachery hidden? Whichever the case, Clouet's date matches Rilliet de-Constant's account, which explains the movement of possible staff, and most certainly baggage, as well as, the mystery of who (*General Bourmont*) delivered the intelligence to Gneisenau that directly led to the concentration of the Prussian army.

Although Clouet wrote to defend Bourmont's conduct (and by association his own), it is certainly mysterious why he would publish an incriminating timeline a few years into the reign of Louis-Philippe, when the protection afforded by the Bourbon's was no longer available; when the veterans of Waterloo were returning to France. Did Clouet have a hidden agenda?

Bourmont and his entire treacherous party never admitted to delivering intelligence to the Prussians. The letter Bourmont sent to Gérard announcing his defection even went as far to say, "... No one shall see me in the ranks of the enemy. He shall obtain from me no information capable of injuring the French Army, composed of men who I love and for whom I shall never cease to bear a lively attachment."[121] Houssaye easily refutes this lie, as once among the Prussians, Bourmont spoke freely to all that would listen.[122] Even Gautherot, who was a fawning admirer of Bourmont, admits that Bourmont spoke freely, yet strained to qualify Bourmont's statements as being harmless based on their timing.

---

120   See "Lettow-Vorbeck" on page 277, "Pages 2196 – 199"
121   Houssaye, *1815, Waterloo*, p. 63
122   Ibid.

The above theory of a defection on June 14 has problems. It will never be possible to reconcile the various accounts of June 14 into the morning of June 15 for Bourmont and his staff. Could Bourmont's absence not have been noticed? It is true that the troops spent the day marching, and it's possible that, once Hulot's brigade arrived at Florennes, no one of rank saw the General. Yet, while Hulot and Bourmont were close (and there is some evidence that Hulot did not interfere or react quickly to Bourmont's actions) Hulot fought bravely during the campaign, which makes it hard to believe he wouldn't have said or done anything if Bourmont and his staff had disappeared on June 14th.

Yet, Bourmont's duty to the King demanded that he act, did it not? Had he abandoned the army on June 14th to spread the alarm, he would have likewise warned Napoleon that the surprise was compromised. So? Would that not have been better than harmlessly defecting on the morning of Napoleon's attack, and after (Gautherot reminds us) the first shots had been fired? If Napoleon had been successful in Belgium, would the King have received Bourmont well after having scurried back to England?

Considering how well the Bourbons rewarded Bourmont (he became a Marshal of France under Charles X), one might assume that Bourmont did a bit more than sneak away... which, considering his loyalties, actually *increased* the effectiveness of his division for the upcoming campaign. However, if one cannot accept Rilliet de Constant's account (and many do not) and, if it seems a stretch that Bourmont and staff rode to Namur, and then were present around 11 pm to speak with Gneisenau, before riding back in order to defect sometime between 2am and 6am, then another scenario must exist.

The next theory is that Bourmont sent someone ahead in his place... or, just as possible, someone could have ridden ahead, possibly escorting the servants and baggage, and then took it upon himself to betray the French army.

Anne Louis Antoine Clouet

Not only does Tulard's 1800+ page *Dictionnaire Napoléon* lack an entry for Clouet, but he is not even mentioned in Bourmont's entry, which is barely an eighth of a page. Maybe this was a conscious choice to show scorn for their treason. Regardless, we would be wise to examine Clouet more closely.

Our first encounter with Clouet was when he angrily met with Ney during Napoleon's march on Paris. Let's revisit this scene exactly as recorded by Levavesseur, one of Ney's aides:

> *Suddenly, at 6 o'clock in the evening, Clouet enters. This officer had left the Marshal to accept, by the king's word, a hereditary family charge. At the news of the return, he left, on March 12, from Tours, in order to resume his title with his former Marshal. Learning of the defection from Ney, he had no less continued on his route, hidden by a disguise, and he had arrived to us with great difficulty, while crossing the countries insurgent in the name of the Emperor: "Where is the Marshal," he says sharply, "where is the Marshal? I want to speak to him." And he hurries quickly into the room that I show him. There, I hear a most spirited scene taking place. Undoubtedly, Clouet maintained toward the Marshal the same language as me, but with more animated expressions, without however using the same feelings of acknowledgement, pain, and interest. Clouet escapes from the Marshal's room, enters Dutour's office, grabs a blank sheet of paper, and gives to himself an order thus conceived:* My aide-de-camp Clouet has been given the order to go at once to Paris with my cook and a servant. By order of the Marshal, signed. *Then he affixes the Marshal's seal on the sheet and leaves.*[123]

This is a very telling event, packed with interesting anecdotes. Clouet is decisive and emotional. He took risks - he traveled in disguise! Also, he had no problems forging a document in the name of Marshal Ney. Clouet had a firm commitment to his cause, and for it he did not lack boldness.

Bourmont, on the other hand, was not as decisive. As Ney was in the process of switching allegiances to Napoleon, Bourmont was silent. It took him several days to leave Ney and travel to Paris. However, he sought a role in Napolen's army, and he was clearly in communication with both Fouché and the King.[124]

---

123 Levavasseur, *Souvenirs Militaires d'Octave Levavasseur*, 1914, p. 280. http://gallica.bnf.fr/ark:/12148/bpt6k6367503q.r=Octave+Levavasseur.langEN

124 Lettow Vorbeck, *Napoleons untergang 1815*, 1904, footnote bottom of page 249 referencing a letter written by Artois, number 65 starting on page 131 of *Louis XVIII et les Cent Jours à Gand*, Volume 1, states: *Romberg and Malet, abridged notes. No. 4. P. 133/4. "Send very quickly an officer very securely, for him to establish a personal confidence, to let him know the intentions*

Did serving the King also require betraying the men he led? Bourmont's letters to his wife show someone tortured over the right course to take. It is clear that he sought to retire from his command on June 1st. Clouet claimed that he talked him out of it, which seems probable.

Various aspects of the events of June 14th/15th relating to Bourmont and his staff were documented by several parties, including Clouet's, which he wrote in 1832. None of them agree; Clouet's account disagreed on time, date, and even the number of cavalry troopers who accompanied their party differ by more than double! It makes one wonder: *was he even there?*

Clarity may be gained by the following observations.

Bourmont and Clouet were rewarded for their actions with commands even before Napoleon had abdicated. The second restoration was a period of extreme anti-Bonapartism, fueled by the Ultra-Royalists. In October of 1815, Clouet was appointed Colonel of *légion départementale de la Somme*, and was clearly at home with the Ultras. On his own initiative, Clouet founded a secret society for the purpose of probing the loyalty of his officers.[125] The King did not approve, and removed him from active service on May 9th, 1816.

With the July Revolution of 1830, Louis-Philippe would completely change the dynamic relating to Napoleon's memory. The army would be led and staffed by veterans of the Empire, including Soult as Minister of War. Those that went to Ghent or betrayed France in 1815 were systematically rooted out, such as Du Barail, the traitor of the 18th of June. Clouet himself was retired on August 19th, 1831.

In 1832, we see Clouet write his justification of Bourmont's behavior, which likewise excuses himself. Clouet states that Hulot stayed with Bourmont until 3 am on June 14th, and that Hulot was aware of their actions. Was this on June 14th, before an all day march to Florennes? Or is he wrong about the date, referring instead to the 15th, when we have correspondence from Bourmont to Hulot dated at midnight (Hulot writes he left them at 11 pm). Certainly, 17 years later details would not be remembered crisply. Why would he have tried to minimize their actions of 1815, yet said they left on June 14th which would only implicate them further?

---

of the King, (illegible words) and also to assure that we count on him entirely and request from him information on his division and on the journey of General Gérard's Corps."

125 Quintin, Danielle and Quintin, Bernard, *Dictionnaire des Colonels de Napoléon*, 2013, pp. 213-214. It should be also noted that Clouet also participated with Bourmont in the *Duchesse de Berry*'s uprising against Louis-Philippe, and was duly sentenced to death in absentia. One cannot deny the man's motivation!

Those that served with Bourmont and Clouet during the Bourbon years also left us interesting anecdotes.

In his memoirs, Marshal MacMahon tells the following story, related to him by Clouet when the two served together in Algeria:

> *You know that several days before Waterloo, I was called away by Bourmont to leave the army and to join the King in Ghent. On the day of the battle, I was in Brussels. I heard a sharp cannonade and I moved to the side from where it came. I saw a swirl of dust and a mass of English crews fleeing in full gallop towards Brussels; the drivers shouted that the battle was lost and the entire English army in rout. I experienced, I acknowledge it, an enormous satisfaction. At last, we French, we have defeated the English! I pushed ahead and I realized on the contrary that we were defeated! I scanned the battle field and descended from my horse near the square where the guard had fought. I bandaged myself, as I could, the serious wound of an old Sergeant of the Guard. This procedure finished, I took my purse and gave it to him saying: "It is all that I have but it can be useful to you."*
>
> *This Sergeant looking at me intently, he shouted: "But it seems to me that I know you?" – "Yes," I could not stop myself from saying, "you have seen me, aide-de-camp of Marshal Ney." – "You, aide-de-camp of Marshal Ney! You are then this traitor of Clouet? I want to take nothing from you!" He threw my purse that I had just given him and ripped off the bandage that I made. Since this time, at each anniversary, this fact is recalled to my memory and then I try not to cry."*[126]

Poor Clouet - suddenly he was simply a pawn of that *traitor* Bourmont, and not a year goes by that he does not cry for those very veterans he was trying to have arrested in 1816! Were his emotions further heightened by the moon-lit scenes of devastation; which allowed him to so easily make out details on a battlefield still occupied by thousands of Wellington's army and scoured by hundreds of Prussian cavalry looking for prey?

---

126 MacMahon, Edme Patrice Maurice comte de, *Mémoires du Maréchal de Mac Mahon : duc de Magenta. Souvenirs d'Algérie,* Plon, 1932

June 15th

Yet in *Mémoires du Chancelier Pasquier*, starting on page 191, we have the following:

> *It was a singular assembly that this ministry, which we feared the energetic resolutions and that however contained so many seeds of division, well made to render any unity of action impossible. M. de Polignac and M. de La Bourdonnaye, jealous of each other, each one sought for his side to seize the presidency. M. de Polignac, accustomed to march in measured steps, energetic toward his goal with a persevering address; M. de La Bourdonnaye, impetuous, violent, wants to bring a hard fight; M. de Bourmont, decided well to stay with the one of the two who appears to have the best chances. Frantic player, debt-laden, he had decided to remain in power. He showed brilliant valour in the Wars of 1813 and 1814, but no superior quality. The best years of his youth took place with the adventures of the last war of the Chouans. He developed the habit of plots, never acting openly. During the seven or eight years that I saw him at the Chamber of Peers, I do not remember him saying a word; he did not even talk with his neighbors. He had, however, found a way to gain the confidence of the Dauphin; it was all the more remarkable with the return of Spain, he was on rather bad terms with this prince. He was the first who had refused to observe the ordinance of Andujar. As for being firm, which is one of the first merits of the soldier, especially one who made his way through the civil wars, he did not possess it. Who would believe that at the time of committing one of the most serious actions of his life, the day before the Battle of Waterloo, he hesitated until the last moment, and that he was called away by the energetic pleas of his aide-de-camp, M. Clouet?*[127]

Pasquier does not say where he gained this insight, but how interesting that now it is *Clouet* who was the mastermind! But, is that not believable? Clouet, who was clearly motivated, decisive, and bold – did he push Bourmont to stay with the army so that, once near the frontier, their defection could take place? And if so, is it possible that it was *Clouet* who

---

[127] Pasquier, Etienne-Denis, *Mémoires du Chancelier Pasquier*, Plon, 1895, pp. 191-192
https://books.google.com/books?id=EhFx1aFGrZgC

rode to the Prussians carrying a letter in the name of Bourmont and sealed with Bourmont's crest?

But did not Clouet leave a letter with Bourmont for Gérard on June 15? According to the accounts, Bourmont gave two letters to the troopers to return to Gérard, one of which was Clouet's:

Florennes, June 15, 1815

> *My general, the reasons which determine the departure of M. de Bourmont are also mine, and it must be that they are quite powerful so that I am resolved to leave an army filled with my friends, and commanded by a leader whose noble character and great talents inspire at once respect, dedication, and confidence without bounds. My friends will tell you, my General, all that it costs me to follow this party. I must have this intimate conviction that I make for the good of my country, for giving up all that one finds under your orders. I am with greatest sorrow and a deep respect,*

Colonel Clouet[128]

If anything sticks out from Clouet's letter to Gérard, it is that nothing sticks out – there is no detail. It could have been written and dated at any time, and given to Bourmont to disguise the fact that it was *Clouet* who rode to Namur to tip off the Prussians. Bourmont then apparently delivered two letters, which for many, definitively proves that Bourmont and Clouet were together and defected on the morning of June 15th, after the first shots were fired.

Bourmont, the Invisible Man

Certainly, there is little proof of anything, but a simple fact remains: Gneisenau ordered the concentration of the Prussian army on the night of June 14th, which would have required something more impressive than a simple deserter. A letter, carried by Clouet, indicating an advance via Charleroi, and signed by Bourmont (who was working for the King and was

---

128 De Wit, Pierre, *The 4th corps and the division of Delort*, p. 2 http://www.waterloo-campaign.nl/15-june-1815/

known to be leading a division of IV Corps which had just marched across the country from Metz), most certainly would have done the trick, even if it was forged. And covering that up would certainly explain the significant differences in Clouet's account of the events – *he couldn't remember because he was not there.*

The details of Bourmont's defection during June 14th and 15th will probably never be known. But what has been demonstrated is that the conventional account of a "meaningless" morning defection is almost assuredly false. And, if Bourmont had not demonstrated the decisiveness, motivation, or anti-Napoleon lust required to betray thousands of his countrymen, as his apologists argue, then Clouet more than certainly did. If not a French general, then someone on behalf of a French general betrayed the French army on June 14th, 1815.

Would the same have happened if IV Corps had been near Mariembourg with Vandamme's III Corps between Bourmont's 14th Division and the frontier? Escorting baggage and servants, it seems doubtful. Already, one has to accept that some ruse was required to escort baggage and servants past the French outposts even with Bourmont's headquarters at Florennes. For a *Général de Division* or his senior staff, this was possible. Riding from the rear through an Infantry Corps and past the French outposts with servants and baggage without attracting attention was not.

The impact of treason on Napoleon's plans was undeniably devastating. Soult's mangling of Napoleon's plans is no longer inexplicable.

Center Column

Marshal Mortier, one of the few friends Soult could claim in the army, gave up command of the Imperial Guard while still in Beaumont on the morning of the 15th. He claimed an attack of gout, which made it impossible for him to ride a horse or function.

Mortier, to whom Louis-Philippe expressed such strong devotion[129], had been heroic in the 1814 campaign. Napoleon had often protected the

---

129 Mortier was killed during an assassination attempt on Louis-Philippe in 1835, which devastated the King and drove him to tears.

guard to his own detriment; notably at Borodino in 1812, where a decisive victory was possible with their commitment. However, watching his guard melt away during the Russian Retreat had been a sobering lesson, and in 1814, the Guard would be liberally used in many combats and instrumental in many victories.

Is it possible that Soult realized that leading the Imperial Guard, in a campaign he was actively undermining, was not a safe place to be for his dear friend?

In his memoirs, Napoleon stated that the loss of Mortier caused him great harm.

Vandamme

Due to Soult's muddled orders on the 12th, General Dominique Vandamme had become the vanguard of the center Column. Indeed, he is the first general named in the Order of Movement!

Vandamme was passionate... though his peers may have preferred to consider him a brash, quarrelsome jerk.[130] During 1815, it is said Vandamme wouldn't even shake Soult's hand. As Houssaye writes:

> *Soult, before his appointment has been officially announced, sent an order to Vandamme; that irascible general retorted by writing to Davout the following letter, remarkable for its delicate sarcasm: "I have received a letter from the Duke of Dalmatia in which he announces himself as chief of the headquarters staff. I think it my duty to send it to your Excellency before replying to it. As the Duke of Ragusa might send me the same announcement, I must consider this as not having taken place, until informed of the appointment by your Excellency or by an Imperial decree."*[131]

---

[130] In Volume 4 of Grouchy's Memoirs (though compiled after Grouchy's death), the author speaks repeatedly of Vandamme's unwillingness to follow Grouchy's orders. While Grouchy was always trying to rehabilitate his own reputation, it should be noted that Davout was also aware of Vandamme's nature, and had warned Napoleon of it.

[131] Houssaye, Henry, *1815, Waterloo*. Translated from the 31st edition, London, 1900, pp. 34-35 http://books.google.com/books?id=xWBAAAAAYAAJ

Marshal Marmont, the Duke of Ragusa, had betrayed Napoleon in 1814. Add insightful to Vandamme's qualities!

Considering the animosity between Vandamme and Soult - and Vandamme's well-known temperament - one might wonder how Vandamme would react to any mishap that was Soult's responsibility.

Vandamme's Orders

On the morning of June 15th, Vandamme did not receive any orders. And, predictably, he did nothing about it; in spite of the expectations that the orders of the previous day had set.

Impact of Vandamme's Lost Orders

Vandamme's delays cost at least 3 hours, probably more.[132] While Napoleon pushed units of the Guard to Charleroi, in order to support the leading Cavalry and used them to storm the city, ultimately there was insufficient infantry when needed later in the day to accelerate the action beyond Charleroi at Gilly, which would only commence at 6 pm. Though the Guard had ended up preceding III Corps, Napoleon was reluctant to use it. Eventually, Vandamme and Grouchy pushed through Gilly with Napoleon's urging and settled for the night south of Fleurus.

Lobau's VI corps was scheduled to leave an hour later and follow Vandamme's III Corps. When VI Corps ran into III Corps, VI Corps was forced to stop and it waited for more than an hour. Colonel Janin was sent ahead to determine what the problem was, and found their camp, "…as quiet as if they were to remain there: the soldiers cleaned their arms, adjusted or mended their belongings, and I surprised the officers by announcing that the army, gathered and pressed to their left, wait to depart to continue its march halted in a rather unpleasant way by their inaction." He went on to explain:

> *I waited yet a long time, and, not being able to understand the reason for this delay, I headed towards the headquarters of Count Vandamme, when I met an officier-général who, when I announced*

---

132 See Mauduit, who listed Vandamme's delay as his 1st fatality of the campaign.

> to him the subject of my concern, told me that the orders addressed to General Vandamme in the night had not reached him, because the senior officer, who was the lone carrier, had fallen off of his horse, and had broken his thigh before being able to fulfil his mission. At the same time General Rogniat, who walked to the head of the large park, came forward, and received, I believe, the same information. It is true that in his Considérations sur l'art de la guerre this general, having true appreciation of the facts, merely says that Napoleon stopped in Charleroi, either that he was delayed by the bad weather, or by other reasons. If he did not believe he had to reveal these reasons was it because he did not find the degree of certainty necessary to be presented as historical documents? I would be tempted to believe this, because the explanation given by General Gourgaud is far from consistent with what I saw and which I have just reported. It is no less certain, as was very well noted by the expert and judicious author whom I have just mentioned, that all success depended on the speed of this first movement, that nothing was to be neglected to ensure its execution.[133]

How did *who* know that the orderly had fallen and broken his leg? If this were true, then when did it happen? Hours prior? And if it was already known, why hadn't those that knew retrieved the orders and delivered them, or, at the very least, informed Vandamme?

One way to clear the matter would be if we knew the identity of the messenger and we could pursue his history. Fortunately, while only a few of the messages in the Register of the *Major-Général* that Grouchy published in 1843 bothered to include the name of the messenger, the movement order of June 14 has an attached table which identifies the messenger for each formation:

> *Ramorino carried to d'Erlon*
> *Macarty carried to Reille*
> *Faviers carried to Vandamme*
> *Poirot carried to Lobau*
> *Bénard carried to Gérard*

---

[133] Janin, M.E.J. *Campagne de Waterloo,* starting on page 6.

June 15th

Gentet carried to Drouot and Mortier, Duc de Trévise
Vaucher carried to Grouchy
Lefébure carried to Ruty and Rogniat

Mauduit included in his book an order of battle which included a breakdown of the staff of the *Grand Quartier-Général*. From it, we find *Capitaine Ramorino, Chef de bataillon Gentet, and Chef de bataillon Lefébure* on Soult's headquarters staff. Some names are not included in Mauduit; such as, Macarty, Poirot, and Vaucher. It could be that Mauduit's list is incomplete, or that these individuals belonged to the staffs of the recipient organizations who had, by common practice, delivered their reports for the day and remained to return with the next day's orders. Two names are included that have similar spellings, but are not exact: *Chef de bataillon Bernard* and *Capitaine Favier*. Was Capitaine Favier the carrier of Vandamme's orders who, according to legend, fell from his horse and broke his leg?

The website: http://waterloo1815.olympe.in/main.php# allows one to search the Waterloo casualties using data compiled from over 100 sources. It identifies, as a member of Soult's staff, Favier as *Capitaine Benoît Favier*, born in La Mure on February 2nd, 1792 and died on November 29th, 1834, and who was, "… wounded at Waterloo with two lance thrusts in the neck."[134] If Benoît Favier was the messenger that carried the movement orders to Vandamme, either during the late night of June 14th or the early morning of June 15th, then one can only assume his injury (so severe that it prevented him from completing his mission to Vandamme), must have contributed to his inability to avoid not just one, but two blows from Prussian lancers on June 18th. As Benoît died in 1834, prior to the publication of the copy of the *Registre du Major-Général*, he was not alive to either confirm or deny any role as a member of Soult's headquarters staff.

---

134 Benoît Favier's dossier, found online below, also identifies his rank as *"Capitaine l'Etat Major,"* which would support his being a member of staff, as well as, his service record, which indicates both his service in the 1815 Campaign and his 2 lancer wounds.
http://www.culture.gouv.fr/public/mistral/leonore_fr?ACTION=RETROUVER&
FIELD_1= NOM&VALUE_1=FAVIER&NUMBER=10&GRP=0&REQ=
%28%28FAVIER%29%20%3aNOM%20%29&USRNAME=nobody&USRPWD=
4%24%2534P&SPEC=9&SYN=1&IMLY=&MAX1=1&MAX2=1&MAX3
=100&DOM=All

Napoleon labeled the whole matter as "un funeste contretemps," which translates loosely to *bullshit*.[135]

It is not surprising that others have questioned the veracity of this story.[136] What is surprising is that more have *not*. While Vandamme's response fits his character, the episode's entirety simply does not make sense. Such complete indifference on the day of hostilities! However, lacking a better explanation, this story has been repeated without question.

There have been other explanations. In Gourgaud's account of 1815, Vandamme took the wrong roads. In Karl Bleibtreu's *Englands grosse Waterloo-Lüge*, the theory is that Vandamme was upset that Napoleon took his headquarters in Beaumont, and thus he deliberately dragged his feet, providing the broken leg as an excuse. In Grouchy's *Relation succincte de la campagne de 1815*, the Appendix titled *Events de 1815* has a footnote stating the orders had arrived very late because they were taken to where Vandamme had spent the previous night. If true, the orderly would have only gone where he was told. Unfortunately, none of these explanations comes with any substantiating detail.

Janin is the closest thing we have to an explanation from someone who was there, and it's clear even he isn't totally sure.

When examined against the backdrop of treason and Soult's bungling of Napoleon's final concentration orders, another explanation becomes possible. Soult arranged Vandamme to be the lead infantry Corps in the central Column, but Napoleon did not approve. Countermanding orders were sent, but too late to prevent III Corps redeploying to the center:

> On the 13th the entire 3rd army corps, of which the 22nd regiment was part, having been assembled as though for review by its chief commander General Vandamme, stepped out for the distant frontier, leaving Chimay a quarter of a league to the left and going through the forest of Fagne. This march, both slow and troublesome because

---

135 The author has since learned that it translates to "a fatal mishap," but was unwilling to edit the text.
136 See De Wit's explanation; he also finds it lacking credibility http://www.waterloo-campaign.nl/bestanden/files/june15/obs.fr.intro.pdf

the column comprised 15,000 men of all arms, led us a half-league beyond Beaumont. There we bivouacked for the night.[137]

Napoleon, not wishing III Corps to march back to the right, which could have been demoralizing as well as fatiguing, then canceled the countermanding order:

As General Vandamme has reached Beaumont, I no longer think he should return to Philippeville, as it would exhaust his troops. I prefer that this general camp in the first line a league and a half from Beaumont. I will review them tomorrow.

The 6th corps will therefore be placed a quarter of a league to the rear.

In this case, the Armée de la Moselle will concentrate tomorrow on Philippeville with the cuirassier detachment coming from Alsace. Make these changes by general order.[138]

Soult could not guarantee that Vandamme would be left in the central column, but, considering the timing of events on the eve of the campaign, it was a reasonable bet. No matter how Napoleon reacted, damage would be done… and if nothing else III Corps would not be between Bourmont and the frontier for almost two days, even if they returned to the right column on June 14th.

With Vandamme now in the center column, the General who had suggested that Soult was a traitor and refused to shake his hand, was now, on the morning of the campaign, left without orders. Janin hears a detailed explanation, while the unnamed source has left Vandamme blissfully unaware.

One of the common refrains from the campaign is that Berthier, *Major-Général* prior to 1815, would have avoided this mishap by sending multiple orderlies. Of course, this will never be known; however, it is not true that this was always the case under Berthier, nor is it true that there were never lost transmissions under Berthier. In Chesney's study of the

---

137 *Journal du general Fantin des Odoards, Etapes d'un officier de la grande armée, 1800-1830*, Paris, 1895, p. 428 quoted from "The Concentration of the French Army" by Philippe de Callatay, published in *First Empire*, #102, translated by John Hussy

138 *Porte-feuille de Buonaparte: pris à Charleroi le 18 juin 1815*, The Hague, 1815 p. 98

Waterloo Campaign, he likewise takes up the question of Berthier's performance, documenting several mishaps.[139] No human institution is perfect. Interestingly, and probably an indication of the capacity of the General Headquarters, on June 16th we find Soult writing to Napoleon, requesting funds for his orderlies to acquire needed extra horses:

> *Charleroi, June 16, 1815.*
>
> *SIRE,*
>
> > *The service that General Staff Officers have to actively fulfill each day requires a great number of horses, that most cannot afford, for lack of pecuniary means.*
> > *I have, therefore, the honor to propose to Your Majesty to grant as extraordinary gratification to the Adjudants, Commandants, and General Staff Officers listed in the attached statement, the sum of eight hundred francs for the Adjudant-Commandants and that of six hundred francs for the Staff Officers.*
> > *I request Your Majesty to inform me of your decision on this subject,,*
>
> *Major General,*
> *Duke of Dalmatia*[140]

Apparently, resources were limited. This may be true, as on May 27th, Napoleon had written to Soult the following:

> *Paris, May 27, 1815.*
>
> > *Our army is no longer the same force as in the past years, it is probable that I will find myself with only one command. Therefore you may organize your crews accordingly and having only a third or a quarter of what Prince de Neuchâtel* (Berthier) *had. I did the same for mine.*

---

139 Chesney, Charles, *Waterloo Lectures*, starting on page 88.
140 "Soult to Napoleon" on page 401

June 15th

> *I have ordered the Minister of War to place at your disposal the sum of 50,000 francs for our secret expenses. You will take these funds so as to send money to the division generals who will need to make these types of expenditures.*[141]

At this time in 1815, Napoleon was not anticipating the need to move between multiple fronts or to control multiple armies. Resources, especially horses, had been difficult to come by; thus, it is no surprise that there had been such a dramatic decrease in the horses available for the headquarters. The frequent criticism Soult received for not using multiple orderlies for each piece of correspondence during the campaign never takes into account whether sufficient horses were available during 1815. The above pieces of correspondence suggest that they were not. History has been very willing to simply condemn Soult's performance, with the lack of duplicate messages as *the* compelling evidence. If only using one orderly was a matter of necessity, then it is possible Soult wasn't as grossly incompetent as has been argued.

One should also consider that, on the evening of the 14th of June, Napoleon and the headquarters were at Beaumont. III Corps was at Clermont, less than 10 kilometers forward. Vandamme was in the very middle of the French army, with light cavalry divisions between III Corps and the frontier, and flanked by II Corps on the left and IV Corps on the right. Vandamme was arguably in one of the safest parts of France on the evening of June 14th. In fact, this detail warrants repeating - the Imperial headquarters and III Corps were both still in FRANCE! III Corps was far less than an hour's ride away. This was not Prussia, Poland or Russia steaming with Cossacks - this was FRANCE! There simply was no reason to believe that the dispatch to Vandamme was at risk.

However, tragedy is always possible. Every year in the United States, people die by getting tangled in, and ultimately strangled by, their bed sheets.[142] It's exactly because of these possibilities that one should take extra precautions; undoubtedly, sending extra orderlies to Vandamme could have prevented this failure. But if extra orderlies were to be used for the June 15th

---

141 *Dernières lettres inédites des Napoléon Ier* Volume 2, p. 529, No. 2311
https://books.google.com/books?jtp=525&id=m67SAAAAMAAJ#v=onepage&q&f=false
142 http://www.forbes.com/sites/timworstall/2014/05/12/important-economics-lesson-spurious-correlations-are-spurious/

Order of Movement, one would expect the priority to be the formations on the wings, which were a considerable distance away from headquarters.

Maybe Napoleon was right… maybe it was just fate.

Another possibility is that Soult created an opportunity for havoc, and let Vandamme do the rest.

Left Column

The left column encountered none of the difficulties the center and right had faced.

General Reille's II Corps moved out promptly at the appointed time. By 7 am, Thuin had fallen. Marchienne-au-Pont fell and the Sambre was crossed by 1 pm. Gosselies was taken by 5 pm, and Girard's 7th division pursued the Prussians as far as Wangenies, directly west of Fleurus. Frasnes was occupied by 9 pm. Elements of Reille's Corps had covered over 30 kilometers while beating back the Prussian outposts.

The sounds of the combat at Gilly and the presence of the Prussians in mass at Fleurus presented a significant concern. If II Corps had advanced in strength on Frasnes or beyond, with a Prussian army massing in its right rear and an Anglo-Dutch army still unaccounted for, it ran a very real risk of isolation and destruction. Thus, most of II Corps was halted around Gosselies, while Girard's 7th division had been left west of Fleurus to observe the Prussians. Bachelu's 5th Division and the Imperial Guard light cavalry moved forward and the cavalry occupied Frasnes.

Hence, the advance of II Corps was also a victim of Vandamme's delay. Without the delay, III Corps would have pushed through Gilly and beyond Fleurus. This, in turn, would have led to II Corps advancing in strength beyond Gosselies, possibly to Frasnes or beyond.

D'Erlon's I Corps did not leave promptly, but this did not make a significant impact. The 90 minute delay, and the distance between I Corps and II Corps, was more than made up by the delays II Corps faced battling tenacious Prussian resistance.

At 10 am, Soult sent orders to d'Erlon instructing him to cross at Marchienne au Pont and to send reconnaissance towards Mons and Nivelles. Regardless of what Napoleon expected Wellington to do, he would have been very mindful of the flanks of his army while they advanced. Had Wellington chosen to concentrate at Mons, and had this already been underway, then it posed a significant threat to both the French army's rear and to their lines of communications.

At 3 pm, Soult sent the following order to d'Erlon:

> *In front of Charleroi, June 15 (three in the afternoon).*
>
> *Count d'Erlon, the Emperor orders Count Reille to march on Gosselies and to attack there an enemy corps that appeared to stop there. The intention of the Emperor is for you to march on Gosselies to support Count Reille and assist in his operations. However you must continue to guard Marchienne and you will send a brigade on the Mons road, recommending its commander to guard itself very militarily.*
>
> *Marshal of the Empire, General Staff,*
> *Duke of Dalmatia.*[143]

D'Erlon's First Request

With the above order, d'Erlon was ordered to support Reille's advance. At the same time, as it was I Corps' role during the advance of securing the flank, d'Erlon was to send a brigade (2 regiments, half of a division) towards Mons, continuing to recognize not only the need to observe the flank, but also to provide enough strength to delay any enemy advance, thereby providing the time necessary to react to enemy movements.

Per the Order of Movement, d'Erlon had left the 1st Division at Thuin and intended to leave the 3rd Division at Marchienne-au-Pont. Given this new order, he was unsure whether he was to maintain the garrison at Thuin, considering he was to, "still need to keep Marchienne…" Thus, at 4:30 pm, d'Erlon sent the following report to Soult, seeking clarification:

---

143 See "Soult to d'Erlon at 3 pm" on page 387

Marchienne-au-Pont, June 15, 1815 at 4:30 in the evening

Your Highness,

I received the two letters that your Excellency has done me the honor of writing to me today. The first was given to me in Montigny-le-Tigneux and I just received another at Marchienne. Under yesterday's general order I left a brigade of cavalry in Solre and Bienne-sous-Thuin, and my infantry division at Thuin, Lobbes, and Aulnes abbey.

My other troops begin to arrive at Marchienne, as soon as the last units of the 2nd Corps has filed past, I will have them cross the Sambre, I will place a brigade on the Mons road, another brigade will remain ahead of Marchienne and with the two other infantry divisions I will march on Gosselies.

I saw the position of Thuin; it is very strong as it is, but given what the localities are, we cannot establish a bridge head there.

I ask Your Excellence to let me know if I should still leave troops at Thuin, Solre, and surroundings.

Deign, Your Highness, to accept my deep respect,

Lieutenant General Commander in Chief of the 1st Corps Count d'Erlon[144]

From this report, we can see that, despite d'Erlon's morning delay, I Corps was now waiting for II Corps to complete its crossing of the Sambre. II Corps had not yet been impacted by Vandamme's delays, which proves that d'Erlon's initial delay was inconsequential. D'Erlon indicated that he would march on Gosselies with two infantry divisions, and asked specifically if he should bring the division and cavalry left in the rear at Thuin across the Sambre.

Was it clear, as some contend[145], that d'Erlon was to bring his entire corps across the Sambre? Considering that he was ordered to continue garrisoning Marchienne-au-Pont, and to send a brigade down the road

---

144 See "D'Erlon to Soult at 4:30 pm" on page 388
145 Ropes is severly critical of d'Erlon.

to Mons, one could suggest that it was not. D'Erlon chose to continue to satisfy his role protecting the flank of the army, and he sought clarification.

None came.

D'Erlon's Second Request

Early in the evening d'Erlon sent Soult another report, again asking about the divisions that he had left in the rear:

Jumay, June 15, 1815

Your Highness,

> *In accordance with the Order of Y.E. as of today, 3 pm, I was directed to Gosselies. I found the 2nd corps established there; consequently I placed my fourth division behind this village, and my second in front of Jumay, the cavalry brigade is in the latter place. The 3rd Division remained in Marchienne and the 1st in Thuin, my other cavalry brigade is in Solre and Biel-sous-Thuin, which disperses my troops very much; I pray Y.E. to kindly let me know if I must recall those I left behind. The reconnaissance party that I sent to Fontaine-l'Eveque learned that 1500 Prussians, who were there this morning with three pieces of artillery, left at noon heading on Marchele-le-Chateau; they took with them a lot of cattle. I await the order for tomorrow which will be carried by the officer who will have the honor to give this letter to Y.E. I ask acceptance of my deep respect.*

(Signed) Count d'Erlon[146]

As the 15th ended, d'Erlon's Corps was positioned exactly as his report stated, with the 1st Division in the vicinity of Thuin, and the 3rd division at Marchienne-au-Pont. While every other Corps in the *Armée du Nord* was reasonably consolidated, I Corps was distributed across over 20 kilometers.

---

146 See "D'Erlon to Soult around 8 pm" on page 390

One can also note that the officer who delivered this order to Soult was identified by d'Erlon as the one who would remain at the imperial headquarters and return the following morning to Jumet with the following day's orders as was the common practice.

Ney Takes Command

In the afternoon of the 15th, Marshal Ney had arrived at the front and was given command of the left wing. His exact orders on the 15th are unknown; for 200 years a debate has raged on whether Marshal Ney was instructed to seize Quatre Bras[147]. This was the beginning of the narrative of Ney's culpability in the campaign, which has served to utterly distract the real subterfuge that was happening right under Napoleon's nose.

Ney had a few aides, and had apparently collected orderlies from the light guard cavalry division on his wing. He certainly lacked the full complement of staff one would expect in order to command two Infantry Corps and a Corps of Cavalry. Furthermore, he did not know the positions of his forces. During the afternoon, he scrambled to gain control of his wing, but even at the end of the day, his results were incomplete, as seen in his 11 pm report to Soult:

> *Gosselies, June 15, 11 pm*
>
> *Marshal,*
> *I have the honor to report to Your Excellence that, in accordance with the Emperor's orders, I went this afternoon to Gosselies to dislodge the enemy with General Piré's Cavalry and General Bachelu's Infantry. The enemy made only a slight resistance; we exchanged 25 to 30 cannon shots; he withdrew through Heppignies on Fleurus.*
> *We took 5 to 600 Prussian prisoners from General Zieten's Corps.*

---

147 See Ropes, Jomini, Houssaye, Charras, and many others for detailed analysis of whether Ney was ordered to occupy Quatre Bras on the 15th of June. Grouchy claims to have heard Napoleon admonish Ney for failing to on the 15th. Berthezene claims to have heard Soult admit to it. *Documents Inédits* was assembled by Ney's son in large part to refute the charge. In this case, the primary sources of both sides have agendas and make demonstrably false statements. Not coincidentally, most authors from the 19th century come down on the side of their political bias.

June 15th

Here is the position of the troops:
General Lefebvre Desnouettes with the Lancers and the Chassuers of the Guard at Frasnes.
General Bachelu with the 5th Division at Mellet.
General Foy with the 9th Division at Gosselies.
General Piré's Light Cavalry at Heppignies.
I do not know where to find General in Chief Reille.
General Count d'Erlon informs me that he is in Jumet with the greater part of his Army Corps. I have just transmitted the arrangements to him, prescribed by the letter from Your Excellency, dated today.
I am enclosing in my letter a report from General Lefebvre-Desnouettes.
Accept, Marshal, the assurances of my highest regards,

Marshal Prince de la Moskowa, Ney[148]

While Ney was in command of the left wing, it is unclear exactly when he had full operational control of I Corps. Based on the correspondence, d'Erlon was still reporting and seeking direction from Soult late into the night of the 15th. Furthermore, the information Ney has was utterly wrong – d'Erlon did *not* have most of I Corps assembled at Jumet. Soult knew this, and, seemingly in response to Ney's report, he sent the following order to d'Erlon near midnight:

To Count Erlon, Commander of the 1st Corps
Charleroi, June 15, 1815

Count, the intention of the Emperor is that you rally your corps on the left bank of the Sambre, to join the second corps at Gosselies, according to the orders Marshal Prince de la Moskawa will you give on this subject.
Thus, you will recall the troops you have left to Thuin, Sobre, and surroundings; you must however always have many parties on your left to scout the Mons road.

---

[148] See "Ney to Soult around 11 pm" on page 397

Marshal of the Empire, Major General,
Duke of Dalmatia

Soult finally gives clarification – the entirety of I Corps is to cross the Sambre, including the troops at Thuin, which Soult knows, from the previous reports, have remained behind. Curiously, this order was not present in the copy of the *Registre du Major-Général*, later provided by Grouchy.

CHAPTER 11
JUNE 15TH, EVENING

NAPOLEON WAS VERY PLEASED WITH the outcome of the 15th of June. He believed that the majority of his army had crossed the Sambre and that the Allies were retreating. If they were to give battle, he believed he would have both a numerical and a quality advantage.

His confidence was high. The surprise of the Anglo-Dutch was absolute; not a single British soldier was observed on June 15th. A single Prussian corps, which was known to be headquartered at Charleroi, had been engaged and had been pushed back.

That evening, an Army Bulletin (reproduced in the Select Correspondence of the Appendix) was sent to Paris and published on June 18th in the *Moniteur*. Typical of Napoleon's Army Bulletins, a rosier picture of events was presented for public consumption. As Pierre DeWit points out:

> *-the 2nd corps Reille wasn't at Ham-sur-Heure, but at Leers-Fosteau.*
> *-Reille didn't attack the enemy at 3.00 am but around 4.00 am*
> *-Napoleon was at 1.00 am certainly not at Jamioulx-sur-Heure*
> *-Domon sabred down one company just south of Charleroi and took here about 160 prisoners*
> *-Pajol entered Charleroi around 12.30 pm*
> *-the 3rd corps of Vandamme started leaving Charleroi after 4 pm, and not around 3 pm*
> *-the French attack on Pirch II, near Gilly, started at 6 pm and not at 5 pm*
> *-neither the 26th nor the 27th Prussian infantry regiments took part in the action near Gilly.*

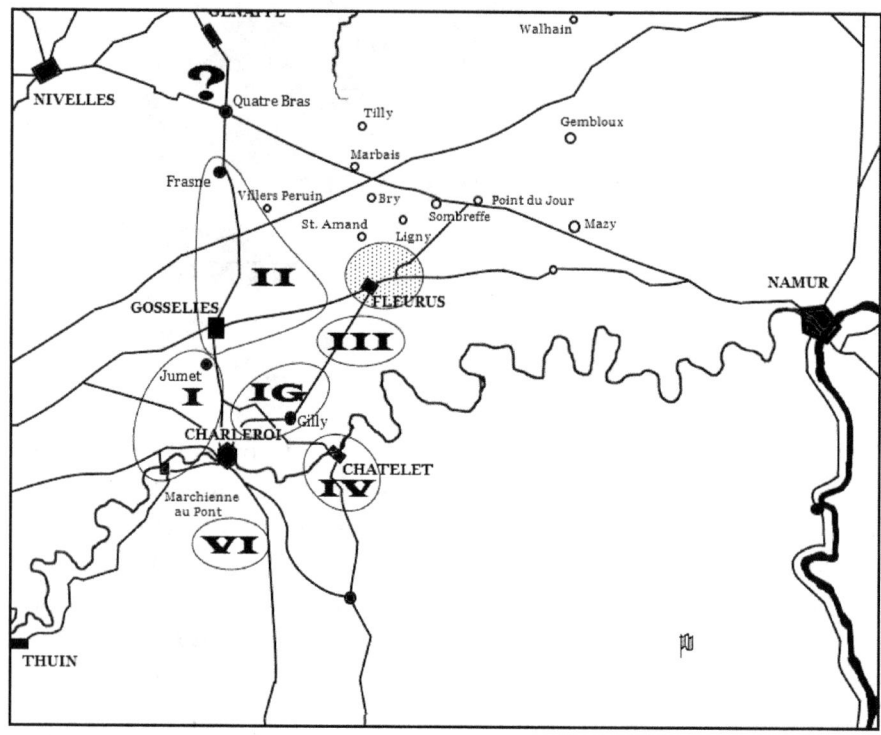

Figure 8 – Napoleon's understanding of the French and Allied dispositions at the close of June 15th. Note the scarcity of Allied forces.

*-Reille didn't attack Gosselies with Jéromes division. Additionally, the prussians were not followed on the road to Brussels.
-Napoleon entered Charleroi around 9 pm in stead of 8 pm
-Prussians losses are exaggerated as well as the French, but the other way around
-Ney was not at Quatre Bras on the 15th of June.*[149]

Much of the inaccuracy is simple exaggeration, a rounding of any element of time or conflict in favor of the French. Some of it could also be honest mistakes. Ney headquartered at Quatre Bras and the French being the master of all of Fleurus stands out not only as inaccurate, but potentially delusional. Note that in 1794, the French Republic had won a great victory at Fleurus, and thus the name carried significance. Quatre Bras, however, carried no significance at this time.

---

149 From http://waterloo-campaign.nl/bestanden/files/june15/fr.avond.pdf

June 15th, Evening

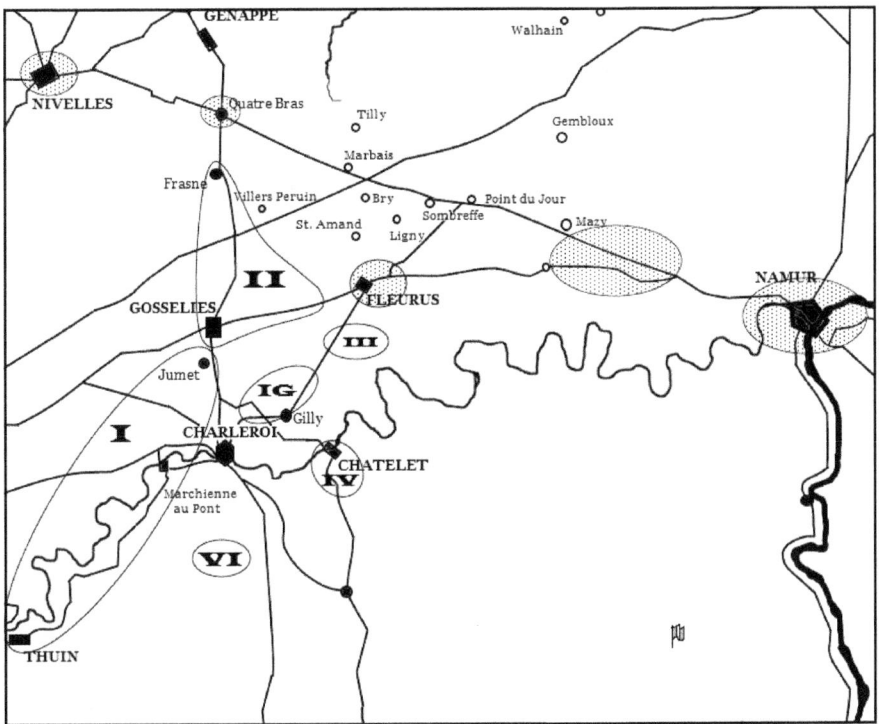

Figure 9 – Reality of the French and Allied dispositions at the close of June 15th. Note the Anglo-Dutch army was not retreating and the two additional Prussian Corps.

Realities of June 15th

As far as what was learned about the Allied forces, the French had pushed the Prussian I Corps back, but forces from no other Prussian Corps had been engaged. Dutch-Belgium battalions had been encountered at Frasnes and pushed back to Quatre Bras, but no British units had been seen.

The location of the Allied forces was largely a mystery. Napoleon had some idea of the disposition of the Allied armies before the campaign; he also knew that the French concentration would not have gone unnoticed. The location of the Guard was always of prime importance, which also explained why Napoleon waited as long as possible to move them to the front, and did so by forced marches. Napoleon seems to have expected the Allied armies to retreat, based on his orders on the morning of the 16th, and he was certain that the surprise gained the French at least one day's march. However, he was very mindful of the possibilities. The Meuse and the Sambre provided some protection on the flanks, but the left was problematic. North of the Sambre there were ample roads; if Wellington had somehow started concentrating in the vicinity of Mons or Binche, on the 14th or 15th, it was theoretically possible he could have cut across the rear of the French advance with a large part of the Anglo-Dutch army. What Napoleon was not aware of was that Wellington's response to the invasion was slow. Napoleon had gained more than a day on Wellington , which meant that Napoleon would be able to operate against Anglo-Dutch forces with an overwhelming numerical superiority, if he so chose.

But whatever Napoleon gained against Wellington, it was lost against Blücher.

The treason of June 14th led to the concentration of the Prussian army before the French had crossed the frontier. Though the Prussian IV Corps had not responded to the initial order, the Prussian II Corps was already bivouacked near Mazy, and the III Corps around Namur. The Prussian army was closing in on its concentration point of Sombreffe.

The Prussians had won the race. No matter how it was enabled, as this was their goal in event of invasion through Charleroi, one can easily argue that the Prussians were thus far executing the most effectively among the three armies. Just how bad was this for Napoleon?

While one army hesitated, another had forced march late into the night or early morning in order to meet a superior foe. Napoleon's expectation for the campaign was thwarted; however, due to the uneven allied response to the invasion, the Prussians were risking destruction.

Unfortunately, for Napoleon, there were other factors working against him.

If not for Vandamme's delays, the French would have most likely occupied Fleurus (if not Sombreffe) on the evening of the 15th. This would have enabled possession of the Namur-Nivelles road by early on the 16th. By greatly impacting communications between Wellington and Blücher, this would have likely eliminated any thoughts of Allied operations along the Nivelles-Namur road during June 16th.

Additionally, had Vandamme and III Corps led the center column, as was intended, Reille and II Corps would have also concentrated further north without the concerns of the Prussians in their right rear. If Quatre Bras had been taken on June 15th, or early on June 16th, this would have

June 15th, Evening

only compounded the Nivelles-Namur road situation. Wellington may not have even advanced south of Genappe. Napoleon would have achieved the separation of the Allied armies, thus possessing a tremendous advantage.

The brilliance of his campaign had been stolen due to the acts of traitors.

But despite the disruption of Napoleon's original vision, he still had a tremendous advantage. Delays of ones troops was nothing new, nor was the unexpected movements of the enemy. And, despite the concentration of the Prussians and the delays of Vandamme, Napoleon would be presented with a battle on June 16th, in which the destruction of the bulk of the Prussian army was a real possibility. In fact, this battle and the events surrounding it are the key reason the details of June 14th and 15th have been largely glossed over by historians. But by doing so, they have missed the final fatality that robbed Napoleon of his chance for a decisive victory.

It is clear that Napoleon went to his death having never realized the true extent of I Corps' deployment.

In 1818, Gourgaud's account of Waterloo was published. Napoleon and Gourgaud had spoken extensively about the campaign; thus, at the very least, it revealed a common understanding of events at that time.[150]

In Gourgaud's account, the following positions are given for the French army on the evening of the 15th:

> *The left wing of the French army, commanded by Marshal Ney, had its head quarters at Gosselies, and its vanguard at Frasnes; General Reille's corps was stationed between Gosselies and Frasnes, having one division (Girard's) at Vagnies, in the direction of Fleurus; General d'Erlong's corps was between Marchiennes and Julmet.*
>
> *The centre, consisting of Vandamme's corps and Grouchy's reserves of cavalry, lined the woods opposite of Fleurus.*
>
> *General Gérard's corps, forming the right wing, had passed the Sambre, and was in front of Châtelet.*
>
> *The imperial guard was escheloned, between Fleurus and Charleroi. The sixth corps in front of the latter town. Kellerman's*

---

150 Some claim that Gourgaud's account was dictated by Napoleon.

corps of cuirassiers, with the great part of artillery, on the left bank of the Sambre, behind Charleroi.[151]

Obviously, after the campaign, Napoleon was aware that Ney had not occupied Quatre Bras on the 15th. Even with the hindsight, I Corps stands alone as inaccurately reported. The 1st division of I Corps was 20 kilometers from Gosselies, which was its initial destination on the 16th. On the 15th, the farthest any infantry made was 36 kilometers, but that included fighting the Prussians, which undoubtedly slowed the progress. Davout's march to Austerlitz covered approximately 50 kilometers per day, which is considered an extreme example. Basically, the tail of I Corps was at least a half day behind II Corps.

In the Memorial of Saint Helena (either accepted as dictated or written by Napoleon and later published in Napoleon's Correspondence), Volume 31, Napoleon states that on the evening of the 15th of June, I Corps, "was between Marchiennes and Jumet." This is likewise incorrect.

Is it possible Napoleon just forgot?

No. If there was any single quality for which Napoleon was known, it was his memory.

Napoleon had an unbelievable range of intellectual ability. His power of concentration was enormous as was his memory for detail and facts. It is argued that when on campaign in 1805 one of his subordinates could not locate his division, while his aids searched through maps and papers, the Emperor informed the officer of his unit's present location, where he would be for the next three nights, the status and resume of the units strength as well as the subordinates military record. This out of an army with seven corps, a total of 200,000 men, with all the units on the move.[152]

Another equally impressive example:

---

151 Gourgaud, Gaspard, *The Campaign of MDCCCXV*, London, 1818, pp. 51-52.
152 Dean, Peter, *Napoleon as Military Commander: The Limitations of Genius* http://www.napoleon-series.org/research/napoleon/c_genius.html

June 15th, Evening

In his Memoirs, Chaptal relates the following anecdote about General Bonaparte, then First Consul.

"I saw all your reports," Bonaparte wrote to his minister, "they are correct. However, you forgot two four-pound guns in Ostend."

And Chaptal wrote:

"I was utterly amazed that, among the thousands of pieces of artillery positioned along the coastline in fixed and mobile batteries, his memory could still recall two four-pounders."[153]

Napoleon offered his own explanation for his amazing memory in this exchange, captured by Las Cases from Saint Helena:

A propos of good memory and fond recollections, I must here note down a remark of the Emperor, which I omitted to mention at the time it was made. One day at dinner, while describing one of his engagements in Egypt, he named numerically the eight or ten demi-brigades which had been engaged. On hearing this, Madame Bertrand could not refrain from asking how, after so long a lapse of time, he could possibly recollect all these numbers. "Madam, this is a lover's recollection of his former mistresses," was Napoleon's reply.[154]

Regarding I Corps on the evening of June 15th, Napoleon didn't need to remember the bivouac location of every regiment. The detail that he was unaware of was whether the 1st division of I Corps was at Thuin, which was more than 15 kms from I Corps' headquarters and more than 10 kms from the crossing at Marchienne-au-Pont. The distances by road were even greater. Are we to conclude that Napoleon did not care about the disposition of the *Armée du Nord*? Had he slipped so far in his year of exile that it was good enough to know that a Corps of his army was somewhere *over there*?

As can be seen from the correspondence, Soult knew exactly where each division of I Corps had bivouacked, and he gave d'Erlon the order to cross the Sambre late at night on the 15th; an order that was kept from the *Registre du Major-Général*. One might think that this could just be an example of Soult's sloppy staff work (for which he has been so often criticized);

---

153 From http://www.napoleonicsociety.com/english/chap20a.htm
154 Las Cases, *Memorial de Sainte Hélène*, Volume 2, Bliss, 1823, p. 122

however, if this were true, wouldn't Napoleon have at some point learned the actual dispositions?

It is simply not believable that, at some point during the night/morning of June 15th/16th, Napoleon did not crawl over his maps and place a pin for every division, using the latest reports.

There is yet another clue to Napoleon receiving misinformation on the night of June 15th. In his book on the 1815 Campaign, Gourgaud included this footnote about Ney's position:

> *It will naturally be asked, why Ney did not establish himself at Quatre Bras. It would appear, that the recollection of his conduct in 1814, and lastly in March 1815, had occasioned a kind of mental derangement, which manifested itself in all his actions. Though the bravest of the men in battle, Marshal Ney frequently committed mistakes in his field dispositions. Being informed by his light cavalry, that the enemy had but a small force at Quatre Bras, he thought it most prudent to stop on a line with the cannonade, which he heard on his right, and dispatched Girard's division, as an advanced guard, to Fleurus. Wishing it however to appear, that he had executed his orders, he reported to his Majesty, that he was occupying Quatre Bras by an advanced guard, and that his main body was close behind.*[155]

Here, Gourgaud states that Ney, "reported to his Majesty, that he was occupying Quatre Bras by an advanced guard, and that his main body was close behind." While it is possible that this was done by Ney in person, as his aide Heymes claims that he returned to Charleroi around midnight to meet with Napoleon, this, like many of Heymes claims, is questionable. But even more damning: Ney's 11 pm report written from Gosselies (quoted earlier) makes *no* mention of occupying Quatre Bras.

As Gourgaud states, while no one dared question Ney's bravery, his reputation in other matters was less than stellar. Soult, Ney's enemy dating back from Spain, had a particularly low opinion of Ney. It cannot be debated that Napoleon was misinformed about the dispositions of I Corps. Had Soult likewise misinformed Napoleon of Ney's occupation of Quatre Bras, the impact would have been profound. It would have strongly reinforced the

---

155 Gourgaud, Gaspard, *The Campaign of MDCCCXV*, London, 1818, p. 50.

notion that the Anglo-Dutch army had retreated in the face of the French advance. This would completely explain the mystery of why the Bulletin incorrectly stated Ney's occupation of Quatre Bras. As will be revealed, the morning hours of the 16th of June find Napoleon seemingly over confident, lacking urgency, and *basing his plans on a completely false premise.* Soult, as the failings of the left wing were discovered, laid the blame on Ney.

As seen by Gourgaud's comments, the idea of Ney failing was something that was readily believed.

Yet, what is evident in the correspondence between Soult and the left wing, is that Napoleon was actively deceived on June 15th, 1815.

PART III
CRESCENDO OF DOOM

CHAPTER 12
JUNE 16TH

THE DAWN HOURS OF THE 16th were largely administrative. Napoleon wrote his brother in the morning, "Confiscation of the property of traitors who are rallied in Ghent is required." If only he knew the traitors in Ghent were the least of his concerns.

With the crossing of the Sambre, Napoleon organized his army into two wings and a reserve.

Morning on the Left Wing

Early on the 16th, Napoleon sent an artillery colonel attached to the Imperial HQ staff (V. Belly de Bussy), to inquire about the situation on the left wing.[156] Why was he not satisfied by the information supplied by Soult's staff?

On or before 5am, Soult sent the following to Ney:

Charleroi 16 June 1815

Marshal, Emperor has just ordered the Count of Valmy, commander of the 3rd Cavalry Corps, to assemble and lead it to Gosselies where it will be available. The intention of his Majesty is that his Guard Cavalry that was placed on the road to Brussels, remain behind and join the rest of the Imperial Guard; but so that it does not make a retrograde movement, it can, after being substituted on the line, remain slightly to the rear, where orders will be sent in the

---

156 Houssaye, Henry, *1815 Volume 2, Waterloo*, p. 136

movement of the day; for this General Lefebvre-Desnouettes will send an officer to take the orders.

Please inform me whether the First Corps has made its move, and what is this morning the exact position of the 1st and 2nd Corps, and of the two attached cavalry divisions, while noting what is in front of you and what you learned.[157]

Ney answered sometime around 7am, which included reiterating his misunderstanding of the location of I Corps.[158] Sometime between 8am and 9am Napoleon sent the following letter to Ney:

Charleroi, June 16, 1815,

My cousin, I send my Aide-de-Camp General Flahaut to you, who brings you this letter. The Major General should have given you orders but you will receive mine first because my officers move faster than his. You will receive the day's movement orders, but I want to write to you in detail, because it is of the highest importance.

I am sending Marshal Grouchy with the 3rd and 4th Infantry Corps to Sombreffe; I am taking my Guard to Fleurus, and I will be there in person before midday, I will attack the enemy if I find them there, and I will clear the roads as far as Gembloux. There, according to what will happen, I shall come to a decision, perhaps at three o'clock in the afternoon, perhaps this evening. My intention is that, immediately after I have made up my mind, you will be ready to march on Brussels. I will support you with my Guard who will be at Fleurus or Sombreffe, and I wish to arrive at Brussels tomorrow morning. You will march this evening; if I make up my mind at an early hour then you will be informed of it during the day and then this evening will go three or four leagues and reach Brussels tomorrow by seven o'clock in the morning.

---

157 See "Soult to Ney around 5 am" on page 403
158 Houssaye quotes a fragment of this order in his footnotes, but earlier, when substantiating Ney sending a report on June 15th. Houssaye quotes: "The 1st Corps is at Julmet. My report of yesterday mentions it." He says this on Note 3 of Chapter 1 Book II. He refers to the report once again in Note 6 of Chapter III Book II, and, in both notes, indicates that the report was found in General Gourgaud's papers. Pierre De Wit failed to find this correspondence in the archives of Gourgaud.

June 16th

You can arrange your troops in the following way:

The first division, two leagues in front of Quatre Bras, if there is no harm; six divisions of infantry around Quatre Bras, and a division at Marbais, so that I can draw it to me at Sombreffe, if I need; it would not otherwise delay your march;

Count of Valmy's Corps, who has 3,000 Elite Cuirassiers, will be placed at the intersection of Roman and Brussels roads, so that I can draw it to me if needed. As soon as I take my course of action, you will send him the order to come join you.

I will want to have the Guard Division with me, commanded by General Lefebvre-Desnoëttes, and I am sending you two divisions of Count of Valmy's Corps to replace it. But, in my current endeavor, I prefer to place Count of Valmy so as to recall if I need him, and I do not wish to cause General Lefebvre-Desnoëttes to make unnecessary marches, since it is likely that I will decide this evening to march on Brussels with the Guard. However, cover Lefebvre's division with d'Erlon and Reille's Divisions of Cavalry, in order to save the Guard: if there was a skirmish with the English, it is preferable that it is on the Cavalry of the line rather than on the Guard.

I have adopted as a general principle, during this campaign, to divide my army into two wings and a reserve. Your wing will consist of four divisions of the 1st Corps, four divisions of the 2nd Corps, two divisions of Light Cavalry, and two divisions of the Count of Valmy's Corps. That should be roughly 45 to 50,000 men.

Marshal Grouchy will have about the same force and will command the right wing.

The Guard will form the reserve, and I will move to one or the other wing, according to circumstances. The Major General gives the most precise orders so that there is no difficulty in obeying such orders that you receive; the corps commanders will take my orders directly when I am present.

According to circumstances, I will diminish one wing or the other, to strengthen my reserve.

You understand the considerable importance in taking Brussels. This may also lead to incidents, because such a swift and abrupt movement will isolate the English army from Mons, Ostend, etc. I want your arrangements to be well made, so that at the first order your eight divisions can go quickly and without obstacles to Brussels.

Napoléon.[159]

Here Napoleon's plan for the campaign comes to life.

Militarily, he pushed his army between scattered forces; he was prepared to respond to any opportunity. He expected the Allied armies to retreat, as there would be great danger to try to concentrate within Napoleon's reach. But if they did give battle, he would have the immediate advantage. This is a perfect demonstration of Napoleon's art of war.

Politically, his goal was to seize Brussels, a thunder clap which would reverberate across Europe. For this purpose, he had printed up proclamations to the Belgian people before even crossing the frontier.

Remarkably absent is any order to attack Quatre Bras. There is not even a written order to *occupy* Quatre Bras! The order is written as though Quatre Bras was already occupied, consistent with the Bulletin of the previous evening. Napoleon directs how Ney's eight divisions - the entirety of I Corps and II Corps - are to be deployed, including pushing a division two leagues beyond Quatre Bras on the road to Brussels. Napoleon was happy that his left wing could settle in and rest, in preparation for a forced march to Brussels through the night. The lack of urgency on the morning of the 16th is directly related to Napoleon's inaccurate facts of progress.

Napoleon expected that Ney could execute the proscribed movements and be ready to march by 3 pm, if, by that time, Napoleon had decided to advance on Brussels with the left wing.

Napoleon thought that there was only a single Prussian Corps around Sombreffe; thus with the right wing under Grouchy, comprised of the III and IV Corps plus 3 corps of Cavalry, as well as the Guard, he planned to attack and scatter that force. Then, with his Guard and the left wing under Ney, he could dramatically seize Brussels. It is clear that Napoleon believed the Anglo-Dutch forces had retreated.

VI Corps, which was always part of the central reserve, was left at Charleroi protecting the army's baggage and communications. Napoleon remained very aware of the potential for Wellington to advance in the large gap between the left wing and Charleroi. At the same time, VI Corps could

---

159 See "Napoleon to Ney before 9 am" on page 409

be drawn to either wing, if necessary. VI Corps' position was necessary because ,in Napoleon's mind, I Corps would rapidly vacate the gap between Quatre Bras and Charleroi.

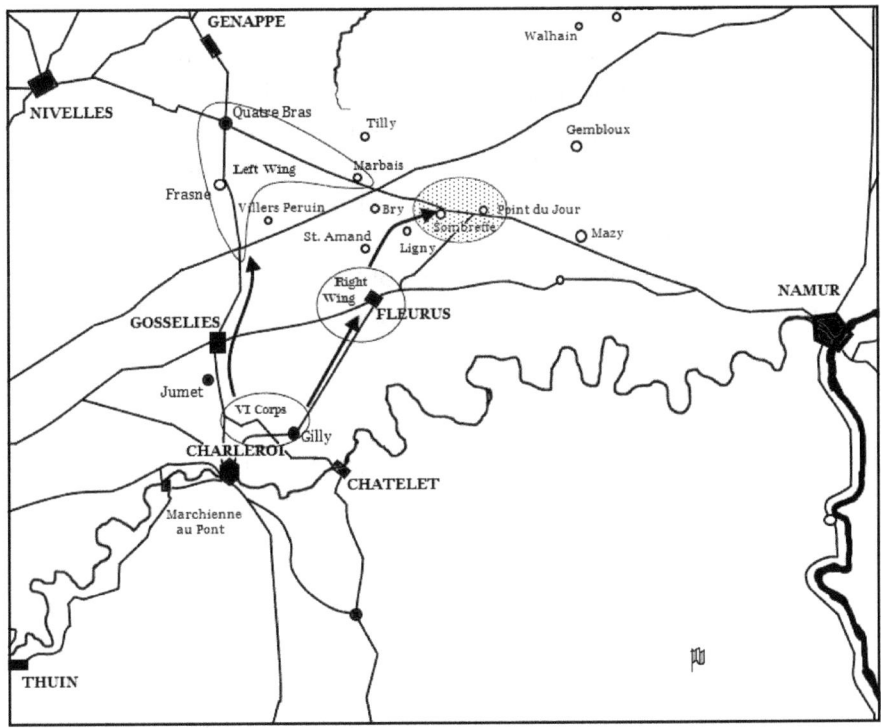

Figure 10 - Napoleon's vision on the morning of June 16th

The bearer of this dispatch, Flahaut, wrote a letter in 1857, attempting to explain this absence of directions on occupying Quatre Bras:

> *But as regards orders for the movement of troops, I was directed to give them to Marshal Ney by word of mouth. I therefore gave him as from the Emperor the order to move to Quatre Bras, to hold this important point in force, and (should the enemy allow him to do so) to support with every man at his disposal the Emperor's offensive against the Prussian army.*[160]

---

160 *The First Napoleon - Some Unpublished Documents from the Bowood Papers*, 1925, p. 116

The problem with this explanation is that Napoleon had not yet decided on an offensive against the "Prussian army."[161] At this point, Napoleon believed that he only faced a single Prussian corps which had been driven back on the 15th. In his 9 am letter to Grouchy, he estimates the Prussians to be no more than 40,000 men. It seems that maybe Flahaut's recollection, after 40 years, has been blurred by the events as they actually unfolded.

Thus, one could read the dispatch carried by Flahaut to mean that Napoleon thought the Quatre Bras position was unoccupied. More sinisterly, it could instead be read that Napoleon believed Ney had already occupied the position - which would explain the Bulletin, yet leave the origin of such false information unresolved.

Napoleon's letter referenced the order of the day that Soult would send. Presumably, it would be identical. Soult sent this order to Ney around 8 am:

Charleroi, June 16, 1815

> *Marshal, the Emperor orders that you have the 2nd and 1st Army Corps, as well as the 3rd Cavalry Corps that was placed at your disposal and direct them to the intersection of the roads known as the* Trois-Bras *(Brussels road), where they will take their position. At the same time you will send a reconnaissance, as forward as possible on the road to Brussels and Nivelles, where the enemy has probably retreated. H.M. wishes that, if there is no harm, you establish a division with cavalry at Genappe, and orders that you march another division in the direction of Marbais to cover the space between Sombreffe and Trois Bras. You will place, close to this division, the cavalry division of the Imperial Guard commanded by General Lefebvre-Desnouettes, as well as the 1st Hussars Regiment which was detached yesterday towards Gosselies.*
>
> *The Corps that will be at* Marbais *will also plan to support the movements of Marshal Grouchy on Sombreffe, and support you at the position at the Trois Bras, if that becomes necessary. You will recommend to the General who will be at Marbais, to scout well in all directions, particularly those of Gembloux and Wavre.*

---

161 See Houssaye, *Waterloo 1815* footnotes (pp. 344-345) for a detailed overview of Napoleon's letters to Ney and Grouchy and their meaning vis a vis the plans for the 16th of June.

If, however, General Lefebvre-Desnouettes' Division is too engaged on the Brussels road, you will leave it there and replace it at Marbais by the 3rd Cavalry Corps, that will be under command of the Count of Valmy, and by the 1st Hussars Regiment.

I have the honor to advise you that the Emperor will march on Sombreffe, where, according to the orders of H.M., Marshal Grouchy must move with the 3rd and 4th Infantry Corps, and the 1st, 2nd and 4th Cavalry Corps. Marshal Grouchy will occupy Gembloux.

Please report to me as well as to the Emperor about your arrangments, to execute the order that I send to you as well as all that you will have learned about the enemy.

H.M. desires me to tell you to prescribe to the Generals commanding the army corps to keep their troops united, and send isolated men back to their units, to maintain perfect order in the troops and rally all the artillery carts and ambulances that have been left behind.

Marshal of the Empire, Major General,
Duke of Dalmatia[162]

Soult, aware of the distribution of the left wing, immediately makes it clear that Ney must "direct" his forces to Quatre Bras, and then carry out the reconnaissance and positioning that Napoleon wished. Napoleon stated in his letter that he expected his aide-de-camp to reach Ney first; Napoleon couldn't simply be *seconding* an existing order. Quite plainly, the orders are different, though the final results are similar. This is the first sign that Napoleon had a disconnect with his left wing, which would unfortunately grow throughout the day with fatal consequences.

The charade of the left wing abruptly ceased with the arrival of an officer of lancers, who revealed that the enemy was massing at Quatre Bras.[163] Right before leaving for Fleurus to deal with the gathering Prussians, Napoleon had Soult send Ney the following order:

---

[162] See "Soult to Ney before 8 am" on page 407
[163] Margerit's *Waterloo*, p. 256, footnote 2 states, "The report of the adjutant Bussy, dated Frasnes, six in the morning, also reported a small gathering enemy at Quatre Bras." I do not know when this report was received by Napoleon.

Charleroi, June 16, 1815.

Marshal, a Lancer officer has just told the Emperor that the enemy is present en mass at Quatre Bras; assemble the Corps of Counts Reille and d'Erlon and that of Count of Valmy who is at this moment en route to join you; with these forces you must attack and destroy all the enemy corps that present themselves; Blücher was in Namur yesterday and it is not credible that he moved troops towards Quatre Bras, thus you are opposed by only what comes from Brussels.

Marshal Grouchy will execute the movement on Sombreffe that I announced to you, and the Emperor will go to Fleurus; it is there that you will address your new reports to H.M.

Marshal of the Empire, Major General,
Duke of Dalmatia[164]

Additionally, Napoleon sent Colonel Janin, Lobau's adjutant, to the left wing in order to get details, and to let Ney know that VI Corps was at Charleroi and could be called upon if needed. Once again, Napoleon was acting on his own to gather intelligence on the left wing. Whether Napoleon had given Ney orders to seize Quatre Bras on the 15th, or just that morning, he expected the Anglo-Dutch forces to retreat. The presence of enemy forces at Quatre Bras was not expected.

As Napoleon was heading to Fleurus, he had just learned that what he thought he knew about the left wing was not true. At the same time, while the Prussians had been encountered in force, it was still a complete mystery as to where Wellington would concentrate his forces. Napoleon was very concerned about his exposed left and the risk to his lines of communication. VI Corps was his safeguard against such a maneuver, as it could be ordered to either wing once additional intelligence was received.

At this same moment (around noon), Ney was advancing towards Quatre Bras with the divisions of II Corps. He had received the orders of both Napoleon and Soult in the late morning, and then issued his own orders which he communicated to Soult in the following report:

---

164 See "Sout to Ney before 10 am" on page 412

June 16th

Frasne, June 16, 1815 at 11 o'clock in the morning.

To His Excellency Marshal Duke Dalmatia, Major General,

I receive at this moment your instructions for the movement of the 1st and 2nd Infantry Corps, and for General Piré's Light Cavalry Division and the two Cavalry Divisions of the 3rd Corps.

Those of the Emperor have already reached me. Here are the placements that I have just ordered:

The 2nd Corps, General Reille, will have a division behind Genappe, another at Bauterlet, and the two others at Quatre Bras.

A Light Cavalry division of General Piré will cover the 2nd Corps' march.

The 1st Corps will set up as follows: a division at Marbais, two others in Frasne, a Light Cavalry Division at Marbais, two divisions of Comte de Valmy at Frasne and Liberchies.

The two Divisions of Light Cavalry of the Guard will remain in Frasne where I establish my headquarters.

All of the information reveals that there are about 3000 enemy infantrymen at Quatre Bras and very few cavalry. I think that the arrangements of the Emperor for the subsequent march on Brussels will be carried out without great obstacles.

Marshal Prince de la Moskowa,

Ney[165]

The left wing was acting without urgency, arguably by design. At noon on June 16th, the plan was to march on Brussels, possibly through the night, once Napoleon eliminated the danger to the French army's line of operations. The Prussians that occupied Fleurus (though would later fall back on Sombreffe) needed to be dealt with, and the Anglo-Dutch army was yet to be seen. However, Napoleon most certainly thought that he would learn of Wellington's maneuvers once he turned his attention to the left wing and drove on Brussels, which was Wellington's headquarters. And, one should keep in mind, that while Napoleon drove against the Prussians, he kept

---

165 See "Ney to Soult at 11 am" on page 415

VI Corps at Charleroi for exactly the purpose of dealing with anything unexpected on the left.

The controversy in the popular history of Waterloo is whether Napoleon ordered Ney to seize Quatre Bras prior to the morning orders of June 16th.[166] Although there is material that supports both sides of the argument, the truth will never be known. The impact of Ney occupying Quatre Bras is profound, as it may have ceased cooperation between Wellington and Blücher on June 16th. Both Napoleon and Gourgaud claim that Napoleon gave Ney instructions to seize Quatre Bras verbally on the June 15th. Whichever the truth, this is one Waterloo mystery that does not involve Soult.

But as we have seen, Soult played an active role in keeping Napoleon misinformed on the status of the left wing. At noon, I Corps was still at Gosselies, but its rear divisions had closed up. The trailing divisions of II Corps, which were positioned in and to the east of Gosselies, had only just received Ney's orders to advance, and were moving through Gosselies, and heading north. I Corps was delayed behind II Corps. Thus, one could argue that I Corps' disposition on June 15th was irrelevant. This is probably why no one has ever cared about Napoleon's understanding of I Corps' disposition on June 15th. Regardless, it remains a basic fact that Soult knew something that Napoleon did not.

While waiting at Gosselies, d'Erlon launched a reconnaissance mission, triggered by a report of the enemy to his left.[167] This was a continuation of his mission to monitor the left flank. The reconnaissance found nothing, but it delayed I Corps' advance. Thus, d'Erlon wrote Soult a report from Gosselies. I Corps' march commenced around 3 pm.

Houssaye, who read the report, says it was sent between 1 pm and 3 pm. Based on what's known, this seems reasonable. Houssaye said he found the report in Gourgaud's papers, but Pierre de Wit has stated that he did not

---

166 One challenge that exists when trying to decipher what happened is that Memoirs can not only be inaccurate, written to place the author in the best possible light, and/or trying to help one general against another, but they can also be more or less re-written. Complete fabrications written by ghost writers or ancestors exist in French, but are rare. It is surprising that the last one published in 2006, *Jean-Louis de Crabbé, colonel d'empire*, is sometimes quoted (and listed in bibliographies) as an authentic memoir, but other than his various positions and their dates gathered from his personnel file, the rest (as noted in the preface) is a fictional account of his experiences.

167 Houssaye, Henry, *1815, Waterloo*, London, 1900, p. 117. Footnote 41 states that the information came from a report from d'Erlon to Soult, sent from Gosselies before 3pm. The report was found in General Gourgaud's papers.

find it in that collection. If d'Erlon was updating Soult due to a delay, then it is probable the report was sent closer to 3 pm. Either way, d'Erlon would have given Soult an indication of his march status, as he did on the 15th. The report would have taken around an hour to reach Soult on the right wing north of Fleurus. Altogether, Soult would have learned, sometime between 2 pm and 4 pm, that I Corps was at Gosselies, and was either commencing its march or waiting for II Corps. Thus, no later than 4 pm, Soult knew that I Corps was positioned on the Charleroi-Brussels road, with its head about 4-6 kms north of Gosselies in a column that was at least 5 km long.

Not to be forgotten are the additional traitors. During the morning, Chief of Staff of General Durutte's 4th division of I Corps, Colonel Gordon, and ADC Chef de Battalion Gaugler, deserted, and then made their way to Quatre Bras.[168]

Morning on the Right Wing

In the early morning, orders to advance to Sombreffe were issued to III Corps and IV Corps. The Guard was ordered to Fleurus, and VI Corps was ordered to a reserve position above Charleroi. VI Corps was positioned such that it could support either the right or left wing. The Cavalry reserve (except Kellerman's heavy cavalry corps ordered to the left) was ordered to Sombreffe.

As Ney was put in command of the left wing, Grouchy was put in command of the right wing. Foreshadowing his weakness for this role, Grouchy tried to refuse, but was overruled.

Napoleon believed that there were no more than 40,000 Prussians at Sombreffe, a single corps, and believed it was a rear guard that would be retreating. This Prussian force, Zieten's I Corps, would have been forced to retreat if the army concentration had not been ordered the evening of the 14th.

Napoleon planned to attack and push the Prussians back beyond Gembloux. With the French army sitting on the Nivelles-Namur road, and with Wellington north of Genappe and Blücher at Namur or Gembloux, Napoleon would have eliminated the ability for the Prussians and Anglo-Dutch armies to coordinate their actions. Then, leaving the right

---

168 From http://www.waterloo-campaign.nl/bestanden/files/june16/frlinkervleugel.pdf

wing to secure his flank, he would take his reserve and drive to Brussels with the left wing. What Napoleon was unaware of was that Gneisenau had already ordered the concentration of the Prussian army at Sombreffe. The Prussian I Corps was in position around Sombreffe, II Corps would arrive in the late morning, and III Corps in the early afternoon. A Prussian army of over 90,000 men and over 200 guns awaited Napoleon. The IV Prussian Corps had not reacted to the concentration orders immediately, and would end up a day behind the main Prussian army.

During the morning, the III and IV Corps, as well as the Guard, moved to Fleurus, while the VI Corps remained in reserve near Charleroi. Some criticize Napoleon's lack of use of VI Corps at Ligny. However, as previously noted, in the absence of intelligence of the location of the Anglo-Dutch army, VI Corps was fulfilling a crucial role. Wellington did eventually order a concentration at Quatre Bras.

Not to be forgotten are the additional traitors. While performing reconnaissance on the Prussians massing around Sombreffe, Colonel Laderiac of Marshal Grouchy's staff went over to the enemy and asked to join the King in Ghent.[169]

Battle of Ligny

Having arrived at the battlefield, Napoleon teased Gérard (who had vouched for Bourmont) about the prior day's desertion. Napoleon is said to have joked, "the blue are always blue and the white always white."[170] Bourmont's actions were not a surprise; however, how he had been put in the position to execute his plan was never connected.

Sometime around 1 pm, Soult received Ney's report of 11 am (previously cited). While Quatre Bras was not occupied, it was lightly defended, and there was every indication that Ney's forces were largely consolidated, although one division of I Corps was not accounted for. There was no reason for Soult to conceal this report, as it simply reinforced Napoleon's

---

169 *Monatshefte für Politik und Wehrmacht*, 1906, p. 611
http://books.google.com/books?id=fZ0jAQAAIAAJ
170 Blue was the color of the revolution, white was the color of the Bourbons.

June 16th

inaccurate view of the left wings dispositions. In fact, this report could be the foundation of Napoleon's growing belief that Ney was failing.

By early afternoon, Napoleon realized that he faced more than just a rear guard, but the bulk of the Prussian army. This presented a golden opportunity, which once again validated Napoleon's majesty in war. Lightning maneuvers against a numerically superior enemy had produced a battle in which Napoleon had both superior numbers, quality, and position. He planned to engage the enemy, and then, once he pinned them, bring a flanking maneuver from the left wing that could lead to its destruction.

At 2 pm, Soult sent the following order to Ney:

> *Before Fleurus, June 16, at two o'clock.*
>
> *Marshal, the Emperor desires me to inform you that the enemy has assembled a corps of troops between Sombreffe and Bry, and at 2:30 pm Marshal Grouchy will attack the enemy position with the 3rd and 4th Corps. The intention of His Majesty is that you attack what is before you, and that after having vigorously pressed them, you will turn back on us so as to envelop the enemy corps that I just mentioned. If this corps is overthrown first, then His Majesty will maneuver in your direction, to hasten your operations as well.*
>
> *Inform the Emperor of your dispositions and what occurs on your front.*
>
> *Marshal of the Empire, Major General*
> *Signed, Duke of Dalmatia*[171]

Because Napoleon was expecting to flank the Prussians, his battle plan was fairly simple: a frontal assault that would both pin the Prussians and suck in their reserves. This would assure maximum damage when the Prussians were enveloped. Napoleon told General Gérard, after giving him the order to attack Ligny, "It is possible that in three hours the issue of the war will be decided. If Ney carries out my orders well, not a single gun of the Prussian army will escape; it is caught red handed."[172]

What Napoleon didn't know was that at 2 pm, Ney was just arriving at Quatre Bras, and II Corps was strung out on the march. I Corps was

---

[171] See "Soult to Ney at 2 pm" on page 418
[172] *Napoleon's Memoirs*, Soho Book Company, London, 1986, p. 510

still south of Gosselies, not even in Ney's operational control. The lack of urgency on the left wing was now creating a danger for Napoleon's plans. Napoleon was largely responsible for the lack of urgency, though only because he was misinformed. Had he known the truth, there is every reason to believe that his orders to the left wing would have been dispatched in the predawn hours.

The battle would begin around 3:00 pm. In June of 1815, the sun set at around 8:30, though combat could, and did, go later at times. This gives approximately a six hour window. Napoleon calculated that the envelopment should take place around 6 pm, from the Nivelles-Namur road, thus coming from the north-west and hitting the right rear of the Prussian army. At this point in time, Napoleon must have believed that Ney had both I Corps and II Corps in his operational control near Quatre Bras.

In Las Cases' *Mémorial de Sainte Hélène,* when discussing the mistrust of the soldiers toward their superiors, in light of the treason of 1814 and 1815, the following incident is related:

> *At the moment, when the first cannon shots were firing near Saint Amand, an old corporal approached the Emperor and said; "Sire, beware of General Soult; be assured that he is a traitor." – "Fear nothing," replied the Emperor, "I can answer for him as for myself."*[173]

Napoleon relates the battle:

> *At three o'clock in the afternoon, the 3rd Corps assaulted the village of Saint-Amand. A quarter of an hour later, the 4th Corps assaulted the village of Ligny, and Marshal Grouchy bent back the left of the Prussian Army. All the positions and houses situated on the right of the ravine were taken, and the enemy army thrown back on to the left bank.*[174]

At 3:15, with the battle heavily engaged and going as planned, Napoleon had Soult send another order to Ney:

---

173 Las Cases, Emmanuel, *Memorial de Sainte Hélène*, 1823, p. 141
174 *Napoleon's Memoirs*, Soho Book Company, London, 1986, p. 510

June 16th

Before Fleurus, on the 16th at 3:15

Marshal, I wrote to you, an hour ago, that the Emperor would attack the enemy at 2:30 pm, in the position that it took between the village of St. Amand and Bry, at this moment the action is in full swing. H.M. charged me to say to you that you must maneuver immediately, so as to envelop the enemy line and strike his rear. This army is lost if you act aggressively. The fate of France is in your hands; thus do not hesitate a moment to carry out the movement that the Emperor orders and is aimed at the heights of St. Amand and Bry to contribute to a possible decisive victory, the enemy has been caught in the act, at the moment when they look to join the English.

Major General, Duke of Dalmatia[175]

Note that Napoleon continued to send orders to Ney, whom he expected to have operational control of both I and II Corps, as well as the various cavalry divisions under his command.

Around this time, a report from Lobau arrived, as a result of Napoleon's prior request to send Janin to gather information about the left wing:

Sire,

In accordance with Your Majesty's orders, I sent Adjudant-Commandant Jeanin to the corps commanded by Marshal Ney. This officer found these troops positioned from the surroundings of Gosselies to beyond the village of Frasnes. He has a lot of experience in war and thinks that the enemy is not in very great force; but it is difficult, because of the forests, to judge precisely.

The previously mentioned Colonel talked with several superior officers, and he finally interrogated deserters, and none of the individuals questioned brought the number of the enemy beyond 20,000 men; when this officer left the site, there were only skirmishers engaged, these in a rather small number.

---

[175] See "Soult to Ney at 3:15 pm" on page 418

> *I am still positioned in front of Charleroi where I will remain until given new orders. It would be good if Your Majesty wanted to replace the battalion that I have in town for police and the large numbers of baggage; to protect the wounded etc; this position cannot, it seems to me, remain completely devoid of troops.*
>
> *Charleroi, June 16, 1815*
>
> *Lieutenant General, Aide-de-Camp of the Emperor, Commander in Chief of the 6th Corps*
>
> *Lobau*
>
> *P.S. Colonel Jeanin reports that Colonel Tancarville, Chief of Staff of Cte of Valmy, said to him that the emissaries who came to Cte D'Erlon reportedly said to him that the enemy was marching today from Mons to Charleroi. Your Majesty will surely be able to fully appreciate the value of this information.*[176]

This report indicates that Ney may have been facing 20,000 of the enemy. While this number was inaccurate at the time Janin made his observation, it had since become true.

This altered Napoleon's mental picture. Originally, with Quatre-Bras sparsely occupied, Napoleon had no idea where the various elements of the Anglo-Dutch army had concentrated. A bold maneuver, one which Napoleon would have probably considered himself if in Wellington's shoes, would have been to concentrate the forces surrounding Mons at Binche, and then fall upon Charleroi or march up the Roman road hitting the French in the flank. Hence, believing I Corps to be north of the Roman road near Quatre Bras, Napoleon left VI Corps near Charleroi to protect the baggage and the rear, especially of the left wing. Leaving VI Corps behind - or, as many have incorrectly stated, "forgotten about" - was not a mistake at all. Hearing that Ney now faced a considerable force, Napoleon must have become comfortable enough with the notion that the Anglo-Dutch army would not concentrate at Quatre Bras, and carry out a flanking maneuver;

---

176 See "Lobau to Napoleon around 1 pm" on page 416

thus it was now safe to call VI Corps to the front. Soult sent Lobau the order for VI Corps to come to Fleurus.

Napoleon then decided that Ney would need to delay Wellington and send whatever could be spared to Ligny to affect the envelopment. At 3:30 pm, Soult sent Ney a duplicate of the 3:15 pm order. Napoleon may have included a direct order to d'Erlon in one of the orders to Ney.

As we have seen previously, d'Erlon, and much of I Corps, were at Gosselies at 3 pm. Clearly Napoleon was not aware of this; otherwise this knowledge, and the Janin report, would have completely altered his plans. There would have been no force for Ney to dispatch down the Nivelles-Namur road. And an even more sinister possibility exists: if d'Erlon had written his report to Soult before 2 pm, then Napoleon was sending orders to Ney to maneuver on the Prussian rear, while Soult knew that more than half of Ney's force was nowhere near Ney, nor the location where Napoleon desired Ney to launch the envelopment.

The slow movement of the left wing during the 16th was not Soult's doing. However, it is clear that Soult knew more than he shared with Napoleon - information which would have clearly altered Napoleon's plans.

Napoleon continues:

> *The village of Ligny was taken and retaken four times, Count Gérard covered himself with glory there and displayed as much bravery as talent. The attack was weak at the village of Saint-Amand, which was also taken and retaken; but it was carried by General Girard, who, having received the order to advance by the left of the ravine with his division, the 3rd of the 2nd Corps, brought into play there that intrepidity of which he had shown so many examples during his military career. He overthrew at the point of the bayonet all who thought to oppose his advance, and took possession of half the village; but he fell, fatally wounded.*[177]

Napoleon began to shift forces to his left in preparation for the attacks which would require the Prussians to deploy on their right to meet; the very flank he expected to hit in the rear when Ney's forces arrived.

---

177 *Napoleon's Memoirs*, Soho Book Company, London, 1986, p. 510

Suddenly, at around 5:30 pm, a corps of 20,000 or more was spotted north of Villers Peruin and marching on Fleurus, behind the French lines! Had a Prussian corps maneuvered between Sombreffe and Quatre Bras and enveloped the French? Or had Wellington been bold enough to send a corps of the Anglo-Dutch army from Mons to march between Quatre Bras and Charleroi!? This was one of Napoleon's concerns from the beginning of the campaign; it was also what Vandamme thought at the time, and now it had happened!

Whatever this force was, it couldn't have been sent by Ney. Ney's forces were farther north; thus, the orders to Ney would result in French forces coming down the Nivelles-Namur road (which passed through Quatre Bras) then appearing in the rear of the Prussian army. Any Prussian forces attempting that wide a flanking maneuver (which would now be emerging behind Vandamme), would have certainly been intercepted by the forces sent by Ney.

By 5:30 pm, Soult would have received d'Erlon's report from Gosselies. Thus, Soult was aware that from 3 pm until 5:30 pm, I Corps and its 5+ km column had been marching north from Gosselies. Soult may not have known exactly where I Corps was, but its location certainly eliminated any possibility of the unknown force coming from the west. Furthermore, I Corps was the closest French troops to the unknown force. But, just as he had not informed Napoleon of I Corps' position during the afternoon, Soult continued to stay silent.

At the sight of this unknown force, units of Napoleon's left flank actually panicked and retreated. Napoleon suspended his attack maneuvers, instead positioning to meet this threat, while sending out reconnaissance.

After an hour wait, the unknown force was identified as I Corps, which was "inexplicable" according to Napoleon. Had Soult kept Napoleon informed of I Corps' maneuvers, their identity may have been unfortunate and not what Napoleon had planned, but far from "inexplicable." Had Napoleon known the identity of the corps, he may have taken advantage of their arrival, instead he was busily engaged in a battle, maneuvering troops to meet the unknown threat. Once the situation was discovered, it was too late. I Corps had begun to march away.

Many have asked: since Napoleon ordered French forces from the left, and possibly even sent a direct order to I Corps itself, why would he be surprised at its appearance? This ignores what Napoleon was being told.

On his map, the unknown force was not I Corps or II Corps. Napoleon had not forgotten that he'd asked for troops from the left, nor had his staff forgotten. They were all expecting the force dispatched from Ney to appear from farther north. The reason for the collective shock was that, having boldly invaded between two armies, the worst case scenario was now seemingly materializing. Napoleon had been actively deceived. It bears repeating: this force was coming from a location on Napoleon's map (mental or otherwise) that were void of French forces, but not from the possibility of an Anglo-Dutch force. Because Napoleon could easily imagine such a bold maneuver (and had made these same types of maneuvers throughout his career), it was paralyzing.

Regardless, with the crisis averted, Napoleon returned to the attack. He now realized that there would be no envelopment, and no destruction of the Prussian army, but there was still a victory to be won.

Napoleon concludes:

> *The Guard thereupon resumed its march on Ligny. General Pecheux, at the head of his division, crossed the ravine; Count Gérard, the whole of the Guard, infantry, cavalry, artillery and cuirassiers, and Milhaud's division supported his movement. All the enemy reserves were overwhelmed at the point of the bayonet; the centre of his line was pierced.*[178]

The battle was won, but too late for an effective pursuit. Night fell, and most French units bivouacked on the battlefield. The Prussians established a reasonable rear-guard, and then began their retreat. At a council of war after the battle - and with some consideration of retreating east to await the Austrians and Russians - it was decided instead to retreat to Wavre in the north, thus to remain in cooperation with Wellington, who later called the decision to retreat on Wavre the "decisive moment of the century."

The time lost due to d'Erlon's unexpected appearance at the rear of the French lines prevented Napoleon from dictating his terms on the victory. The cavalry he had massed, along with the Imperial Guard, could have easily followed up the breaking of the Prussian center with scattering the

---

178 *Napoleon's Memoirs*, Soho Book Company, London, 1986, p. 511

Prussian right and seizing the key northern points in the rear of the Prussian lines that would have compelled a retreat to the east.

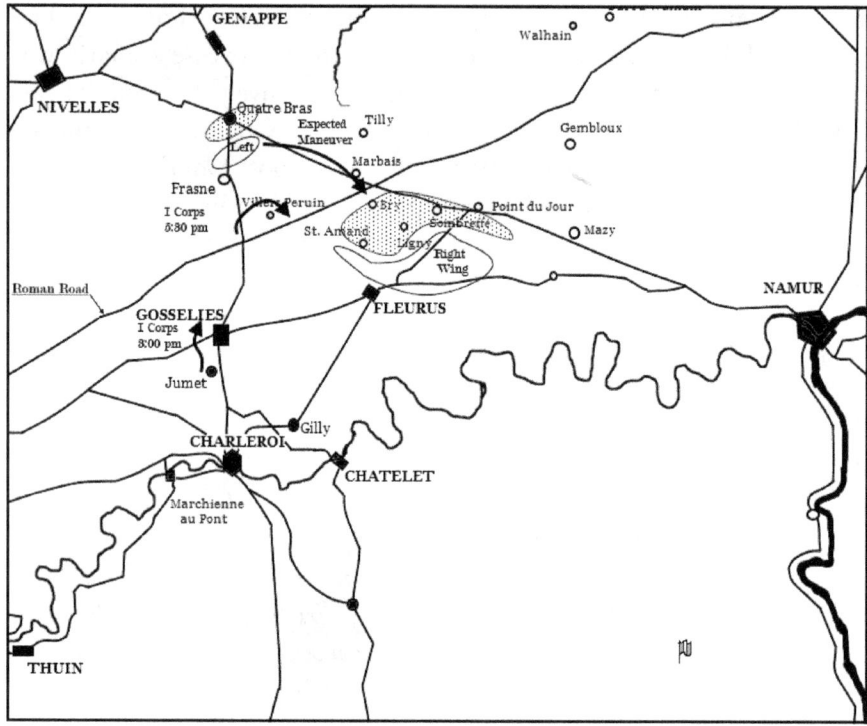

Figure 11 - Situation at 5:30 pm on June 16th

Battle of Quatre Bras

Ney did not move on Quatre Bras with much urgency. However, the need for urgency is only obvious in retrospect. While there is room to criticize Ney, it must be remembered that he inherited a left wing that had, by no fault of his own, been left spread across 24 kilometers as the crow flies. Had I Corps crossed the Sambre on the 15th, it's a fair assumption that Ney would have been far more confident to undertake aggressive actions, both late in the day on the 15th and early on the 16th, as he would have had more strength to deal with the various concerns he had about being positioned so far in front on the French army. Here, we can see the ongoing impact of Soult's subtle actions.

Reille, who had faced Wellington in Spain and was well aware of how Wellington concealed forces, was quite cautious. Responding to the orders from Napoleon and Soult (only received in the late morning), Ney began advancing towards Quatre Bras at around 1:30 pm.

Napoleon begins:

> *His sharp-shooters were engaged at two o'clock, but it was not till three o'clock when the cannonade of the battle at Ligny could be heard in all its ferocity, that he really got to grips with the enemy. The prince of Orange and his division were soon overthrown; but it was supported by the Prince of Brunswick's Division, and the 5th English Division, which arrived helter-skelter. These two divisions had left Brussels at ten o'clock in the morning and had covered eight leagues; that had neither artillery nor cavalry.*
>
> *The fight was renewed with vigour; the enemy had the superiority in numbers, since Marshal Ney's 2nd Line was three leagues in the rear, but the French artillery and cavalry were in much greater numbers. The Brunswick troops, repulsed, like those from Nassau, left plenty of dead, among whom was the reigning prince of Brunswick. The 42nd Highland Regiment of Picton's division, having formed itself into a square in order to withstand a charge by the cuirassiers, was smashed in and cut to pieces; its colonel was killed; its colours taken. The French sharp-shooters were already arriving at the farm of Quatre Bras when the 1st English Guards Division and Alten's 3rd Division came up at the double on the Nivelles road; they too were without artillery and cavalry.*[179]

Ney learned of d'Erlon's march to Ligny, and, deprived of his reserves, he was not able to match Wellington's growing forces. He withdrew to Frasnes by 8:30 pm D'Erlon's I Corps, minus its cavalry and the division of Durutte left at the left of the French line at Ligny, arrived at 9:00 pm, having not contributed to either battle fought that day.

---

179 Ibid, p. 513

Opportunity Lost

Napoleon had launched his army between Wellington and Blücher, and had expected each to withdraw. However, he'd made allowances that either Allied army might give battle, and, if this happened, it would necessarily be to Napoleon's advantage so early in the campaign, while the French were concentrated and the Allied forces were not. Napoleon realized that had the Anglo-Dutch and Prussian armies been able to concentrate together in the North around Brussels, he would have been at a severe disadvantage. Though this explains his surprise at the Allied aggressiveness, it does not mean that he was unprepared.

Early in the afternoon, Napoleon formulated a plan based on his understanding of the dispositions of his army. Had his information matched reality, the brilliant plan would have produced a brilliant success. D'Erlon was not concentrated with II Corps and was not within Ney's control. In fact, considering its trailing division was more than 35 Kilometres march from Thuin through Frasnes and on to Marbais in the Prussian rear, this division would not have been able to execute that maneuver and arrive in time to contribute to the battle of Ligny unless it would have been executing on that goal without pause since dawn. However, at dawn, there was no battle of Ligny yet imagined.

But Napoleon did not necessarily require the envelopment be carried out by I Corps. Orders were sent to Ney to affect the maneuver, leaving the composition to Ney's discretion. Only in mid-afternoon when Napoleon learned that Ney was facing a sizable force was I Corps chosen by Napoleon to deliver the coup de grace, with the assumption, as Houssaye suggests, that as it was trailing II Corps. II Corps would have been best positioned to meet the enemy and screen I Corps' movements. Had Napoleon known I Corps' actual disposition, he could have ordered Ney to use his plentiful cavalry to screen II Corps, and could have had Ney fall with at least two divisions on the Prussian rear. I Corps could have then proceeded directly to Quatre Bras, where it could menace and pin any attempt by Wellington to follow. Whatever Napoleon's plan would have been, the fact is that on the 16th of June, 1815, the expectation was always from the Quatre Bras–Namur road. This is where Napoleon was convinced that Ney had concentrated his forces. Hence, when d'Erlon arrived in the French rear, it paralyzed Napoleon's army, paused the climatic attack, and robbed precious time.

June 16th

Thus, even as the envelopment and destruction of the Prussian army was taken off the table, so was a decisive victory and a routing of the Prussians. If Napoleon had simply known reality, the battle would have been won earlier, probably with the commitment of more troops such as VI Corps, and a pursuit in the remaining daylight that would have driven the Prussians east. Based on the historical results of June 16th, one can confidently say that had Napoleon known the truth - captured in Soult's correspondence - then Napoleon would have separated the Prussians from the Anglo-Dutch army and the theatre of advance towards Brussels.

The movements of I Corps are one of the most studied aspects of the Waterloo campaign, and even today, while there are many solid theories[180], no one knows for sure exactly what happened. The focus on I Corps' march from the Brussels road to Ligny and then back to the left wing has, like many of the Waterloo controversies, provided a complete distraction from the root cause of the fatality. This work will not explore this issue at all, and instead will focus on undermining of Napoleon's plans.

First, we have seen the machinations that Soult went through to slow walk I Corps' advance on the 15th. When Soult finally gave the confirmation order to d'Erlon that all of his corps should cross the Sambre, it was kept out of the *Registre du Major-Général*. Was it kept out when dispatched, or removed later? We'll never know, but that Napoleon was not made aware of it is an indisputable fact.

Second, we have seen how even as Napoleon learned, with great surprise, that d'Erlon was not concentrated at Jumet, what he must have been subsequently told by Soult was that d'Erlon was really "in column from Marchiennes to Gosselies." This is what Gourgaud and Napoleon left in their accounts of the campaign. This, combined with Ney's delays, thus explained the disposition, and satisfied Napoleon on why his plan failed. Napoleon would repeatedly lament how Ney and his 40,000 men couldn't sweep aside the resistance at Quatre Bras, while Ney never had more than three divisions of infantry until the close of the day. Fate, as Napoleon would repeat over and over again, was simply not on his side during this campaign, mixed in

---

180 See Houssaye's footnotes, De Wit's http://waterloo-campaign.nl/bestanden/files/june16/derlon.2.pdf, Uffindell's chapter "The Fatal Peregrinations of D'Erlon" from *The Eagle's Last Triumph*, http://www.napoleon-series.org/military/battles/waterloo/c_waterlood'erlon.html, and almost every detailed study of the campaign.

with a heaping helping of Ney's failures. This was readily accepted as Ney had previously demonstrated failures with Napoleon's strategic designs.[181]

Finally, we have confirmation that Napoleon had been misled. In Gourgaud's diaries, printed after his death, Napoleon comments on d'Erlon and the events of the 16th:

> *The movement of d'Erlon did me much harm. Those around me thought it was an advance of the enemy. D'Erlon was a good staff officer. He could maintain order; but that was all. He ought on the 15th to have sent me word that he was at Marchiennes.*[182]

These candid discussions were never meant to be published, and were not part of any plan to bolster Napoleon's legacy. This is the simple confirmation that what Napoleon was led to believe, even after the events unfolded, was **false**. What d'Erlon reported to Soult on the 15th was accurate and correct.

During the 16th, information came into the general headquarters that may have illuminated I Corps' disposition during the day.

- Ney's report of 7 am, found in Gourgaud's papers, and confirmed by Reille in his account in *Documents inédits*, (also quoted by Houssaye).
- D'Erlon's report from Gosselies, which would have been sent from 1pm – 3pm, found in Gourgaud's papers (Houssaye wrote of this as well).
- The Report that Ney would request from Reille and D'Erlon, which, Ney promised to forward to headquarters, in Ney's report on the 16th.

Combined with the information d'Erlon sent on the 15th, Soult was well aware that I Corps was farther south than Napoleon was led to believe. As the early orders on the 16th did not express urgency, nor the expectation of a major battle, he should have likewise realized that I Corps would not have hustled to Frasnes or Quatre Bras. As it was, II Corps was likewise

---

181 At the battle of Bautzen, Ney was to envelop the allied armies. Napoleon's plans had been worked to perfection. But instead of attacking the rear of the allied army, Ney became preoccupied with taking a village that was at the far end of the line, thus strategically was of no importance. Had he followed through on Napoleon's intent, a large part of the Allied army would have been encircled and destroyed, and the village would have fallen in due course.

182 Gourgaud, Gaspard, *Talks of Napoleon at St. Helene with General Baron Gourgaud*, A.C. McClurg & Co, Chicago, 1904, p. 188

not aggressively moving forward, so there was nowhere for I Corps to go. Finally, I Corps paused to pursue intelligence, and d'Erlon sent a report to headquarters to communicate this fact.

Why then, when the unknown force arrived on the Ligny battlefield, did Soult not offer the explanation that the force in question *could* have been I Corps, as it was coming from a direction which was consistent with everything I Corps communicated, from the evening of the 15th and through the day on the 16th? Had Napoleon known I Corps was considerably south of Ney and out of his effective control, something Soult may have *always* been aware of (though, at the very least, made aware of it by d'Erlon during the afternoon), we can also assume that Napoleon would have given far different orders and formulated far different expectations. Soult let Napoleon stumble through the day blind. Yes, the French were on their way to winning a battle, but it was not going to be what Napoleon envisioned, a result that could have knocked Blücher's army out of the current campaign.

Reading the above reports on the events of the 16th of June would be very illuminating. Unfortunately, this is not possible. They are each *missing*.

Both reports found in Gourgaud's papers and discussed by Houssaye were present in the 1890's, but today they cannot be found. Reille's report can be found in the archives,[183] however, d'Erlon's report has never been seen.

Just as Soult's gross corruption of Napoleon's June 10th orders were hidden by early authors of the campaign, we now find key dispatches - that were once known - have gone missing. While there are numerous pieces of correspondence from the campaign that have never been seen (unsurprising considering the chaos the French defeat produced), it cannot escape attention that there is an eerie consistency in which information incriminating to Soult has been glossed over, found then lost, or never seen.

Someone was, and quite possibly still is, hiding something.

---

[183] Service Historique De l'Armée de Terre, Vincennes, Paris, nr. C15/22, as reported by De Wit

CHAPTER 13

JUNE 17TH

PURSUIT

IN THE EARLY MORNING OF the 17th, Flahaut returned from Quatre Bras and reported his observations of Ney during the 16th. Napoleon was furious!

> *"Ney went crazy: I entrust to him 40,000 men, and he does not unite them; there are eight hours without doing anything; he does not crush the English, nor give the final blow to the Prussians! And he added such a fault to disobey my orders: he stops the Count d'Erlon marching on Saint-Amand and prevents me from destroying the Prussian army! If I do not owe him so much for his past service, I would shoot him on the spot." And with an indescribable accent which betrayed the pain, he repeated several times: "He has lost France."*[184]

---

184 This account comes from an article by Colonel Baron Stoffel written in 1905. Stoffel was working on a book on the Waterloo campaign, but died before its completion. Subsequently, excerpts were published. This article was written about the operations on June 17th, and appeared in the *Revue Militaire Générale, Tome V, Janvier à Juin 1909*.
« Le maréchal Ney est devenu fou : je lui confie 40.000 hommes, et il ne les réunit pas; il reste huit heures sans rien faire; il n'écrase pas les Anglais, ne vient pas donner le coup de grâce aux Prussiens ! Et à pareille faute il ajoute celle de désobéir à mes ordres : il arrête le comte d'Erlon en marche sur Saint-Amand et m'empêche de détruire l'armée prussienne! Si je ne lui devais pas tant pour ses services passés, je le ferais fusiller sur-le-champ. » Et, d'un accent inexprimable où perçait la douleur, il répéta plusieurs fois : « Il a perdu la France. » Stoffel describes his sourcing for this account thusly:

Baron Stoffel reported the above. Apparently Soult was the sole witness to the outburst, and he told Monthion who then told Stoffel's uncle. While the above is mostly consistent with Napoleon's criticisms of Ney after the campaign, one cannot discount that Soult had every reason to put the focus of the events of June 16th clearly on Ney.

One should consider how Soult chose to respond to Napoleon's outburst. First, he could have pointed out that the left wing was spread out over such a wide area partly because of Soult's failings in communicating to d'Erlon on June 15. Second, he could have mentioned that Ney did not receive orders until the late morning during a time when Napoleon did not expect one significant battle, let alone two. Third, he could have mentioned d'Erlon's delays while pursuing intelligence of Anglo-Dutch movements to the west of Gosselies, a fact communicated to the general headquarters at the Ligny battlefield which demonstrated that Ney not only lacked the division of Girard that fought at Ligny, but the entire I Corps of d'Erlon which at mid-afternoon was actually closer to Napoleon than Quatre Bras.

Of course, Soult realized that first, Napoleon was never aware of the left-wing's dispositions, and this was probably not a good time to share this critical information. Second, Soult may have known that Ney *had* received orders to occupy Quatre Bras prior to the morning of the 16th, and thus his delays were inexcusable. If Ney had not received orders to occupy Quatre Bras prior to the morning orders of June 16th, then it is difficult to find fault in Ney's conduct. Third, Soult had never shared d'Erlon's status or reconnaissance delays on the previous day, and as it would have made

---

Cette scène n'eut d'autre témoin que le maréchal Soult qui la raconta aussitôt au général Bailly de Monthion, chef d'état-major général. Celui-ci, à son tour, la raconta à mon oncle qui servait sous ses ordres depuis plusieurs années et qui jouissait de toute sa confiance. Elle transpira d'ailleurs, le jour même, dans le grand quartier général.
Translation:
This scene had no other witness than Marshal Soult who immediately told General Bailly de Monthion, Chief of the General Staff. The latter, in turn, told my uncle who served under him for several years and who enjoyed his confidence. This transpired by the way, the same day, in the Army Headquarters.
How maddening is it that to get such powerful insights such as the one above we must rely on the nephew of someone who served with Monthion who passed down a story told to him from Soult, who apparently was the only eye-witness. This is not strong substantiaion, but in this case, Napoleon's words *are* consistent with his complaints of Ney's performance after the campaign.

a dramatic impact on the execution of the battle of Ligny, it was probably best to keep that to himself.

So instead, Soult did the only sensible thing, and at 8 am, Soult sent the following to Ney:

Fleurus, 17 June 1815

Marshal,

> *General Flahaut, who arrived at this moment, discloses that you are uncertain about yesterday's results. I believe however you were already acquainted with the victory that the Emperor has won. The Prussian army was routed. General Pajol is in pursuit on the Namur and Liege roads. We have already taken several thousand prisoners and 30 cannons. Our troops performed well. A charge of six battalions of the Guard and some Service Squadrons, and General Delort's Division, pierced the enemy line, brought the greatest disorder in its ranks, and cleared the position.*
>
> *The Emperor travels to the Bry Mill where the main road leads from Namur to Quatre Bras, it is therefore possible that the English Army can take action to engage you; if that were so, the Emperor would go directly by the Quatre Bras route, while you would attack in the front with your divisions which must be assembled by now, and this army in an instant would be destroyed; thus, inform H.M. of the exact position of the divisions and all that occurs in front of you.*
>
> *The Emperor has seen with regret that you did not succeed yesterday: the divisions acted separately; so you have experienced losses. If Counts d'Erlon and Reille's Corps had been together, not a man of the English corps that attacked you would have survived; if Count d'Erlon had carried out the movement on Saint-Amand that the Emperor ordered, the Prussian Army would be completely destroyed and we would have taken perhaps 30 thousand prisoners. General Vendamme and Gérard's Corps and the Imperial Guard were always together; we expose ourselves to reverses when detachments are made.*
>
> *The Emperor hopes and wishes that your seven infantry divisions and the cavalry are together, and that they do not occupy more*

than a league of ground, to have them well in hand and ready to employ them as needed.

The intention of H.M. is that you take a position at Quatre Bras, as you were ordered; but if it is not possible, immediately report the details and the Emperor will go there as I have told you; if on the contrary there is only a rear-guard, attack it and take the position.

Today it is necessary to finish this operation and to fill the munitions, to rally the isolated soldiers, and to return the detachments. Give orders accordingly and assure that all casualties are bandaged and directed to the rear. Some have complained that the ambulances have not performed as they should.

The famous partisan Lützow, who was taken prisoner, said that the Prussian Army was lost and that Blücher had exposed the Prussian Monarchy for a second time.

Duke of Dalmatia[185]

Soult blamed everything on Ney, and made sure it was included in the *Registre du Major-Général* as well.

While most historical focus has been on who diverted I Corps to the Ligny battlefield and all the confusion that led to the recall, Napoleon blamed Ney. It was Ney who had over 40,000 men and just needed to push aside a few thousand Dutch, seize the Quatre-Bras, and then hold off Wellington while completing the envelopment. This admonishment is embodied in the above correspondence. Whether Napoleon dictated it to Soult, or whether Soult wrote it on his own, it clearly establishes the thoughts at the Imperial Headquarters, and there can be no doubt that Soult contributed to this belief.

The truth, which Napoleon did not know, was that Ney had made it clear in his reports of the 15th that he had not gained complete operational control of the left wing. How could he have? The divisions were spread over 25 kilometers, and d'Erlon was still being directed by Soult until the late evening. Further, on the 16th, d'Erlon had communicated to Soult his position at Gosselies in the mid-afternoon. The situation of the left wing was partially Soult's doing, and more importantly, Soult had the correct intelligence which was withheld from Napoleon.

---

185 See "Soult to Ney at 8 am" on page 420

June 17th

But in this dispatch, and in his discussions with those around him captured in their memoirs, Napoleon is sure to place the full blame of the events of the previous day on Marshal Ney.

Soult's orders have been criticized for lacking clarity in 1815, but they have been understood exactly as he desired by posterity. Despite all of Soult's documented acts, rewriting orders, and withholding information, from this point forward it would all be forgotten or lost, while Ney stood alone as the cause for the failures to date.

Ney would not be alone for long.

It was late morning, which has been often criticized for having been too late, that Napoleon gave orders to Grouchy to pursue the Prussians with the III and IV Corps. He gave verbal orders, and followed these with a written dispatch by the hand of Bertrand as Soult was not present at time of dictation. The significance of the order written by Bertrand is that Grouchy would deny its existence for decades after the battle. Further, Bertrand never spoke up against Grouchy. The order was first published in 1840[186], and then later turned up in a biography of Grouchy, *Notice Biographique sur le Marechal de Grouchy* published in 1842. Grouchy may have inadvertently included the order in his papers he made available, considering how long he had denied anything like it existed. Regardless, it is telling that secrets such as this were that easy to keep.

Napoleon led the VI Corps and Guard to Quatre Bras, and upon arriving launched the pursuit of Wellington's forces which had begun withdrawing north towards Brussels. According to Gourgaud, Ney claimed his lack of attacking was, in part, due to having received false reports the Prussians had been victorious at Ligny. The truth of this is not known, but Soult's correspondence definitely expresses doubt on whether he, as *Major-Général*, had kept Ney informed.

---

186 In Pierart's *Drame de Waterloo*, a footnote on pages 238-239 identifies that the order was printed by the printer Bauduin in Paris, and that the order is dated at 3:00pm. Interesting to see this order printed in the year of Napoleon's remains returning to France. Based on the timeline for June 17th, which De Wit meticulously reconstructs, this order was most like written around noon. See http://www.waterloo-campaign.nl/17-june-1815/ Parts 1 and 2. A later time would be favorable to Grouchy who was accused of a lethargic pursuit of the Prussians.

Napoleon led the chase of the English with personal command of some squadrons of cavalry and horse-artillery. Following him was I Corps, II Corps, VI Corps and the Guard. In the afternoon the rain started and continued through the night. Upon arrival south of Mont St. Jean near Plancenoit, Napoleon feared that Wellington would not give battle, and retreat until achieving a chance to combine with the Prussians. Thus, Napoleon deployed heavy cavalry and artillery in a manner sufficient for the Anglo-Dutch army to reveal its presence; it was more than a rear-guard.

Thus, on the evening on the 17th, Napoleon believed there would be a major battle the following day. Most of the French army was around Genappe. The night was miserable with constant rain and many units did not reach their bivouacs until very late.

Napoleon issued an order of battle for the following day, though its text has not survived.

What was Napoleon planning? For an idea, we can look back on Napoleon's career.

Castiglione, Italy 1796

There are many examples of Napoleon concentrating troops prior to a large battle.

On August 4th, 1796, Count Wurmser advanced towards Castiglione with over 20,000 men. Wurmser had already lifted the siege of Mantua, and was expecting a decisive victory against the French. Napoleon was outnumbered, and had been for the entire campaign. However, time and time again, he had pushed his men through forced marches and counter marches to achieve equal or better odds on the battlefield. Realizing that a major encounter was imminent, in the early morning of the 4th he ordered remote forces to march to both flanks of his army.

On August 5th, the Austrians attacked. Just as the troops Napoleon had called to the battlefield arrived, the French achieved numerical superiority and counter attacked. Wurmser, realizing his army was about to be enveloped, ordered a retreat. With the victory, Napoleon would remain the master of Northern Italy.[187]

Throughout his career, Napoleon would frequently order a concentration of troops at the moment he recognized a great battle was imminent. "When you have resolved to fight a battle, collect your whole force. Dispense with nothing. A single battalion sometimes decides the day."[188]

Bernadotte and Davout were ordered to Austerlitz, and in Davout's case, this meant a march of over 100 km in just 48 hours.

Davout and Bernadotte were ordered to fall on the rear of the Prussians at Jena, but instead Davout ended up facing the main Prussian army at Auerstadt while Bernadotte skilfully managed to avoid either battlefield.

Davout and Ney were ordered to Eylau.

Napoleon lead several Corps to Friedland once Lannes had engaged the Russians.

Napoleon considered his maneuvers at Eckmuhl, where he had rapidly sent reinforcements to help Davout throw back an Austrian attack, one of his finest feats.

Ney was called to Bautzen where he could have trapped and destroyed an Allied army had he not become preoccupied with the tactical situation, foreshadowing his performance at Quatre Bras.

In 1814, the entire campaign was, like in Italy, Napoleon furiously pushing his numerically inferior forces around in order to achieve a local advantage. He was very successful and won numerous victories. Wellington himself said, "Excellent – quite excellent. The study of it has given me a greater idea of his genius than any other."[189]

Just the previous day, once Napoleon recognized the Prussians were concentrating at Sombreffe with the intention of giving battle, Napoleon's first thought was calling forces from his left wing in order to take the Prussians in the flank.

Thus, one might wonder why, during the evening of the 17th as Napoleon realized Wellington was deploying at Mont St. Jean, apparently with the

---

187 David Chandler, in his *Campaigns of Napoleon*, uses the Battle of Castiglione as an exemplary action in his chapter discussing Napoleon's art of war.
188 https://archive.org/stream/officersmanualnaoonapo#page/72/mode/2up Maxim XXIX
189 Uffindell, Andrew, *Napoleon 1814 The Defense of France*, p. 107, quoted from another source.

intention to give battle, he had not recalled some or all of Grouchy's forces which could have arrived on the flank of Wellington's line. This would have been completely consistent with Napoleon's manner of waging war.

Orders to Grouchy during the night of the 17th/18th

Considering Napoleon's history, it is therefore not surprising that Napoleon claims in his memoirs that he *had* issued a recall order to Grouchy:

> *At ten o'clock in the evening, I sent an officer to Marshal Grouchy whom I supposed to be at Wavres, in order to let him know that there would be a big battle the next day; that the Anglo-Dutch army was in position in front of the forest of Soignes, with its left resting on the village of La Haye; that I ordered him to detach from his camp at Wavres a division of 7,000 men of all arms and sixteen guns, before daylight, to go to Saint-Lambert to join the right of the Grand Army and co-operate with it; that, as soon as he was satisfied that Marshal Blücher had evacuated Wavres, whether to continue his retreat on Brussels or to go in any other directions, he was to march with the bulk of his troops to support the detachment which he had sent to Saint-Lambert.*[190]

The above order is perfectly consistent with Napoleon's actions his entire career. After receiving updates from Grouchy during the night, Napoleon goes on to say, "A second officer was sent to him, at four o'clock in the morning, to reiterate the order which had been dispatched to him at 10 o'clock at night." In Gourgaud's account of the 1815 Campaign, the above orders are likewise mentioned.[191]

Grouchy claims he never received these orders. When one considers his zeal for Napoleon, even despite his flawed performance, there is little evidence that he was a traitor. However, Napoleon's account of the orders to Grouchy during the night of 17/18 have largely been dismissed by historians. While it's possible this story is simply Napoleon trying to protect

---

190 *Napoleon's Memoirs*, Soho Book Company, London, 1986, p. 517-518
191 Ibid., p. 518

his reputation, there is no reason to dismiss it out of hand. There are many possible explanations.

First, the orderlies could have been traitors. As has been shown, the French army was infected with numerous traitors, many of them members of staff. In fact, he even theorized this very point as noted by O'Meara:

> *I asked Napoleon if he thought that Grouchy would have intended to betray him. 'No, no,' he replied, 'but there was a lack of energy on his part. There was also treason in the General staff. I believe that some of the staff officers that I had sent to Grouchy, betrayed, and passed to the enemy; however I am not sure having not seen Grouchy since.'*[192]

Many of the known traitors were members of staff, and there must have been traitors in the Army or various Corps and Divisions staffs of the *Armée du Nord* that were never revealed to history. Here Napoleon indicates the orders to Grouchy were sent through Soult and the General Staff. That the officers chosen may have betrayed is a completely plausible explanation.

Second, consider that Napoleon expected Grouchy to have made more progress on the 17th, it is very possible that the initial order was dispatched via a route that carried the messenger in harm's way close to Wavre. This could have easily led to capture.

Third, there is evidence that both may have happened. In Grouchy's *Relation Succincte de la campagne de 1815* published in 1843, the following testimony of an individual named Letourneur[193] can be found:

> *Letter from M. A. de NEUFRELLE-BAVENT to MARSHAL GROUCHY,*
>
> *In response to that by which requested clarification on a conversation of M. LETOURNEUR of Caen, on the campaign of 1815.*
>
> *Mr Marshal.*

---

192 O'Meara, Barry, *Napoleon in Exile*, 1853, p. 237, http://books.google.com/books?id=d4oQAAAAYAAJ&source=gbs_navlinks_s
193 In *Mémoires du maréchal de Grouchy*, Volume 4, 1874, the name given is Letourneux.

I saw Mr. Letourneur which had the honour to write to you lately, I urged him to do new research, which he did with alacrity.

M. Letourneur has asked me to let you know that he has found no date for the fact that interests you. It is possible, he said, he had known it, but today his memories are quite vague on this subject.

M. Letourneur thanks you, Mr. Marshal, to kindly allow him the honour to address the "Fragment historique relatif à la campagne de 1815."

I will kindly beg you to accept all the regrets, I feel unable to be useful in this circumstance, and assurances of the deepest respect with which I have the honour to be, etc, etc.

Signed a. NEUFRELLE-BAVENT.

STATEMENT BY MR. LETOURNEUR
Inhabitant of Caen.

Letter from M. Letourneur, inhabitant of Caen containing the statement that orders of the Emperor, to the Marshal de Grouchy, and drawn in pencil, were handed to Marshal Blücher by the officer who was a messenger, either that he had been taken prisoner, or he had deserted to the enemy.

Mr Marshal.

Reading in the newspapers a claim that you have issued against an assertion by Mr. General Berthezène, I thought I should, in the interests and honor of our Normandy, in yours also, Mr. Marshal, let you know a circumstance which will perhaps not have any scope in the discussion raised by general Berthezène.

This is the great historical fact of Waterloo, which has long divided opinion since 1815, and to which your name relates with a celebrity that parties have not always sufficiently respected.

So here is what happened to my knowledge, by pure chance.

In 1815, during the stay of the Prussian troops at Caen under the orders of Marshal Blücher, the municipal administration sent home with a billet, a nephew of the old general, called Lanken; He

June 17th

was cavalry NCO in the Hussars, I believe, and could be 20 to 22 years old.

A son of the Marshal, attached to the staff of his father, came very often to visit his parent, in the company of another officer named Vousseaux, young man also well raised, appearing as the other two, having received a distinguished education... These gentlemen spoke French perfectly, the last two, especially, infinitely better than the young Lanken.

One day, I had invited them to take the punch, and we talked of events that had led the Prussian army in France, and of the disasters of the day of Waterloo particularly: the son of the old Marshal tells me these words that I transcribed the same evening on an album:

"The loss of the battle of Waterloo is generally attributed to the fact that Mr. Marshal Grouchy would not execute the orders of the emperor... It is a great mistake! and this is what has happened under my eyes, at the headquarters of Marshal Blücher: A staff officer of the imperial general headquarters was brought to Marshal Blücher...Was he made prisoner, had he betrayed? This is what I don't know, but he is one who was carrying an order, written in pencil, to Marshal Grouchy, saying that the Marshal had to walk on the point where the Emperor stood and let six thousand men in the front of the Prussian army, to hide his movement and keep it in check while he would move. That Marshal Blücher, with this document, had done exactly the same maneuver... This is why the Emperor kept repeating, seeing off a corps from the side where it was waiting for Mr. Marshal Grouchy: it is Grouchy! It is Grouchy!"

It is permissible to think that one would encounter in Berlin some members of the family of the old Marshal Blücher, which would easily indicate where you would find today Mr Blücher, Vousseaux and Lanken.

If this letter, Mr. Marshal, can have the slightest interest to you, please make such use of it that may please you.

In sending it to you personally, I only have in mind to pay tribute to the truth, and my sole purpose is to prevent that a personal opinion, or an error long reproduced, continues, especially after the fight which will be engaged under the watchful eye of French public opinion.

Please accept, etc, etc.
Signed Ch. Letourneur.[194]

According to the account in this letter, the story of the recall order, that had either been intercepted or delivered by a deserter, was told by one of Blücher's sons. This son would be Gebhard Lebrecht Friedrich Blücher. In 1815, he was a captain of cavalry attached to his father's staff.

His companion was another officer, Vousseaux. However, this is clearly a French spelling. The German equivalent of this name is Wussow. On Blücher's staff during the 1815 campaign was Seconde Lieutenant Johann George Philipp von Wussow.[195] He played a significant role, especially in helping organize the retreat after Ligny. However, his most interesting mission was informing Wellington of the status of the battle of Ligny in the early evening of June 16th.

> *Throughout the course of the afternoon the combatants could clearly hear the roar of the artillery at Sombreffe. The Duke of Wellington subsequently expressed his desire to Generalmajor Karl, Freiherr von Müffling, the Prussian liaison officer attached to his headquarters, to receive a report on the state of the contest, and towards 7:00pm Seconde-Lieutenant Johann von Wussow, an officer serving on the Prussian General Staff, arrived at the crossroads. As Freiherr von Müffling knew that the young officer spoke fluent French, he ordered him to repeat the message that he had been given directly to the duke.*[196]

In the Appendix is a detailed account of this mission in Wussow's own words, including his direct interactions with Wellington.[197] The existence of the fluent-French speaking Wussow is at the very least a corroborating detail of the Letourneur letter.

---

194 Grouchy, Emmanuel, *Relation Succincte de la campagne de 1815 en Belgique*, 1843, pp. 20-23, https://books.google.com/books?id=aowUAAAAYAAJ&
195 Many thanks to Oliver Schmidt for making this connection. See Seconde-Lieutenant Johann von Wussow.
196 Franklin and Emleton, *Waterloo 1815 (1): Quatre Bras*, Osprey Publishing, 2014, p. 79.
197 See "Seconde-Lieutenant Johann von Wussow" on page 309

June 17th

This account is also corroborated by a Major Zach, of the Baden Staff, in a Waterloo study translated and published in the *Journal des Sciences Militaires* 1840, prior to Grouchy's publication above:

> *It should also be attributed to the fatality that the orders to march on Saint-Lambert that had been sent to him by Napoleon were not received at 10 pm and at three in the morning. The officer carrying the first mail and on its way to Wavre, fell into the hands of the Prussians, and the charge of second dispatch was probably killed on the way.*[198]

Houssaye refutes the possibility of the recall orders. He states that there is no record of the above account in any of the German sources.[199] Yet other events, like the capture of a Prussian orderly on the day of the battle of Waterloo, he believes though it is equally undocumented.

Houssaye never considered the possible infidelity of Soult. As this work has shown, Soult was clearly dishonest in his dealings with Napoleon during the campaign. This is but another example. The fact that Napoleon reports language that is inconsistent with what Soult has left as evidence is a further indictment of Soult. The most likely explanation is that on the evening of the 17/18th, while Napoleon was trying to recall Grouchy in what could have been a decisive maneuver in his favor, Soult assured that this would not be executed. Apparently one dispatch was sent to the Prussians where its content provided valuable intelligence. The second was probably never dispatched. On the 16th, before Napoleon expected a great battle, he had used members of his own staff to carry detailed letters to Ney and Grouchy. As the orders to Grouchy during the evening of the 17th/18th only needed to arrive during the night, and Grouchy's were taking less than three hours to be received, Napoleon went through Soult.

Houssaye further mentions that Baudus, the royalist that Houssaye curiously relies on heavily, wrote that Soult advised Grouchy's recall, and Napoleon refused. In fact, according to Baudus, who just happened to be an aide-de-camp of Soult and where this story originates from, Napoleon was utterly arrogant and dismissive:

---

198 See "Major Zach" on page 314
199 Houssaye, *Waterloo*, London, 1900, p. 390, footnote 55

> "Because you have been beaten by Wellington, you consider him a great general. And now I tell you that Wellington is a bad general, that the English are bad troops, and that this affair is nothing more serious than eating one's breakfast."
> "I earnestly hope so," said Soult.[200]

The above, if nothing else, is a dramatic example of Napoleon's arrogance and megalomania. Yet, at Saint Helena, Napoleon was extremely complementary of the English troops:

> *It was the good discipline of the English that gained the day. They could advance thirty yards, halt, fire, go back, fire, and come forward again thirty yards, without breaking their line, without any disorder.*[201]

Napoleon's angry retort about Wellington and the English is repeated in numerous sources without attribution. What makes above even more remarkable is that the world was not even aware of this exchange until Houssaye published it in his *Waterloo* work in 1899. He found it in the manuscript notes of Baudus. It was so powerful that Baudus *left it out* of his *Etudes sur Napoléon* published in 1841. Instead, Baudus said this:

> *The Major General, persisting in his view that Napoleon had been wrong to give two whole corps of infantry to Marshal Grouchy, thought it his duty to open the notice of recall on the spot most largely for the next day's business; but his comments about it were no more heard in the evening than they had been in the morning.*[202]

---

200 Houssaye reports them from Baudus' manuscript notes. Houssaye is generally favorable to Napoleon, but why did he see fit to give life to this scene? Houssaye quotes this as having happened after breakfast with the staff, and before Reille and Jérôme entered the farmhouse of Le Caillou where Napoleon had stayed the evening of the 17th. Many attributers thus retell this as an exchange in front of other named individuals.
201 Gourgaud, Gaspard, *Talks of Napoleon at St. Helena with General Baron Gourgaud*, Chicago, 1904, p. 189
202 Baudus, *Etudes sur Napoléon*, Volume 1, Paris, 1841, p. 224

This difference despite the fact that Baudus' manuscript notes closely follow the finished manuscript.[203] Was this simply an issue of style, choosing a dry approach over colorful anecdotes? No, for just a few pages earlier we find Baudus relating the following exchange quoted between Napoleon and a peasant after the battle of Ligny:

> *Do you believe in hell?*
> *Yes! Sire.*
> *Well! If you do not want to go, take care of the wounded man whom I entrust to you, do it well; otherwise God will burn you there because he wants us to be charitable to his neighbor.*[204]

Furthermore, in A. Brialmont's *Histoire du duc de Wellington*, Volume 3, page 288, published in 1857, one finds the following:

> *At Waterloo, always with the same sentiments in regard to the one who he had called "a General of Sepoys," the Emperor said to Soult: "Because Wellington has defeated you, you believe that he is a great general," and on this day Wellington won a victory over him more decisive than those of Jena, Austerlitz, and Wagram!*[205]

Brialmont probably found this quote from Chateaubriand, who says this in *Mémoires d'outre-tombe*, Volume 4, page 11, published in 1849:

> *Many lies and some rather curious truths were expressed about this catastrophe. The word: The guard dies but does not surrender, is an invention that one does not dare to defend anymore. It appears certain that at the beginning of the action, Soult made some strategic observations to the Emperor:*
> *"Because Wellington has defeated you," Napoleon answered him curtly, "you always believe that he is a great general." At the end of the combat, M. de Turenne pressed Bonaparte to retreat to avoid falling in the hands of the enemy: Bonaparte, left to his thoughts*

---

203 Shared by Jean-Marc Largeaud who has reviewed both.
204 Baudus, *Etudes sur Napoléon*, Volume 1, Paris, 1841, p. 222
205 A. Brialmont's *Histoire du duc de Wellington*, Volume 3, 1857, p. 288, https://books.google.com/books?id=nx7ELfGoRUkC

like a dream, blamed himself at first; then suddenly, in the middle of his rage, he leaps on his horse and flees.[206]

It is likely that Chateaubriand learned the above anecdotes from royalists on the French staff, such as Turenne or even Baudus. We cannot ignore that the most explosive part of the quote as related by Houssaye remains missing. Since Houssaye found this in Baudus' notes, it is possible that two separate incidents were strung together. However, it's just as possible that Napoleon did say the first part of the quote, and that the most damning portion was added on. And one cannot preclude the possibility that it was entirely made up considering its substantiation is weak to none.

What is maddening is that the veracity of the exchange with Soult has seemingly never been challenged. Baudus was no fan of Napoleon, and Soult's own words demonstrate his willingness to condemn the man. But the unfortunate fact is that when it comes to the history of 1815, anything that is unflattering to Napoleon is seized and spread like a gospel delivered by the hand of God.

This anecdote is believed because it is *wanted* to be believed.

But obviously, if Napoleon did attempt to send recall orders to Grouchy, then the entire episode is a complete fabrication. This may explain why Napoleon's biting retort to Soult never appeared in any source published contemporaneously with living Waterloo veterans… maybe Baudus didn't trust it himself.[207]

One plausible explanation is that Baudus was Soult's mouthpiece to explain why a maneuver one would expect from Napoleon didn't happen. If Soult was betraying Napoleon, the last thing he wanted to leave for posterity was the question, "Why didn't Napoleon recall Grouchy before Waterloo as he had ordered Ney to maneuver on Ligny and had ordered similar maneuvers so many times previously?" The above anecdote would have been a quick story to tell Baudus, for if Baudus had witnessed it, why would he not have used it? Had Soult planted this seed with Baudus during the evening of the 17th and morning of the 18th, it would have been prior to

---

206 Chateaubriand, *Mémoires d'outre-tombe*, Volume 4, 1849, p. 11, https://books.google.com/books?id=T_Q-AAAAcAAJ

207 If one was to read the author's notes, one would find numerous additional charges against Soult, including a quote from a document where Soult sought to overthrow Louis-Philippe in exchange for a higher position! This additional material was not included in this work because it could not be substantiated to the author's satisfaction.

Napoleon's subsequent orders to Grouchy and the entire concept becoming one of Waterloo's greatest controversies. Baudus had a bomb-shell refutation, and if revealed at a time of many living veterans, may have invoked an unwelcomed response and scrutiny.

Soult had told Monthion of Napoleon's disgust with Ney's performance on June 16th. That story was consistent with Napoleon's later words. Just as Soult was sure to relay a story (and leave correspondence) that blamed Ney for the distribution of the left wing, he now tells another anecdote criticizing Napoleon for not executing an expected maneuver. But Napoleon did order the recall of Grouchy, and Soult knew this. Thus, Soult hatched a plan that would explain the failure of the recall orders sent during the night of the 17th and early morning of the 18th. Soult would have only done this had he known in advance that the recall orders were never going to reach Grouchy.

And it worked, probably far greater than Soult ever imagined. Not only did Soult get away with treason, but the reputations of those he disdained were forever tarnished.

> *Ted: [after Napoleon explains his new waterslide war strategy] I don't think it's gonna work.*
> *Napoleon: Non?*
> *[pause, then slams his pointer down on the map, scattering playing pieces everywhere]*
> *Napoleon: Triomphe Napoleon!*
> *[translated: Napoleon wins!]*[208]

---

208 *Bill and Ted's Excellent Adventure*, quotes from http://www.imdb.com/title/tt0096928/quotes Several who read this work for me commented that this reference was unnecessary, however I disagree. This comic view of Napoleon as the arrogant/egomaniac has been carried into many serious works on 1815 that suggest he was overconfident to the point of dismissive of his adversaries. Further, many see his writings at Saint Helena to be an extension of this mania as he blames all his misfortune on others. This is untrue on several levels. First, he was both thorough and respected what his foes were capable of as this work demonstrates. Second, while Napoleon certainly made bad choices in personnel, the execution of the campaign was largely undone by others, his confusion and finger pointing was justified though the target of blame was unfortunately misplaced. Had Napoleon's performance received more respect by historians, I'm quite certain that many of the questions this work raises would have been asked long ago.

As long as this is the view of Napoleon that persists, the world will chose to believe those anecdotes that paint him the fool.

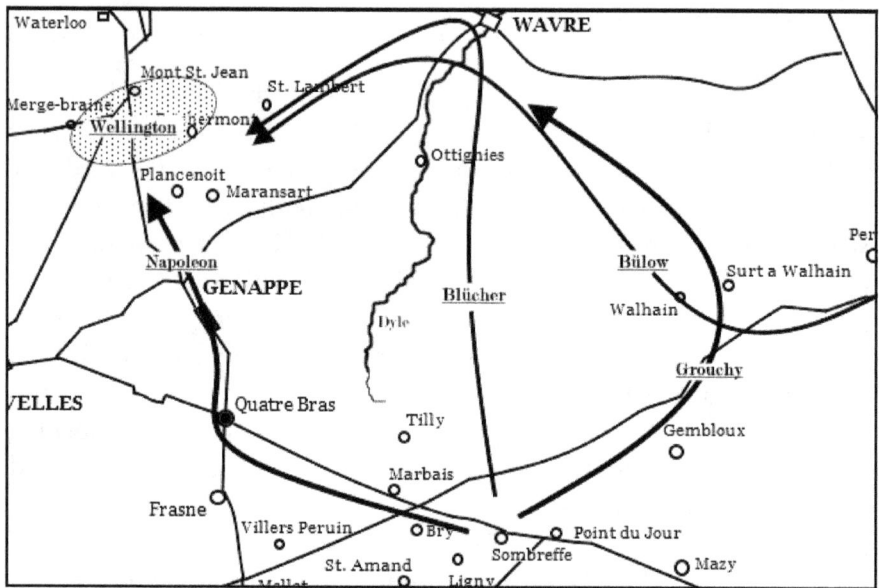

Figure 12 – Movements of June 17th/18th

CHAPTER 14
JUNE 18TH

THE RAIN WOULD END AROUND dawn, and the battle of Waterloo would be fought on June 18th, 1815.[209]

Morning

Around 2 am, Grouchy's report of 10 pm was received.[210]

Gembloux, June 17, 1815, at ten o'clock in the evening

SIRE,

> *I have the honor to report to you that I occupy Gembloux where the Fourth Corps begins to arrrive; the Third is in front of this town, and part of my Cavalry is in Sauvenière.*

---

209 The controversies surrounding just what time it was when any particular event happened at Waterloo are significant. As the most studied and written about battle in European history, possibly world history, it is inevitable that there would be more disagreements if for no other reason that there are more authors, more memoirs, and probably quite a few inaccurate watches. This study is one of correspondence and its content where time only needs to be approximate.
210 The times of Grouchy's correspondence, and the times when Napoleon received them is also very controversial. The timeline presented here is thus largely Grouchy's and Napoleon's, though Grouchy most certainly altered times to aide his reputation. For this work, those details are not critical.

The Prussian Corps, about thirty thousand men in strength, who were still here this morning, carried out his retreat movement toward Sauvenières. According to various reports, he appears to have arrived at Sauvenières, part of the Prussian Army would be divided: a column would have marched to Pervès-le-Marchez, another would have taken the Wavre road, while passing by Sart-à-Walhain. Perhaps we can infer that some Prussian Corps are going to join Wellington, and that others would be withdrawing to Liege.

A Prussian column with artillery, has taken, in leaving the battlefield of Fleurus, the Namur road. The enemy abandoned for us at Gembloux, a park of four hundred cattle, magazines, and baggage.

General Exelmans has ordered to drive, this evening, six squadrons on Sart-à-Walhain, and three squadrons on Perwez.

If I learn by reports that, I hope, will reach me during the night, that strong Prussian forces march on Wavre, I will follow them in this direction and will attack them as soon as I meet them.

Generals Thielmann and Borstell are part of the army that Your Majesty fought yesterday: they were still here this morning, admitting that twenty thousand of their men had been casualties. They requested, while leaving, the distances of Wavre and Perwez.

Blücher was slightly wounded in the arm, on the 16th, which did not prevent him from continuing to command, after being bandaged. He did not continue to Gembloux.

I am, etc, etc.

Marshal Grouchy[211]

Having received this dispatch, Gourgaud says a duplicate recall order was sent at 3 am, though curiously he states the order instructed Grouchy to "pass the Dyle above Wavres." He expected the order to arrive at Gembloux before 6 am, which still seems late to accomplish such a maneuver. Napoleon says the duplicate order was sent at 4 am.

Around 5 or 6 am, Napoleon received Grouchy's report from 3 am, though in his memoirs he remembered it stating 2 am.

---

211 See "Grouchy to Napoleon at 10 pm" on page 425

June 18th

Gembloux, June 18, 1815, three o'clock in the morning.

Sire,

All my reports and information confirm that the enemy withdraws to Brussels, concentrating there, to give battle there, after having joined Wellington.

Namur is evacuated, indicated to me by General Pajol.

Blücher's First and Second Army Corps appear to direct, the First on Corbais, and the Second on Chaumont. They must have left yesterday evening, at 8:30, from Toürrines and marched through the night; fortunately it was so bad, that they would not be able to go very far.

I leave at this time for Sart-à-Valliain, from where I will march to Corbaix and Wavres. I will have the honor to write to you from one and another of these towns.

I am, etc, etc.

Marshal Grouchy

P. S. According to your orders, I write to the General Commandant of the 2nd Division Militaire in Charlemont, to occupy Namur with several National Guard Bataillons and some artillery batteries that he will form in Charlemont.

I leave twenty-five horses here to ensure correspondence with Your Majesty.

The Infantry and Cavalry Corps that I have with me have only one provisionment and a half, so that in the event of a major event it seems necessary to me that Your Majesty will want to draw on the munitions reserves, or indicate to me the places where artillery could go to find supplies.[212]

---

[212] See "Grouchy to Napoleon at 3 am" on page 427 – note that the times of Grouchy's letters is much disputed, but as he is the source of the documents, we can never know the truth. However, Gourgaud wrote his account from Saint Helena without access to documentation other than any copies they received and memory.

Gourgaud says, in reference to the orderlies already dispatched, that, "... there was reason to hope, that the officer would overtake Marshal Grouchy, and that the latter, instead of reaching St. Lambert at noon, might arrive there at ten in the morning: and if, in consequence of the departure of the Marshal, the officer should not find him, it was still certain that he would arrive before Wavres at noon, and that he would have received the first order, which had been written at 10 o'clock on the preceding night, and which informed him of the battle."

Gourgaud speaks of spending the entire day anxiously scanning the horizon for the arrival of Grouchy.

What Napoleon did not know was that Blücher and the entire Prussian army had retreated to Wavre and was in constant communications with Wellington. The battle he was excited to have was only offered because Blücher had promised not only the minimal assistance of one corps that Wellington asked, but his entire army. In reality, the corps of Bülow, which had not fought at Ligny, as well as two other Prussian corps were already on the march to the Waterloo battlefield. Grouchy's pursuit had been slow and confused, and rather than maneuvering between the Prussians and Napoleon's right wing, he had ended up following in the Prussians wake.

Grouchy's failings had nothing to do with Soult, but Napoleon's recall orders, had they been aggressively executed, could have very well interrupted the Prussian movement to Mont St. Jean.

Napoleon had hoped to commence the battle at 9 am The ground was in horrible condition due to the rain, and this was definitely a problem for the movement of troops. In fact, the army was not yet into the battle lines Napoleon had ordered the previous evening.

With his army deploying, and with the daylight offering him the ability to survey the field of battle, Napoleon decided to send even more detailed orders to Grouchy. Immediately prior to a major battle, Napoleon dared not send one of his more trusted aides. When Flahaut had been sent to Ney on the 16th, Napoleon did not expect the battle of Ligny to be fought. However, it's possible Napoleon was already feeling uneasy about the youth, inexperience, and fidelity of the staff; the complaints he would later share

June 18th

with O'Meara while in exile. Thus, a veteran, Zenowicz[213], was given the mission including significant verbal instructions.

While surrounded by hundreds of staff from both the Imperial Palace and General Headquarters, Soult would not be so easily able to affect a failure in dispatching an order of Napoleon's... but he very well could have dispatched one that was incorrectly worded.

Zenowicz has left us this detailed account of this moment:

> *On June 18, 1815, the day of the Battle of Waterloo, I was on duty as senior officer, in the imperial headquarters, and I had orders not to leave Napoleon for a moment.*
>
> *About nine in the morning the Emperor mounted his horse; I followed him. Approaching to the straight line of the army, having spoken a few times to Count d'Erlon he left his suite behind, and accompanied only by the Major General (Marshal Soult), he ascended a small hill, from which one easily discovered the various positions of the two armies. After examining some time with his telescope, without changing place, he addressed a few words to the Major General; then, when he came down from the plateau, the Emperor beckoned me to sit beside him; I obeyed; He then spoke to me, "Here is Count d'Erlon, our right," he said, pointing to the corps of that general; then continuing, after describing a circle with his hand to the right of the line, he added, "Grouchy is marching in that direction, go immediately to him, go through Gembloux, follow in his footsteps; Major General will still give you a written order;" I wanted to point out to the Emperor that he was suggesting that I had to follow a route too long; but without giving me time to finish, he said: "Never mind, you would be caught following the shortest route;" and then pointing to the end of the right side of the line, he said: "You'll come back here and join me, when Grouchy will arrive on the line. I look forward to him being in direct communication and in the line of battle with us. Go, go."*

---

213 Zenowicz had been first assigned to I Corps as Deputy Chief of Staff, but was later assigned to the General Staff on May 23. See Danielle and Bernard Quintin's "Zenowciz", *Dictionnaire des colonels de Napoléon*, 2013

At once the order received, I hurried after the Major General, who was heading now towards the farm of Le Caillou, where the imperial headquarters had spent the night. We arrived at the farm at ten o'clock; the Major General returned to his room and asked for his secretary. The first thing one does while starting to write an order is to put the date and time; it is easy to see that this hour cannot be the time the dispatch was sent: because, before departure, it takes time to write; it also takes time to copy it into the Register of the Major General. All this requires enough time; in ordinary service where the hours and minutes have no role to play, this remark is of no importance; but in a particular case, when one counts the hours and minutes, when an accusation is made against the bearer of an order, it should be possible to restore the facts as they occurred. I repeat, the date of the order which I was carrying was set at ten o'clock; I then retired to the living room. After half an hour of waiting, I joined the General Staff. Still nothing but the date was written; the Major General looked at the map, and his secretary was amusing himself cutting a quill.

I returned to the living room, where I found Mr. Regnault, chief officer of the first corps, who, learning that for twenty-four hours I had always been on duty, and that I had been unable to eat anything, was kind enough to send for a piece of bread and some spirits from his caisson. After my meal, I went back to the Major General: he was busy dictating the order I expected; I once again went to the living room. After half an hour, I was requested; Marshal Soult repeated to me roughly, giving me his written orders, what the Emperor had said. I left immediately.

All the details that I have just entered give ample proof that the observations of the writers on my mission are inaccurate. Some of these writers are excusable though: they could not know the details that I just mentioned on the basis of orders as published; they judged me by the time wrongly fixed of my departure; for others, who sacrificed the truth to their political hatred, I do not have to worry about their biased criticisms, both partial and lacking authority.[214]

---

214 See "On Zenowicz and his Account" on page 321

June 18th

Here is yet another affirmation that on the day of the battle of Waterloo, Napoleon was expecting Grouchy to arrive on the battlefield. But far from some impossible hoped for gesture that was asked for too late, Napoleon, so he thought, had been ordering the maneuver since late on the 17th of June.

There is just one problem… Zenowicz's account and the text of the order written by Soult do not match:

> *In front of the farm of Caillou*
> *On June 18, 1815, at 10 am*
>
> *Marshal Duke of Dalmatia General Staff, to Marshal Grouchy, Gembloux or forward*
>
> *Marshal, the Emperor received your last report dated from Gembloux, you spoke to His Majesty only about the two Prussian columns that went to* Sauvenières *and* Sart à Walhain. *However reports say that a third column which was rather strong went to* Géry *and* Gentinnes *directing to* Wavre.
>
> *The Emperor charges me to advise you that at this moment His Majesty will attack the English army which has taken a position at Waterloo close to the Forest of Soignes; thus His Majesty wishes that you direct your movements on* Wavre, *in order to bring you closer to us, to report operations, and to maintain communications about the Prussian Army Corps pushing before you those which took this direction, and which have stopped at* Wavre *where you must arrive as soon as possible.*
>
> *You will follow the enemy columns which are on your right with some light troops in order to observe their movements and to pick up their stragglers.*
>
> *Immediately inform me of your arrangements and your march as well as the news that you have about the enemy, and do not neglect to maintain your communications with us; the Emperor wishes to have your news rather often.*
>
> *Marshal of the Empire, Major General,*
> *Duke of Dalmatia*[215]

---

215 See "Soult to Grouchy at 10 am" on page 429

This has been enough for most to discount Zenowicz's story, for how can we reconcile it with the **fact** that the text is different? For Houssaye, this was enough to discount Zenowicz. Further, Houssaye goes on to say, "From this order it is clear that the Emperor, at ten in the morning, neither summoned Grouchy to his battlefield, nor expected him to appear there."[216]

The above analysis is insightful. In order for Zenowicz's account to have the faintest authenticity, Soult would have had to outright rewritten Napoleon's order in such a manner as to remove its actual meaning. It would be like ordering a Corps to go to an entirely new position; a gross example of insubordination.

To find such an incredible example, one would need to look no farther back than June 12th, 1815. Just six days prior, Soult had altered Napoleon's orders of June 10th, and had failed to convey Napoleon's intentions to Gérard with the orders of June 5th. Even if Soult was a loyal servant that took liberties with Napoleon's designs, this highlights why it was critical for historians to have revealed Soult's conduct prior to June 15.

Zenowicz's account provides some interesting insights. Soult was able to rewrite Napoleon's order out of view, and while Napoleon and his staff were finalizing the preparation for the battle, Soult was able to drag his feet. This allowed Soult to set the non-urgent tone that enabled Grouchy to respond to the dispatch not only with indifference, but with an affirmation that his current course hovering around Wavre was correct. In fact, when the sound of the cannons were heard, many around Grouchy urged him to march to the guns! He refused, and when this order was received, he felt vindicated. He was following the Emperors orders!

While Soult was slow sending the wrong orders, a task which anyone can see should have taken no time at all, Napoleon was anxiously deploying cavalry on his right flank with orders to scout for and link with Grouchy. Several memoirs[217] affirm that the cavalry on the far right flank was ordered to expect and link with Grouchy, and were given these orders early in the day. If the 10 am order had been the first attempt to bring Grouchy to the battlefield, Napoleon may still have told the cavalry to look for and link with Grouchy's forces upon their arrival. However, it is Napoleon's earnest expectation, repeatedly stated during the battle and observed by many, that

---

216 Houssaye, Henry, *1815 Waterloo*, 1900, note 40, pp. 406-407
217 See "Marbot's Letter on June 26, 1815" on page 319 and "Dupuy's Account of Waterloo" on page 321

Grouchy was coming that is the most compelling evidence that he had issued recall orders prior 10 am.

Napoleon had chosen Zenowicz, depriving Soult from a more simple form of deception. But he could, and he did, drag his feet and author an order in such a manner that historians have actually made fun of Napoleon's inability to deal with such simple matters as time and distance.

Napoleon was an arrogant dunce at Waterloo! So say hundreds of historians...

Soult rewrote Napoleon's orders during the campaign! So say just a handful, while others who clearly knew, and in Houssaye's case one who elaborated on practically everything[218], remained silent.

Afternoon

Around noon, the French attacked. It was a dramatic affair.[219]

Around 1 pm, movement was noticed to the north-east in the direction of Saint Lambert. Could it be Grouchy? No, the cavalry patrols were reporting Prussians.

Napoleon immediately had Soult once again send a dispatch to Grouchy to come to Saint Lambert.

> *Marshal, you wrote to the emperor this morning at 3 am that you will march on Sart Walhain, therefore your plan was to march to Corbaix and Wavre. This movement is consistent with the provisions that His Majesty has provided to you. However the Emperor commands me to tell you that you should always maneuver in our direction and look to draw the army closer, so that you can contact us before any Corps can come between us. I do not tell you direction, it*

---

218 Houssaye's notes are a worthwhile book upon themselves which I greatly encourage the reader to read. The edition referenced in this work has them in English.
219 The Battle of Waterloo has, more than any other event, dominated the analysis and discussion of this campaign. This work will not consider the details of the battle for which there are numerous very good books available. Prior to the first significant combat on June 18th, Napoleon had already been terminally betrayed. We shall keep our focus on exposing the traitors.

is for you to see where we are, to adjust yourself accordingly and link to our communications and as to always be capable of falling on some enemy troops who would seek to disturb our right, and crush them.

18 this afternoon at 1 pm

Signed Marshal Duke of Dalmatia[220]

Did Napoleon read this? While it somewhat tells Grouchy to join the main army, it is hardly direct.

However, before the order could be dispatched, a Prussian orderly carrying a message for Wellington that had been captured was presented at headquarters! Just as the story of a French orderly at the Prussian Headquarters during the night, there is no record in any German reports of this Prussian orderly, but he is seen and written about by numerous individuals in the French headquarters staff. The captured orderly informs Napoleon that the Corps of Bülow, 30,000 strong, is arriving.

There, right before Napoleon, Soult must add a post script to the dispatch:

P.S. A letter that has just been intercepted reveals that General Bülow is about to attack our right flank; we believe we see this corps on the heights of St.Lambert. Thus, do not lose one instant to approach and join us, and to crush Bülow, whom you will catch in the very act.[221]

Finally, in front of an anxious staff, Soult is unable to do anything but write an urgent recall to the battlefield... the Prussians had arrived. But what Napoleon did not know is that his previous recall orders had either never been sent, never arrived, or continued to push Grouchy towards Wavre. Grouchy had never been ordered to come to Waterloo.

When Grouchy finally received this order, it was much too late. The battle would be lost by the time he could have arrived. This is his account of receiving the order first published in 1818:

---

220 "Soult to Grouchy around 1 pm" on page 432
221 Ibid.

June 18th

The attack on the Mill of Bielge, made half-heartedly, does not succeed, and I prepared to renew it, while an officer sent by Napoleon gave to me around four o'clock, a dispatch from Major Gal.(Mal. Soult,) which reads: "From the Battlefield of Waterloo, on the 18th, at one o'clock in the afternoon. M. Marshal"[222]

The order is quoted earlier, but it is not necessary to revisit the text. What is significant is what is quoted above, something that Grouchy would correct in later publications.

The battlefield of Waterloo, 18, an hour after noon.

Why would Soult have called it the "battlefield of Waterloo"? While it's true he referred to Waterloo in the 10 am correspondence, it wasn't the Battle of Waterloo until after a victorious Wellington wrote his famous dispatch on the 19th of June. This, along with numerous other details, are delineated by Michel Damiens in an Appendix of his work on the battle of Plencenoit.[223] The appendix is titled, *La letter de 13.00 hrs est-elle une forgerie?*

Damiens makes a very compelling case. Bernard Coppens, author of *Les Mensonges de Waterloo*, likewise believes that it is fake. If true, what does it mean?

It is a fact that what is referenced as the *Registre du Major-Général* is *not* that at all, but simply a copy provided by Grouchy. Thus, any number of items could have been edited or fabricated. Any number of items could have been excised if they proved embarrassing, both by Soult before giving to Grouchy, or by what Grouchy chose to reveal to the world.

There is an ongoing debate on whether the Prussians were observed around 1pm at all, or whether the French were totally surprised by Bülow's attack. Thus, fabricating a story, such as adding a post-script that was not there originally or making sure the text of the orders directed Grouchy to Wavre, could serve the purpose of protecting the reputation of not only Napoleon, but the French army. This might explain why even Baudus and

---

[222] Grouchy, Emmanuel, *Observations sur la Relation de la Campagne de 1815*, Philadelphia, 1818, p. 17 , https://books.google.com/books?id=DghAAQAAMAAJ&

[223] Damiens, Michel, *La bataille de Plancenoit*, 2012, https://www.scribd.com/doc/112839794/La-bataille-de-Plancenoit

those unfavorable to Napoleon claim the 1pm sighting and dispatch. If so, this is a very large conspiracy.

So many questions arise from this event.

Why would Napoleon claim he sent an order to do something that could easily, and has been, refuted by the text of the order? This has served to impact his reputation negatively, and put his entire memoirs in doubt. Would he really be so naive to think he could get away with this?

Why would Grouchy alter the text of an order that Soult could have easily refuted, and therefore further destroy a reputation he was trying to salvage?

But Soult remained quiet on the entire matter. If his words were fabricated, his silence would have been a party to the deception. Were Soult and Grouchy in an unholy alliance? Did Soult aide Grouchy in his efforts by silence in exchange for Grouchy's efforts to aide Soult? We know Grouchy did not reveal any parts of the order book prior to June 13th, and only many decades after the campaign.

Suffice it to say that the controversies and mysteries surrounding the 18th of June have spawned entire books in themselves. What is important for this work is to simply point out that many believe there is something suspicious about the correspondence of the French army that has been revealed by its veterans. As Mauduit pleaded, the one man who could have done the most to clear up these mysteries was Soult, and he chose not to do so. As this work has demonstrated, Soult had motivations far stronger than any other French officer to see the mysteries of 1815 remain unsolved.

Regardless of the contents, it is certain Napoleon sent dispatches to Grouchy on the 18th of June. Everything Napoleon sent to Grouchy on the battlefield on the 18th of June was predicated in his mind that Grouchy had already been previously told to close towards the main army. Instead, Grouchy ended up following a rear guard, with the entire Prussian army between him and Napoleon.

Soult had made sure he stayed there.

Grouchy believed Napoleon made a simple time-distance mistake, for there is no way an order sent in the afternoon could have been acted upon in time for Grouchy to carry out the mission of attacking Bülow. So this

June 18th

is what we are left to judge – Napoleon making a *gross* miscalculation on the speed of delivery and subsequent execution of an order, or Napoleon believing he had sent at least three recall orders already and that Grouchy would already be on the march.

The battle continued to rage.

Late in the day, and with the French engaged with almost twice their strength, Napoleon decided to launch a final desperate attack by his Guard.

At this point, the campaign was lost. The French army had suffered far too many losses; thousands of irreplaceable horses littered the slopes of Mont St. Jean.[224] Even had the Guard attack been successful, there was nothing to follow it up with. There would be no thunderclap from Brussels reverberating across Europe.

But even so, Napoleon was betrayed once again.

Captain Du Barail, having used the excuse of wishing to examine the enemy line, suddenly spurred his horse through the astonished allied skirmishers while crying out, "Vive le Roi!" He climbed the enemy ridge seeking the first allied officer he could find.[225] Colonel Colborne described it thusly:

> *However, soon after I had received this order I heard a great noise and clamour in the direction of Hougoumont, and observed the Nassau Regiments, I believe, running in disorder out of the wood; and supposing that Hougoumont would be abandoned and our flank would be exposed, I formed columns from squares, and wheeled into two lines, and this formation being completed, we faced about and retired in two lines through the Belgian Guns under the command of Colonel Gaeld [?], and as we were ascending the hill a French*

---

[224] Ney had launched hours of futile cavalry charges during the late afternoon, without infantry support, and never once destroying the artillery that was repeatedly captured. This, and many other events litter the Waterloo legend.

[225] Mauduit, *Histoire des derniers jours de la Grande armée*, 1854, Volume 2, footnote starting on page 345.

> *Colonel of the Cuirassiers galloped out of the French ranks, holloaing out "Vive le Roi," repeatedly, and rode up to me, addressed and said, "Ce — Napoleon est la avec les Gardes. Voila l'attaque qui se fait." This Officer remained with me for some time.*[226]

Du Barail was not the only traitor to ride to Wellington's line that day. General Chasse reported a Cuirassier defecting at some point in the battle as well.

The guard was defeated. In the 200 years since the battle of Waterloo, the formation of the Guard attack has been debated and discussed far more than Soult's actions during the campaign have been analyzed. Consider how absolutely ridiculous that is. Whether the reader finds the charge of treason against Soult credible or not, it is a fact that Soult rewrote Napoleon's orders of June 10th. Yet the formation of the guard attack at a point in time when the campaign was already lost gets more attention.

At this same moment, the Prussian I Corps attacked, and those French on the ridge of Mont St. Jean turned into a mob.

"Sauve qui peut! We are betrayed!"

Napoleon wanted to put himself at the head of his defiant Old Guard battalions and lead a charge!

But Soult, alone remaining calm amongst the chaos, took hold of the reins of Napoleon's horse and selflessly led him away from the battlefield.

"Sire, the enemy has already gained too much, they must not get you."

Few care to mention that Soult saved himself in the process.

---

[226] Siborne, *Waterloo Letters*, London, 1891, p. 283

CHAPTER 15
Aftermath

NAPOLEON AND HIS PERSONAL STAFF retreated through Charleroi and onto Philippeville on the 19th. Soult remained at Philippeville and began to rally the army of Waterloo. Word of the disaster had been sent to Grouchy, along with orders to retreat. Napoleon wanted to go to Laon, rally the army, link up with Grouchy, and continue to battle to protect the homeland. However, his staff advised him to go back to Paris and deal with the intrigues that were already well known, and would only inflame with news of the defeat.

Napoleon arrived in Paris in the early morning hours of the 21st, and immediately began to blame Ney for the loss of the campaign, as well as for the Battle of Waterloo. Though some advised him to seize the Chambers, dissolve it, and rule as a dictator, Napoleon declined. *No matter what*, he did not want French to fire upon French. At the same time, Fouché was already maneuvering for Napoleon's downfall.

During the 21st and into the 22nd, debates raged in the Chambers. Realizing that it would take violent acts to remain on the throne, Napoleon abdicated in favor of his son.

By the 22nd, Soult had made it to Laon while continuing to gather the remnants of the army of Waterloo. There, he wrote Napoleon:

Laon, June 22, 1815.

To His Majesty the Emperor,
Sire, I asked Mr. Lieutenant General Dejean go immediately to your Majesty to inform about the fermentation prevailing in the army, especially among the leaders and generals; it is so important

that a clash may happen next, and anarchic projects which have been designed are no longer kept hidden.

General Piré said today that within a fortnight the government would be changed, this opinion seems generally accepted, and I am confident that among twenty generals, there are eighteen who share it. General Piré went a few hours later to Paris with a letter from Prince Jerome, I did not give him the authorization!

Other generals also left the army to go to Paris; General Kellermann, and Tromelin, Rogniat are in this case, and I was told that there were others who were ready to go.

The example is contagious, and it is likely to be imitated by the corps commanders and individual officers, especially if the Minister of War within twenty-four hours does not give the order to return to the army or to another destination.

Everyone discusses about public interest, and the troops begin to make critical observations on military measures or orders of movement which are given; it was reported that when the 11th chasseurs received the order of the General Subervie to stop in Vervins with the rest of the 5th Cavalry Division, the commander and officers of this corps responded: "That they would do nothing, that the position was bad and that they were betrayed, and they withdrew!"

I have also been told that the main agitators put into deliberation if I would be forced to condescend to their projects, and that it was possible this night, that the group I gathered in Laon, should compel the guards to withdraw. There is no exception, and it is said that all army corps and even the Imperial guard first, are in the same situation.

There may be some exaggeration in this, but it is nonetheless true that there is a great commotion in the army, and that the troops have never been more ill-disposed.

The name of ORLEANS is in the mouth and heads of MOST GENERALS!

All this appeared to me of a too big of importance to delay informing your Majesty about it, so I requested General Dejean to come to report directly, as well as about the information he himself collected.

Signe: Duc De Dalmatie

Soult, *the firm supporter*, graciously imparted upon Napoleon an account of all the bad generals and (gasp!), a faction are in favor of the duc d'Orléans!

And had Louis-Philippe ascended to the throne and by chance, thought that Soult could serve France in some role in the Orléans monarchy, then with a heavy heart, Soult would have done his part for his country. Of course, Soult never expressed this sentiment.

With Napoleon leaving the political scene, a provisional government was organized, of which *Fouché* was elected President. At long last, Fouché's goal complete! Now he just needed to secure it permanently… which meant avoiding a Bourbon restoration. He continued his intrigues, working with all sides, saying what each wanted to hear.

Soult continued to rally the forces from Waterloo. Why shouldn't he? As he would later write in his *justification*: "… Marshal of France could not leave his sword in its sheath when the entire army took up arms to defend the country!" Now, he would unsheathe his sword to prove these virtuous claims!

Thus, on June 23rd, Soult sent to Davout the status of the army, and concluded by saying:

> *It is also noted that since the abdication of Emperor the functions of Major General have ceased in the person of Duke of Dalmatia. One prays to consider his mission fulfilled, and that after having sent orders relating to the abdication of the Emperor, he will cease to give; he will command the army till the arrival of Marshal Grouchy, and he is no longer able to continue his services for health reasons.*

And so went his elaborate display of virtue to "defend the country." It lasted until the enemy crossed the frontier.

On June 25th, 1815, Marshal Grouchy arrived at Soissons, having led the victorious right wing of the *Armée du Nord* in a successful retreat from Belgium. There he took over command of the army with orders to rush to the defense of Paris in the face of the advancing allied armies. Thus relieved,

Soult dutifully turned over the *Registre du Major-Général* to Grouchy and quickly made it to Paris, where one could find the best doctors.²²⁷

On June 26ᵗʰ, Marshal Ney wrote a letter to Fouché, defending his conduct during the campaign. It began:

> *The most defamatory and the most lying rumours have been circulated for some days among the public upon my conduct in this short and disastrous campaign. The public journals repeat them and seem to give credit to the most odious calumny. After having fought for 23 years, and shed my blood for the glory and independence of my country, they dare to accuse me of treason! Me it is, whom they point out to the people, and even the army, as the author of the disaster which it has just encountered.*²²⁸

The rest of the letter is his account of the campaign, which suffered from his limited perspective. It was true in that Ney had led from the front, and had been heroic. This is what the soldiers saw, as well as the arriving Prussians at Waterloo when it was Grouchy they had expected. How could a *defeated* foe appear while Grouchy could not? That was easy to understand. Wounded veterans - still in their uniforms covered in grime and blood - were seen at the cafés of the Palais Royale cursing Grouchy's failures. And so began Grouchy's battle with posterity.

For the entire French nation, Waterloo would become a national wound which only slowly healed into *la défaite glorieuse*.²²⁹

In early July, *President* Fouché, while in discussion with Wellington, lamented over how the Allied Sovereigns, specifically those of Russia and Prussia, would not support restoring the Bourbons to the throne. Fouché implied/suggested that the Chamber should offer the crown to the duc

---

227 There is no evidence Soult visited a doctor upon his arrival at Paris. It's likely the excuse about his health was a ruse in order to quickly gain Paris and have a prominent role in the politics.
228 http://www.napoleonbonaparte.nl/newspaper/dedham/letter_from_ney_to_fouche.html
229 See Jean-Marc Largeaud's *Napoléon et Waterloo: La défaite glorieuse de 1815 à nos jours*

d'Orléans. The discussions continued, including discussions of pardons, of which Fouché undoubtedly would need.

What Fouché did not know was that Wellington had already been making arrangements with Louis XVIII, and the situation had already been decided. Long before his Britannic majesty had implied Britain had no intention of imposing any form of government on France, a Bourbon restoration had been decided. Wellington was imposing the Bourbons on France with the cautious, unenthusiastic support of the allied Sovereigns. Louis XVIII would return at the head of a large occupying army. While Fouché had been making patsies out of many, Britain now needed *their* patsy in order to peacefully establish their ally, the Bourbons, on the throne.

Thus, during the meeting, while Fouché was trying to manipulate Wellington into affecting his plans:

> *Talleyrand leaned forward. 'The King offers you a full and complete amnesty,' he said. Then he added: 'At the same time, he offers you the Ministry of Police. Do you accept?'*
> *Fouché looked at him, his face entirely devoid of expression. 'Yes,' he said.*[230]

While Fouché played with the truth in attempting to avoid a Bourbon restoration, it was generally believed by many in France that the cause of the Bourbons was lost. The throne had been lost twice, and the first restoration had not even survived a year. Indeed, one of Louis's motivations in returning to Paris quickly, even marching with an occupying army, was to beat any moves by the Orleanist party, of which M. Boulay de la Meurthe told the Chamber he had proof.

England would subvert the will of the French people in the name of peace. Empires, it seemed, could not be tolerated, unless they were British.

Napoleon surrendered to England, and would end up imprisoned at St. Helena.

---

230 Cole, Hubert, *Fouché The Unprincipled Patriot*, McCall, 1971, p. 282 Also see Hamilton-Williams, *The Fall of Napoleon: The Final Betrayal* for and interesting take on these events

A Royal decree of July 24th would seek the arrest of Ney and Grouchy. Grouchy fled to America and settled near Philadelphia. Ney was caught, and after a trial where Bourmont cemented his dishonor with lies, was condemned to death. Ney was executed on December 7th, 1815. The firing squad was composed of royalist officers who disguised themselves for the opportunity to slay a dragon.[231]

Soult fled to Germany and eventually settled near Düsseldorf, but not before writing his *Mémoire justificatif de M. le maréchal Soult, duc de Dalmatie* where "Buonaparte" was described as a creature and a tyrant. For example, here is how he described his reaction to being named *Major-Général*:

> *I was groaning in the bosom of my family and my friends at my country's sad fate, when I heard I'd been nominated to the position of Major-Général, and got the order to leave for the army. I obeyed, not as a creature of Buonaparte would have done... The whole army knows very well I'd always only had reasons to complain of this man, and no one more frankly detested his tyranny, whilst serving with zeal and fidelity. I obeyed, not as an enemy of the King might have done; from him I have never received anything but signs of esteem and confidence, and I do not know how to be ungrateful.*[232]

Despite Soult's pleas of undying loyalty to ~~the King~~ Napoleon the King, he still found himself on the July 24 decree and was forced into exile.

---

[231] Taylor, George, *Scholarship and Legend, William Henry Hoyt's research on the Ney Controversy*, printed in the South Atlantic Quarterly, Volume LIX, number 3, summer issue of 1960.
William Henry Hoyt did a tremendous amount of research and invested significant sums in researching the story of Peter S. Ney, the teacher who came to the Carolinas and claimed to be Marshal Ney. His research included examining the notes of Michel Louis Felix Ney, the Marshal's son, who researched his father's execution and identified a Monsieur de Réclade as an émigré who disguised himself as a veteran in order to both guard the Marshal and man the firing squad.
He also quotes Fournier Verniuil's *Curiosité et indiscrétion* where a M. Granger also claimed to disuguise himself to gain a spot on the firing squad.
Capitaine Coignet, in his memoirs, also named a Saint-Leger, who had followed the king to Ghent, and a Tourville who had been with the *gardes du corps*, who likewise claimed to have disguised themselves in order to gain a spot in the Marshal's firing squad.
[232] *Mémoire Justificatif de Monsieur le Maréchal Soult*, Paris, 1815

Mauduit offers a detailed account of his "escape"[233] which chronicles the royalist game Soult played where the Marshal "… returned on several occasions to HIS CONSTANT LOYALTY TO THE KING." Soult maintained a constant loyalty to the king, forced Napoleon to abdicate *which by definition meant Napoleon first had to lose*, and was ready to draw his sword once again to defend the Bourbon Monarchy!

Fouché was a useful pawn for the Bourbons. He had put together the proscription list, though at the King's urging tried to get all those on it out of the country. In 1816, he was first given an ambassadorship, and then finally exiled. No one doubts his treason, and in his memoirs he is almost gleeful about his subterfuge.

Guizot would always be the *Man from Ghent*,[234] which would haunt his political career; however, the full depth of his treason was never revealed, despite the existence of incriminating correspondence. Silence during this period was easy to obtain.

Bourmont and his staff were haunted by their actions. Villoutreys would be disparagingly referred to as "Villoutraître" with the word "traitor" added to his name. While rewarded by the Bourbons, they found themselves ostracized once Louis-Philippe gained the throne in 1830.

Gourgaud accompanied Napoleon in exile, and, after he departed Saint Helena in 1818, he published his Waterloo account, *Le Campagne de 1815: ou Relation des operations militaires qui ont eu lieu en France et en Belgique, pendant les cent jours*.[235] While clearly a product of his conversations with Napoleon, it was still Gourgaud's work. Bertrand's diaries revealed Napoleon's criticisms of the work, though his own narrative would be very similar.

---

233   See "Mauduit's suggestions of Treason" on page 249, "Page 527 Volume 2"
234   See "François Guizot's Troubles" on page 273
235   Gourgaud, G. *La campagne de 1815: ou Relation des opérations militaires qui ont eu lieu en France et en Belgique, pendant les cent jours*, London, 1818
http://books.google.com/books?id=mHRJAAAAMAAJ
Also see :
Gourgaud, G., *Campagne de 1815: opérations militaires en France et en Belgique*, Paris, 1818
https://books.google.com/books?id=M9aoOB8PupUC

Gourgaud's account clearly pointed to the failings of both Ney and Grouchy.

Though Ney was silenced, his family was not. His brother in-law, Charles-Guillaume Gamot, would waste no time, and responded that same year, 1818, with a publication of his own, *Réfutation en ce qui conerne le Maréchal Ney*.[236] In this work, the full text of several orders from the campaign was quoted. Gourgaud's work lacked such documentary evidence, and it is unknown exactly what Napoleon and his entourage had available to them. Based on their memoirs and accounts, it was clear that while they had the advantage of being some of the most important eye witnesses, they lacked the full accounting of records necessary to reconstruct minute details.

Though in America, Marshal Grouchy also wasted no time in responding to Gourgaud, and likewise published a response in Philadelphia in 1818, *Observations sur la relation de la campagne de 1815, publiée par le général Gourgaud, et refutation de quelques unes de assertsions, d'autres écrits relatifs à la bataille de Waterloo*. The work was published in Paris in 1819.[237]

Grouchy shared a few pieces of correspondence in these early accounts, but far less than one would have hoped considering he should have had the single biggest repository of authentic records for the *Armée du Nord*.

In 1819, the July edition of *The Edinburgh Magazine and Literary Miscellany*, contained this passage rich with irony:

> FRANCE. – *The Paris papers of the 19th June contain an account of an extraordinary discussion which took place in the Chamber of Deputies on the preceding day. M. de Bignon, who was minister of foreign affairs during the last short reign of Bonaparte, had, it seems, published a speech, in which he threatened the government which the revelation of a particular fact of which he had the knowledge, when the proper time should arrive. M. de Bignon, in his capacity of minister for foreign affairs, signed, along with the other commissioners, the treaty of Paris, and it is supposed that this communication*

---

236 http://books.google.com/books?id=vX1JAAAAcAAJ
237 Pierre De Wit has a thorough accounting of Grouchy and his families efforts to defend the Marshals reputation, see: http://www.waterloo-campaign.nl/bestanden/files/notes/june19/note.2.pdf

has a reference to certain conversations which passed previous to the signing of this convention, the object of which was to secure good treatment to those who had supported Bonaparte's government. In reference to this, M. de Case, in the debate on the budget, called upon him to explain himself. M. de Bignon declined until the Chamber should be engaged in deliberations on the propriety of recalling the regicides. Then, he said, only then, could the information which he possessed be properly made public. To this the Keeper of the Seals replied, that they never would be engaged in any such deliberations, which declaration was hailed with applause by the one party, while it was received with corresponding disapprobation by the other.

A certain General Morand, who had in the year 1816 been condemned to death par contumace, *on a charge of having, in the preceding year, issued a proclamation at Nantes in favour of Bonaparte, was again tried before a council of war at Strasburg on the 5th of June. He admitted having issued the proclamation, but pleaded the commands of the Secretary at War as his justification. The plea was admitted, and the former sentence annulled.*

Marshal Soult, who is one of the six exiles recently permitted to return to France, has lost no time in taking advantage of this royal clemency, having arrived in Paris the 10th of June last.[238]

Bignon's secret was that the King had claimed to be a party of the Treaty of Paris, signed by Bignon, in order to save a Paris monument from destruction by the Prussians. This treaty also called for amnesty for those who followed Napoleon. The King would deny being bound to the Treaty while executing Ney. Yet, while the Chamber of Deputies would be shaken by Bignon's threat, the man *actually* responsible for Ney's demise would slip into Paris ready to begin his second life.

And not without notice is the gem about General Morand, who had been sentenced to death for *words*! This is how so many of the answers to the mysteries of this campaign have been lost - stifled during the years immediately following the campaign, when their mention meant the possibility of death - and eventually their questions forgotten to history.

---

238 *The Edinburgh magazine, and literary miscellany,* July, 1819, p. 70
https://books.google.com/books?id=4NsEAAAAQAAJ&

In 1820, Napoleon's account of the campaign was published in *Mémoires pour server à l'histoire de France en 1815*. In his obervations, Ney's and Grouchy's conduct continued to be sanctioned.

Grouchy again responded and published *Doutes sur l'authenticité des Mémoires historiques attribués à Napoleon et prémière refutation de quelques-unes des assertions qu'ils renferment*. This document was the basis for a letter, written on April 1st, 1820 in Philadelphia, which was submitted to *The Monthly Magazine* and printed on July 1st, 1820.[239] In this letter Grouchy revealed that the majority of his records from the campaign, including the "book of orders and correspondence of the Major Gen. chief of the staff, the organ of communication between the Commander and Chief and his general officers" was in the possession of his family in France and he warned that this "will furnish me, upon my return to my native country, with materials to confute and overwhelm my detractors."

The editors were not impressed.

Colonel Janin's account, *Campagne de Waterloo*, was also released in 1820. It likewise was meant to address Napoleon's criticisms of subordinates, such as Ney. At once, it is evident that the early works from French authors had strong agendas. While having an agenda does not necessarily invalidate the accuracy of any given work, it does help explain the great number of inconsistencies.

Napoleon died on May 5th, 1821, but his account of the campaign would echo through the 19th century on the strength of his identity alone. Thus, Ney's failures on the 15th and 16th, and Grouchy's on the 17th and 18th continued to be the focus of debates and take center stage in books.

Grouchy returned to France in 1821. He was reinstated by Louis the XVIII, though without his Marshal's baton and no longer as a Peer of France.

Grouchy sparred with several ranking officers and peers through the 1820s, and this culminated in 1829 with the publication of *Fragmens historiques rélatifs à la champagne de 1815, et à la bataille de Waterloo. De l'influence que peuvent avoir sur l'opinion les documents publiés par M. le comte Gérard*. Anyone hoping it would contain the original correspondence he boasted of was disappointed. However, Grouchy continued to boldly contend that

---

239 *The Monthly Magazine*, No. 341, July 1, 1820, p. 489
https://books.google.com/books?id=a20EAAAAQAAJ&

he had not received any written orders from Napoleon on June 17th, and that the order book and correspondence of the *Major-Général, which he possessed*, proved that.

While Grouchy was the popular villain, Ney was the choice of the more thoughtful student of the campaign, who could understand the nuance of how the failure to take Quatre Bras on June 15th (when it was practically empty) could lead directly to an inconclusive victory at Ligny on June 16th, which in turn led to catastrophe at Waterloo. The famous Jomini was particularly active in this perspective and engaged in discussions with both Grouchy and Ney's heirs.

In July of 1830, Louis Philippe, the Duc d'Orléans, was finally seated on the throne of France, and before the year was out, Marshal Soult would be once again Minister of War. In 1831, Louis Philippe restored Grouchy's Marshal's baton and made Grouchy a Peer of France.

Grouchy once again answered to *Minister* Soult.

Soult became the most significant member of the French government during Louis Philippe's reign and served as Minister of War from 1830-1834 and 1840-1844, and as Prime Minister from 1832-1834, 1839-1840, and 1840-1847. Many veterans of Waterloo owed their restoration to the French army directly to Marshal Soult. D'Erlon shared the following letter in his memoirs:

Paris January 7, 1831

M. General,
I am pleased to announce that I have decided that you would be put on the lists of the active officers of the army. This measure had to be delayed because it was important to know with precision the effects of the order of 26 August 1830 on the abolition of convictions and decisions of the government, imposed for political actions since July 7, 1815 and the need to consult the Garde des Sceaux (Minister of Justice), to see and identify (evaluate political motives of judgements). The opinion of the Minister is that, after this order and the judgment of the Cour de Cassation of June 11, 1825, you were back

in the fullness of your rights, and that there was no objection to see you regain your rank in the army.

I applaud this interpretation, which gives back to the army one of his bravest generals, and I will give orders accordingly.

Signed: Marshal Duke of Dalmatia[240]

In 1840, Louis Philippe sent Guizot to London with a request to return Napoleon's remains to France. The British government agreed, and Napoleon was interred in Paris in December.

That same year, Ney's son, Michel Louis Félix Ney, the 2nd Duc d'Elchingen, published *Documents inédits sur la campagne de 1815*[241]. For students of the campaign, this was a gold mine and it easily became one of the most referenced French works in the mid-late 19th century. It contained a detailed account from Colonel Heymès, one of Ney's aides-de-camp. It had numerous orders from the campaign, including some shared by Grouchy and even labelled "Extraits du registre du Major-Général." Even Soult apparently confirmed the lack of Ney being ordered to Quatre Bras on June 15th!

Reille, commander of II Corps, also contributed a detailed analysis of his command's movements, as well as vouched for the validity of some of the orders. In all, it was one of the first campaign studies that approached the topic with scientific vigor. However, it had a very strong agenda, and some of it remains contested to this day. For example, whether Ney visited Napoleon on the night of June 15th in Charleroi, as claimed by Heymès. It is also known that evidence that did not fit the narrative was left out of the final work. For example, a letter from General Pierre David Édouard de Colbert-Chabanais of the Lancers indicated that Quatre Bras was empty for a period of time, yet Ney still did not occupy the position. The latter can be found in the National Archives.[242]

The reality remained that the primary sources - those who witnessed the events –could not agree on really basic facts.

---

240 *Le Maréchal Drouet, Comte d'Erlon Vie Militaire*, p. III
241 Ney, M. L., *Documents inédits sur la campagne de 1815*, 1840
242 Houssaye, *1815*, London, 1900, p. 71, and footnote 54 on p. 341 tells of the letter from Colbert to the Duke d'Elchingen on May 15, 1829 which was omitted from Documents inédits."

Aftermath

In 1842, in *Notice Biographique sur le Maréchal de Grouchy, &c.*, edited by E. Pascallet, the written order from Napoleon to Grouchy, transcribed by Bertrand in Soult's absence, on June 17th was published.[243] John Codman Ropes devotes an appendix in his *The Campaign of Waterloo: A Military History* to examining this order and others that demonstrate that Grouchy was not always honest.

In 1843, Grouchy finally published a complete record of the campaign! His *Relation succincte de la campagne de 1815 en Belgique, et notamment des mouvements, combats et opérations des troupes sous les orders du maréchal Grouchy, suivie de l'exposition de quelquels-une des causes de la perte de la bataille de Waterloo. Pièces et documents officiels inédits jusqu'à ce jour, et qui légitiment les dispositions qu'a dû prendre le maréchal Grouchy par suite des ordres de l'empereur* contained the correspondence between Grouchy and Napoleon, the correspondence between Grouchy and his subordinates, supporting accounts of his actions from numerous subordinates, and most importantly, the "*Copie du Registre d'ordre et de correspondance du major-général, à partir du 13 Juin, jusq'au 26 Juin, époque à laquelle le M^{al}. SOULT remit au Mal. GROUCHY le commandement général de l'armée.*" The Order Book!

Grouchy explained in a letter to Baron Baudrand: "…an unexpected circumstance had made me retrieve all the official documents that had been misplaced for twenty five years."[244] Yet, he claimed as late as 1829 to be in possession of the order book! Once again, it seemed that the more Grouchy spoke in his defense, the more he contradicted his own previous claims.

Soult never published a word on the Waterloo campaign.

Interestingly, the copy of the order book Grouchy published *only started on June 13th, 1815* - after critical events covered had occurred. Further, numerous orders known to be given during the campaign were absent.

Prime Minister Soult expressed no opinion on Grouchy's publication.

Grouchy died on May 29th, 1847.

---

243 In Piérart's *Le Drame de Waterloo*, 2nd edition published in 1868, the footnote on pages 238-239 indicates the order was published in 1840 by the printer Bauduin.
244 De Wit, Pierre, *Grouchy's Defence*, page 3.
http://www.waterloo-campaign.nl/bestanden/files/notes/june19/note.2.pdf

That same year, Soult retired from government. Shortly afterwards, Louis Philippe appointed him Marshal General of France, *ahead of all of France's armies*, where he joined the ranks of such illustrious heroes as Turenne, Villars, and Saxe. Certainly now Soult had equaled all that Napoleon had done.

Though in one aspect, Soult had achieved even more. At the dedication of a display of his military exploits at Versailles, Soult made it known that he was most proud of his defense of Toulouse where he had faced and arguably defeated Wellington.[245] Napoleon, even though the age bears his name, had famously failed in his one opportunity against the duke.

1847 also saw the first publication of *Les Derniers jours de la Grande Armée, ou souvenirs, documens et correspondance inédite* by Hippolyte de Mauduit, who had served in the Old Guard in 1815. Mauduit accused Soult of betraying Napoleon and the *Armée du Nord* during the campaign in Belgium. Neither Soult nor his heirs would object or respond.

In 1848, France once again had a revolution. Louis Philippe abdicated, and the Second Republic was formed. But, just as with the first revolution, stability was fleeting. Once again, a Bonaparte, Louis Napoleon, would seize control, first as Head of State, and finally in a coup on the anniversary of Austerlitz, December 2nd, 1851. Louis Napoleon ruled the Second Empire for 18 years.

Soult died on November 26th, 1851.

In 1864, Grouchy's son Alphonse turned over to the *Biblioltheque Nationale* a **copy** of the *Registre d'ordre et de correspondance du major-général*. It was identical to what his father had published in 1843.

The **original** *Registre d'ordre et de correspondance du major-général* had been lost!

---

[245] Hayman, Peter, *Soult: Napoleon's Maligned Marshal*, Arms and Armour Press, London, 1990, p. 209

Despite Grouchy and his heir's best efforts, his role as the principle cause of defeat of the Waterloo campaign became ingrained in the French culture. In 1869, the following was casually referenced in a French grammar lesson:

> *Les alliés auraient été vaincu à Waterloo, sans un malentendu du général Grouchy.*[246]

Poor Grouchy.

Once again, they had taken away his Marshal's baton.

---

246 Lecomte, Emmanuel and Ménétrier, Abbé, *Exercices Français adaptés à la Grammaire française*, 1869, p. 135
Translated: *The allies would have been defeated at Waterloo without a misunderstanding of General Grouchy.*

PART IV
DESCENT INTO MEDIOCRITY

CHAPTER 16
Closing Arguments

Typically, in a trial, when one is accused of a heinous act, a passionate defense would be expected. When one is accused of negligence, then if not a denial, an excuse. If one is held responsible for a failure, in the absence of an argument, an apology.

Soult faced all of the above after 1815, and said nothing.

After Napoleon's first abdication, Soult initially found himself excluded from the King's army. However, before 1814 closed, Soult had not only gained the King's favor, he had been named Minister of War. In this position, Soult did not hesitate to persecute the veterans of Napoleon's armies, men he had formerly led.

When Napoleon returned, Soult did not hesitate to condemn him in a public fashion. Yet, Soult soon found himself under suspicion of arranging the army in Napoleon's path and was dismissed.

On March 26th, Soult's initial meeting with Napoleon was reported to be heated, with Soult expressing great disapproval. Soult claimed in the justification of his conduct that he resisted numerous overtures to serve Napoleon since he hated Napoleon's tyranny. It may very well be true that Soult resisted the March 26th meeting with Napoleon. But if so, what changed?

During the King's flight from Paris, many officers and soldiers loyal to the King followed the royal court to Ghent. But Bourmont's request to serve in Napoleon's army was a clear signal that in late March the strategy had changed. An unknown number of Royalists stayed with the army, and many would defect during the upcoming hostilities. Bourmont was given command of the 14th Division, and would be the Waterloo campaign's most famous defector.

In early April, Soult aggressively sought a role in Napoleon's army, despite his later claims to the contrary. Napoleon's long time right hand man, Berthier, had declared for the King and was out of the country. As one of Napoleon's most respected Marshals, and having had some experience with the function in 1813, Soult was a logical choice for the most important role of *Major-Général*. One cannot deny that Soult's motivation for this prestigious post could have been nothing more than his famous ambition. Yet at the same time, as a veteran of over 20 years of almost constant war, Soult was perfectly aware of how imperfect a science the control of armies was in the face of the enemy. Even the most successful campaigns had their mishaps, delayed or lost orders, and misunderstandings. If Soult wished to see Napoleon defeated, then gaining the position of *Major-Général* would give him the ability to make the destruction of Napoleon's army a near certainty.

After numerous pleading letters to Davout, Soult earned the ability to deliver both a signed and verbal oath to Napoleon. On May 9th, Soult was named *Major-Général* of the army Napoleon would lead personally.

To gain clarity on Soult's motivations, one need look no farther than his actions during the campaign in Belgium.

It is undeniable Soult's performance as *Major-Général* crippled the *Armée du Nord*.

The question is why.

The conventional history suggests simple incompetence by a man more experienced in leading an army than administering one. There is much to support this argument. Orders were imprecise, locations mangled, and the paperwork itself apparently lacking in completeness demonstrating a lack of the rigor for which Berthier had been famous. It is highly likely that

Soult was mediocre or worse in the chief of staff position. But this does nothing to explain what the record demonstrates. On the contrary, Soult masterfully destroyed one of Napoleon's greatest maneuvers, and then slyly undermined Napoleon's efforts on each day of the campaign all the while keeping Napoleon's wrath focused on others.

It is worth delineating certain events that history has either offered no explanation for, or more often failed to acknowledge.

On June 3rd, Napoleon wrote to Soult:

Give me a plan of movement for the Corps of Général Gérard or the Moselle, concealing it as much as possible from the enemy, for this corps to march on Philippeville. It should be returned there on the 12th, marching as quickly as possible.

At this point, Napoleon had set the commencement of hostilities to be June 14th, the anniversary of his victory at Marengo.

According to Lettow-Vorbeck, who may have seen the original correspondence, Soult sent Gérard an order on June 5th that was received on June 7th "…to start marching on the 7th and to reach Rocroi on the 13th, in seven stages of 3 miles each, via Stenay, Meziéres." Regnault suggests IV Corps began departing on June 8th, but nevertheless seconds Lettow-Vorbeck's account. Further, whatever Soult said to Gérard did not convey the urgency of Napoleon's directive for instead of marching quickly, Gérard had each division commence their march a day apart.

What Soult ordered was a dramatic change to Napoleon's plan: the wrong place on the wrong day.

On June 10th, Napoleon issued his final concentration orders which would have resulted in three columns, each with two infantry Corps, converging on Charleroi starting on June 14th. Any doubt of Napoleon's intentions with the IV Corps were removed as Napoleon wanted them at Mariembourg by the 13th. This was an easy adjustment had IV Corps been targeting Philippeville by June 12th. It would be a more difficult adjustment had IV Corps been targeting Rocroi, a half day's march south, by the 13th. It was an impossible adjustment considering IV Corps' actual march.

However, Soult had far larger adjustments in mind.

On June 12th, Soult reported to Napoleon that in response to his orders of the 10th, Soult had ordered VI Corps to Beufort, and III Corps and IV Corps to Beaumont thereby completely eliminating the right column. Soult's orders were clearly written, successfully delivered, and promptly executed. Soult was not bumbling in his role as *Major-Général*, he was deliberately sabotaging Napoleon's plans.

Soult further reported to Napoleon that in response to Gérard's slow advance, Soult had directed Gérard to make up for lost time as to be at Rocroi on the 13th and to operate via Chimay and onto Beaumont. Finally conveying the urgency to Gérard is commendable, but it was still not what Napoleon had ordered.

The final evidence that Soult's actions were completely contrary to Napoleon's wishes, lest one believe there were conversations or missing correspondence that would have approved of Soult's actions, was that Napoleon instantly countermanded Soult's orders as soon as he became aware of them. VI Corps returned to Beaumont. IV Corps, though it had begun to divert to Chimay, was redirected to the right column. However Napoleon chose to keep III Corps in the center as it had already gone too far and he did not want the men to tire backtracking to their previous location.

As a result of Soult's actions, Napoleon was forced to delay the campaign by one day, until June 15th. This alone was extremely damaging. Defectors were leaving the army daily and giving the Allies intelligence. Each day that the concentrated army, including Napoleon and his guard, were near the frontier was a day that the entire plan could be discovered.

And in one of the great coincidences in the history of war, it just so happened that Soult's machinations put the campaigns most famous traitor in the vanguard of the right column nearest to the frontier with a clear path to the enemy.

What could Soult have done differently that would have damaged Napoleon's efforts more?

The Prussian chief of staff, Gneissenau, informed by the treason of a French general of the advance via Charleroi, in the late evening on the day the campaign should have started, issued orders at 11:30 pm for the Prussian army to concentrate at the position of Sombreffe. While this put the Prussian army at great risk, it also eliminated one of the outcomes Napoleon had prepared for – the occupation of Brussels with minimal loss. It would have been a thunderclap across Europe, the importance of which can be judged most readily by Wellington's dogged determination to prevent. Understanding the importance of the King in Ghent, the conduit of intelligence and intrigue that was fostered in France from Belgium, and the tremendous impact to the French morale a decisive victory would instil, Wellington and Blücher had previously planned concentration points for their armies based on Napoleon's route of attack, should he do so.

Brussels was to be defended in all cases.

On June 15th, the right column was negatively impacted when Bourmont and his staff defected. More importantly, it failed to cross the Sambre due to having failed to reach its intended position even given an extra day.

On June 15th, the center column was delayed by hours when III Corps failed to receive its orders. Even if the conventional history is correct and this was negligence or a mistake on Soult's part, one can now see just how minor an event it was when stacked up against Soult's clearly deliberate actions.

On June 15th, Soult failed to communicate I Corps' dispositions to Napoleon. One could debate there was little impact to the execution of the campaign due to Napoleon's ignorance, but that misses the point. This is one of the clearest examples of Soult's deceit and active measure to conceal. Furthermore, the time it took for I Corps to assemble at Jumet may have been a contributing factor to Ney's slow advance on the morning of June 16th. It is certain that Ney was uncharacteristically cautious. But it is also certain that due to Soult's actions on June 15th, his command was dispersed over a very wide area.

On the afternoon of June 16th, Soult once again failed to communicate I Corps' disposition to Napoleon. Ney took the blame for Napoleon's plan failing, but this plan was formed in the afternoon and based on incorrect information.

On the night of June 17th and into June 18th, Soult failed to send Napoleon's recall orders to Grouchy. There is evidence that at least one orderly either defected or was captured by the Prussians. The idea that Soult did something improper is supported by the fact that what Soult sent during the day on June 18th was a complete change to what Napoleon had ordered and communicated to others on the battlefield.

For the past 200 years, it has been Napoleon's credibility that has been questioned. But in light of the above actions, it is clear that it is Soult that deserves scrutiny.

There is simply no reasonable conclusion other than Soult intentionally and actively betrayed Napoleon.

CHAPTER 17
Conclusion

For supporters of Napoleon, the Waterloo campaign was, and remains to this day, maddening. For his detractors, it has been ample fodder to fuel the narrative of a declining yet arrogant Napoleon.

Why did Napoleon leave Davout in Paris when Berthier served both in the field and as Minister of War through 1807? It is especially more frustrating since this was going to be a short campaign and only a couple days travel from Paris.

Why didn't Ney take Quatre Bras when he had the chance, which he had for many hours!?

What happened with d'Erlon and his useless marches on the 16th!?

Why was half the day wasted on June 17 instead of immediately pursuing the Prussians?

What happened with Grouchy and his pursuit on the 17th/18th!?

And really, why was the battle of Waterloo waged so poorly? One could almost write a book about it...

The above questions and events, and those are but a fraction, have been rehashed in countless books on the Waterloo campaign over the last 200 years. And deservedly so. The drama of 1815 is unparalleled, and the controversies alluded to above continue to be debated.

And yet the most central events that made the greatest impact on the campaign get nary a word.

This work has two theses.

The first and most controversial is that Marshal Soult, Napoleon's *Major-Général* during 1815, was a traitor.

The second is that Napoleon was betrayed in 1815 on a *massive* scale. During the entire Revolutionary, Republican, and Napoleonic wars no nation faced a fraction of the betrayal in a single military campaign than France faced during the preparation and waging of the campaign in Belgium. While this treason is well known, its impact has been blunted over time.[247] This is unfortunate, because Napoleon's plan was destroyed by treason.

Most Waterloo histories start their discussions on June 15th. Many that start earlier completely skip over the muddling that Soult did to Napoleon's original dispositions. Houssaye seems to have purposely omitted these maneuvers as he similarly kept the name of the traitor Du Barail out of his book to protect the reputation of Du Barail's son.[248]

While some early French historians were quick to highlight Bourmont's treason on the 15th as a cause of the defeat, most recent histories have pointed out that this came after the Prussians had begun their concentration. This completely ignores the possibility of nefarious actions on the 14th that were only enabled by Soult's machinations. Lettow-Vorbeck is clear that it was the information the Prussians received on the 14th of June from a French General that enabled their rapid response: an order given before hostilities to concentrate on the agreed to position in case of a French advance through Charleroi. A gain of at least a half day during a campaign where mere hours at Ligny or Waterloo made all the difference is nothing to ignore. It seems Bourmont's actions are worthy of consideration after all.

The explanation for Vandamme's delay has been accepted and repeated with little critical thought despite the lack of evidence. Regardless, Vandamme's performance leaves a lot to be desired. The previous day's

---

247 Some give it credit for making the army fragile. I don't agree. Where was the French army fragile? At Waterloo, where it fought a combined army almost twice its size, attacked a suberbly defended position, defended against far superior numbers, saw Guard battalions almost destroyed to a man, and finally broke after *repeated* set backs… yet even then two Old Guard battalions stopped the allied advance cold while much of the army marched away. There is no doubt certain formations routed, and that darkness combined with the Prussian cavalry created a mob, but the *Armée du Nord* was not fragile at all. It simply was unable to both attack and defeat twice its number while being underminded by constant treason. It is time these men get their due.

248 "Les Traîtres de Waterloo", *Revue Napoleonienne*, Volume 7 http://books.google.com/books?id=SIEkAQAAIAAJ

order made it clear he was expected to have III Corps on the move by 3 am. In the absence of movement orders prior to that time, one would expect a prudent leader to be pursuing an explanation. But for all Vandamme's strengths as a fighting general, his attitude problems were well known, and would manifest themselves throughout the campaign as they did his career. While Soult could not absolutely predict Vandamme's response when the movement orders failed to arrive, it was certainly a safe bet that considering Soult and Vandamme's relationship, Vandamme would be far from prudent.

Alone, the loss of Vandamme's movement order seems like just one of those countless episodes thrown off by the friction of war. Yet, as the misfortunes pile up, they always lead back to Soult… the General that rides to the enemy is positioned in the vanguard through Soult's orders that can only be described as a tortured misapplication of Napoleon's intent… the Corps that doesn't receive orders just happens to be led by one of Soult's greatest enemies and the personality who would most likely respond with inaction… even the one individual that falls ill at the start of the campaign, Mortier, just happens to be someone who was personally close to Soult.

Could Mortier have been warned that leading the Guard in this campaign was undoubtedly going to be a role of the greatest danger? Soult must have known that at some point, his actions were going to create difficulties, and thus Napoleon's elites were likely to be required in a desperate manner against unfavorable odds… exactly as they were.

Soult's actions early in the campaign would have received significantly more attention if, paradoxically, they actually hadn't in some ways *aided* Napoleon! By delaying the French advance, and accelerating the Prussian concentration, on June 16th Napoleon was presented a chance for a decisive battle over the isolated Prussian army. The events that enabled the battle of Ligny have avoided scrutiny, as though it was an inevitable circumstance of the invasion. However, without Soult's machinations, the French would have occupied Fleurus on the first day of the campaign, which would have also been the 14th of June. With the Prussians twelve hours behind their historical schedule, the French would have clearly occupied the Sombreffe position in strength, and seized the Namur-Nivelles road that runs through Quatre Bras, before the Prussians concentrated. It's even possible the Prussian I Corps could have been significantly mauled. This was the campaign Napoleon had planned for and expected. The Allied armies would have been separated on the first day, and the likelihood of either giving battle on the second day is greatly diminished. Had they, their risk of destruction would have been greatly increased.

Soult could not have guessed that slowing the French advance while accelerating the Prussian concentration (not to mention delaying the French invasion by a full day), would have created an opportunity for decisive victory. Eventually, Soult's treason would have to be damaging. And thus Soult, seizing upon d'Erlon's uncertainty on the 15th, allowed I Corps' advance to be delayed, while Napoleon is given false information. Napoleon eventually learns that I Corps was further south than he thought, something he attributes to a failing in the reporting of d'Erlon. Not only did Napoleon in exile lack access to the correspondence that proves everything he was told was false, so did generations of historians. Soult did his best to cover his tracks by making sure his order to d'Erlon late in the night of 15th to bring up I Corps' rear divisions was not included in the *Registre du Major-Général*. Whether it was removed, or never recorded, we will never know.

As a veteran of more than 20 years of war, Soult was completely aware that during the campaign there would be instances of poor communication that would offer opportunities for sabotage. Soult certainly could not rewrite every order Napoleon sent. With d'Erlon, Soult was able to mislead Napoleon while leaving scant evidence. It would take decades for the archivists of France to gather the correspondence and for historians to reconstruct the truth, but by then, instead of asking why Napoleon was so clearly misinformed, the focus has remained on the question of Quatre Bras and Ney. This is a shame because Ney's possession of Quatre Bras was relevant only due to Soult's earlier actions.

Napoleon realized the good fortune he gained by the Prussians offering battle. He even went as far to say in his memoirs, contrary to his correspondence, that he did not intend to seize Sombreffe on June 15th as he knew that would have prevented the battle. Napoleon's ego and revisionism aside, the point here is that all the misfortune of June 15th was quickly forgotten with the first cannon shot at Ligny. But while many say that had d'Erlon come to Ligny it would have led to decisive results, there is an equally strong argument that I Corps could have never carried out Napoleon's intended maneuver based on the realities of its dispositions.

Suffering from bad information, Napoleon formulated a plan that was beyond execution. Napoleon addressed orders to Ney to flank the Prussian position as he expected both I Corps and II Corps to be concentrated near

Conclusion

Quatre Bras. As Napoleon learned that Ney was facing a significant force, he may have called out to I Corps directly. As it turns out, Ney's lack of aggression and Reille's caution contributed to d'Erlon's position being farther south than Napoleon thought. Additionally, d'Erlon likewise paused on his march to pursue a report of the enemy to the west, and reported this fact to Soult along with his position at Gosselies.

On June 16, Soult did not take much of a role in the advance of the left wing. It was slow and ineffective, and Ney has received a tremendous amount of focus and criticism for his performance. While Soult was fundamentally responsible for how dispersed the left wing was on the morning of the 16th, Soult was not responsible for Ney failing to dispatch a force to fall on the rear of the Prussians. Thus, once again, Soult's actions avoid scrutiny.

Soult was aware of I Corps' position, and kept Napoleon in the dark. Had Napoleon known the truth in the morning, he most certainly would have altered his plans. With d'Erlon farther south, and thus blocking the approach from Mons, Lobau wasn't necessary near Charleroi to protect the rear and possible enemy advances against the western flank. Additionally, when Napoleon did decide to bring forces to Ligny, he would have most likely gone directly to d'Erlon earlier and in a clear manner, and most importantly, avoiding the surprise that paralyzed the French at Ligny for more than an hour and robbing Napoleon of a decisive victory.

The history of d'Erlon's movements dominates the discussions of the 16th. To this day, no one is sure what happened, but it is quite clear that regardless of all Soult's actions to thwart Napoleon, had d'Erlon come in force to either Quatre Bras or Ligny a significantly positive impact could have been made.

Napoleon was not faultless during the campaign. His delays during the morning of the 17th have garnered great criticism. Both the battle of Ligny and Waterloo have been criticized for their lack of imagination, though these claims ignore the surprises that interrupted Napoleon's actual plans at each battle.

Once the Prussians escaped Ligny and retreated upon Wavre, the Anglo-Dutch army and Prussians were effectively joined. They were in active communication, and maneuvering together to their mutual support on the 18th. Grouchy's performance was far from acceptable, and this has created another villain that has dominated the study of this campaign.

As Napoleon closed in on a battle with Wellington, there is evidence that Napoleon attempted to recall Grouchy to Waterloo, which would have been completely consistent with his career. The evidence is scant, but this is not surprising considering Soult's treason. The orders to Grouchy, late in the evening or predawn hours, Napoleon would have dispatched via Soult and the orderlies of the general headquarters reserving his smaller staff for missions he felt were more time critical. Soult assured these orders would not be delivered and likewise were kept from the *Registre du Major-Général*. Soult's manipulation of Napoleon's intent during the day on the 18th, and the slow dispatch of Zenowicz, is more evidence of his infidelity.

Marbot, who substantiates Napoleon's expectation of Grouchy's arrival on the right flank at Waterloo, and Zenowicz, whose story is unequivocal about Grouchy's recall, have both had their integrity challenged. Marbot's biography is colourful and exaggerated. Zenowicz had some legal issues and was discharged from the army for a few years. Both were also pro-Napoleon, and that alone motivates many historians to eliminate their testimony. It is wise to consider the integrity of sources, but if doing so, where does Soult's integrity compare?

Did Soult have a sincere moment during 1815?

His written words against, then for, then against Napoleon within the span of six months prove him to be a liar. This may have been the result of political expediency, fine, but then what was the motivation? What did he wish to gain, and to what lengths would he have gone to gain it? We don't have to ask whether he would be willing to rewrite Napoleon's orders because we know for a fact that he did on June 12th.

There remains another compelling source. Gourgaud's diaries were never meant for the public eye and were finally published in 1899. They quote many conversations with Napoleon, and in them, Napoleon is highly critical of his own performance during the campaign. This is far from the stuff of legacy building! And here, Napoleon once again speaks of the recall orders to Grouchy during the night of the 17th and early morning of the 18th.

While Soult never specifically denied the recall orders during the night of the 17th/18th were sent, their absence from the *Registre du Major-Général* is a fairly strong statement from Soult that he did not send them, at least in good faith. He most certainly went through the motions, and was convincing enough to never garner Napoleon's suspicions, though Napoleon did suspect that there may have been disloyalty amongst Soult's orderlies.

But in discussing the *Registre du Major-Général*, we must recognize that what has been passed down is terribly flawed. There is no way to know what orders were originally in the order book, or what their original form was. We do know that Grouchy and his heirs fought tenaciously to salvage the Marshal's reputation, and were not always honest.

Most of the "primary-source" materials that we base the study of this campaign on has been handed down by those with strong agendas. Some materials were later collected from private archives, and they probably have the greatest claim to authenticity. But the bottom line is that it is not possible to make any definitive claim based on the existing materials alone. The absence of an order means nothing, and no one living can vouch for the existing materials.

Recently, historians have begun to challenge the authenticity of existing materials. Michel Damiens has challenged two pieces of correspondence. In his *Le 17 juin 1815, La foudre enrayée ou le plan oublié*, he concludes after a lengthy and exhaustive analysis that the Bertrand letter to Grouchy written at Ligny on June 17th is a fake.[249] In his *Le bataille de Plancenoit*, Damiens devotes a detailed appendix of over 30 pages claiming the order to Grouchy from the Waterloo battlefield on June 18th at 1pm is a forgery.

Whether Damiens' analysis of the above pieces of correspondence is correct or not, the greater point is that there were clearly nefarious actions taken in dealing with the original materials from this campaign. It is known that there are missing orders – what is not known is how many. Likewise, there have been orders found that were not recorded – what is not known is why. Grouchy had a clear agenda, and most certainly tinkered with dispatch times or wordings, but only on that correspondence dealing with his actions on June 17th and beyond. Could Soult have likewise taken proactive measures to hide his actions during the campaign? Could Soult have influenced what Grouchy or others revealed during Louis Philippe's reign?

Of course Soult could have. There is no other reasonable explanation. But certainly if Soult was of such questionable character who would act in such nefarious ways then it would be known and written about by others.

---

249 Michel Damiens has numerous publications on the 1815 campaign here: https://www.scribd.com/michel_damiens

And it has. In *Dictionaire Napoléon*, the massive 1800+ page book written under the direction of Jean Tulard, one of France's most esteemed historians on the Napoleonic era, the following are the first and last paragraphs of the entry on Soult, written by the respected military historian Jacques Garnier:

> *SOULT (Jean de Dieu, duc de Dalmatie), 1769-1851, maréchal de France. Few characters are more difficult to understand than that of Marshal Soult. The judgment of his contemporaries of him is not always gentle. Thus Marshal Marmont: "I had, for the character of Marshal Soult, the common conviction and keeping with his reputation; thus I had little confidence in his loyalty. Junot, with whom I was always very close since my early youth, and who had true and deep attachment for me, said to me, at the moment when we separated in Castille: "You will have frequent associations with Soult. Your points of contact will be multiplied. Stand up to him, act with prudence; take precautions; because, I give you assurance of it, if he can, at whatever price, bring you great misfortunes, he will not miss it! It is because I had the occasion to know him well that I advise you." "Général Thiébault: "Lieutenant General Count Delaborde, spirit of Porto, said to me in Burgos (1809) while speaking about Marshal Soult and in his own words: "This guy is from the race of the crows, he fears the powder." The general of Girard's division, killed at Waterloo, told me that in Andalusia, the Marshal having been pressed by him to go to the angle of a wall to see one of the enemy's operations, he went there on four legs." General Lamarque: "In passing through the first salon of M. Marshal Soult, I examined this beautiful painting of the Assumption of the Virgin, most outstanding masterpiece, they say, of all, by Raphaël, and I recall a story that someone told me and I relate in turn. It is said that a patron, admiring this painting, dared to ask the Marshal what he had paid for it. "It costs me only two cordeliers. - How is that? - Yes, two Cordeliers." And His Excellency told the patron that two monks found compromised in a conspiracy were going to be hung, when the community offered to redeem them with this beautiful painting. The Marshal was moved, he accepted the painting and the two cordeliers were not hung."*
>
> *...*

Conclusion

> *He was a good general, composed, with a sharp eye, but his character seems not to have been at the height of military form. He was the "adulator" of all the powers, and was even accused of removing from the archives the documents which were likely to disserve him. His morals were not safe from criticism: he was certainly one of the marshals who had taken the most plunder of the conquered countries, especially of Spain.[250]*

The entire entry paints an even darker picture of the Marshal.

The battle of Waterloo is one of the most dramatic in history. It is studied and written about far more than the campaign in general. It has been re-fought on table tops and in computers a million times. It has dominated our imaginations in a way that the final concentrations of the French army could never do. Yet, by the time Ney launched the French Cavalry on Wellington's lines, one could argue that Napoleon's chance for a history changing victory had already slipped away.

During the time that Mauduit, and other living veterans, were questioning Soult's fidelity, they simply did not have access to the records that would demonstrate Soult's bad acts. Thus, they were left with anecdotal accusations that did not gain traction, while Ney and Grouchy's actions and the drama of the battle are the centerpiece of modern discussions.

Soult could not have been more fortunate. By keeping silent, the attacks on his fidelity and competence could never compete with all the incidents of the campaign. As the veterans of the battle began to die off, the passion against Soult died with them.

Soult's behavior in 1815 has always been portrayed as that of an opportunist whose loyalties were gained at the cost of a ribbon. But he went beyond simple oaths. As Minister of War for King Louis XVIII, he persecuted men he had fought beside for 20 years! It is simply too easy to consider Soult a charlatan.

Soult's actions persecuting Napoleon's veterans drove many to hate him. What Soult did has never been given the justice it has deserved. If Soult's motive was to achieve preeminence in France in a political or military role,

---

250 Jacques Garnier, "Soult." *Dictionnaire Napoléon sous la direction de Jean Tulard*, 1989, pps. 1584-1586.

then the destruction of an army rabidly loyal to one's chief antagonist would have been a necessary goal.

Soult's memoirs of the 100 Days and the Waterloo campaign are a closely guarded family secret.[251] He published nothing during his lifetime, and apparently rarely spoke, of the Waterloo campaign. Interestingly, in 2007, a huge trove of Soult's correspondence went to auction. The French Ministry of Defense eventually put a claim on it, as the French law allows, and acquired it. 33 Volumes covering the years of 1794 - 1814, yet not a word about 1815. So almost 200 years later, whatever Soult did in 1815 is still kept from the public eye.

Did the distant heir that put this material up for auction really care what Soult said or did in 1815? Or, is it possible this material does not exist? Has it been intentionally concealed or destroyed? The legal term for this is *Consciousness of Guilt*, and in the absence of the materials, one can only conclude that there is something to hide.

Soult did offer an opinion on the Waterloo campaign at least once:

"Ney was the evil genius of the campaign; he neglected his orders at Quatre Bras, and again at Waterloo; he attacked Wellington's position beyond la Haye Sainte contrary to orders and too soon; but he is dead, he was unfortunate. I do not like to speak of his errors."[252]

Soult had to know of the criticism of his job during his lifetime, but never got embroiled in any discussion publicly. Did he agree? Did he appreciate the job of *Major-Général* after Waterloo? Did his experience give him an appreciation of running the bureaucracy of an army at war?

---

251 Paddy Griffith wrote in regards to Soult's memoirs on the Restoration and Hundred Days, "We are told that the manuscripts are 'well guarded' by the family – but it would be helpful to see more of them in print." Indeed, what are they hiding?
Griffith, "Soult", *Napoleon's Marshals*, Edited by David G. Chandler, Macmillan, New York, 1987
252 Bruce, H. A., *Life of General Sir William Napier*, London 1864, p. 505
A chapter of this book is devoted to meetings Napier had with Soult during the latter's visit to England.
http://books.google.com/books/download/Life_of_General_Sir_William_Napier_K_C_B.pdf?id=wxU6AAAAcAAJ

CONCLUSION

Hardly, for late in his life speaking of Berthier and Clarke:

> *Old women – Catins. The Emperor knew them and their talents; they were fit for tools, machines, good for writing down his orders and making arrangements according to rule; he employed them for nothing else. Bah! They were very poor. I could do their work as well or better than they could, but the Emperor was too wise to employ a man of my character at a desk; he knew I could control and tame wild men, and he employed me to do so.*[253]

How does one interpret such a remark? I would suggest that if he is being honest, then he is all but admitting he was acting as a traitor in 1815. Otherwise, delusional seems appropriate.

Napoleon certainly had a high opinion of Soult. Soult's career started under the command of others, including Napoleon's nemesis Moreau. Yet Napoleon recognized a great talent in Soult. Soult was appointed chief of the Camp of Boulogne where the *Grande Armée* was forged. Soult was one of the first appointed Marshals, and given the decisive role at Austerlitz. Soult many times held the center of the line for Napoleon in battles, and when Spain became a crisis, it was Soult that Napoleon sent there when only the one of the best would do.

Soult, as a Marshal of the Empire, was competent.

After Waterloo, when Soult would serve under Louis-Philippe and enter politics, he would once again rise to the top, and have one of the longest terms as Prime Minister of France while serving in that capacity three different times.

Soult, as a French political figure, was competent.[254]

Yet for two weeks in June, of 1815, we are told that the act of putting Napoleon's thoughts and plans into words was beyond his grasp:

> *Soult, I have studied the dispositions of the enemy, as well as our own, and have determined the time is now to spring my trap… move this unit from A to B!*

---

253 Ibid, p. 510
254 "Indefatigable" is what Guizot would write. For those wondering if Soult was able or energetic enough to fulfill the duties of *Major Général* in 1815, one must only study his political life for the decades that followed.

> ...
> *Soult!*
>
> *Oh, Sire, our August Emperor, forgive me! I was lost in the magnificence of your presence, in the sublime perfection of your plans, in the elegant beauty of your designs. Here, Sire, I have written the dispatch, and have, per your instructions, directed the unit move to C.*

Yet that is what we are supposed to believe. Houssaye didn't buy that:

> *One must read in his* Memoirs *(ii. 206) the portrait he draws from his own model of the ideal head of the staff. If it be true that, when he discharged these functions in the Lefebvre division, he was so active, so diligent, so prudent, he had somewhat altered in 1815. However, during the campaign, Soult was not as much below his task as was presumed. His greatest fault was in sometimes writing his orders without precision and clearness, and in not ensuring their rapid transmission. As for the charge of negligence and want of foresight brought against him, it is just to say that Bailly de Monthyon, who had been appointed to assist him as chief of the staff, is also responsible for these to a certain extent.*[255]

We could seek Monthion's opinion of what transpired in 1815, but as with Soult, he has left us with no memoirs nor is quoted by anyone.[256] The cult of silence of so many of the high ranking French officers of the Waterloo campaign is one of the lasting mysteries.

Regardless, here in this work is a significant lot of relevant correspondence. One can only judge for themselves whether the demonstrated fatalities were that of simple error, or gross misconduct.

But is it possible that Napoleon could have traitors so close to his person and be unaware of it? Napoleon had an opinion on this:

---

255 Houssaye, *Waterloo*, p. 318
256 Monthion has left various anecdotes that have been commented on, typically by a third party. But as far as the great mysteries of the campaign, he has left no insight.

Conclusion

There are fewer traitors in the world than you think, but on the other hand, there are numbers of weak men who yield to circumstances far more powerful than themselves.

Fouché is the only real traitor I have met; Marmont, the wretched Marmont who injured me more than Fouché, was not a traitor. He was misled by vanity and the hope of playing a great part, and he believed that by abandoning me, and depriving me of the means of overwhelming the coalition in Paris, he was saving France from a great catastrophe. But he did not betray me as Fouché did.

Who is Napoleon fooling!? Was he really that naïve to believe there were not traitors in his company? Did he think he had some mesmerizing control of all around him?

Others knew better:

Napoleon never lost anyone on his own initiative - never, never, never! It was necessary, when once you were known to him, to commit faults, nay even crimes, over and over again, twenty, thirty times, before he could bring himself even to punish. No, never; the Emperor never lost anyone on his own initiative. But wicked people sometimes deceived him. He had many false friends; many person opposed him who owed everything to him…[257]

Those were wise words from someone who knew Napoleon well.

They are the words of Soult.

If a criminal case was brought against Soult, the verdict could only be not-guilty. There is no proof of treason, no way to claim that we know what was in that man's heart *beyond a reasonable doubt*. But likewise, if a civil claim was brought where the burden was simply the *preponderance of the evidence* of his culpability, how could it be argued otherwise?

I believe there is *clear and convincing* evidence that Marshal Soult betrayed Napoleon in 1815. I don't believe there is an example in this man's

---

257 Bruce, H. A., *Life of General Sir William Napier*, London 1864, p. 507

life which supports an argument that the events that are documented in this work were a product of simple negligence by a sincere individual. This is not to suggest he was Berthier's equal, or even a good *Major-Général*. The fact is Soult could be both a mediocre *Major-Général* and a traitor. One simply cannot explain rewriting orders and concealing information as a product of mediocrity. Thus, while repeated historians have lamented that Soult failed to send multiple couriers to Vandamme to transmit orders *over a distance of just a few miles and within the borders of France,* few have focused on why Vandamme was in the central column, and how especially unfortunate it was that it was the stubborn and fiery *Vandamme* whose orders were lost.

And how could this have gone undiscovered by the veterans of Napoleon's last army? Certainly, with the disdain for Soult, the stated belief by some that he *would* betray Napoleon, and Mauduit's outright accusations, there must have been some that discussed the possibility in private circles. For this, we must remind ourselves of the political environment in France. As Peter Hofschröer wrote when discussing the British historian Siborne's efforts to produce an accurate history of the campaign and battle:

> *Siborne also endeavoured to get input from the French. He wrote to Marshal Lobau, commander of the VI Corps at Waterloo, asking for information and requesting permission to send a circular to surviving French officers. When he got no reply, Siborne had friends at the British Embassy in Paris go and visit him in an endeavour to get a response. They were not successful – the theme of Waterloo was taboo in France, even twenty or thirty years afterwards.*[258]

Twenty or thirty years after Waterloo, the French discussions on this campaign did not and could not discuss the details that reveal Soult's treason. Mauduit, who lived the events, and *felt* Soult's conduct, could not offer any details… just colorful exclamations of frustration. The details were yet to be discovered in the completeness required to make a charge. But by then, Soult was the target of political scorn and no longer a prominent figure of Waterloo. Grouchy would take the baton, and with his own contradictions and self-serving memoirs, dig a hole his reputation has yet to emerge from.

---

258 Take from: http://www.richardgilbert.ca/achart/public_html/articles/wellington/siborne.htm

Conclusion

Ney has gone down in history as a brave idiot, the *sans brains*, which is utterly unjust. Just as the royalists of Paris would lament, *if we had only known*, when they would finally read of Ney's heroics in Russia, we can only hope this work will help others understand that Ney was thrown into a very difficult situation; a campaign commenced with active combat yet little staff. Ney was extraordinarily dependent on the main headquarters, and was utterly let down. Ney was betrayed, just as Napoleon, just as every French soldier in 1815.

The cult of silence was not motivated purely to keep great secrets. For some, Waterloo was a deep wound during a period that was rife with conflict. General Foy summarizes what may have been a prevailing thought when discussing his notes with General Auguste Petiet, who was a member of Soult's staff during the campaign in Belgium:

> *General Foy wanted to review the notes that I agreed to trace each day during the campaign of 1815, to etch in my memory the important facts that I witnessed or which I had been able to report with accuracy to the Emperor's headquarters. General Foy ensured me, when returning them to me, that the summary description of the campaign operations was reported perfectly according to his recollection, then he added: "You are young, General, let these notes lie dormant for twenty more years. In twenty years, it will be history; in twenty years partisan hatred will have faded; in twenty years we will raise alters to an exceptional man, today unrecognized, for whom evil persists. Finally, in twenty years France will go, if she must, to arms, to wrest from England the mortal remains of the martyr of Sainte-Hélène, with acclamations of all of Europe!"*[259]

One could still wonder how Soult could not have been discovered. Even without the documentary evidence that took decades to gather, there had to be other officers in the French army that were intimately aware that there was inconsistencies in popular accounts.

For example, consider d'Erlon. He was aware of his Corps' disposition during the 15th and 16th. During the course of the campaign there was little

---

[259] Petiet, Auguste, *Souvenirs militaires de l'histoire contemporaine*, 1844, p. 167
http://gallica.bnf.fr/ark:/12148/bpt6k6507348f/

time for a debriefing which would have cleared the matter for Napoleon, and after the defeat the two would never meet. Why didn't d'Erlon raise questions of what information Napoleon had been operating on?

After Waterloo, d'Erlon was sentenced to death, and thus he fled to Bavaria under the name of "Baron Schmidt." In his memoirs he speaks of being visited by members of the Bavarian army that had served under him, but he does not speak of any gathering of Waterloo veterans. In 1825 he was allowed to return to France, but did not have his position restored with the army, something he desperately wanted. Thus, he remained in Bavaria with his family. Did he read the accounts of Waterloo? Was he aware of their inaccuracies relating to his movements? Who knows, but in the aftermath of Waterloo during the Bourbon rule, his focus appears to have been on starting over.

In 1829, d'Erlon responded to a request by Ney's son to explain the movements of I Corps on the 16th of June:

Paris, February 9, 1829.

You ask me, Prince, for information about the events of my army corps on the day of June 16, 1815.
I am sending them to you without delay:
Towards eleven o'clock or noon, M. Marshal Ney sent the order to me for my army corps to take up arms, and to lead it on Frasnes and Quatre-Bras, where I would receive further orders. My army then began moving immediately after having given the order to the general who commanded from the head of the column, to march quickly; I advanced to see what occurred at Quatre-Bras, where the army corps of General Reille appeared to be engaged. Beyond Frasnes, I stopped with the generals of the guard, where I was joined by General Labédoyère, who showed me a pencilled note that he carried to Marshal Ney, and that commanded this Marshal to lead my army corps on Ligny. General Labédoyère advised me that he had already given the order for this movement, in making a change of direction to my column, and indicated to me where I could join it. I took this route at once and sent my chief of staff to the Marshal, General Delcambre, to advise him of my new destination, M. Marshal Ney imperatively charging in reply that I return to Quatre-Bras, where

he was heavily engaged, expecting the cooperation of my army corps. I had therefore to assume that it was an urgency, since the Marshal took upon himself to summon me again, though he had received the note about which I spoke earlier.

I ordered, consequently, the column to countermarch; but despite all of the diligence that we made for this movement, my column could not appear behind Quatre-Bras with the approach of the night.

Was it General Labédoyère's mission to change the direction of my column before seeing the Marshal? I do not think so; but, in any case, only this circumstance was the cause of all the marches and countermarches that paralyzed my army corps during the day of the 16th.

D. Count D'Erlon[260]

His letter is extremely terse and is notable in that he assigns responsibility for I Corps diversion to the Ligny battlefield to Labédoyère who, executed after Waterloo, is not available to comment. While d'Erlon responded, he was certainly very careful in doing so. With Charles the Xth on the throne, and probably hopeful for eventual reinstatement, d'Erlon had every reason to tread carefully in regards to the events of the Waterloo campaign.

After the 1830 Revolution, d'Erlon rushed back to France eager to regain his position with the army. As was previously seen, Soult, as Minister of War and a key member of Louis Philippe's government, brought d'Erlon back into the folds of the army.

Soult! What a gracious man! Though Soult was humiliated by d'Erlon in the trial of Exelmans and later sentences d'Erlon to death after Napoleon returns, Soult now welcomes d'Erlon back as one of France's bravest generals and restores him with his rank back in the army. And Soult makes it clear that it is Soult that is giving the order. Whatever motivations d'Erlon may have had to reveal anything damaging against Soult was instantly eliminated.

D'Erlon would serve in Algeria and upon his return command the Twelfth Military Division until April 9, 1843 when d'Erlon was appointed a Marshal of France. In his memoirs, in discussing the events of June 16th, he states the following:

---

260 Ney, *Documents Inédits sur la Campagne de 1815*, Paris, 1840, pp. 64-65

> *I ask the reader to carefully study the paragraph that follows, because it matters that the truth is finally known.*
>
> *The Emperor, heavily engaged at Ligny, sent an aide-de-camp to Marshal Ney, for him to say to lead the first corps on Ligny, in order to turn the right wing of the Prussian army. This officer met the head of the column of the first corps, which arrived in Frasnes, and, before having transmitted the orders of the Emperor to Marshal Ney, took this column in the direction of Ligny.*[261]

As the above account was not unknown, what does d'Erlon mean when he asks the reader to "...carefully study the paragraph that follows, because it matters that the truth is *finally* known." What is there to study? By 1844, it was well known that I Corps had been diverted to Ligny, and it was generally believed by the orderly carrying an order from Napoleon. I believe d'Erlon is urging us to notice that the messenger had run into I Corps on the Charleroi-Brussels road *as it arrived at Frasnes*. Why was it still that far south, and out of Ney's operational control? Why didn't Napoleon know this? D'Erlon is begging us to finally recognize where Napoleon had been misled. As d'Erlon knew first hand I Corps' disposition on June 15th and his interactions with Soult including his correspondence in the afternoon of June 16th, d'Erlon had to have figured out that Napoleon had been misinformed. Soult was too powerful to directly confront, but he must have desperately wanted "... that the truth is finally known."

Regardless, d'Erlon will go on to criticize Napoleon for the lack of direct orders, and Ney for his recall. The criticism of the lack of direct orders is once again a call for analysis. While Napoleon was sending orders to Ney, I Corps was actually closer to Napoleon than it was to Ney. For the time, this was certainly politically correct. D'Erlon died on January 25th, 1844, never once offering an explanation for why Napoleon incorrectly stated the dispositions of I Corps in his memoirs for the evening of the 15th of June, 1815.

This is what faced the French officers after Waterloo. For 15 years, Bourbon censorship with a very real threat of death if the wrong position on Napoleon was taken. After the 1830 revolution, though the veterans of Napoleon are welcomed back into the army, they find themselves answering to Soult as Minister of War and a senior member of the government. This

---
[261] *Le Maréchal Drouet, Comte d'Erlon Vie Militaire*, 1844, p. 95

Conclusion

also explains the cult of silence. The officers that knew the most, such as d'Erlon, simply never had a reason to share anything controversial. Their positions, income and the welfare of their families were best served by shutting up and taking their secrets to the grave.

Unlike many of his peers, Soult had no financial concerns. Well known for plundering in Spain, Thiébault leveled the following charge:

> *His plunder was brought to my attention by the spoliation of the rich abbeys of Austria during the campaign of Austerlitz, by the share of all profits made per month by M ... in charge of the services of the army of Naples, which was commanded by the Marshal: the last payment of these profits which amounted to 300 or 400,000 francs was made in Paris to the Marshal; by the millions stolen in Andalusia and by the 25 millions that, according to the statement made in 1815 by the Duke of Wellington to the Count of Valencia, the Marshal had at the Bank of England; by the mass of paintings he removed in Seville and with which he had the impudence to cover the walls of his Paris hotel and of the castle he just built in Languedoc.*[262]

Thiébault hated Soult, and thus we must consider his attacks carefully. But there is no doubt to Soult's plundering as his children auctioned off what remained of his well-known collection after his death and made over 1.5 million francs. If Soult had a fortune in England, then it is easy to imagine that had he ever been at risk of discovery in 1815, he would have simply gone to a hero's welcome in England where he would have lived as the king he so wished to become.

Soult, who never ceased throwing ladders on the ramparts of life, ultimately achieved his goal. Though not quite a monarch of his own country, he had held the post of Prime Minister. He had achieved all that was possible in France.

But despite all that Soult accomplished in his life, and all that he did to emerge from Napoleon's shadow and achieve his own greatness, his treason has only contributed to his own obscurity.

---

262 *Mémoires du Général Baron Thiébault*, Paris, 1895, p. 468

For when visitors come upon one of his paintings adoring the walls of some museum in France, visitors stumble over their guides looking to answer the question that has come to signify his place in history.

"Who is that?"[263]

---

[263] In the movie *Dirty Rotten Scoundrels*, a portrait of Marshal Soult hangs above the bed of Ruprecht, a deranged imbecile played by Freddy, Steve Martin's character, in order to chase away a woman being scammed by Lawrence, Michael Caine's character.

Appendices

APPENDIX I
Instead of Soult

To understand the full impact of Soult on the Napoleon's plans, let us consider possible results if an obedient and diligent individual had been employed as the *Major-Général* of the *Armée du Nord*.

The following are the assumptions of the French advance:
- The campaign will commence on June 14th, per the original design.
- French are slightly farther from the frontier which would reduce the progress by 1-2 hours. However, as formations stopped their advance historically at various times, this is not absolute.
- I Corps would be much farther behind II Corps, and thus would leave on time and never be waiting on II Corps at bridges or key roads. As was shown in the text, d'Erlon's decision to not break camp at the appointed time, far from being an act of negligence, was actually a decision of experience. His historical mistake was one of indecision in the face of a difficult decision with two battles raging on June 16th.
- VI Corps would lead the center advance diligently.
- III Corps would lead the right advance diligently.
- IV Corps would have, per Napoleon's instructions, been ordered to reach Mariembourg by the 13th. The corps would advance diligently – Bourmont would undoubtedly still defect, but as with the traitors of I Corps (Gordon, Gaugler) would need to wait until closer to the Allies.

The following are the assumptions for the Prussian concentration:
- There would be no 11:30 pm concentration orders as Bourmont is now well behind the frontier with III Corps between him and the

Prussians. There is simply not time for him to perform his treason on the eve of the campaign.
- With the French hitting the frontier positions 1-2 hours later, and the concentration orders being dispatched 4 or so hours later from Namur, we'll estimate Blücher's orders to concentrate, and directly to Sombreffe, would have been sent around 11 am. Note that the original order flow sent at night was not as smooth or prompt as possible. But, much of the time the riders were carrying the 11pm orders the units were asleep. Thus, for simplicity, we'll assume that carrying orders more smoothly during the day will offset the use of the dead time of the early morning June 15th orders.
- A single precise order would be sent to Bülow, and there would be no hesitation or delay by the Prussian IV Corps.

The historical results of the Anglo-Dutch concentration will be used. Nothing would have changed Wellington's caution of what he believed Napoleon would do.

It should be noted that beginning the campaign a day sooner, one could easily argue for even greater surprise and delays on the Allied side, especially along the frontier.

For the French, the left Column would have probably achieved the historical result. The Anglo-Dutch forces Napoleon feared were the ones from the west, in the direction of Mons that could maneuver to his rear on an advance to Brussels.

The big change would be the center and right. In the center, with a prompt advance, the leading cavalry would have had enough infantry from VI Corps to quickly push through all resistance. This combined with III Corps prompt advance to the Sambre, probably redirected to Chatelet once Charleroi was taken, would have compelled the Prussian I Corps to retreat rapidly. By night fall, Fleurus would have been occupied with a significant presence thrown beyond.

The Imperial Guard would have bivouacked around Charleroi, and IV Corps would likewise around Chatelet.

For the Prussians, there is real risk I Corps would have been seriously mauled. It would have been all a matter of fine timing on the various

APPENDIX I – INSTEAD OF SOULT

axis of advance as to whether battalions to brigades would have been cut off. Regardless, whatever remained would have fallen back to the Sombreffe position.

By the late evening of the 14th of June, or early morning on the 15th of June, II Corps would have made just west of Namur, and III Corps would have gathered just on the other side of the Meuse. IV Corps would be concentrated around Hannut.

The Anglo-Dutch would have had the 2nd Netherlands Division at Quatre Bras, with Wellington leading the reserves from Brussels. The units farther forward were falling back, and the units to the north and west were moving east and south.

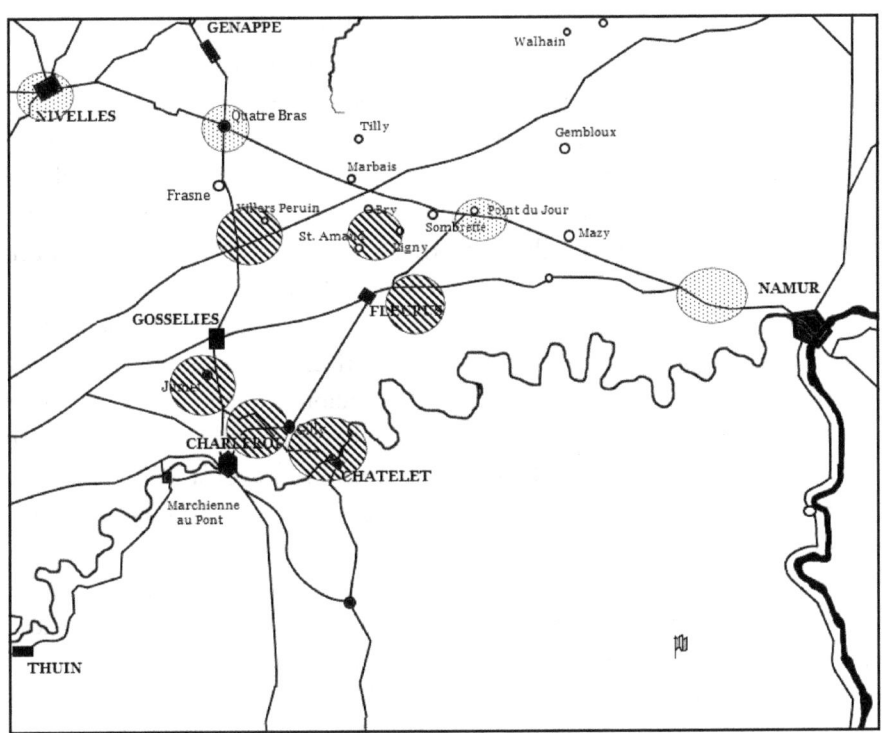

Figure 13 – Position of French Army with loyal Major-Général

Looking at Figure 13, one can instantly see how dramatically different the campaign could have been. This is what Napoleon expected, and now one understands why his orders early in the campaign were written with the expectation of allied retreat. The French have interposed between the two armies, and communications are impacted. With the French light cavalry vanguards cutting the Nivelles-Namur road, Blücher and Wellington are in sporadic communication.

There is no battle of Ligny, and no meeting between Blücher and Wellington. There is no Prussian concentration at Sombreffe. Consider, the Prussian I Corps may be intact, it may be mauled, or it may have been largely destroyed. In all cases, it is in no position to hold the line as the balance of the Prussian army falls in. Napoleon, in his early orders historically, was prepared to attack the Prussians as far to the east as Gembloux if they stood their ground, in order to open up an advance on Brussels.

Without the Prussian concentration in its right rear at Fleurus, II Corps can be presumed to move quickly north and seize Quatre Bras. I Corps follows, and Napoleon has his left wing augmented with a heavy Cavalry Corps holding his designs there. Everything would depend on the Prussians.

Is Blücher so committed to battle the Gembloux-Mazy line becomes a battlefield? But would he even have the ability to establish his army there before being overwhelmed? Or does the shattering of the pre-existing concentration plans lead to a rallying farther north where they can maintain communications with Wellington and defend Brussels?

While many modern historians diminish the chances Napoleon had in this campaign and do not see the potential impact of seizing Brussels, Wellington proves its importance by his tenacious defense of the city historically. We can assume that as Wellington became aware of the situation with the Prussians, he would likewise fall back. However, if he chose to fight a battle of Waterloo, there would be no Prussian assistance, with the rains of the 17th now working to Napoleon's favor.

If this was a wargame, an Allied player with perfect intelligence would feel like they possessed all the advantage having Napoleon between their two armies, but had this been the historical result of the first day of the campaign, the armies of Wellington and Blücher would be at great risk of individual destruction. However, even Napoleon acknowledged in his later writings that had the allied armies simply retreated away and combined, he would have been in quite a predicament.

If one disagrees with my hypothetical dispositions, then they should understand that I do as well. It would take many detailed simulations that could somehow capture the uncertainties of the hundreds of men involved as part of the various staffs to truly get an idea of the possibilities. However, even if reasonable adjustments are made to the hypothetical dispositions, which could easily go either way for any formation, it should still be clear that the historical campaign was an out-lier – a product of Soult's treason.

But, a great irony is that Soult's treason accelerated the advance of the Prussians, while doing nothing to the Anglo-Dutch. Thus, on the 16th, Napoleon got a decisive battle opportunity that may not have existed without the treason. Of course, the treason on the 16th prevented the type of decisive victory that could have won the campaign.

When bungling Napoleon's final concentration orders, putting Bourmont on vanguard of the right column and then both overloading and delaying the central column with Vandamme, Soult could not have guessed it could have ended up helping Napoleon's cause. How could anyone guess that? Of course, over the days of the campaign, "thwarting the will of Napoleon", to paraphrase Mauduit, was eventually going to be fatal. But, the 16th of June, the battle of Ligny, Ney failing to seize Quatre Bras, and d'Erlon's inexplicable maneuvers have captured the attention of all subsequent historians. This has all but eliminated analysis of the early stages of Napoleon's final campaign. When one adds the drama of June 18th with Grouchy's wanderings, then it is not surprising that the Battle of Waterloo itself has been written about in far more detail than all the days preceding it.

Soult's conduct during the campaign, though almost always mentioned, has never seriously been analyzed.

APPENDIX II
ACCOUNT OF EXELMANS AFFAIR

Sir John Richard Hall's account of Soult's prosecution of Exelmans:

> *No sooner was Soult installed at the War Office than he took up the question of the half-pay officers with an uncompromising vigour. He decreed that in the future they must live at their native towns or villages. Those of them who had not been born in Paris would be required to leave for their birthplaces without delay. Soult, furthermore, decided to initiate this reform by making a striking example. A few weeks before he had taken up office the police had arrested a doctor who was traveling through France to Naples, where he held a post at Murat's Court. Among the papers found in this man's possession were two letters written by General Exelmans, the Inspector-General of Cavalry. One was addressed to King Joachim himself, and in it Exelmans, who had been Murat's Aide-de-Camp, congratulated him on the fact that the Powers at Vienna had decided to leave him in undisturbed possession of his kingdom. "Had they not done so," added the General, "a thousand French officers trained in Your Majesty's school would have flown to your assistance." Exelman's other letter was directed to Murat's Aide-de-camp, and contained a reminder that there were certain arrears of pay owing to him. Dupont, after consulting with Louis, had sent for General Exelmans and had cautioned him to be more guarded in his language for the future. The matter had, in short, been treated as nothing more than an indiscretion. Soult, however, though the case had been dealt with and settled by his predecessor, determined to reopen it in a very different spirit. Exelmans was deprived of his appointment and placed on half-pay. This brought him within the provisions of*

Soult's recent regulation on the subject of officers so circumstanced. He was accordingly directed to leave Paris and take up residence at Bar-sur-Ornain, his native town. The General was a cavalry officer with a splendid record of service, but somewhat of a swashbuckler, and with a strong theatrical vein in his character. He was the last man to submit tamely to treatment of this kind. He protested that he had not been to Bar-sur-Ornain for twenty years, that Paris was his home except when away on duty, and that moreover, his wife was in an interesting condition and could not travel. As he persisted in refusing to obey the Minister's order, he was placed under arrest in his own house. The affair became the talk of the town, the Liberals, especially, espousing his cause warmly. Lafayette and Lanjuinais visited him, Madame de Stael wrote to congratulate him on his firm attitude. Soon all Paris heard that, when the police had entered the General's house, he had bared his breast and told them to kill him, that every cupboard and drawers had been ransacked, that Madame Exelmans had fainted, and that her husband had made his escape over the wall at the back of the house, leaving behind him a letter addressed to the President of the Chamber, in which he entrusted his family to the protection of the Assembly and protested against the treatment to which he had been subjected. A few days, however, after his sensational flight, General Exelmans surrendered himself to the military authorities and was sent to Lille to be tried. On January 23rd, 1815, he duly appeared before a Court Martial. In addition to the charge of refusing to obey an order of the Minister of War four other offences were alleged against him. The letter which he had written to Murat was described as an act of espionage, and he was, further, charged with speaking in a disrespectful manner about the King. The trial was soon over. Exelmans was unanimously acquitted on all counts. Soult had only succeeded in making him a popular hero.[264]

---

264 Hall, Sir John Richard, *The Bourbon Restoration*, (London, 1909), pp. 52-53 http://books.google.com/books?id=Aj1BAAAAIAAJ

APPENDIX III
Questions of Treason

Janin's Rebuttal to the Impact of Treason

Janin played a key role during the campaign, and left some valuable recollections. He was also critical of Napoleon, and did not believe treason played a significant role in the campaign. He was an eye witness to this history, yet like all veterans, lacked access to the correspondence that we have available to us today. Regardless, it seems only fair to offer his observations on the campaign as a rebuttal of sorts, starting on page 45 of his *Campagne de Waterloo*:

> *Scholars have already elaborated on, in an illuminating critique, and even in the interest of art, the errors made in this campaign; I have not made the presumptuous claim to exceed or even to equal them, but I believe I must present, based on a fact yet too recent to be familiar, some new considerations: I also believe I must respond to unjust recriminations published in Napoleon's name, and whose praise of disappointed ambition attempts to malign the conduct of an army to which, made an abstraction of the primitive cause that gave him existence, any Frenchman must be honored to have belonged.*
>
> *In summary: fate that Napoleon remained on the defensive, that he is resolved to attack, the fight could engage only on the northern border.*
>
> *The enemy could easily be informed of the movements of the army towards this point without the help of treason.*

The desertion of a very small number of individuals cannot as a result be regarded as the main cause, nor even as a notable cause of the disasters of this campaign.

The first real cause is the delay of the march of the advanced guard corps, ordered by General Vandamme. This general is not responsible if he did not receive the orders that were addressed to him.

The first duty of a general is to take all possible steps to make the orders arrive and to ensure that they can in fact arrive. It is because this condition was not met that on the 15th the army could advance in the direction of Fleurus approximately only one league beyond Charleroi.

Every indication is that Marshal Ney did not accept precise enough orders, nor instructions detailed enough for the operations with which he was charged. Nevertheless, by driving, on the 15th, his advanced guard until before Frasne, he did all that he could reasonably do: he was then within four miles of Charleroi, and not as claimed at the level of the canon noise fired on his line.

The direction that he gave to Gérard's division in this circumstance is proof of his insight and his dedication: if he did not have an effect, it is because he was too distant, or, more precisely, too forward of the corps' center with which he held the left.

The marshal's occupation of Quatre-Bras could only have regrettable results, because it was too isolated. Bringing a corps of twenty thousand men between an army of sixty thousand and another of seventy thousand, without support and away from any assistance by four to five miles, is one of these gigantic undertakings that for one random success will produce a thousand defeats.

Count d'Erlon's corps remained at Marchiennes-au-Pont: it is not proven, it is even very improbable that this delay can be traced to the Marshal.

On the 16th, Napoleon attacked the Prussians hard by their right and weakly by their left, facilitating their junction with the English, which had to be avoided. Blücher's position, being the same as that of Prince Waldeck in 1690, most certainly would maneuver as did Marshal de Luxembourg. To say that the attack on Saint-Amand was halted by the appearance of Erlon's corps from behind is an

Appendix III – Questions of Treason

excuse which itself is not valid under the slightest examination. The proximity of this corps, on the contrary, favors the plans of Napoleon.

The Marshal's position was somewhat unfavorable, he did not acquire any less glory on the day of the 16th by stopping the English army with a force at least double of his; he thus prevented it from achieving its union with the Prussian army, and the goal of Napoleon was fulfilled in this respect. If he did not have more decisive accomplishments for his side, it is not the Marshal's fault.

It is indisputable that the Fleurus matter ultimately was reduced nearly to insignificance as far as its results; regardless of what some official journals stated, Napoleon judged himself by it, and what proves this is the time wasted with acknowledgements and fumbling in the morning of the 17th.

General Grouchy's detachment can only be explained by the interpretation concerning the proximity of the English army; his retreat had to determine the recall of this detachment. In any event he was essential to ensure communication with the main corps.

It is generally unfavorable to plan a battle line on the extension of its line of operations by forming too sharp of an angle with this line, because the slightest reverse can create a loss and find the enemy in control of the most essential communications, and this consideration at least impedes the general from easily using his reserves. Based on this concept, we had a prelude to the Battle of Waterloo with the occupation of the Hougoumont woods; the two pronged attack on this important post and the English center gave our line this faulty direction. The failure experienced on the center is not attributable to Napoleon, but he could have repaired it in time had he not been occupied with the attack at the woods to the extent that his reserves were concentrated.

Marshal Ney did not make an error in advancing his cavalry, in the absence of infantry to support and rally his infantry in rout; but the fault is that this cavalry was committed too heavily and for too long a time, because the infantry reserves were not there ready to replace those who were beaten, and this error is the consequence of the omission of the concept described above. In truth the reserves quickly moved ahead and were distracted from their destination by the unexpected arrival of the Prussian corps, but it is no less true that their separation had already caused greater damage than the speed and precision of their movement was completely able to restore.

The army, or more accurately, all the individuals of the army, acted with the devotion of those who never gave a greater example, and no one can mistake the patriotic sentiments that inspired them.

I could add more comments, but I fear to be overcome by the emotional intensity that I feel: I especially hesitate to give additional incentive to the partisanship, to which, after having had the pleasure to escape since my return to France, I want and must always remain foreign.

In conclusion of this writing, I learned that M. Gamot, brother-in-law of Marshal Ney, formally denied all allegations brought against him, and that he has propagated the questions which gave rise to the knowledge that any friend of the truth and national glory so deeply desires. He had just been taken from the unfortunate family for whom he had become the father and support. Young people and noble orphans, do not be overcome by this latest stroke of fortune. Adversity hardens big hearts, it is there that they are strengthened, it is at this school that you will learn to support the luster of a name that is associated with a long list of great and beautiful acts; only one fault had tarnished it, but by paying with his head, by paying to atone the last drop of this blood so often shed for the country, your father left you to inherit all of the glory that he had acquired for you: preparing you in study and reflection to educate with dignity. Can this wish by one of his former soldiers reach you, revive your courage and sweeten the bitterness of your regrets!

Traitors of 1815

Betraying, or deserting, one's country in time of war is a huge action to take. In 1815, the situation was not so clear. A royalist would have sincere loyalties to the King. Someone could also object to Napoleon's rule as being despotic. And for some, treason was an opportunity for personal gain or advancement. Whatever the motivation, in 1815 there were many traitors, including from the Army, and worst of all, during hostilities.

Appendix III – Questions of Treason

Soldier desertion has been a common event for most armies throughout history, and it was for all armies that fought in 1815. However, this is a list dominated by officers.

Considering Soult's persecution of Imperial Army veterans while serving as the King's Minister of War, it is not hard to believe that Soult considered his treason in 1815 as nothing more than working for the other side, albeit always with an eye towards his own reward.

One has to consider that for every known instance, there were probably many others.

Minister of Police Joseph Fouché – March 1st, 1815 through June 22nd, 1815

François Guizot – Resigned as Secretary-General of the Ministry of the Interior upon Napoleon's return, but subsequently brought intelligence to Ghent, leaving Paris on May 23rd, 1815.

Tabarie, Head of Recruitment services in Ministry of War – Paid spy of Ghent. From *Les Royalistes contre l'Armee (1815-1820)*, as well as in Volume X of Wellington's *Supplementary Despatches*, p. 135.

Sigismond du Pouget de Nadaillac – During the first restoration was made a Colonel and an aide-de-camp of the Minister of War. Brought some form of intelligence to Wellington, from *Notes on Conversations with the Duke of Wellington, 1831-1851* by Stanhope.

Adjutant Commander Count of Boulogne Lascours – Paid spy of Ghent in the defence ministry. From *Les Royalistes contre l'Armee (1815-1820)*

Chef d'escadron Moriez – 6th Lancers, Reille notifies Defence Ministry of desertion on April 29.

Battalion Commander Bois-David – 17th Line, d'Erlon notifies Defense Ministry on April 29; name published on May 12 in Moniteur

Capitaine d'Andre – 1st Lancers, arrived in Ghent on May 13, 1815. From *Le Marechal Davout, Prince D'Eckmuhl, Un Dernier Commandement*.

Colonel Marie-Joseph-Andre-Augustin de Capriol de Saint-Hilaire – 28th Ligne, I Corps. During concentration march from Valenciennes, as the 28th Ligne passed Orchies, he left for Ghent and was replaced by Colonel Saint-Michel. From *Memoires de Canler: ancien chef du Service de Sureté* by Louis Canler, 1862, page 10.

Capitaine Dambray – 1st Lancers, son of Chancellor Dambray. Deserts on May 15th

Colonel Arnaud de Saint-Sauveur – deserts and Davout orders arrest on June 5th. Ends up as Captain in Chasseurs of Garde Royale. From *Les Royalistes contre l'Armee (1815-1820)*.

Adjutant Doisonville – 7th Hussars, name published on May 12 in Moniteur

Capitaine Naylies – name published May 12 in La Gazette de France, ends up Chasseurs of Garde Royal.

Sous-Lieutenant Buisseret – name published after May 12 in La Gazette de France, ends up in Chasseurs of Garde Royale.

Colonel and two Soldiers – In a history of the Kings German Legion, the following example is used as an example of frequent defection: at Comines, north west of Lille sitting on the river Lys, two French soldiers were coaxed into crossing sides. The Colonel demanded their return, before crossing over himself a few days later. See Bernhard Heinrich Schwertfeger's *Geschichte der königlich Deutschen Legion, 1803-1816*, Volume 2, page 272.

Captain Jallot – 11th Chasseurs à Cheval, letter to Duc de Feltre giving information about strength and spirit of Imperial army on June 12.

Trooper of 5th Lancers – Mentioned in a June 13th report of Baron de Collaert, found in *Prins Frederik der Nederlanden en zijn tijd* by de Bas. http://babel.hathitrust.org/cgi/pt?id=wu.89097621346;view=1up;seq=713

Major Adrim – Named by *Niles Weekly Register, Volume 12* as being bribed by Paris Royalists and having deserted on June 13.

Drum-Major – Mentioned by Jomini and Lettow-Vorbeck, possibly from the Guard, which alerted Zeiten of imminent attack on the night of the 13th. Is this Major Adrim?

General Bourmont – General of the 14th Infantry Division of IV Corps, went over the enemy on morning of June 15, and also responsible for giving intelligence to Prussians on June 14th.

Colonel Clouet – Bourmont Chief of Staff

Chef d'Escadron Adjudant Charles Villoutreys – ADC to Clouet

Capitaine d'Andigne – ADC to Bourmont

Lieutenant d'Trelan - ADC to Bourmont

Capitaine Sourdat – Adjudant part of Bourmont's staff

Lieutenant of the 11th Chasseurs – mentioned as crossed over to the enemy in the Bulletin of June 15th but not identified.

Colonel Gordon – Chief of Staff to General Durutte, 4th Division I Corps, went to the enemy the morning of the 16th.

Appendix III – Questions of Treason

Commander Gaugler – ADC to General Durutte, 4th Division I Corps, went to the enemy the morning of the 16th.
Colonel Laderiac – Grouchy's Staff went to the enemy on the 16th.
Six members of the General Staff - "were said" to have gone over to the enemy after the battle of Ligny on the 16th according to Captain Coignet, see his memoirs, page 169 from the 1st edition published in 1851.
Capitaine Du Barail – Went over to the Anglo-Dutch lines at battle of Waterloo on the 18th prior to attack of Imperial Guard as recorded in personnel dossier at Ministry of War archives. Other troopers are reported to have done the same.

Mauduit's suggestions of Treason

About the possibility that traitors existed amongst orderlies of the various head-quarters staffs, starting on page 170 of 2nd edition:

> *Si jamais il y eût de l'incurie dans l'expédition des ordres de mouvements, donnés à une armée, ce fut dans cette malheureuse journée du 16 juin, et nous sommes encore à nous demander s'il n'y eût pas autant de perfidie que de maladresse dans la manière dont ce service si important lut fait et dirigé pendant toute cette campagne.*
>
> *Ainsi; pendant que des généraux, des officiers supérieurs ou autres employés aux divers états-majors de l'armée, passaient sans scrupule dans le camp ennemi, d'autres plus infâmes encore, ne restaient peut-être dans nos rangs que pour rendre leur trahison plus profitable et plus méritoire!...*
>
> *Nous avons repoussé longtemps l'idée de la possibilité d'un pareil crime, mais cette accusation terrible nous échappe malgré nous; car rien encore n'a pu chasser cette espèce de cauchemar qui nous poursuit depuis que nous avons consacré nos veilles à chercher la vérité! sur la révolution des Cent-Jours.*
>
> *A chaque pas, nous avons rencontré des traîtres sous les deux cocardes, et des partis soudoyant la trahison. Comment alors s'étonner si le germe en resta parmi nous, s'il dut produire des fruits empoisonnés?*

Nous le disons donc avec douleur, mais avec la conviction la plus profonde : il y eût peut-être autant de trahison que d'incurie dans le service des dépêches, avant comme après avoir franchi la frontière.

Que chacun fasse son examen de conscience, et plus d'un, en se reportant à cette fatale époque, devra, nous n'en doutons pas, se sentir déchiré par le remords, car il aura contribué, non-seulement à nos désastres, mais encore à l'humiliation de la France, en paralysant ou livrant à l'ennemi, des dépêches confiées à son patriotisme, comme à son honneur.

Suivons maintenant, pied à pied, les opérations du premier corps, que la fatalité ou la trahison ont empêché ce jour-là de nous assurer la plus éclatante des victoires modernes, en nous donnant pour trophées Wellington ou Blücher avec l'une ou l'autre des deux armées qu'ils commandaient.

Translated:

If ever there was negligence in the dispatch of the movement orders, given to an army, it was on this unfortunate day of June 16, and we still ask ourselves whether there was as much treachery as clumsiness in this respect which was so important a service to be read and guided during this entire campaign.

Thus, while generals, senior officers, or other employed in the various army staffs, passed without scruple in the enemy camp, others yet more infamous, remained in our ranks only to make their treason more profitable and more meritorious! ...

We rejected for a long time the idea of the possibility of a similar crime, but this terrible accusation escaped us despite us, because nothing still could expel this kind of nightmare that follows us since we devoted our vigils to finding the truth! for the Hundred Days revolution.

With each step, we met traitors under the two cockades, and the parties bribing treason. How then can we be surprised if the germ remained among us, if it had produced poisoned fruits?

We therefore say with pain, but with deep conviction: perhaps there was as much treason as negligence in the dispatch services, before and after crossing the border.

Appendix III – Questions of Treason

For each one examines his conscience, and more one, while referring to this fatal time, will have, we don't doubt, feel torn by the remorse, because it will have contributed, not only to our disasters, but more to the humiliation of France, while paralyzing or delivering to the enemy, the dispatches trusted to its patriotism, its honor.

Let's follow now, step by step, the operations of the first corps, that destiny or treason was prevented this day from ensuring us the brightest of modern victories, while we give our trophies to Wellington or Blücher with one or the other of the two armies which they commanded.

Page 193

Hommage à qui de droit, et surtout aux officiers subalternes et aux soldats! mais blâme et blâme sévère aussi a qui n'y fit pas son devoir! !! Anathème enfin aux traitres et aux transfuges de cette journée mémorable!...

Il est étrange, on en conviendra, que de Fleurus ni de Frasne, on ne se soit pas réciproquement rendu compte des résultats de la journée, par des rapports ou des communications officielles, si indispensables cependant pour les opérations due lendemain.

L'Empereur, le croirait-on, n'apprit que, dans la matinée du 17, et seulement par le retour du comte Flahaut, ce qui s'était passe aux Quatre Bras, alors qu'il eût été du devoir du prince de la Moskowa de lui en faire parvenir le rapport, au moins sommaire, si non détaillée, avant le point du jour. N'eut-il pas dû y avoir toujours en route, et d'heure en heure, des officiers allant du quartier impérial à celui du prince de la Moskowa et vice-versa, comme l'eut certainement exige le prince Berthier?...

De son côté, le maréchal duc de Dalmatie, qui se montra, pendant toute cette campagne, si peu à la hauteur de ses éminentes fonctions, ne parait pas avoir mieux compris de quelle importance il était que le commandant en chef de l'aile gauche connut le résultat de la bataille de Ligny, pour sa gouverne à l'égard de l'armée anglaise, car, chose inouïe! Nous trouvons une étrange NAIVETE dans la lettre adressée, le 17 juin A MIDI, de Fleurus au prince de la Moskowa par le duc de Dalmatie, sur la bataille de Ligny, dont le Marechal Ney se plaignait avec raison d'ignorer les résultats :

« *JE CROIS CEPENDANT VOUS AVOIR PREVENU DE LA VICTOIRE QUE L'EMPEREUR A REMPORTEE, etc. etc. etc.,* » *JE CROIS CEPENDANT!... Oui! voilà comment le major-général de 1815 a expliqué son étrange silence envers le maréchal Ney !...*

De deux choses l'une, ou le major-général a eu recours à un mensonge pour couvrir une aussi coupable négligence, ou l'officier, porteur de son message, est encore allé le remettre à Wellington ou a Blücher, ainsi que paraissent l'avoir fait les officiers expédiés au maréchal Grouchy dans la journée et dans la nuit du 17 et que celui-ci affirme n'avoir point vus.

Quel génie pouvait désormais lutter contre tant d'incurie, d'insouciance, de mauvais vouloir, de rivalités jalouses, de trahisons patentes ou secrètes, alors surtout que les éléments allaient aussi se liguer contre nous tous, pauvres soldats, qui ne cherchions qu'à venger la patrie de ses humiliations de 1814?...

Tant de mauvaises directions, de lenteurs, de retards prolongés, inexplicables encore pour la plupart, se continuant et renouvelant sans cesse dans le service de l'état-major-général, ont trop souvent rendue nulle et sans effet la volonté de l'Empereur.

Translated:

Homage to those concerned, and especially to the subordinate officers and the soldiers! but also blame and severe blame to those who did not perform his duty there !!! Anathema finally to the traitors and the defectors of this memorable day! ...

It is strange, one must admit, that of Fleurus nor of Frasne, we reciprocally will not realize the results of the day, by reports or official communications, if essential however for the operations necessary on the following day.

The Emperor, it is believed, only learned, in the morning of the 17th, and only by the return of Count Flahaut, who was going to Quatre Bras, whereas it had been up to the Prince of Moscow to forward the report, at least in summary, if non-detailed, before

Appendix III – Questions of Treason

the dawn of the day. Had he not always had to be en route, and hour by hour, the officers going from the imperial quarter to that of the Prince of Moscow and vice versa, as had certainly demanded Prince Berthier? ...

For his part, Marshal Duke de Dalmatie, who showed, during all of this campaign, so little to the level of his eminent duties, does not appear to have understood how important it was that the commander in chief of the left wing know the result of the Battle of Ligny, for his direction in regard to the English army, because, some incredible thing! We find a strange NAIVETY in the letter addressed, on June 17 TO MIDI, from Fleurus to the Prince of Moscow by the Duke de Dalmatie, on the battle of Ligny, about which Marshal Ney complained with reason to be unaware of the results:

"I BELIEVE NEVERTHELESS YOU HAVE ANTICIPATED THE VICTORY THAT THE EMPEROR HAS WON, etc. etc. etc.," I BELIEVE NEVERTHELESS! ... Yes! here is how the major general of 1815 explained his strange silence towards Marshal Ney! ...

One of two things, either the Major-Général had recourse to lie to cover such culpable negligence, or the officer, bearing his message, went on to give it to Wellington or to Blücher, as well as appearing to have the officers dispatched to Marshal Grouchy in the day and in the night of the 17th and that he affirms not to have seen.

What genius could from now on fight against negligence, carelessness, ill will, jealous rivalries, evident or secret treason, then especially as the elements were also in league against us all, poor soldiers, who only seek to avenge the homeland for it's humiliations of 1814? ...

So many bad directions, slowness, prolonged delays, unexplainable still for the most part, continuing and renewing unceasingly in the service of the general staff, too often nullified and without the will of the Emperor.

Footnote on Page 372 Volume 2

Un écrivain qui a entrepris de justifier les actes militaires du maréchal Grouchy pendant les Cent-Jours, porte à cette occasion une très grave accusation contre l'officier chargé de cette dépêche, et voici en quels termes il la porte:

« *Cette rédaction, au moins étrange, ne put recevoir sa véritable explication, car l'officier porteur de la dépêche était* TELLEMENT IVRE, *qu'il fut impossible d'en tirer aucun éclaircissement.* » *(Revue de l'Empire, année 1842, page 402).*

Il est de l'honneur de cet officier, s'il vit encore, de repousser une pareille accusation; comme il est de l'honneur aussi de l'officier envoyé en mission le premier de tous au maréchal Grouchy, dans la journée du 17, d'expliquer comment il n'est point parvenu à sa destination, tandis qu'on l'accuse d'avoir livré volontairement à Blücher, en passant à l'ennemi la dépêche importante qui lui avait été confiée, et dont la communication décida, nous a-t-on écrit, la marche précipitée de Bulow sur notre flanc droit.

Ou donc M. le duc de Dalmatie avait-il été prendre ses officiers d'état-major, pour avoir eu autour de lui des traitres, des ivrognes ou des imbécilles, montés sur des mulets?

Translated:

A writer who undertook to justify the military actions of Marshal Grouchy during the Hundred Days, brings on this occasion a very serious accusation against the officer charged with this dispatch, and here are the terms that it bears:

"This writing, strange at least, could not receive his true explanation, because the officer carrying the dispatch was SO DRUNK, that it was impossible to draw any clarification from it." (Revue de l'Empire, year 1842, page 402).

It is the honor of this officer, if he yet lives, to return a similar accusation; as it is also the honor of the officer sent on the first mission of all to Marshal Grouchy, on the day of the 17th, to explain how he has not arrived at his destination, while being accused of having voluntarily delivered to Blücher, passing to the enemy the important dispatch that had been entrusted to him, and whose communication decided, written to us, the march hastened from Bulow on our right flank.

Appendix III – Questions of Treason

Or had therefore M. Duke de Dalmatie taken his staff officers, having been among traitors, drunkards or imbeciles, mounted on mules?

Page 420 Volume 2, Footnote (b)

Nous ignorons à qui doit en revenir la triste responsabilité. Est-ce au major-général ou à ceux qui, ayant reçu des ordres, ne les auraient pas exécutés à temps ou avec intelligence ? Car, dans cette malheureuse campagne, que de fautes à reprocher à l'état-major de l'armée, fautes que nous n'aurions pas eu à déplorer avec le maréchal Berthier, dont l'activité était si précieuse et si rare, qui savait deviner la pensée de l'Empereur et dont la ponctualité dans l'exécution de ses ordres était telle qu'il eut envoyé vingt officiers, au lieu d'un, au maréchal Grouchy pour le forcer, au besoin, à hâter sa marche et l'empêcher, comme nous l'avons dit, de s'amuser à manger des fraises, lorsqu'il ne devait pas laisser à l'armée prussienne le temps de reprendre haleine.

Si quelque chose a dû et doit encore surprendre, c'est le silence gardé par M. le maréchal Soult sur cette campagne de 1815, dont, mieux que personne, il a dû connaître tous les mystères, et il en aurait d'importants et de curieux à dévoiler !.. On ne saurait considérer son mémoire justificatif, comme un document militaire de l'époque ; il a pu satisfaire alors les calculs personnels de M. le maréchal, mais non certes l'armée, dont il fut le major-général. Sa conscience aurait-elle des reproches à se faire ?.. Tant pis, car l'histoire alors sera inexorable pour le major-général de la grande armée, s'il vient à être prouvé qu'il n'a pas rempli ses éminentes fonctions loyalement, comme avec intelligence et dévouement.

Il serait donc utile à l'histoire, aussi bien qu'à la réputation de M. le maréchal duc de Dalmatie, qu'il voulut bien rassembler ses matériaux, recueillir ses souvenirs et surtout faire connaître, avec la PLUS SCRUPULEUSE VERITE et sans restrictions, tout ce qu'il doit savoir sur cette campagne ; car, à l'exception de quelques ordres donnes et signes par lui, il n'est nulle part question de sa coopération ; nous serons peut-être même le premier à le mettre en scène à cette occasion.

Translated:

We are unaware of to whom must return the sad responsibility. Is it for the Major-Général or those who, having received the orders, would not have carried them out in time or with intelligence? Because, in this unhappy campaign, the faults to reproach the army staff, faults that we would have had to deplore with Marshal Berthier, whose activity was so valuable and so rare, who could guess the thought of the Emperor and whose punctuality in the execution of its orders was such that he sent twenty officers, instead of one, with Marshal Grouchy to force him, as needed, to hasten his march and to prevent him, as we said, from having the enjoyment to eat strawberries, when he had to deny the Prussian army time to take another breath.

If something had and must still surprise us, it is the silence kept by M. Marshal Soult on this 1815 campaign, from whom, better than anyone, he had to know all the mysteries, and he would have the important and curious ones to reveal!.. One could not consider his Mémoire Justificatif, as a military document of the era; it could satisfy the personal calculations of M. Marshal, but certainly not the army, of which he was the Major-Général. His conscience would make the necessary reproaches? Too bad, because history then will be inexorable for the Major-Général of the grand army, if it suddenly has been proven that he did not fulfill his eminent duties honestly, with intelligence and devotion.

It would therefore be useful for the history, as well as for the reputation of M. Marshal Duke de Dalmatie, that he wanted to gather his materials, collect his memoirs and especially make known, with the MOST SCRUPULOUS TRUTH *and without restrictions, all that he must know about this campaign; because, except for some orders given and signals from him, his cooperation is not mentioned; we will be perhaps the first to demonstrate this for the occasion.*

Page 527 Volume 2

Après de telles génuflexions, de telles palinodies, le maréchal Soult n'était-il pas, en effet, en droit de s'écrier contre l'application qui lui était faite de l'ordonnance du 24 juillet ?.. Ne devait-on pas,

Appendix III – Questions of Treason

des lors, élever ce zélé défenseur de la légitimité, a la haute dignité de connétable de France, en reconnaissance du dévoument dont il fit preuve après la chute de l'Empereur, dévoument que nous allons raconter, puisque, par modestie sans doute, M. le maréchal n'en a parlé, que par allusion, dans son Mémoire Justificatif; les détails que nous allons rapporter, nous les tenons de M. le lieutenant-général Brun de Villeret, qui nous en a garanti l'exactitude.

Apres nos désastres dc Waterloo, le maréchal duc de Dalmatie, qui était allé chercher un asile dans les montagnes de la Lozère, arriva subitement, le 7 juillet, chez le général Brun de Villeret, son ancien secrétaire-général, et qui, pendant les Cent-Jours, s'était retiré dans sa terre du Malrieu prés Mende.

Le maréchal se présenta au général, la cocarde blanche au chapeau, et sa première parole fut: « qu'il venait dans l'intention de prendre part à l'insurrection royaliste du midi. »

Le maréchal en informa aussitôt les autorités constituées de la commune et chargea le même jour deux personnes que lui indiqua le général Brun de Villeret de se rendre à Mende pour en instruire le Conseil Royal institue dans cette ville. Ces ouvertures furent, comme on le pense bien, favorablement accueillies; on lui envoya donc des députés pour l'inviter à venir au chef-lieu. Le maréchal accepta avec empressement et annonça qu'il s'y rendrait aussitôt l'arrivée de ses bagages, c'est-à-dire dans deux jours. Mais dans cet intervalle, les têtes s'étaient montées, en raison du rôle qu'avait joué le due de Dalmatie pendant l'interrègne. La fermentation augmentait, des rassemblements de gardes nationaux se formèrent dans différentes localités pour arrêter le maréchal au Malrieu. Afin de prévenir ces mesures violentes, le maréchal se décida à partir pour Mende, sur-le-champ, c'est-à-dire le 10 juillet, et il demanda au général Brun de Villeret de lui fournir une escorte pour sa sûreté. Celui-ci l'accompagna lui-même à la tête de quelques détachements de gardes nationaux, et il eut à lutter en route contre des détachements d'autres communes qui voulaient s'emparer de sa personne.

Arrivé à Mende, Le Marechal se mit à la disposition du Conseil Royal, qui lui fit donner sa parole de ne pas sortir de la ville jusqu'à ce que le gouvernement eût donné des ordres à son égard. Mais le Conseil Royal, craignant des excès de la part de quelques têtes

exaltées, le fit détenir dans l'hôtel de la préfecture, jusqu'à ce qu'un ordre du ministre de la police vint terminer cet incident, en ordonnant de délivrer des passeports a M. le due de Dalmatie, pour se rendre dans la commune ou il lui plairait de résider, et il partit pour Saint-Amans, le 2 août, et y arriva le 7.
Le lendemain de son arrivée à Mende, le 11 juillet, le maréchal Soult comparut devant le Conseil Royal du département, composé de MM. de Pressac, préfet; l'abbé de Fayet, chargé de pouvoirs du due d'Angoulême; le comte de Corsac, général commandant le département de la Lozère; le comte de Chambrun, inspecteur général; le vicomte de Lescure, chef d'état-major; d'Angles, colonel du régiment des gardes nationales d'élite, ancien colonel; Chapelain, sous-préfet de Mende; Reboul, conseiller de préfecture.
Devant ce conseil, le Maréchal se plaignit des mesures de surveillance exercées contre sa personne, et fit l'expose de sa conduite.
Cet expose fut écrit sous la dictée du maréchal Soult, et signe de sa main; voici ce curieux document historique :
« Il dit que, depuis son retour à Paris, venant de l'armée, jusqu'au moment de son départ pour les départements du Midi, qui eut lieu le 3 juillet, il avait constamment représenté, soit à la Commission du Gouvernement provisoire, soit à la Chambre des Pairs dans des comités particuliers, soit à un conseil de guerre qui fut tenu au faubourg de La Villette, le 1er juillet, a neuf heures du soir, auquel tous les maréchaux de France, présents à Paris, furent appelés, soit à différents membres de la Chambre des Représentants, ou soit à d'autres personnes en place, qu'APRES AVOIR FORCE Napoléon a ABDIQUER, L'ON AURAIT DU ENVOYER SUR_LE_CHAMP un députation à S. M. Louis XVIII, pour lui porter DES ACTES DE SOUMISSION, AU LIEU DE PROLONGER LES MAUX DE LA France EN ENTRETENANT LA NATION ET L'ARMEE DANS DES ILLUSIONS CHIMERIQUES ; QU'IL VOYAIT AVEC PEINE QU'ON PRENAIT DES DISPOSITIONS POUR DEFENDRE PARIS, ou toute l'armée se trouvait concentrée ; QU'IL NE CROYAIT PAS QUE LA VALEUR DES TROUPES, ni la bonté des lignes que l'on avait élevées sur les deux rives de la Seine pussent préserver la capitale de l'invasion dont elle était menacée ; qu'il était à craindre que les

troupes, MEME LES NOTRES, DONT L'INDISCIPLINE ETAIT TRES GRANDE NE SE PORTASENT AU PILLAGE ET NE COMMISSENT D'AUTRES EXCES.

En conséquence, il paraissait à l'opinant qu'il n'y avait pas un instant à perdre pour ordonne l'évacuation de Paris, et pour porter l'armée sur la rive gauche de la Loire, quand bien même la négociation que était ouverte serait sans résultats.

Il s'assura dans la nuit suivante, que les troupes étaient retirées ; IL EUT LA SATISFACTION D'AVOIR CONCOURU A SAUVER LA CAPITALE pour qu'à son arrivée le Roi LA TROUVAT INTACTE. Il s'était déterminé à partir pour les départements du Midi, OU IL SAVIT QUE L'INSURRECTION ETAIT PREPAREE, POUR RENDRE CETTE INSURRECTION GENERALE et LA DIRIGER DANS LES INTERETS DU BIEN DU SERVICE DE SA MAJESTE, JUSQU'A L'ARRIVEE des S. A. R. MONSEIGNEUR LE DUC D'ANGOULEME, VERS LEQUEL IL SE PROPOSAIT DE SE DIRIGER ET DE PRENDRE SES ORDRES... »

Puis, le maréchal Soult raconta les circonstances de son voyage, revint à plusieurs reprises sur SA CONSTANTE FIDELITE AU ROI, ET DEMANDA ACTE DE SES PAROLES, dont procès-verbal fut dresse et signe par lui, maréchal duc de Dalmatie, et les membres du conseil!!!...

Notre plume nous échappe des mains et nous laissons à chacun de nos lecteurs le soin de caractériser comme il l'entendra, une pareille monstruosité politique !....

Translation:

After such genuflections, such chants, Marshal Soult was not, indeed, right to cry out against the application that was made for him, the ordinance of July 24? Should we not, consequently, raise this zealous defender of legitimacy to the high office of Constable of France, in recognition of dedication of which was proof after the fall of the Emperor, dedication that we will relate, since by certain modesty, M. Marshal spoke about it, only by allusion, in his Mémoire Justificatif; the details which we will report, we have them from M. Lieutenant-General Brown of Villeret, which guarantees it's accuracy.

After our disasters at Waterloo, Marshal Duke de Dalmatie, who had gone to seek refuge in the mountains of Lozere, arrived suddenly on July 7, at the home of General Brun de Villeret, his former secretary-general, and who, during the Hundred Days, withdrew to his land in Malrieu near Mende.

The marshal presented himself to the general, white cocade on his hat, and his first word was: "that he came with the intention to take part in the royalist insurrection of Midi."

The marshal at once informed the authorities from the commune and the same day charged two people that told him General Brun de Villeret went to Mende to inform the Royal Council to be established in this town.

These overtures were, as it is thought, favorably accepted; we thus sent deputies to invite him to come to the administrative center. The marshal accepted readily and announced that he would go there immediately upon the arrival of his baggage; this is, within two days. But in this interval, the heads were assembled, because of the role that was played [by] Duke de Dalmatie during the interregnum. Fermentation increased, assemblies of national guards were formed in various localities to halt the Marshal at Malrieu. In order to prevent these violent measures, the Marshal decided to leave for Mende, at once, on July 10, and he asked General Brun de Villeret to provide him an escort for his safety. He accompanied this himself at the head of several detachments of national guards, and he had to fight on the way against detachments of other communes that wanted to seize his person.

Arriving at Mende, the Marshal placed himself at the disposal of the Royal Council, which made him give his word not to leave the city until the government had given the orders for his regard. But the Royal Council, fearing excesses on behalf of some exalted heads, made him remain in the hotel of the prefecture, until an order of the minister of the police conclude this incident, while ordering the delivery of passports to M. Duke de Dalmatie, to go within the commune where he pleased to reside, and he left for Saint-Amans, on August 2, and arrived there on the 7th.

APPENDIX III – QUESTIONS OF TREASON

The next day after his arrival at Mende, on July 11, Marshal Soult appeared before the Royal Council of the department, composed of MM. de Pressac, prefect; Abbey de Fayet, responsible authority for Duke de Angouleme; Count de Corsac, Commander General of the department of Lozere; Count de Chambrun, Inspector General; Vicount de Lescure, Chief of Staff; d'Angles, Colonel of the regiment of the elite national guards, former colonel; Chaplain, sub-prefect of Mende; Reboul, prefecture counselor.

Before this council, the Marshal complained about the surveillance measures used against his person, and presents his conduct.

This account was written under the dictation from Marshal Soult, and signed by his hand; here is this curious historical document:

"He said that, since his return to Paris, coming from the army, until the time of his departure for the departments at Midi, who was there on July 3rd, he had constantly represented either at the Commission du Gouvernement Provisiore, or at the Chambre des Paris in the particular committees, or at a war counsel held at Faubourg de La Villette, on the 1st of July, at nine o'clock in the evening, to which the Marshals of France, present in Paris, were called, either with various members of the Chamber of Representatives, or with others present, AFTER HAVING FORCED Napoleon TO ABDICATE, ONE WOULD HAVE TO SEND A FIELD ENVOY, a delegation to S. M. Louis XVIII, to bring him ACTS OF SUBMISSION, INSTEAD OF PROLONGING THE SORROWS OF France BY KEEPING THE NATION AND THE ARMY IN CHIMERIC ILLUSIONS; THAT HE SAW WITH GRIEF THAT ONE MADE ARRANGEMENTS TO DEFEND PARIS, where the entire army was concentrated; THAT HE DID NOT BELIEVE THE VALUE OF THE TROOPS, nor the kindness of the lines that we have raised on the two banks of the Seine that can protect the capital from the invasion from which she was threatened; that he was concerned that these troops, EVEN OURS, WHOSE INDISCIPLINE WAS VERY GREAT NOT TO BRING PILLAGE AND NOT COMMIT OTHER EXCESSES.

Consequently, he appeared to consent that there was not an instant to lose to order the evacuation of Paris, and to bring the army on the left bank of the Loire, when even the negotiation which was open would be without results.

He made sure the following night that the troops were withdrawn; HE HAD THE SATISFACTION TO HAVE CONTRIBUTED TO SAVE THE CAPITAL so that on his arrival the King WOULD FIND IT INTACT. He was determined to leave for the departments of Midi, WHERE HE KNEW THAT THE INSURRECTION WAS READY, TO TAKE THIS GENERAL INSURRECTION and DIRECT IT IN THE INTERESTS OF THE GOOD OF HIS MAJESTY'S SERVICE, UNTIL THE ARRIVAL of S.A.R. MONSEIGNEUR DUKE D'ANGOULEME, TO WHICH HE PROPOSED TO LEAD AND TAKE HIS ORDERS..."

Then, Marshal Soult recounted the circumstances of his trip, returned on several occasions on HIS CONSTANT FIDELITY TO THE KING, AND ASKED FOR CERTIFICATION OF HIS WORDS, whose statement was drawn up and signed by him, Marshal Duke de Dalmatie, and the members of the council!!! ... Our quill escapes our hands and leaves us to each of our readers the care to characterize as they will hear it, the same political monstrosity!....

On Traitors

Napoleon speaking on traitors:

The question did not depend on the conduct of an individual, however important he might be. It should be decided by the loss or gain of a battle, and had I, by accusing Fouché, anticipated that event, I should but have disturbed the stability of my government. I was obliged to have patience and wait, but I let Fouché see that I was not deceived. He has avenged himself for my contemptuous forbearance, but after Waterloo even without the presence of a man so dangerous as Fouché I should have been lost. Traitors are rarer than you think. Great vices and great virtues are the exceptions. Men, in general, are weak, and changeable because of their weakness, they seek their advantage wherever they can, advance their own interests without intending to injure others, and, on the whole, are more deserving of pity than blame. They must be taken and made use of as they are, and impelled to something higher when it is possible. Of this you may be sure, contempt will never elevate them. To induce them to exert their capabilities, you must lead them to believe themselves better than they are. In the army, cowards are made brave by telling them they are so. The only way to deal with men is to affect to believe that they possess the virtues with which you wish to inspire them.

In these words, one can find wisdom, but also the seeds of naiveté that allowed Napoleon to be deceived by so many.

APPENDIX IV
Traitors and Royalists

Royalists against the Army

In Edmond Bonnal de Ganges' book, *Les royalistes contre l'armée d'après les archives du Ministère de la guerre : 1815-1820*, he documents the Bourbon efforts to undermine Napoleon :

http://books.google.com/books?id=BVLR6avoI2MC

Page 37-38:

Pour amener la chute de Bonaparte, la cour de Gand acheta deux concours militaires à Paris dans les bureaux de la guerre, le premier, celui de Tabarié avoué par Wellington dans sa correspondance; le second, celui de l'adjudant-commandant comte Boulogne de Lascours attaché au cabinet du prince d'Eckmuhl, aveu d'un rapport royaliste intercepté par notre gendarmerie et envoyé directement au ministre. Dans les deux cas, l'opinion ne fut qu'un prétexte, l'argent fut le mobile. L'émissaire qui donne le nom de Lascours déclarait qu'il fallait de l'argent, beaucoup d'argent, qu'à ce prix on aurait tout provenant du cabinet.

 Le fils du chancelier Dambray, capitaine du 1er Lanciers, déserta vers le 15 mai. Le chef d'état-major colonel Arnaud de Saint-Sauveur s'enfuyait de sa division, Davout ordonna son arrestation le 5 juin. Le 3, il écrivait à Lecourbe : « Nous devons éloigner de nos rangs tout être équivoque », *l'ennemi cherchant des traîtres. A Montmédy,* *le sous-préfet empechait l'exécution des ordres militaires sur la place. A Belfort, on tenta de corrompre Lecourbe comme Barbanégre à Huningue. Comment s'étonner lorsque le duc de Bellune écrivait au duc de Berry le 1er mai, qu'il fallait tirer le canon et qu'un général le mandait, le 8, à Wellington.**

Sur ces infamies et ces tristesses, il y a une conclusion à tirer. Elle n'est pas de nous celle-là ; elle émane d'un général en chef illustre dans la guerre, devenu maréchal de France aprés 1830, le comte Lobau. Lorsqu'il connut les appels a la désertion multipliés dans les troupes impériales cantonnees sur la frontiére, il repondit a leurs offres insultantes (80 francs pour un cavalier monté et 20 pour tout fantassin qui rejoindrait le camp d'Alost) par cette apostrophe :

« Voila le prix que mettent ces miserables à un vainqueur d'Austerlitz et de la Moskowa ! »

* : Le Moniteur du 12 mai livra au public le nom d'officiers passant à l'ennemi : Boisdavid chef de bataillon au 17e de ligne, Doisonville adjudant-major au 7e hussards. Ulterieurement les capitaines de Naylies, d'Andre, sous-lieutenant de Buisseret. La Gazette de France imprima les noms de ces derniers.

Translated:

To bring the fall of Bonaparte, the court of Ghent bought the help of two officers in Paris in the bureaux of the war, the first, that of Tabarié acknowledged by Wellington in his correspondence; the second, that of the Adjudant-Commander Count Boulogne de Lascours attaché to the cabinet of Prince d' Eckmuhl, admission of a royalist report intercepted by our gendarmerie and sent directly to the minister. In both cases, the sentiment was only a pretext, money was the motive. The emissary giving the name of Lascours declared that money was needed, much money, that at this price we would have everything from the cabinet.

The son of Chancelier Dambray, Captain of the 1st Lancers, deserted on about May 15. The chief of staff Colonel Arnaud de Saint-Sauveur fled his division, Davout ordered his arrest on June 5. On the 3rd, he wrote to Lecourbe: "We must keep away from our

Appendix IV – Traitors and Royalists

ranks all that are suspect", the enemy seeks the traitors. At Montmédy, the sub-prefect prevented the execution of the military orders on the square. At Belfort, they tried to corrupt Lecourbe like Barbanégre at Huningue. How surprised when the Duke de Bellune wrote to the Duke de Berry on May 1, that it was necessary to fire the canon and that a general sent word, on the 8th, to Wellington.*

Of these infamies and these sorrows, there is a conclusion to draw. It is not us; it emanates from a famous staff general in the war, becoming Marshal of France after 1830, Count Lobau. When he found that the calls for desertion multiplied within the imperial troops stationed on the frontier, he responded to their insulting offers (80 francs for a cavalier and 20 for any foot soldier which would join Camp d'Alost) by this quote:

"Here is the price that these wretches place on a winner of Austerlitz and Moscow!"

Le Monitor of May 12 delivered to the public the names of the officers passing to the enemy: Batallion Chief Boisdavid of the 17th line, Adjudant-Major Doisonville of the 7th Hussards. At a later date Captain Naylies, Andre, Second Lieutenant of Buisseret. La Gazette de France printed the names of the latter.

Treasonous Correspondence with Ghent

Excerpts of the correspondence at Ghent found in *Les Cent-Jours a Gand*, Volume 2 published in 1902 and written by M. Albert Malet.
http://books.google.com/books?id=Facf9oBJHqYC

No. 9.

Goltz to Hardenberg.

Ghent. June 2, 1815.

Your Royal Highness,

I take advantage of the first occasion that I have to convey to Your Highness, with the attached copy, a letter that I received from M. Duke de Feltre. The interesting details that it contains were provided to him by Mr. Guizot, secretary general in the ministry of the interior who got them directly from an employee in the office of Marshal Davoust. This M. Guizot has only arrived in Paris three days ago, where he continued his duties under the new Carnot ministry, with the intention of serving the Royal cause. We have ended however by dismissing him, because we are suspicious of him. Being known in Paris as a man of intellect and a very good observer, I asked that he give me a brief recollection of the state of France, and finding this extremely interesting I hurried to have it, through the attached copy, in front of Your Highness. I think fit to see that it agrees very well with the reports which I had the honor of making for him, during my stay in Paris since I returned there. I believe that I must yet add the following information, that I found and that I am able to record.

The public spirit is generally rather bad in Burgundy, but it is only partly so in Champagne, Alsace, Lorraine, and in the departments of Seine-et-Marne, Marne, and Aisne. In Dauphiné, the Jacobins have the advantage, and people only talk of the Republic there. The inhabitants of almost all the other provinces are royalist. There is not at this moment in France, not only no true party for the King of Rome and a regency; but it no longer exists even for the Duke d'Orleans, for whom the Jacobins makers do not assume, since the latest events, the courage necessary to sit on and maintain a usurped throne. France, in fact, is divided now by only two parties, that of the Bonapartists, to which Jacobins are associated by personal interest and because the majority of the army is in the hands of Bonaparte, and that of the royalists, having less energy than them, because they are less malicious, but who are without comparison the most numerous, and who request once again, unanimously, King Louis XVIII. The constitutional moderates are included in this party, because they believe with reason that Bonaparte, if he is maintained, will restore the early or later constitution; that any other sovereign by the choice of l'armée or the Jacobins will not offer any guarantee for the stability of conditions, and that King Louis XVIII after having proven his manner of thinking, by the constitutional

Appendix IV – Traitors and Royalists

charter that he has given to the nation without being forced, I will include in their plans consolidation of the work that he has started. Those who are elected from the constitutionals for the assembly of the Champ de Mai proposed to form an opposition to the Jacobins and the deputies of the army who must be part of it. But there is a fear that, not finding large enough numbers, they could not be actually useful to the cause of the King when the allied armies have achieved some success. It is more than likely that if the Jacobin leaders at present are not afraid to lose their fortunes and even their lives, as a consequence of the restoration of the legitimate dynasty, they would at once give up Bonaparte. Thibaudeau, famous Jacobin, said to Guizot, several days before his departure: "Your party is better than ours! Well, he replied, why do you persist in remaining in the position where you are? Because, he answered, we made too much of being able to indulge in forgetting the past without having a sufficient guarantee of it in advance."

We could not therefore conceal that there are two main things to do to avoid war, that will break out and be long and bloody:

1. Encourage the royalists in France with the hope of the return of Louis XVIII, and by the consideration for him, without however declaring officially that the allied powers want to force the nation to restore this sovereign.

2. Prevent, if possible, the allied troops from conveying feelings of indignation and vengeance that French control has inspired in them; because that can produce only a lack of discipline and countless excesses, that the French, more miserly with their properties and their money than with their lives, withstand with more difficulty than any other nation, would undoubtedly determine the mass of people to fight for Bonaparte.

The Duke of Wellington is also serious about the need to do this. His army also conducts itself in the most exemplary manner. But this army has until now the immense advantage of being received everywhere, because subsistence and needs for all individuals who form it are paid cash and at a high rate, that will, however, naturally cease with his entry into France. Bonaparte on the other hand, will attempt without a doubt, to obstruct the movements of the allied troops there while directing as many means of subsistence as possible from the east departments towards stores behind the lines, that he will be able to burn in the event of the approach of our armies.

The adjournment of the Champ de Mai seems to have been motivated mainly by the delay that saw many electors return to Paris, hoping that any type of crisis will excuse them from having to decide publicly for or against the current state of affairs.

Particular letters from Paris tell that Bonaparte proposed to go to the army immediately after the Champ de Mai assembly, which had only one or two meetings. Direct warnings from Vendée announce some advantages that the royalists gained there; but they have been forced, by Bonaparte's measures, to raise the standard of revolt against him, before they could be supported by the allied armies offensive, there is considerable fear that they will succumb to the number of troops which were sent to fight them.

Financial difficulties increase every day in France, because of the excessive expenditures for armaments and because taxes are not paid in many departments, so very inconsistently, and in others not at all. At the time of M. Guizot's departure, there was not more than two million in cash in the government treasury. Before finishing this report, I still have to remark to Your Highness that Carnot is now entirely in the hands of the usurper, who is at odds with Fouché, who tries to win over public opinion by easing all of the measures in force, but he is and will be always too cowardly to break openly and from the same vision as Bonaparte.

Mme Duchess d'Angouleme confirmed to me yesterday, when the ministers of Austria, Russia, and England also attended their court, all the confidence that they have in the raised feelings for His Majesty, our august sovereign, and in the valor generally admired of the Prussian army. This princess intends to return to London on the day after tomorrow. I will have the honor of dining with her today at the home of S.M. King of France.

The Duke of Wellington was, in the morning of the day before yesterday, here to hold court, and then proceeded to Alost to see 1,800 to 2,000 men in review who form the King's troop.

Appendix IV – Traitors and Royalists

By the third sheet included here, I had the honor of transmitting to Your Highness several new reports from emissaries or other individuals associated with the cause of the King of France.

Please accept, Your Royal Highness, the assurance of my respectful consideration.

No. 12

Goltz to Hardenberg.

Ghent, June 11, 1815.

Your Royal Highness,

I submit to Your Highness without delay the attached letter that I have just received from M. Duke de Feltre. The interesting notions that it contains were given to him by an officer arriving from Paris, with whom an employee in the office of the ministry of war confided them; but this officer dared not be responsible for carrying paper because of the danger that he risked in being stopped, could only use his memory for the transmission here.

APPENDIX TO DISPATCH No. 12

Clarke to Goltz.

Ministry of War

Ghent, June 10, 1815.

M. Count,

I received yesterday, rather late, the attached information that deserves a great deal of attention. It comes from the offices of the department of war and can show that with the help of all the means that he used, Bonaparte succeeded in increasing his troops quite significantly.

The person who sends these details to me and who is trained and perfectly sure, fearing to be compromised, chose not to give them in writing. They were confided to the memory of an old officer who has just arrived and having the sentiments that one can trust. However, he was less certain of it than what he said to me about the forces of Lecourbe, of Suchet, of Brune, and of the Pyrenees than of the rest. He was given the strength of the corps in round numbers and without fractions, and he said to me that they were raised to the highest because they were counted there in advance of everyone that was intended to join them and who will have joined them at the current time. This officer left Paris on June 4. I am led to think that this status has some exaggeration; this is why I placed the recapitulation here and, next to it, is what I believe is more plausible.

STATUS SENT FROM PARIS		CALCULATION That I Believe MORE EXACT
1st Corps (Count d'Erlon)	25,000 m.	20,000 m.
2nd Corps (Count Reille)	25,000 m.	20,000 m.
3rd Corps (Count Vandamme)	15,000 m.	10,000 m.
4th Corps (Count Gérard)	20,000 m.	15,000 m.
5th Corps (Count Rapp)	20,000 m.	15,000 m.
6th Corps (Count de Lobau)	15,000 m.	10,000 m.
Imperial Guard	20,000 m.	15,000 m.
Corps of General Lecourbe	8,000 m.	6,000 m.
Corps of Marshal Suchet	8,000 m.	4,000 m.
Corps of Marshal Brown, including the garrison of Marseilles	6,000 m.	5,000 m.
Corps of Bordeaux and the Pyrenees	15,000 m.	12,000 m.
Hospital and depots	50,000 m.	50,000 m.
Total	227,000 m.	182,000 m.
Difference	45,000 m.	

Appendix IV – Traitors and Royalists

This reduction does not appear exaggerated to me. It is founded on the first basis according to which I established the strength of the French Army next to the number of the regiments that constitute it. I am very inclined to believe that Bonaparte had five hundred pieces of harnessed cannon. It is to have his artillery in good condition that he would have used a large part of the funds that he was able to procure.

There are several corps of soldiers in retirement in various places, even the soldiers who have wooden legs.

Givet is a place in a bad state. It is certain that it is poorly defended, and the commander, whose name is Bour or Baer, testified, in correspondence with Prince d'Eckmühl (Davoust), to the concern about the capability to resist.

The officer who arrived to see me believed Bonaparte left Paris and thought that he could attack around the 10th, and push towards Namur.

The calculation of the number of national guards is conjectural. We could not obtain it exactly.

P. S. If the name of the commander from Givet, that we could not indicate accurately, was General Bourke, former aide de camp of Marshal Davoust, he would not have to conclude, from the letter that he wrote, that he was disposed to return the place, because he would be the man to defend until the very end.

François Guizot's Troubles

Guizot's trip to Ghent during 1815 would be a troubling cloud over his political career. However, it does not appear his opponents knew the full story of his treason. Had they, one can easily assume his political career would have come to an end once the Bourbon hysteria over all things Bonaparte had subsided. The following account, taken from *The New World, May 4, 1844* edition found in *The New World, Volume 8* published by J. Winchester, almost 30 years after Waterloo, demonstrates why anyone with political aspirations would, and in Guizot's case did, keep their treason in 1815 a secret:

A SCENE IN THE FRENCH CHAMBERS

Recent Paris papers, if they brought no important news, were yet interesting beyond those received from the same quarter during a very long time. During fifty years the French Legislative Chambers have not been the theatre of a scene so violent or so outrageous as that which, on Friday evening se' night, occurred in the Chamber of Deputies, recalling the dreadful period when law, justice, innocence, and humanity were trodden under foot by inexorable faction. Nothing equal to it has occurred since the days of Robespierre.

The circumstances which gave rise to this scene of scandal was the discussion of the paragraph in the address, in which the deputies who went to Belgrave Square are branded *with reprobation. The Legitimist deputies made a better stand than was expected. M. De la Rochejaquelin, M. Bechard, and M. Berryer, severally defended their conduct. They all endeavored to do away with the validity of the oath taken to the King of the French, and sought to establish a distinction between their avowed good wish in favour of the Duke de Bordeaux and their forced allegiance to Louis Philippe. These points were met by M. St. Marc Giradin and by the Minister of the Interior with so much success, that the Royalist deputies began to quarrel amongst themselves, and M. de la Rochejaquelin and M. Berryer contradicted each other in rather unparliamentary terms. The violence of the Carlist deputies raised the temper of the Chamber, and the debate was carried on amid a storm of hisses and cries and exclamations of the most disorderly nature. M. Berryer, who had, up to that moment, conducted himself with moderation, lost his temper, and instead of defending himself, suddenly turned on M. Guizot, and instituted a comparison between his visit to Belgrave Square and M. Guizot's journey to Ghent. "Yes," cried M. Berryer, "what would you have said if I had gone on the very frontiers of the country in the midst of armed enemies to give advice to a King?" "True," chimed in M. De la Rochejaquelin, "we are men of honor! We cannot submit to be* branded *by a minister – by him who went to Ghent – by him who took so great a part in the bloody re-action of 1815, and encouraged the atrocities of the south."*

Appendix IV – Traitors and Royalists

No sooner were these words heard, than the most shameless disorders commenced. The Opposition deputies suddenly quitted their pursuit of the Royalist, and to a man fell upon M. Guizot assailing him with cries and invectives of every sort. M. Guizot ascended the tribune and attempted to explain. His first words were met by an exclamation from Ernest du Girardin – "Why did you go to Ghent?" Then a voice from the left said, "It was treason." Another person roared, "Your object was to organize a foreign war." M. Guizot did not give way. He admitted that he went to Ghent to give advice to Louis XVIII. This admission produced another burst of disorder, which was alone put down by the united exertions of the President and M. Dupin, who entreated that the minister might be heard. M. Guizot then continued to say that he went to Ghent to lay before Louis XVIII the advice of the constitutional Royalists, who foresaw his speedy return to France. Another tumult followed the conclusion of this sentence. One deputy exclaimed, "To cut the throats of the French army." Another said, "You foresaw the disaster of Waterloo." A third cried, "Who can tamely listen to this apology for treason." A fifth, "Marshal Soult was not at Ghent." M. Guizot, however, bravely stood his ground, his Conservative friend rallied in force, and a hearing was again procured; but scarcely had a dozen words fallen from his lips than the row again begun. M. Joly exclaimed, "You had no right to betray us," M. Ledru Rollin declared, "We are indignant at your obstinancy." M. De la Rochejaquelin roared – "You had 300,000 foreign bayonets with you." M. De Chambolle cried out, "All traitors speak like you."

In the midst of this uproar, M. Guizot's voice was heard calmly explaining, that seeing the certainty of the return of Louis XVIII he felt the importance of the King coming back under the banner of constitutional monarchy. The words "constitutional monarchy" again called up the factions of the chamber, but M. Guizot silenced them by declaring that though this clamour might reduce his strength, it should not destroy his courage. M. Guizot continued to argue that the event of 1815 were independent of his journey to Ghent; but M. Chambolle interrupted him by saying, "That all traitors could say the same;" and M. De la Rochejaquelin exclaimed – "You were in the enemy's camp, that cannot be denied." M. Guizot went on to say that his whole life had been devoted to the principle of constitutional monarchy, and then suddenly turning to the gauche, *he exclaimed, "What have you done? Had you not the force of the government in your hands for fifteen years, and what use did you make of it? Was it you who gave France the liberty and order she enjoys today?" This burst received no answer from the Legitimists, but M. Garnier Pages came to their aid, and that of his own party, crying out, "It is we who made the revolution of 1830. You are but a man of yesterday." M. Guizot then resumed, saying that he was not to be blamed if events directed by Providence had gone beyond his wishes; that he had in call cases acted a conscientious and honorable part, supporting the principle he had before avowed against extremes of despotism on the one hand, and ultra-liberalism on the other. His acts were engraved in the history of the country, and he defied his enemies to efface them. After suffering M. Guizot to proceed for some time in this strain, the Opposition made another effort to put him down. M. de Boulay exclaimed, "Your conduct was treasonable." "You gave us Waterloo," added another voice. "It is the language of an Englishman," said a third. M. Guizot however contrived to gain a hearing, and he continued for a considerable period explaining his conduct in a satisfactory manner, and gradually resuming his habitual command of the chamber.*

Reading the above affirms Soult's wisdom for remaining silent on the Waterloo campaign. As a traitor, he had nothing to gain, and everything to lose. Indeed, far from a critical analysis of his performance, the fact that he fought for France during 1815 served him well. As he suspected the Bourbons would not hold the throne, as many did and as some allied powers preferred, then serving Napoleon in 1815 was a politically wise decision.

APPENDIX V
Lettow-Vorbeck

Lettow-Vorbeck

Lettow-Vorbeck's book not only was the first to point out Soult's order bungling, but also has insights to the importance of Bourmont's treason that has generally lost favor.

Note that German mile was approximately 7.4 kilometers.

Passages from *Napoleons Untergang 1815*.

Page 192

> *Der Abmarsch einer größeren Zahl französischer Truppen nach dem Innern wurde bald zweifelhaft, sicher schien jedoch, daß zur Bekämpfung des Aufstandes in der Vendée die junge Garde und auch Linienregimenter von Paris dorthin abgeschickt seien. Das Spiel von der Ankunft Napoleons und eines demnächst zu erwartenden Angriffs hatte seit dem 1. Juni von neuem begonnen; so und so oft wurde das Eintreffen des Kaisers als sicher gemeldet, um gleich darauf widerrufen zu werden. In der Anlage 6 sind die vom 31. Mai bis 14. Juni in den beiden Hauptquartieren eingegangenen Nachrichten sowie die von diesen gemachten Mitteilungen zusammengestellt. Wenngleich die Unvollständigkeit deutlich zu erkennen ist, so bietet die große Zahl der in ihnen enthaltenen Widersprüche doch ein Bild von dem Zustande der Unsicherheit, in dem sich eine Heeresleitung fast stets über die Verhältnisse beim Feinde und dessen Absichten*

befindet. Wie ungläubig man unter diesen Umständen geworden war, dafür bietet Gneisenau das beste Beispiel. Die von zwei Reisenden am 9. überbrachte wichtige Nachricht von dem Marsche des IV. Korps Gérard aus der Gegend von Thionville nach Mézières muß er, nachdem keine Bestätigung eingegangen war, wie so viele andere nicht für wahr gehalten haben, sonst wäre es unverständlich, daß er an demselben 9. an General v. Dobschütz in Trier schrieb: „Der Feind wird uns indessen nicht angreifen, sondern selbst bis an die Aisne, Somme und Marne zurückweichen, um dort seine Kräfte zu konzentrieren", und am 12. in einem Schreiben an Hardenberg heißt es: „Die Gefahr des Angriffs ist fast verschwunden." Hierzu ist zu bemerken, daß dem preußischen Generalstabschef die am Abend dieses Tages sehr bestimmt lautenden Meldungen des britischen Generals v. Dörnberg und eines an der Grenze wohnenden Barons Roisin nicht bekannt waren und vermutlich auch am folgenden Tage nicht bekannt wurden, denn Wellington hat sie bei seinen sehr wechselnden Ansichten über den Feind wahrscheinlich gar nicht mitgeteilt.

Translated:

The departure of a larger number of French troops toward the interior soon became doubtful. However, it seemed certain that the Young Guard and also line regiments from Paris had been sent to the Vendée to fight the insurrection there. As of June 1st, the game of Napoleon's arrival and an attack soon to be expected had started all over again. Time and again, there had been reports on the Emperor's definite arrival, which were withdrawn right after their annunciation. Appendix 6 lists the messages received by the two headquarters in the period between May 31st and June 14th and the reports that had been made about them. Although their incompleteness is clearly recognized, the large number of contradictions contained therein nevertheless illustrates the state of uncertainty, concerning the enemy's affairs and his intentions, in which the Supreme Command was almost constantly. Gneisenau provides the best example of how much people had turned into disbelievers under these circumstances. After having received no confirmation, he cannot have believed the important message delivered by two travelers on the 9th, concerning the march *of the IV. Corps Gérard from the Thionville region to Mézières, to be true, as he was likewise questioning the validity of so many other reports. Otherwise, it cannot be understood that he wrote to General v. Dobschütz in Trier, on the same 9th: "However, the enemy will not attack us, but will retreat even as far as to the Aisne, Somme and Marne, to bundle his forces there." And in a letter to Hardenberg, dating from the 12th, he states: "The danger of an attack has almost disappeared." In this regard, it should be noted that the Prussian Chief of General Staff was not aware of the messages of the British General v. Dörnberg, sounding very determined at the end of the day, and of those written by a Baron Roisin who lived at the border, and he probably did not become aware of them the following day, either, because Wellington probably did not even mention them in his frequently changing views on the enemy.*

Pages 196 – 199

Inzwischen waren von Zieten die Auslassungen eines übergetretenen französischen Tambourmajors eingegangen, die ihn veranlaßt hatten, sein Korps auf schnelle Versammlung vorzubereiten. Die weiteren Meldungen und die Beobachtung einer großen Zahl Wachtfeuer ließen kaum noch einen Zweifel an einer Versammlung ansehnlicher Kräfte bei Maubeuge und an einem Fortziehen der Truppen von Valenciennes dorthin. Leider fehlen die Nachrichten, die nach der Meldung Hardinges vom 14. abends Gneisenau veranlaßen, nun doch an den Marsch zweier Divisionen des französischen Korps zu glauben, diese sollten am 12. bei Sedan und Mézières eingetroffen sein. Der englische Oberst schließt seinen Bericht vom 14. abends an den Herzog: „Hier überwiegt die Ansicht, daß Bonaparte beabsichtigt, die Offensiv-Operationen zu beginnen."

 Man hatte also im preußischen Hauptquartier die Absichten des Feindes durchschaut, nur hielt man den Angriff nicht für unmittelbar bevorstehend und begnügte sich deshalb, die Korps über die Lage zu orientieren und sie aufzufordern, die Vorkehrungen für schnelle Versammlung zu treffen. Die bezüglichen Schreiben gingen an die Generale v. Bülow und v. Thielmann um Mittag des 14. Juni ab, das an ersteren lautete:

„*Die Nachrichten, welche vom Feinde eingehen, besagen, daß Napoleon sich bei Maubeuge konzentriere, und es scheint, er beabsichtigt, die Offensive gegen die Niederlande zu beginnen. Diesem nach ersuche ich Ew. Exzellenz, angesichts dieses eine solche Einrichtung in der Verlegung der Truppen des IV. Armeekorps zu treffen, daß sich dasselbe in einem Marsch bei Hannut konzentrieren kann.*"

Nach Absendung dieser Befehle schrieb Gneisenau an Gruner: „Wir stehen noch immer mit müßigen Kräften, während die Feinde die ihrigen verstärken. Mißtrauische Politik trägt hieran die Schuld."

Nach Mitteilung der von Zieten gemeldeten Nachrichten über den Feind schließt das Schreiben: „Die Befehle sind bereits ausgefertigt, die Armeekorps enger zu konzentrieren und auf alle Fälle bereit zu sein . . ." Augenscheinlich hielt er einen Angriff nicht für unmittelbar bevorstehend.

Wenn sich wenige Stunden darauf Gneisenau veranlaßt sah, die Befehle zur Versammlung der gesamten Armee zu geben, so müssen ihn sehr glaubwürdige Nachrichten hierzu bestimmt haben. Olleck folgt dem Tagebuch von Nostitz, wonach zwei nach Namur in der Nacht zum 15. gebrachte Deserteure mit größter Bestimmtheit ausgesagt hätten, Napoleon werde am Morgen die preußische Armee angreifen. Es können dies keine Überläufer gewöhnlichen Schlages gewesen fein, deren Aussagen ihrem beschränkten Gesichtskreise entsprechend stets nur einigen Wert über ihren besonderen Truppenteil gehabt und sich im übrigen auf Gerüchte beschränkt hatten, die später als übertrieben oder falsch erkannt worden waren. Es handelte sich im vorliegenden Falle jedenfalls um Personen, die Kenntnis von den ergangenen Befehlen für den Vormarsch der französischen Armee am 15. morgens hatten. Unter diesem Gesichtspunkte betrachtet, gewinnen die allerdings erst im Jahre 1861 zu Papier gebrachten Erinnerungen des Major a. D. Ritz, der in der bezüglichen Nacht als Fähnrich im 2. Infanterieregiment die Wache an der Maasbrücke in Namur hatte, an Bedeutung. Er gibt an, daß gegen 11 Uhr abends bei ihm ein Trupp von 5 bis 6 Reitern eingetroffen sei. Beim Examinieren derselben habe einer geantwortet, er sei preußischer Stabsoffizier und verlange, zur Wohnung des Fürsten geführt zu werden, weil er einen französischen General bei sich habe, der diesen in einer sehr

APPENDIX V – LETTOW-VORBECK

wichtigen Angelegenheit zu sprechen wünsche. Ritz glaubt selbst, daß man die Bezeichnung „General" vielleicht gebraucht habe, um ihn zum Verlassen der Wache zu bewegen, was er anfänglich verweigert hatte. Im Übrigen erscheint es höchst wahrscheinlich, daß es seiner Angabe gemäß französische Offiziere waren.

Da Blücher bereits sein Nachtlager ausgesucht hatte, wollte Gneisenau ihn nicht wecken und schrieb persönlich an Thielmann und Bülow. Der Befehl an ersteren 11 1/2 Uhr lautete ganz bestimmt: „Da der Feind sich an der Grenze konzentriert hat und wahrscheinlich eine Offensive beabsichtigt, so ist es nötig, daß die Armee sich gleichfalls konzentriere. Ew. Exzellenz wollen demnach sogleich nach Empfang dieses Schreibens Ihr Armeekorps bei Namur auf dem linken Maasufer vereinigen. . . . Bei Dinant lassen Sie ein leichtes Bataillon und zwei Schwadronen stehen, welche die Vorposten gegen Givet und längs der Grenze bilden und sich im Fall eines überlegenen Angriffs aus dem rechten Maasufer nach Namur zurückziehen.

Auf dem linken Maasufer, Dinant gegenüber, hält das II. Armeekorps die Vorposten mit einem leichten Bataillon und zwei Schwadronen, die, wenn sie gedrängt werden, sich auf dem linken Maasufer nach Namur zurückziehen. Die Vorposten des III. Armeekorps müssen mit denen des II. Korps die Verbindung unterhalten. Die Kranken Ihres Korps dirigieren Sie nach Lüttich. Die Truppen in Dinant und Huy haben von hier aus direkt Marschordre nach Namur erhalten, um jeden Zeitverlust zu vermeiden. . . . Das Hauptquartier des Fürsten Blücher ist vorläufig noch Namur."

An den dem Patent nach älteren General v. Bülow befleißigte sich der Stabschef in der Schreibweise einer wenig angebrachten Höflichkeit, die, wie sich zeigen wird, mit Veranlassung gab, daß der Befehl nicht sogleich ausgeführt' wurde.

„An den General v. Bülow nachts 12 Uhr:

Ew. Exzellenz gebe ich mir die Ehre ergebenst zu ersuchen, das unter Dero Befehl stehende IV. Armeekorps morgen, als den 15. d. Mts., bei Hannut in gedrängte Kantonierungen konzentrieren zu wollen. Die eingehenden Nachrichten machen es immer wahrscheinlicher, daß die französische Armee sich uns gegenüber zusammengezogen hat und daß wir unverzüglich ein Übergehen zur Offensive von derselben zu erwarten haben.

Ew. Exzellenz ersuche ich zugleich, den Kommandanten in Lüttich anweisen zu wollen, daß er von morgen an keine der Armee nachgehende Truppe oder Leute auf Huy und Namur instradiert, sondern daß er solche auf dem linken Maasufer, und zwar auf der alten Römerstraße, dirigiert. Zugleich würde es wohl am passendsten sein, wenn die in den Quartierständen sich befindenden Kranken des IV. Korps nach Aachen zurückgebracht würden. Hierbei würde ich dann Ew. Exzellenz ersuchen, den Kommandanten von Lüttich zugleich anzuweisen, daß er die Hospitäler von Lüttich möglichst räume und die Kranken nach Aachen und Jülich zurückschaffe.

Bis auf weiteres bleibt das Hauptquartier des Feldmarschalls noch in Namur. Das Hauptquartier Ew. Exzellqnz dürfte sich wohl am zweckmäßigsten in Hannut befinden, und ersuche ich Ew. Exzellenz zugleich, zur Brief-Kommunikation einen Brief-Ordonnanzposten in Hanret zwischen hier und Hannut stellen zu lassen.

Graf v.Gneisenau."

Der in Namur befindliche General v. Pirch I. erhielt die mündliche Weisung, ein Bataillon, zwei Eskadrons bei Dinant auf Vorposten und ein Bataillon in Namur zu belassen, im übrigen das Korps zwischen Mazy und Onoz in einem Biwak zu vereinigen. — Pirch beließ das Füsilierbataillon/21, und zwei Eskadrons 6. Dragoner unter Oberst v. Borcke bei Dinant, entledigte sich der kranken Menschen und Pferde, der nicht etatsmäßigen Bagage und ließ die zusammengebrachten Lebensmittel ins Magazin in Glimes schaffen, „von wo aus dieselben den Truppen teils durch die Proviantkolonnen, die dort bei Glimes stehen, teils durch Vorspann nachgeschafft werden".

Zieten kannte bereits seinen Sammelpunkt Fleurus.

Tatsächlich gelang es auf Grund dieser Befehle, am 16. noch vor dem Angriff Napoleons drei Armeekorps bei Sombreffe zu vereinigen, und auch das IV. Korps hätte bei Ausführung der ihm zugegangenen Weisung dort noch rechtzeitig eintreffen können. Hierbei darf aber nicht übersehen werden, daß dies nur infolge der in der Nacht zum 15. erhaltenen bestimmten Nachrichten möglich war. Wären die Befehle erst am 15. um 9 Uhr morgens nach dem Eintreffen der ersten Meldung Zietens ergangen, dann wäre eine rechtzeitige Versammlung so weit vorwärts ausgeschlossen

Appendix V – Lettow-Vorbeck

gewesen, und sie hätte weiter rückwärts geschehen müssen. Ohne diesen Verrat von Angehörigen der französischen Armee*) wäre also die von Napoleon beabsichtigte Überraschung noch in höherem Maße geglückt, als es schon jetzt der Fall war. Wie wenig man im preußischen Hauptquartier vorbereitet war, erhellt auch daraus, daß die Übermittlung der Befehle nach Lüttich eine ganz unverhältnismäßige Zeit brauchte. Der erste Befehl langte um 5 Uhr morgens nach 17 Stunden, der zweite um Mittag des 15. nach 12 Stunden dort an. Bei einer Entfernung von 53 km und geregeltem Relaisdienste hätten sie nach etwa 6 Stunden eintreffen müssen.

Nach Brüssel bestand eine solche Relaisverbindung, aber nichts deutet darauf, daß man die in der Nacht erhaltenen wichtigen Nachrichten dorthin hat gelangen lassen. Die am Vormittag des 15. von Wellington und Müffling an Kaiser Alexander bezw. Gneisenau gerichteten Schreiben erweisen jedenfalls, daß sie zur Zeit ihrer Abfassung in dem 72 km von Namur entfernten Brüssel noch nicht eingegangen waren.

*) Major Ritz schließt aus dem Ankommen der Reiter am rechten Maasufer, daß sie dem IV. Korps angehört und wahrscheinlich in Beziehung zu General Bourmont gestanden haben, der bekanntlich am nächsten Morgen mit seinem Stabe überging. Diese Vermutung des Majors gewinnt an Wahrscheinlichkeit durch die Angaben eines Mr. Marcellin, der Paris am 4. Mai verlassen hatte und am 11 dem Prinzen von Oranien unter anderem berichtet, daß er aus einer Unterredung mit dem Adjutanten Bourmonts schließe, dieser habe nur Dienst genommen, um dem Könige, sobald er Gelegenheit fände, Soldaten zuzuführen. Er kommandiere jetzt nur eine Division in der Gegend von Besançon und suche Offiziere an sich zu ziehen, der denen er wisse, sie dienten Napoleon nur widerwillig.

Translated:

In the meantime, Zieten had received accounts of a defected French drum major which prompted him to prepare his corps for a quick gathering. The subsequent messages and the observation of a large number of campfires left hardly any room for doubting the gathering of a substantial number of forces at Mauberge and the marching of the troops from Valenciennes to there. Unfortunately, the messages which, according to Hardinge's report from the evening of the 14th, made Gneisenau change his opinion, finally prompting him to believe in the march of the two divisions of the French corps which supposedly arrived in Sedan and Mézières on the 12th, are lost. The English colonel ends his report to the duke, written in the evening of the 14th: "Here, the opinion prevails that Bonaparte intends to initiate offensive operations."

Hence, the Prussian headquarters had understood the enemy's intentions. However, they did not think that the attack was imminent and hence were content with informing the corps about the situation and prompting them to make arrangements for a quick gathering. The respective letters were sent to the generals v. Bülow and v. Thielmann on June 14th at noon. The message to the first was:

"The news we receive on the enemy states that Napoleon concentrates his troops at Mauberge. It seems he intends to start the offensive against the Netherlands. Therefore, I ask Your Excellency to arrange the deployment of the forces of the IV. Army Corps, so that it is able to concentrate in a march at Hannut."

After having sent these orders, Gneisenau wrote to Gruner: "Our forces are still idle, whilst the enemies are reinforcing theirs. Distrustful politics are to be blamed."

Having communicated the news on the enemy reported by von Zieten, the letter ends: "Orders have already been given to concentrate the Army Corps more tightly and to be ready in all cases . . ." Obviously, he did not think there was an impending attack.

If a few hours later, Gneisenau found it necessary to order the gathering of the entire troops, very reliable news must have prompted him to do so. Ollech follows Nostitz's diary, which states that two defectors, brought to Namur during the night of the 15th, had stated with great firmness that Napoleon was about to attack the Prussian army the following morning. These cannot have been any ordinary defectors whose statements, according to their restricted horizon, would only have had some value regarding their specific part of the troops, and would otherwise have been restricted to mere rumors, later to be recognized as exaggerated or wrong. In the present case,

Appendix V – Lettow-Vorbeck

these were persons knowledgeable of the orders that had been given concerning the advance of the French army on the morning of the 15th. From this point of view, Major retd. Ritz's memoirs, which, however, were only put down on paper in 1861, become more important. In the respective night, he had stayed on guard at the Meuse bridge in Namur, as a cadet in the second Infantry Regiment. He states that a squad of 5 or 6 horsemen had arrived at his post at about 11 PM. Whilst being examined, one of them had replied that he was a Prussian field-grade officer and asked to be taken to the prince's lodgings, because he was accompanied by a French general who needed to speak to the latter in a very urgent matter. Ritz himself believes that the term "general" might have been used to make him leave his post which he had refused to do initially. Furthermore, it seems highly probable that these were indeed French officers, according to his statement.

As Blücher had already chosen his night-quarters, Gneisenau did not want to wake him up and personally wrote to Thielmann and Bülow. The order given to the latter, at 11:30 pm, was definitely: "As the enemy is concentrated at the border and probably intends to start an offensive, it is necessary for the army to concentrate as well. Therefore, Your Excellency must unite your Army Corps at Namur, at the left bank of the Meuse, immediately after receipt of this letter.... At Dinant, you will leave a light battalion and two squadrons forming the outposts against Givel and along the border, which shall, in case of a superior attack from the right bank of the Meuse, withdraw to Namur.

At the left bank of the Meuse, opposite Dinant, the II Army Corps holds the outposts with a light battalion and two squadrons which, if oppressed, will withdraw to Namur, on the left bank of the Meuse. The outposts of the III. Army Corps must stay in contact with those from the II. Corps. You will send those members of your corps who have fallen ill to Liège. The troops in Dinant and Huy have received the order to march directly to Namur from here, in order to avoid any loss of time.... The headquarters of the prince temporarily remain in Namur."

To general v. Bülow, who, according to the patent, was the elder, the chief of staff wrote a letter in such an unbefittingly polite manner that these wordings became one of the reasons why the order was not executed immediately.

"To General v. Bülow, 12 Am:

I humbly ask Your Excellency to grant me the honor to concentrate the IV. Army Corps, commanded by Your Excellency, in forced quartering at Hannut, tomorrow, on the 15th of the month. The incoming messages more and more increase the likelihood that the French Army has concentrated opposite us and that we may have to expect them to start an offensive immediately.

I furthermore ask Your Excellency to instruct the commander in Liège not to send any troop or people following the army to Huy or Namur, but to direct them to the left bank of the Meuse, to the old Roman way. At the same time, it would probably be most suitable to bring the sick members of the IV. Corps from the quarters back to Aachen. In doing so, I would humbly ask Your Excellency to instruct the commander of Liège at the same time to evacuate the Liège hospitals, as far as possible, and to bring the sick back to Aachen and Jülich.

Until further notice, the Field Marshal's headquarters remain in Namur. It would be most appropriate for Your Excellency's headquarters to remain in Hannut and I ask Your Excellency at the same time to set up a decree post in Hanret, located between this place and Hannut, for the purpose of communication by letter.

Count v. Gneisenau."

General v. Pirch I., who was in Namur, was orally instructed to leave one battalion, two squadrons at Dinant on an outpost and one battalion at Namur and otherwise, to unite the corps between Mazy and Onoz in a bivouac. — Pirch left the fusilier battalion/21 and two squadrons of the 6th Dragoon Regiment under Colonel v. Borcke at Dinant, ridded himself of the sick people and horses, the non-budgetary baggage and ordered the collected food to be brought to the magazine in Glimes, "from where the latter was brought to the troops, partly by supplies companies, deployed there at Glimes, partly by advance parties".

Zieten already knew his gathering point Fleurus.

Indeed, these orders made it possible to unite three Army Corps at Sombreffe, on the 16th, still before Napoleon's attack. The IV.

Appendix V – Lettow-Vorbeck

Corps could also have arrived there on time, had the order it had received been executed. However, it must not be overlooked that this was only possible because of the special messages received in the night leading up to the 15th. If the orders had only been given on the 15th, at 9 AM, after receipt of Zieten's first message, a timely gathering so far frontwards would have been impossible and would have had to happen further behind. Without this treason committed by members of the French army*, the surprise intended by Napoleon would have been successful to an even stronger degree than was the case now. The serious ill-preparedness of the Prussian headquarters is also shown by the fact that the transmission of the orders to Liège took an unreasonably long time. The first order arrived at 5 AM, after 17 hours, and the second order arrived on the 15th at noon, after 12 hours. Taking into account the distance of 53 km and ordinary relay services, these orders should have arrived after only 6 hours.

Such a relay connection existed with Brussels, but there is no evidence that the important messages received at night were brought there. Wellington's and Müffling's letters to Emperor Alexander and to Gneisenau, respectively, written before midday of the 15th, show that at the moment they were written, they had not been received in Brussels yet, 72 km from Namur.

* From the arrival of the horsemen at the right bank of the Meuse, Major Ritz concludes that they belonged to the IV. Corps and were probably related to General Bourmont who, as is known, crossed the river the following morning with his staff. The likelihood of this assumption made by the Major is increased by details given by a certain Monsieur Marcellin who left Paris on May 4th and who reports to the Prince of Orange on the 11th, amongst other things, that from a conversation with Bourmont's adjutant, he draws the conclusion that the latter had only entered the service to supply the king with soldiers, as soon as he was given the chance. Now he was only commanding a division near Besançon, trying to attract officers of whom he knew that they served Napoleon only reluctantly.

Pages 219-224

Für die Gruppierung der Korps mußte maßgebend sein der aus der Versammlung beabsichtigte Vormarsch und die hierbei zu benutzenden Wege. Da sich der Kaiser hierüber noch nicht geäußert hatte, schlug Soult in einem Schreiben*) vom 4. vor, in zwei Kolonnen gegen die Sambre vorzugehen und diese so zusammenzusetzen, daß das III. und IV. Korps die eine und die ganze übrige Armee die andere bilden sollten. Anscheinend erfolgte hierauf keine Erwiderung.

\) Diese Mitteilung verdanke ich, wie manche andere, dem bekannten Obersten Baron Stoffel, der seit Jahren ebenfalls mit einem Werke über 1815 beschäftigt ist und mir in liebenswürdigster Weise wiederholt mündlich und schriftlich Auskunft erteilt hat.

Die Arbeit, die der Kaiser dem Generalstabschef übertragen hatte, war eine ganz gewaltige, und man wird diesem kaum einen Vorwurf daraus machen können, daß er erst am 5. Juni dem IV. Korps den Befehl sandte, am 7. abzumarschieren und in sieben Etappen zu je 3 Meilen über Stenay, Mézières, Rocroi am 13. zu erreichen. Der Kommandeur des Korps, General Gérard, sollte aber bis zum 10. in Metz verbleiben, um dem mit der 2. Division der Nationalgarde aus Nancy am 7. abmarschierenden General Rouyer über die Grenzbewachung zwischen Metz und Thionville die erforderlichen Instruktionen zu erteilen. Wahrscheinlich hat Soult wie in der gleichzeitigen Benachrichtigung an Vandamme hierbei den Ausdruck „ablösen" (relever) gebraucht, der es erklären würde, daß Gérard am 7. nur eine seiner Divisionen aufbrechen und die beiden anderen am 8. und 9. folgen ließ. Der letzten Staffel waren auch die Kavallerie und Artillerie des Korps zugeteilt. Vandamme hatte mit dem III. Korps von Mézières links ab nach Chimay zu marschieren, die Truppen sollten derart untergebracht sein, daß drei Stunden nach erhaltenem Befehl aufgebrochen werden könnte. — Die weiteren Ausführungsbefehle von Soult bestimmen: Lobau hat am 9. den Marsch von Laon anzutreten und sich am 13. vorwärts Avesnes auszustellen, damit die Garde hinter ihm Platz finde. Seine noch zerstreute Division Teste soll sich am 11. bei Arras sammeln und am 14. bei ihm eintreffen. Erlon und Reille werden von dem Vorstehenden benachrichtigt und angewiesen, sich bei Valenciennes bezw. Maubeuge zu konzentrieren.

Entgegen den ersten Bestimmungen wird der Marsch der Garden beschleunigt, und wiederum ist es der Kaiser selbst, der alle Einzelheiten anordnet. Am 6. befiehlt er, daß die Artillerie am 9. abends oder 10. früh Soissons verlassen soll. Am Tage darauf weist er Drouot an, alle bereits in Soissons eingetroffenen Truppen am 9. und die im Laufe dieses Tages anlangenden am 10. in Marsch zu setzen. In betreff der beiden am 6. Paris verlassenden Regimenter heißt es: Wenn möglich, sollen sie in zwei Tagen nach Soissons marschieren, sie würden es dann den 9. erreichen; wenn nicht angängig, haben sie sich dem Orte so zu nähern, daß sie am 10. erforderlichenfalls zwischen Soissons und Laon eintreffen. Wie weit der oberste Heerführer in die Details eindringt, zeigt die Bemerkung, er habe mit Bedauern gesehen, daß die am Morgen abrückenden Regimenter nur ein Paar Stiefel gehabt hätten, während hinreichender Vorrat in den Magazinen läge. „Sie sind damit zu versehen, so daß sie zwei Paar im Tornister und ein Paar auf den Füßen haben." Die beiden 4. Regimenter der jungen Garde, deren Bildung am 11. beendigt war, sollten nach demselben Schreiben am 12. die Hauptstadt verlassen und innerhalb vier Tagen das 16 Meilen entfernte Laon erreichen. Sie gelangten nicht mehr zur Armee.

An diesem 7. Juni, an dem sich der wichtige Akt der Kammereröffnung vollzog und das Staatsoberhaupt die Vertreter der Nation mit einer Rede begrüßte, erging noch eine Fülle von Anordnungen aus den verschiedensten Gebieten. Dem Majorgeneral wird wiederholt, worauf bereits in dem Schreiben vom 3. hingewiesen war, daß längs der ganzen Ost- und Nordgrenze jede Verbindung unterbrochen werden soll. „Man übe die allergrößte Überwachung, daß, wenn möglich, kein Brief passieren kann. Sehen Sie die Minister der Polizei und Finanzen, damit sie ihren Agenten schreiben, daß alle und jede Kommunikation unterbunden werde." In einem weiteren Schreiben beauftragt er Soult, sich am Abend des folgenden Tages im strengsten Inkognito nach Lille zu begeben, um alle erforderlichen Maßregeln für die Sicherheit der in erster Linie liegenden Festungen zu treffen und alle etwa noch in ihnen befindlichen Linientruppen ausrücken zu lassen. Alle bis zum 13. bei der Armee anlangenden Bataillone sind den Korps zuzuteilen! Die letzten Nachrichten über den Feind sind zu sammeln, zu diesem Zwecke ist ein Bureau zu organisieren und ebenso eine Kompagnie aus Leuten, die in Belgien die Wege kennen, zu bilden. Die Forstwächter der Ardennen, deren Verbindungen bis über Brüssel hinausgehen, eignen sich besonders hierzu. Soult soll sich am 11. nach Maubeuge und Avesnes begeben und dann dem Kaiser entgegenkommen, der am 12. in Laon einzutreffen gedenkt. Gewiß waren alle diese Aufgaben wichtig, ob es aber rätlich war, sich in den letzten Tagen vor der Entscheidung von dem Chef des Generalstabes zu trennen, darf bezweifelt werden. Einen in die Geschäfte eingeweihten Vertreter gab es nicht, der Kaiser bediente sich in Abwesenheit des Majorgenerals seines Hausmarschalls, des Grafen Bertrand, um Befehle an die Armee zu geben.

Dieser Fall trat am 10. Juni ein. Der Kaiser entschloß sich in letzter Stunde, die endgültigen Bestimmungen über die Ausstellungen des Heeres für den 13. zu geben. Diese Geheimordre hatte folgenden Wortlaut. (Die gesperrt gedruckten Stellen sind vom Verfasser veranlaßt.)

Paris, den 10. Juni.

Tagesbefehl.

Stellungen der Armee am 13.
- Das Hauptquartier und die kaiserliche Garde in Avesnes.
- Der Artilleriepark und Brückentrain vorwärts Avesnes auf dem Glacis.
- Von der Reservekavallerie das I. und II. Korps in Beaumont, das III. und IV. zwischen Avesnes und Beaumont.
- Das VI. Korps in Beaumont und dem Stabsquartier dahinter. Sollte das Korps es für bedenklich halten, bis nach Beaumont zu gehen, so kann es halbwegs Halt machen.

- Das I. Korps Pont s. Sambre. Dies Korps wird die Bewegung, ohne Bavay zu passieren, ausführen. Es wird über Quesnoy marschieren, um sich vom Feinde zu entfernen, es wird seine Bewegung so spät als möglich demaskieren. Da man nicht annimmt, daß es von Valenciennes mehr als einen Tag braucht, so wird es erst am 13. den Marsch bis zur Sambre ausführen.
- Das II Korps vorwärts Maubeuge in Kolonnen auf dem Wege nach Thuin, ohne die Grenze zu überschreiten; es muß suchen, sich möglichst wenig sehen zu lassen.
- III. Korps Philippeville.
- Moselarmee Mariembourg.

Alle Verbindungen über die Sambre werden unterbrochen. Die Soldaten haben für vier Tage Brot im Tornister, ferner ½ Pfund Reis und 50 Patronen. — Die Batterien befinden sich bei den Divisionen, die Batterien der Reserve bei ihren Armeekorps. — Die leichte Kavallerie jedes Armeekorps befindet sich vor dem Korps, jede Ambulanz bei der Division.

Jede Division führt auf zwei Hilsswagen für die Soldaten acht Brotportionen, ferner Biskuit und einen Viehpark für acht Tage mit sich.

Man führt keine ändernden Bewegungen an der Grenze aus, man darf sie an keiner Stelle überschreiten. Man darf keinen Kanonenschuß lösen, überhaupt nichts tun, was den Feind aufmerksam machen könnte.

Bertrand übersandte diese Ordre an Soult, augenscheinlich mit einigen Erläuterungen, denn der Generalmajor fügte dem entsprechenden Befehl an Reille hinzu, der Kaiser werde am 13. morgens in Avesnes sein und wünsche ihn zu sehen, um Nachrichten von ihm zu erhalten. Es steht ferner fest, daß Bertrand die Ordre auch direkt Vandamme zugehen ließ, ebenfalls mit dem Bemerken, er habe sich am 13. zum Empfange des Kaisers in Avesnes einzufinden. Bei der Kürze der Zeit wäre es unbedingt erforderlich gewesen, auch den von dem jetzigen Aufenthaltsort Soults entfernten Grouchy in Laon direkt zu benachrichtigen. Jedenfalls wurde dies versäumt, denn als der Kaiser am 12. mittags dort eintraf, war er nicht wenig erstaunt, den Marschall noch ohne Nachricht zu finden. Der vom 12. aus Avesnes datierte Befehl Soults traf erst später ein. Die in ihren zerstreuten Quartieren befindliche Reservekavallerie wurde nun schleunigst alarmiert, und es gelang, sie im Laufe der Nacht zum 14. noch in die geforderte Aufstellung zu bringen. Hierbei hatten einzelne Regimenter bis an 80 km zurückzulegen, was ohne eine Anzahl gedrückter Pferde nicht abging. Es war dies jedoch nicht der einzige Nachteil, der aus der Trennung des Oberbefehlshabers der Armee von seinem Generalstabschef entstand, wie Soults Bericht an den Kaiser vom 12. aus Avesnes zeigt. Völlig abweichend von der Geheimordre ist darin dem III. und IV. Korps statt Philippeville Beaumont als Standpunkt für den 13. angewiesen, und was noch besonders auffällig ist, ohne die geringste Bemerkung, aus welchen Gründen diese Abänderung getroffen ist. Eine Erklärung für dieses Verhalten ist schwer zu finden. Bei dem Verhältnis des kaiserlichen Herrn zu seinen Generalen erscheint ein bewußter Ungehorsam ausgeschlossen. Vielleicht hat der Umstand, daß der von Soult am 4. gemachte Vorschlag, die Armee in zwei Kolonnen vorgehen zu lassen, keine Ablehnung erfahren hatte, bei ihm den Glauben erweckt, es läge hier von seiten Bertrands ein Versehen vor. Dafür spricht, daß seine Abänderungen wiederum die gesamte Armee bei Beaumont vereinigten bis auf zwei Korps, nur sind dies jetzt entsprechend der Ordre das I. und II. Korps, und sie sollen links statt wie vorgeschlagen rechts des Gros stehen. Die erste Scheu, einen Befehl des Kaisers abzuändern, war überdies schon überwunden, hatten sich doch dessen Anordnungen für das IV. Korps als unausführbar erwiesen.

Als dann der Monarch in Avesnes eingetroffen und die Berichte von Soult und der verschiedenen zu seinem Empfange befohlenen Korpskommandeure entgegengenommen hatte, genehmigte er nicht die von dem Majorgeneral getroffene Abänderung. Dieser war daher genötigt, an Vandamme zu schreiben: „Der Kaiser hat von neuem die Ausführung des Tagesbefehls vom 10. befohlen", das III. und IV. Korps und die 14. Kavalleriedivision haben dementsprechend nach Philippeville zu marschieren. Die beiden letzteren erreichte der Befehl noch rechtzeitig, das III. Korps war jedoch beim Eintreffen des Soultschen Schreibens bereits nach Beaumont in Marsch gesetzt, und sein Kommandeur hatte sich auf den Weg nach Avesnes begeben. Auf diese Weise wurde gegen die Absicht des Kaisers die an sich schon starke mittlere Kolonne noch um 17 000 Mann vermehrt.

Translated:

The decisive factors for the grouping of the various corps had to be the intended advance resulting from the assembly and the routes to be used on this occasion. Since the Emperor had not yet commented on this, Soult suggested in a letter*) of the 4th, to march towards the Sambre in two columns and assemble them in a way that the 3rd corps and the 4th corps would form one column, and the entire remainder of the army would comprise the other. Apparently, there was no reply on this.

*) I owe this piece of information, such as many others as well, to the well-known Colonel Stoffel who for years, has been working on a book about the year 1815 and who very kindly and repeatedly gave me information, orally and in writing.

The work the Emperor had assigned to the chief of staff was a tremendous one, and one can hardly blame the latter that only on June 5th, he issued the order to the 4th corps to start marching on the 7th and to reach Rocroi on the 13th, in seven stages of 3 miles each, via Stenay, Mézières. The commander of the corps, General Gérard, nevertheless was to remain in Metz until the 10th, in order to give the necessary instructions concerning the surveillance of the border between Metz and Thionville to General Rouyer who was to march out of Nancy on the 7th, with the 2nd division of the national guard. Probably Soult had used the term of "relieve" (relever), such as in the simultaneous notification to Vandamme, and this would explain why, on the 7th, Gérard had only one of his divisions march off, and had the other two follow on the 8th and the 9th. The cavalry and artillery of the corps were also assigned to the last squadron. Vandamme was to march with the 3rd corps from Mézières to the left, towards Chimay; the troops were to be accommodated such as to enable them to get marching within three hours after receiving the orders to *do so.* – *Soult's further executive orders determined: Lobau was to start marching off from Laon on the 9th and to position himself on the 13th in front of Avesnes so that the guard would find their place behind him. His "Teste" division which was still dispersed was to gather near Arras on the 11th and reach him on the 14th. Erlon and Reille are notified of the above and instructed to concentrate near Valenciennes, or resp., Maubeuge.*

Contrary to initial orders, the march of the guards is accelerated, and it is again the Emperor who himself gives orders on all details. On the 6th, he orders that the artillery is to leave Soissons on the 9th, in the evening, or on the 10th, early in the morning. On the following day, he instructs Drouot that all troops who already have arrived in Soissons are to march on the 9th, and that all troops arriving in the course of this day must march on the 10th. As far as the two regiments leaving Paris on the 6th are concerned, it says: If possible, they are to march towards Soissons within two days which they would then reach on the 9th; if not possible they were to approach the place in a way enabling them to arrive between Soissons and Laon on the 10th, if necessary. The extent to which the chief military leader gets involved in the details, is shown by his remark that he regretted to have seen that the regiments leaving in the morning had only a few pairs of boots whereas there was a sufficient supply in the magazine. "They must be equipped with these so that they will have two pairs in their satchels and one on their feet." According to the same letter, the two 4th regiments of the young guard whose formation was concluded on the 11th, were to leave the capital on the 12th and to reach Laon at a distance of 16 miles, within 4 days. They never reached the army.

On this 7th June, on which the important act of opening the chamber took place and the head of state greeted the nation's representatives with a speech, numerous orders from the most varied areas were still being issued. The major general is reminded of what he has been instructed already in the letter of the 3rd, that all connections are to be broken along the entire eastern and northern border. "One must exercise the strictest surveillance so that, if possible, no letter will be able to pass through. Go see the Ministers of Police and Finance so that they may write to their agents to interrupt each and every

Appendix V – Lettow-Vorbeck

communication." In another letter, he instructs Soult to come to Lille on the evening of the next day, strictly incognito, in order to take all measures for the safety of the fortifications located in the first line and to move off any line troops who might still be found in them. All battalions reaching the army until the 13th must be assigned to the various corps! The latest intelligence on the enemy is to be gathered, and a bureau established for this purpose, as well as a company consisting of people knowing their way around Belgium. The forest guards of the Ardennes whose connections go beyond Brussels are especially suited for this. Soult is to go to Maubeuge and Avesnes on the 11th and then come up to meet the Emperor who intends to arrive in Laon on the 12th. Certainly, all tasks were important but it might be doubted whether it was advisable to part with the chief of staff during the last days before the decision. There was no successor who would have been in the know of operations; in the absence of his major general, the Emperor availed himself of his own Grand Marshal, Count Bertrand, to issue orders to the army.

Such an occasion arose on June 10th. At the last hour, the Emperor decided to issue the final orders concerning the deployment of the army on the 13th. This secret order was worded as follows:

Paris, June 10th

Order of the Day

Positions of the Army on the 13th.
- Headquarters and Imperial Guard in Avesnes.
- Artillery and Bridge forward Avesnes on the Glacis.
- Of the Reserve Cavalry, the 1st and 2nd corps in Beaumont, the 3rd and 4th between Avesnes and Beaumont.
- The 6th corps in Beaumont and Headquarters beyond. In case the corps should have reservations to move up to Beaumont, it may stop halfway.
- The 1st corps s. Sambre. This corps will carry out the movement without passing Bavay. It will march via Quesnoy in order to move away from the enemy, and it

will reveal its movement as late as possible. Since it is not assumed that the corps will need more than one day from Valenciennes, it will complete its march up to the Sambre only on the 13th.
— The 2nd corps forward to Maubeuge, in columns, on the way to Thuin, without crossing the border; it must take care to be seen as little as possible.
— 3rd corps Philippeville.
— Moselle Army Mariembourg.

All connections across the Sambre are interrupted. The solders have bread for four days in their satchels, in addition to ½ a pound of rice and 50 cartridges. - The batteries are with the divisions, the reserve batteries are with their army corps. - The light cavalry of each army corps is positioned in front of the corps, each ambulance with the division.

Each division carries, on auxiliary carts, 8 portions of bread for the soldiers, in addition to biscuits and livestock for eight days.

No modifying movements are carried out at the border, it must not be crossed at any point. No cannon shot must be triggered, nothing may be done that could alert the enemy.

Bertrand sent this order to Soult, apparently with some explanations since the general major added to the corresponding order to Reille that the Emperor would be in Avesnes on the morning of the 13th, wanting to see him to receive news. In addition, it is certain that Bertrand sent the order directly to Vandamme, too, also stating that the latter was to appear on the 13th, for the Emperor's reception. As time was short, it would have been necessary to also inform Grouchy directly who was at a distance to the current location of Soult. Anyway, this was omitted because when the Emperor arrived there at noon on the 12th, he was rather surprised to find the Marshal still without news. The order from Avesnes dated on the 12th arrived only later. The reserve cavalry in their dispersed quarters was now quickly alerted and succeeded, still in the night of the 14th, to take their required positions. With this, individual regiments had to cover up to 80 km, which did not happen without a number of horses being *exhausted. Yet this was not the only disadvantage resulting from the separation of the army's commander in chief from his chief of staff, as proven by Soult's report from Avesnes to the Emperor of the 12th. In complete deviation from the secret order, the report instructs the 3rd and 4th corps to position themselves on the 13th in Beaumont instead of Philippeville and, something which is especially blatant, without any remark on the reasons for this change. It is difficult to find an explanation for this behavior. In view of the relations between the imperial lord and his generals, intentional disobedience seems to be impossible. Maybe the fact that Soult's suggestion, which he made on the 4th, to the extent that the army should advance in two columns, had not been rejected, had caused him to believe that there was an error here on the side of Bertrand. This is supported by that fact that his changes united the entire army again near Beaumont, except for two corps, but these are now the 1st and the 2nd corps, according to the order, and they are to be positioned on the left of the bulk, instead of the right as suggested. Initial reluctance to change an imperial order had already been overcome anyway as the Emperor's instructions for the 4th corps had already proven unfeasible.*

When the Emperor then arrived in Avesnes and received the reports from Soult and various corps commanders ordered to attend the reception, he did not approve the major general's change. The latter thus was forced to write to Vandamme: "The Emperor again ordered to carry out the order of the day for the 10th," and the 3rd and 4th corps as well as the 14th cavalry division had to march to Philippeville accordingly. The two latter ones received the order just in time but the 3rd corps had already been marching on Beaumount when Soult's letter reached them, and its commander was on his way to Avesnes. This way, and against the Emperor's intention, the central column – which had already been strong – was augmented by another 17,000 men.

Appendix VI
Gourgaud's Diaries

Published in 1899, they were never meant to be seen. Thus, nothing said in these pages was written to enhance Napoleon's legacy. From here we can see the suspicions of Soult, the understanding that there had to be treason within the general staff, and what Napoleon was led to believe about d'Erlon which we know to be false.

>Page 174 Volume 1:

>>*Le Mouvement d'Erlon m'a fait bien du tort; on croyait autour de moi que c'etait l'ennemi. D'Erlon est un bon chef d'état-major, a de l'ordre, mais voila tout. Il aurait dû, le 15, m'envoyer dire qu'il était à Marchiennes.*

>>*The movement of d'Erlon caused me much harm; those around me thought it was the enemy. D'Erlon was a good staff officer. He could maintain order; but that was all. He ought on the 15th to have sent me word that he was at Marchiennes.*

What is most fascinating about this comment is that Napoleon is regretting that d'Erlon failed to properly inform him of his dispositions on June 15th. Napoleon was told something which clearly led Napoleon to believe I Corps was further north on June 16th and within Ney's operational control, and when his plans did not come to fruition, Napoleon must have been told something else. Here he suggests it was that d'Erlon was further south. While the distance wasn't great, the timing of the events on June 16th only required some modest explanation. Undoubtedly Napoleon would have challenged Soult, even if briefly considering they were in the midst of hostilities, on the status of the left wing after the battle of Ligny and the failings of his plan. Soult's explanation clearly held Ney largely responsible, and Ney's lack of aggression on June 16th supported this argument. Further, Soult must have also blamed d'Erlon for not giving accurate information, which Napoleon repeats here and also repeated in his memoirs. As seemingly innocuous as this statement may be, considering the correspondence that we have between d'Erlon and Soult, this is absolute proof that Soult was lying to Napoleon during the campaign.

Page 484 Volume 1:

> *Le grand maréchal se fâche et parle du mémoire du maréchal Soult, qu'il trouve fort bien. Louis XVIII finira par le rappeler.*

> *The grand marshal is angry and speaks about the memoir of Marshal Soult, that he finds very good. Louis XVIII will eventually recall him.*

Page 490 Volume 1:

> *J'ai lu la défense de Soult. L'Empereur assure qu'il n'a pas trahi. La première fois qu'il le vit, le 26 mars 1815, il avait l'air sérieux et avoua que le roi l'avait complétement gagné. Il avait toujours cru que l'expédition de Sa Majesté n'aurait pas de suite, que ce n'était qu'une affaire de gendarmerie. Il pensait que l'Empereur ne voulait que passer en Italie : il a pu se tromper ainsi, parce qu'il ne connait pas bien les Alpes. Il estimait que le roi pouvait compter sur les troupes. Louis XVIII lui avait dit: « Ah! c'est là une terrible affaire! tout dépend des premiers régiments que rencontrera Bonaparte! » Le roi est le seul qui ait bien jugé l'affaire. Puis, l'Empereur ajoute que Soult ne connait ni la France, ni les révolutions; il désire, à présent, se faire employer à nouveau et ne veut pas, surtout, que l'on puisse croire qu'il a trahi, à Waterloo.*

> *I read the defense of Soult. The Emperor assures that did he not betray. The first time he saw him, March 26, 1815, he looked serious and confessed that the king had completely won him. He had always believed that the expedition of His Majesty would not succeed, it was*

> *only a matter of the police. He thought that the Emperor wanted to go to Italy: he was wrong because he does not know the Alps well. He believed that the king could rely on the troops. Louis XVIII had told him: "Ah! this is a terrible thing! all depends on the first regiments that meet Bonaparte!" The king is the only one who understood the case well. Then the Emperor added that Soult knows neither France nor the revolutions; he desires now to be employed once again and does not want, above all, that we believe he betrayed at Waterloo.*

Despite the suspicions that Soult may have aided Napoleon's return in 1815, Napoleon denied it. However, in this candid conversation, Napoleon defends Soult's memory and assures his comrades in exile that Soult would not want them to think he betrayed them at Waterloo. Apparently they had their suspicions.

Page 84 Volume 2

> *L'Empereur ne conçoit pas comment il a pu perdre la bataille de Waterloo. Je lui répète que tous ceux qui s'étaient battus contre les Anglais les redoutaient. Reille lui avait assuré qu'il aurait l'avantage sur les troupes d'infanterie, mais que la cavalerie l'emporterait.*
>
> *« C'était surtout par leur bonne discipline que les Anglais triomphaient. Ils pouvaient s'avancer de trente pas, halte, feu, en arrière, feu, en avant, trente pas, sans se déranger, et en conservant le plus grand ordre. Bien des choses finiront par se savoir. Qui peut avoir donné ordre à, Guyot de charger ? Il est parti avant l'époque que je suppose dans notre narration, mais il est parti sans mon ordre.*
> *— Sire, Votre Majesté se souvient que lorsqu'on aperçut le feu sur la droite, elle demanda à Soult: « Serait-ce Grouchy? », que Soult répondit : « Sire, cela ne m'étonnerait pas, il a dû en recevoir l'ordre; » et qu'alors Votre Majesté avait prescrit d'aller annoncer cela partout, et de faire avancer toute la garde, infanterie, cavalerie, en un grand mouvement. »*
>
> *L'Empereur pense avoir mal fait en prenant Soult pour Major-Général. Il eut mieux fait de choisir Andréossi.*
>
> *« Mais, Sire, si Votre Majesté avait été blessée?*

> *N. — Soult était mal entouré, il avait de mauvais officiers d'état-major; il était craintif; dans la nuit du 18, il m'avait apporté plusieurs rapports effrayants. Soult est un grand ambitieux, mais sa femme le mène.*
>
> *The Emperor does not see how he could have lost the Battle of Waterloo. I tell him that all those who had fought against the British feared them. Reille had assured him it would have the advantage over the infantry, but the cavalry would win.*
> *"It was especially by their good discipline that the English triumphed. They could steps move thirty, halt, fire back, fire ahead, steps thirty, without disturbing, and maintaining the highest order. Many things will come out. Who gave the order to Guyot to charge? He left before the time that I suppose in our narrative, but he left without my order.*
> *- Sire, Your Majesty remembers that when we saw troops firing on the right, you asked Soult: "Could it be Grouchy?" Soult replied: "Sire, it would not surprise me, he had to have received the order;" And then your Majesty had it ordered to go announce it everywhere, and advance the whole guard, infantry, cavalry, in a great movement.*
> *The Emperor thinks he has done wrong by taking Soult for major general. He should have chosen Andreossi.*
> *"But, Sire, if your majesty had been injured?"*
> *N. - Soult was wrong about him, he had bad officers of Staff; we was fearful; on the night of the 18th, he had brought me many scary reports. Soult is very ambitious, but his wife leads him.*

Despite Napoleon's continued faith in Soult's fidelity, he could still recognize that something wasn't right.

Page 370 Volume 2

> *A Waterloo, la garde n'a pas pu se déployer : la bataille a été perdue parce que Grouchy n'a pas rejoint: il aurait fallu avoir la Suchet. Soult avait peur et prétendait que Vandamme avait déserté. On avait perdu un temps précieux à discuter la constitution.*

Appendix VI – Gourgaud's Diaries

At Waterloo the guard was not able to deploy: the battle was lost because Grouchy did not join: we would have needed Suchet. Soult was scared and claimed that Vandamme had deserted. We lost very valuable time to discuss the Constitution

APPENDIX VII
ON CENSORSHIP

During the Bourbon restorations and subsequent July Monarchy, the laws regarding censorship varied and changed over time. The Press, representing works under 20 pages that were quick to produce, distribute, and read, and therefore were powerful tools in spreading danger ideas, was the primary focus. There would be periods of strict censorship where material had to be approved before publication, and then there might be some laws abolished, only to see them re-instituted in reaction to some event. One example is the assassination of the *Duc de Berry*, where press censorship that had been ended in 1819 was re-imposed.[265]

Consider the following during the waning days of the Bourbons:

> *On September 8, 1829, the minister of the interior directed his prefects to protect, by tightening their enforcement of censorship, the ruling dynasty against attempts to "recall the insignia and the memories of the usurpation [Napoleon's rule]." The prefects were instructed that Napoleon could be portrayed in illustrations in which he was depicted as "a general, representing battles and bearing a historic character" since such battles "belong to France and the government which has adopted their glory is far from wishing to forbid their memory." However, the directive continued, "all other portrayals must be strictly banned" such as depictions of "Bonaparte under all forms, in his public as well as his private life," the reproduction of his "isolated feats of arms, incidents or episodes more or less apochryphal and too often in opposition to history," as well as all "lithographs of diverse format which only attempt to recall to the imagination*

---

[265] Goldstein, Rober, *Censorship of Political Caricature in Nineteenth-century France*, Kent State University Press, 1989, pg. 105

and the memory of the people the insignia and the memories of an illegitimate power."[266]

At any time of perceived risk, the voice of the threat was censored. What this climate may have suppressed that is lost to history we'll never know.

Both Napoleon and Napoleon III censored as well. A judgment is not being made. We just need to understand that in the 30+ years after the Waterloo campaign, material that incited Bonapartists against the crown would not have been tolerated. Can one imagine *Napoleon Betrayed : The detailed story of the Bourbons betraying France during 1815 in which thousands of our countrymen were killed* getting a pass during the Bourbon restoration? Or how about *Napoleon Betrayed : The inside story of the Orleanist faction's work with the Allied Powers to defeat France in 1815* during Louis-Philippe's reign?

Thus, while many authors have cited treason as a contributing factor to the events of 1815, the most fertile time to unearth the details that may explain some of the many existing mysteries was lost. Try to imagine Woodward and Bernstein investigating Nixon's role in the Watergate burglary starting after 2000.

Janin's work, *Campagne de Waterloo; ou, Remarques critiques et historiques sur l'ouvrage due Général Gourgaud* was published in 1820. However, this is exactly the type of work that would please the Bourbons as it is refuting Gourgaud, and is critical of Napoleon. Consider the following passage which starts on page 42:

> *Un général doit accepter franchement la responsabilité des événements et des opérations que lui seul dirige. Il y a de la noblesse, de la véritable grandeur à s'avouer coupable des revers ou des succès qui résultent de mauvaises combinaisons. Que doit-on dire d'une conduite opposée ?... Ce fut trop souvent celle de Napoléon. Enfant gâté et idolâtre de la fortune, chaque fois qu'elle le négligea il sembla vouloir se la rendre plus propice en immolant comme en holocauste quelque grande victime sur l'autel de son propre orgueil, je dirais presque de sa vanité : c'est ainsi que dans un grand nombre de circonstances il sacrifia à sa prétendue infaillibilité la réputation des généraux les plus distingués. A Jéna il ne craint point de diffamer*

---

266 Goldstein, Rober, *Censorship of Political Caricature in Nineteenth-century France*, Kent State University Press, 1989, pg. 112

Appendix VII – On Censorship

dans un bulletin officiel les généraux Klien et Lasalle, l'honneur de la cavalerie française : à Fontainebleau il outrage aussi gratuitement le brave et modeste général Lhéritier ; et s'il fallait un dernier et plus grand exemple, je rappellerais, non sans rougir, les infamies qui, jaillissant de la fange du Palais-Royal où elles furent jetées à dessein, souillèrent l'un des noms les plus illustres de l'armée française. Ce que fit alors Napoléon, il le fait encore aujourd'hui par l'organe de son aide-de-camp.

Il fut trahi ! Oui, il let fut par son génie, qui dans cette courte et malheureuse campagne l'abandonna tout-à-fait.

This translates to:

A general must sincerely accept the responsibility for the events and operations that he alone leads. The nobility has the true grandeur to acknowledge culpable reverses or successes that result from poor strategies. What can be said for the opposing leaders? ... It was too often that way for Napoleon. Spoiled child and fortune fanatic, each time neglected he seemed to want a result more favorable through sacrifice on the level of a holocaust of some great victim on the alter of his own pride, I would say mostly due to his vanity: thus in a great many circumstances he sacrificed for his supposed infallibility, the reputation of the most distinguished Generals. At Jena he was not afraid to defame, in an official journal, Generals Klien and Lasalle, the honor of the French cavalry: at Fontainebleau he also gratuitously insulted the brave and modest General Lhéritier; and if we need one last and greater example, I recall, not without shame, the infamies that gushed from the mud of the Palais Royal where they were intentionally cast, defiling one of the most illustrious names of the French Army. Who was Napoleon then, he is portrayed again today by the voice of his aide-of-camp.

He was betrayed! Yes, it was by his genius, that in this short and unfortunate campaign, he was completely abandoned.

Las Cases *Mémorial de Sainte-Hélène* was published in Paris in 1823, and it was certainly favorable to Napoleon. Thus we cannot view censorship as absolute.

For those wishing to reconcile with the government, such as military officers, self-censorship was most likely common.

The following sources were found to be particularly useful in understanding the climate and its impact on the press and print during the monarchies that followed Waterloo:

- http://oll.libertyfund.org/pages/eugene-delacroix-on-press-censorship-during-the-restoration-1814-1822
- Goldstein, Robert, *Censorship of Political Caricature in Nineteenth-century France*, Kent State University Press, 1989; http://books.google.com/books?id=vIA1F2QmoWgC
- Polowetzky, Michael, *A Bond Never Broken: The Relations Between Napoleon and the Authors of France*, Fairleigh Dickinson University Press, 1993; http://books.google.com/books?isbn=0838634826
- Green, J. & Karolides, N., *Encyclopedia of Censorship*, Infobase Publishing, 2009; http://books.google.com/books?id=bunHURgi7FcC

Appendix VIII

Traitors & Prisoners in German Sources

Seconde-Lieutenant Johann von Wussow

The service record for Wussow can be found here: http://archivdatenbank.gsta.spk-berlin.de/ImageLookup/iv_ha_rep_1/IV.%20HA,%20Rep.%201,%20Nr.%2093/Max/00000396.jpg[267]

The relevant portion, expanding the abreviations, is:

> [v. Wussow], Joh[ann]. George Philipp, Cad[ett]. P[orte]E[pée] F[ähnrich Unt[er].Off[izier].
> 1811. 12 Apr[il]. Sec[onde].L[ieutenan]t. b[eim]. Leib Inf[anterie]. Reg[imen]t.
> 1813 22 Dec[ember]. in den Gen[eral] St[ab] b[eim]. 1ten [= ersten] Armée Corps.
> 1815 23 Mart z[um]. G[eneral]. F[eld]. M[arschall]. Fürst Blücher, [means in the latter's staff]
> 1815 9 Juny Pr[emier]. L[ieuntnan]t.
> 1815 3 Oct[ober]. z[um]. Gross[en] Gen[eral] St[ab]. in Berlin
> 1817. 30 Mart Capit[aine].

Von Ollech includes a detailed account of Wussow's mission to Wellington which includes Wussow's own words:

---

267 Many thanks to Oliver Schmidt for providing this link and the subsequent transcription.

Wohl aber hat ein preußischer Generalstabs-Offizier aus dem Stabe Blücher's, nämlich Lieutenant v. Wussow (später kommandirender General), dem Herzoge bei Quatre Bras persönlich rapportirt. Dieser junge Offizier erzählt:

„*Als Major v. Winterfeldt von dem Feldmarschall Blücher bereits nach Quatre Bras abgeschickt worden war, rief mich General v. Gneisenau und befahl mir, eiligst zum Herzog Wellington zu reiten, um demselben "über den gegenwärtigen Stand der Schlacht Bericht zu erstatten".*

Es war ein Glück, daß ich dem Verlauf der Schlacht mit großer Aufmerksamkeit gefolgt war. Das große Vertrauen Gneisenau's ehrte mich, und so stand ich keinen Augenblick an, meinem Pferde im vollen Lauf die Direktion von Brye bei Marbais vorüber auf Thyle und Quatre Bras zu geben. Mein Pferd wechselte ich mit Pferden der Kavallerie-Detachements, welche von Wagnelée bis Quatre Bras die Verbindung mit dem Herzoge unterhielten. Bei dem Dorfe Thyle tritt der Wald (Bois de la Hütte) bis dicht an die Chaussee. Der hier stehende Führer des Kavallerie-Postens machte mir die Mittheilung, daß die Chaussee jenseits des Waldes bereits von den bis Piraumont vorgedrungenen Franzosen besetzt und an jener Stelle der Major v. Winterfeldt von feindlichen Tirailleurs schwer blessirt worden sei. Ich überzeugte mich von der Richtigkeit dieser Warnung und wandte mich deshalb rechts von der Chaussee zwischen Thyle und Ahyle, um dann möglichst bald in die Hauptstraße nach Quatre Bras wieder einzubiegen. Freilich mußte ich auch an der Chaussee das feindliche Gewehrfeuer passiren, aber es gelang mir, wohlbehalten die englischen Truppen bei Quatre Bras zu erreichen. Dort fand ich den Herzog Wellington, der zu Fuß, mit dem Fernrohr in der Hand, den Angriff und die Bewegungen des Feindes beobachtete. General v. Müffling stand an seiner Seite; ihm machte ich zuerst Meldung von dem Auftrage, der mir ertheilt worden war. Der Herzog wandte sich zu mir und ich berichtete ihm:

„*Zur Zeit meines Abreitens vom Schlachtfelde waren sämmtliche Dörfer der von uns besetzten Stellung hinter dem Lignebach, von Sombreffe über Ligny, St. Amand la Haye und Wagnelée, trotz der unausgesetzten Angriffe der Franzosen und des wechselnden Verlierens und Wiedergewinnens, von uns behauptet worden.*

APPENDIX VIII – TRAITORS & PRISONERS IN GERMAN SOURCES

Indessen stelle es sich je länger je mehr heraus, daß die Verluste sehr wuchsen, und da die Aussicht auf eine Unterstützung durch das Korps Bülow's gänzlich geschwunden sei, so werde es höchstens möglich sein, das Schlachtfeld bis zum Eintritt der Nacht zu behaupten: — ein größerer Erfolg stehe nicht zu erwarten."

Bis hierher hatte Lieutenant v. Wussow in der That seinen Auftrag erfüllt. Von der Verabredung zwischen Gneisenau und Wellington, die preußische Armee bei Ligny von Quatre Bras her, wenn möglich, direkt zu unterstützen, hatte Lieutenant v. Wussow keine Kenntniß. Es war daher auch nur seine persönliche Meinung, wenn er mit den Worten schloß:

"Vielleicht könne die kräftige Offensive der Engländer den Kaiser Napoleon verhindern, seine Streitkräfte nachhaltig gegen die preußische Armee zu verwenden."

Dann fährt v. Wussow in seiner Erzählung fort:

"Der Herzog hörte mich mit der ihn charakterisirenden Gemüthsruhe und Kaltblütigkeit an, trotzdem die feindlichen Kanonenkugeln in allen Richtungen um uns her einschlugen, — sprach darauf einige freundliche Worte des Dankes für diese Meldung aus, und da um diese Zeit auf der Brüsseler Straße neue Truppen eingetroffen waren, so gab er Befehle zum erneuerten Vorgehen.

Mich beauftragte der Herzog, dem Feldmarschall Blücher zu sagen, — „daß es ihm bis jetzt zwar sehr schwer geworden sei, dem heftigen Angriff der überlegenen Franzosen Widerstand zu leisten, daß er aber mit der jetzt eingetroffenen Verstärkung — er glaube circa 20,000 Mann zur Stelle zu haben — doch eine kräftige Offensive zu Gunsten der preußischen Armee versuchen werde."

Ich sah noch den Erfolg der englischen Offensive bis zur Wiedereroberung von Piraumont und kehrte dann so schnell zurück, als ich gekommen war. An der Windmühle von Bussy meldete ich mich bei dem General v. Gneisenau und überbrachte die Antwort des Herzogs. Es geschah dies zu der Zeit, als Ligny noch nicht verloren war."

Oberst Hardinge war nicht im Stande, dem Herzoge die Anzeige von dem Ausgange der Schlacht bei Ligny zu machen, weil ihm, im Gefolge des Feldmarschalls, eine Kugel die eine Hand zerschmettert hatte.

Die Abhängigkeit Wellington's von dem Schicksal Blücher's trat am nächsten Tage sogleich hervor. Der Fürst hatte die Schlacht im Interesse der Engländer selbstständig aufgenommen. Der Gegendienst blieb aus, folglich mußte nun auch Wellington die vollständige Konzentration seiner Armee weiter rückwärts suchen.

Above translates to:

But for sure a Prussian General Staff officer from Blücher's staff, namely Lieutenant von Wussow (later Commanding General), has reported in person to the Duke at Quatre Bras. This young officer recounts:

"Already after Major von Winterfeldt had been sent to Quatre Bras by the Field Marshal Blücher, General v. Gneisenau called me and commanded me to ride most urgently to the Duke Wellington to give him "report on the current state of the battle".

It was fortunate that I had followed the course of the battle with great attention. The great trust Gneisenau's honoured me, and so I didn't stay a moment to give my horse at full speed the direction of Brye at Marbais passing by on Thyle and Quatre Bras. I changed my horse by horses of the cavalry detachments, which maintained the connection to the Duke from Wagnelée until Quatre Bras. Near the village of Thyle the forest occurs (Bois de la Hutte) close until the highway. The here standing leader of the cavalry post gave me the information that the highway beyond the forest had already been occupied until Piraumont by the advanced French and at that point the Major von Winterfeldt had been severely injured by enemy skirmishers. I became convinced of the correctness of this warning and therefore I turned to the right of the road between Thyle and Ahyle, then to turn into the main road to Quatre Bras again as soon as possible. Of course, I had also to pass by the enemy gunfire at the highway, but I managed to safely reach the English troops at Quatre Bras. There I found Duke Wellington, who watched the attack and the movements of the enemy on foot, with the telescope in hand. General von Müffling stood by his side; I first gave him report of the mission, which had been imparted to me. The Duke turned to me and I reported to him:

Appendix VIII – Traitors & Prisoners in German Sources

"At the time of my riding away from the battlefield all villages of the position occupied by us behind the Lignebach, from Sombreffe over Ligny, St. Amand la Haye and Wagnelée were held by us, despite the incessant attacks of the French and the alternating losing and retrieval. However, it turns out the longer the more that the losses grew very much and as the prospect of support from Bülow's corps had quite disappeared, it would be at most possible to hold the battlefield until the onset of the night: — A greater success is not expected."

Up to this point Lieutenant von Wussow had in fact fulfilled his mission. About the arrangement between Gneisenau and Wellington, if possible to support the Prussian army at Ligny from Quatre Bras directly, Lieutenant von Wussow had no knowledge. Therefore, it was only his personal opinion as he concluded with the words:

"Perhaps the strong offensive of the British could prevent Emperor Napoleon to use sustainably his armed forces against the Prussian army."

Then von Wussow continues his story:

"The Duke listened to me with his characterising composure and coolness, nevertheless the enemy cannonballs were striking in all directions around us, - then he spoke a few friendly words of thanks for this report and since at this time new troops had arrived at the Brussels road, he gave orders for renewed action.

The Duke instructed me to say to the Field Marshal Blücher, — *"that it had by now indeed become very difficult for him, to resist to the strong attack of the superior French, but with the now arrived reinforcements — he thought about having on the spot circa 20,000 men — he will try a strong offensive in favor of the Prussian army."*

Also I saw the success of the British offensive until retaking of Piraumont and then I returned back as quickly as as I had come. At the windmill of Bussy I reported to the General von Gneisenau and delivered the response of the Duke. This happened at the time as Ligny still was not lost. "

Colonel Hardinge was not able to report to the Duke of the result of the battle of Ligny, because he had shattered one hand by a ball in the wake of the Field Marshal.

Wellington's dependence from Blücher's fate occurred the next day out immediately. The prince had taken up the battle in the interest *of the English on his own. The counter service failed to materialize, consequently now also Wellington had to seek the full concentration of his army further backwards.*

Major Zach

This material is referred to in Grouchy's memoirs, though it appears the translators name is given incorrectly. The article appeared in *Journal des sciences militaires* in 1840, and is a translation of a German work. It appears to confirm that at least some on the German side believed in Napoleon's recall orders of June 17/18, and possibly even had knowledge of the 10 pm order's fate.

Grouchy references this in his 1843 work.

> *Observations sur la bataille de Waterloo (1815).*
> *Extrait des documents militaires laissés par le major DE ZACH, employé à l'état-major badois.*
> *Traduit de l'Allemand*
> *Par M. P. Himly*

Extract military documents left by Major DE ZACH, employed in the General Staff of Baden.

Translated from German

By P. Himly

> *Il faut également attribuer à la fatalité la non-réception des ordres de marcher sur Saint-Lambert qui lui avaient été expédiés par Napoléon à 10 heures du soir et à trois heures du matin. L'officier porteur de la première dépêche, et qui se dirigeait sur Wavre, tomba entre les mains des Prussiens, et celui chargé de la seconde dépêche fut sans doute tué en chemin.*[268]

---

268 Himly, P, "Observations Sur La Bataille de Waterloo (1815)." *Journal des sciences militaires*, 1840, p. 470.

Appendix VIII – Traitors & Prisoners in German Sources

Above translates to:

It should also be attributed to fatality that orders to march towards Saint-Lambert which had been dispatched to him by Napoleon at 10 pm and at three in the morning were not received. The officer carrying the first dispatch, who rode towards Wavre, fell into the hands of the Prussians, and the one in charge of the second dispatch was probably killed on the way.

APPENDIX IX
Evidence Relating To Grouchy's Recall

Baudus

Baudus was one one of the few (only?) of Soult's staff to write about the Belgium campaign in 1815 as part of a greater study of Napoleon. These are the passages discussed in the narrative.

From Volume 1 of *Etudes sur Napoléon*.
Page 222.

> *Crois-tu à l'enfer?*
> *Oui! Sire.*
> *Eh bien! si tu ne veux pas y aller, prends soin de ce blessé que je te confie, fais-le emporter; sans cela Dieu t'y fera brûler, car il veut qu'on soit charitable pour son prochain.*

Translated :

> *Do you believe in hell?*
> *Yes! Sire.*
> *Well! if you do not want to go there, take care of this casualty that I trust to you, do carry it; without this God will make you burn there, because he wants one who is charitable for his next.*

Starting on page 224

Dans la soiree du 17 le quartier-géneral fut établi à la ferme de Caillou; tous les rapports reçus pendant la nuit s'accorderent à dire que les Anglais conservaient leurs positions, et par consequent semblaient disposes à accepter la bataille. Au reste, il etait facile d'en juger par les feux qui couronnaient toutes les hauteurs, spectacle que notre armée ne presentait sûrement pas à ses adversaires, car une partie des corps qui la composaient marchèrent toute la nuit pour arriver à l'emplacement qu'on leur avait désigné, et l'occupèrent à une heure si avancée qu'ils eurent à peine le temps d'allumer des feux pour se sécher.

Le maréchal Major-Général, persistant dans son opinion que Napoléon avait eu tort de donner deux corps d'armée entiers d'infanterie au marechal Grouchy, crut de son devoir d'ouvrir l'avis d'en rappeler sur-le-champ la plus grande partie pour l'affaire du lendemain; mais ses observations à ce sujet ne furent pas plus écoutées dans la soirée qu'elles ne l'avaient été dans la matinée.

Translated:

In the evening of the 17th the headquarters was established at the farm of Caillou; all the reports received during the night agree with the account that the English preserved their positions, and consequently seemed disposed to accept the battle. As for the rest, it was easy to judge by the fires which crowned all the heights, a spectacle that our army surely did not present to its adversaries, because part of the corps marched all during the night to arrive at the site that we had designated for them, and occupied it at one o'clock, so late that they had hardly time to light fires to be dry.

The Marshal Major General, persistent in his opinion that Napoleon was wrong to give two whole army corps of infantry to Marshal Grouchy, believed it was his duty to express the opinion to recall this at once, for the better part of the course of the following day; but his observations on this subject were not heard anymore in the evening than they had been in the morning.

Appendix IX – Evidence Relating To Grouchy's Recall

Marbot's Letter on June 26, 1815

The following letter is supporting evidence that Napoleon was expecting Grouchy to arrive at Waterloo and prepared for the linkage in the morning. However, it appears that he ordered units to link with Grouchy on the far right after ordering the 10 am recall. Had he ordered these units to the right flank before issuing the 10 am recall, it would greatly support Napoleon's claim of issuing recall orders during the night of June 17/18.

However, these troop movements are not easily explained with the actual text of the dispatch sent to Grouchy, and is yet another example of inconsistencies between Napoleon's intent and Soult's execution. Unless one believes the explanation that Napoleon erred with the simple matter of time and distance, then the fact that Napoleon told elements of his army that Grouchy was due to arrive is more evidence that Napoleon had sent recall orders to Grouchy during the night of the 17th/18th.

Marbot's letter:

> *Je ne reviens pas de notre défaite!... On nous a fait manœuvrer comme des citrouilles. J'ai été, avec mon régiment, flanqueur de droite de l'armée pendant presque toute la bataille. On m'assurait que le maréchal Grouchy allait arriver sur ce point, qui n'était gardé que par mon régiment, trois pièces de canon et un bataillon d'infanterie légère, ce qui était trop faible. Au lieu du maréchal Grouchy, c'est le corps de Blücher qui a débouché!... Jugez de la manière dont nous avons été arrangés!... Nous avons été enfoncés, et l'ennemi a été sur-le-champ sur nos derrières!... On aurait pu remédier au mal, mais personne n'a donné d'ordres. Les gros généraux ont été à Paris faire de mauvais discours. Les petits perdent la tète, et cela va mal... J'ai reçu un coup de lance dans le coté; ma blessure est assez forte, mais j'ai voulu rester pour donner le bon exemple. Si chacun eût fait de même, cela irait encore, mais les soldats désertent à l'intérieur; personne ne les arrête, et il y a dans ce pays-ci, quoi qu'on dise, 50,000 hommes qu'on pourrait réunir; mais alors il faudrait peine de mort contre tout homme qui quitte son poste et contre ceux qui donnent permission de le quitter. Tout le monde donne des congés, et les diligences sont pleines d'officiers qui s'en vont. Jugez si les soldats sont en reste! Il n'y*

en aura pas un dans huit jours, si la peine de mort ne les retient... Si les Chambres veulent, elles peuvent nous sauver; mais il faut des moyens promis et des lois sévères... On n'envoie pas un bœuf, pas de vivres, rien...; de sorte que les soldats pillent la pauvre France comme ils faisaient en Russie... Je suis aux avant-postes, sous Laon; on nous a fait promettre de ne pas tirer, et tout est tranquille...[269]

Translated:

I can not accept our defeat!... We were maneuvering like pumpkins. I was, with my regiment, flanked on the right side of the army during almost all of the battle. I was assured that Marshal Grouchy was going to arrive at this point, which was guarded only by my regiment, three pieces of cannon and a battalion of light infantry that was too weak. Instead of Marshal Grouchy, it is Blücher's corps that emerged! ... Judge from the manner that we were arranged! ... We were pressed in, and the enemy was at once on our derrières! ... We could have remedied the problem, but nobody gave orders. The big generals were in Paris making poor speeches. The little ones lose their heads, and things go wrong ... I received a blow by lance in the side; my wound was rather serious, but I wanted to remain to give a good example. If everyone had performed the same way, this would still go on, but the interior soldiers desert; no one stops them, and there is in this country, no matter what anyone says, 50,000 men that we could gather; but then we would need the death penalty for any man who leaves his post and for those who give permission to leave it. Everyone gives leaves, and diligences are filled for officers who are going. Judge if the soldiers remain! There will not be one of them in eight days, if the death penalty does not retain them... If the Chambers choose, they can save us; but we need promised resources and severe laws... We are not sent an ox, nor supplies, nothing...; so that the soldiers plunder poor France as they did in Russia... I am with the outposts, below Laon; we were made to promise not to shoot, and all is quiet...

---

269 Marbot, M., *Mémoires du général baron de Marbot. Polotsk-La Bérésina-Leipzig-Waterloo*, Paris, 1891, pp. 403-404

APPENDIX IX – EVIDENCE RELATING TO GROUCHY'S RECALL

DUPUY'S ACCOUNT OF WATERLOO

Dupuy, in his memoirs, also confirms an expected linkage with Grouchy, but not until much later in the day.

> *Jusque vers quatre heures, nous restâmes paisibles spectateurs de la bataille. Dans ce moment le général Domon vint à moi; le feu des Anglais était à peu près cessé; il me dit que l'affaire était gagnée, que l'armée ennemie était en retraite, que nous étions là pour faire jonction avec le corps du maréchal Grouchy et que nous serions le soir à Bruxelles; il partit.* [270]

Translated:

> *Until around four o'clock, we remained peaceful spectators of the battle. At the moment General Domon came to me; the fire from the English was almost ceased; he says to me that the affair was won, that the enemy army was in retreat, that we were to join there with the corps of Marshal Grouchy and that we would be in Brussels in the evening; he left.*

ON ZENOWICZ AND HIS ACCOUNT

Georges des Despots de Zenowicz published *Waterloo Déposition sur les Quatre Journées de la champagne de 1815* in 1848.

Zenowicz has a clear agenda in his book – the rehabilitation and improvement of his own reputation. Earlier works had been critical of his role in the campaign, and the possible late delivery of the orders he carried to Grouchy.

On dealing with Napoleon, Zenowicz is an admirer, but appears very even handed:

> *Plus tard, l'exécution du duc d'Enghien vint à son tour augmenter le nombre des mécontents. On s'est généralement accordé à regarder*

---

[270] Dupuy, V., *Souvenirs militaires de Victor Dupuy, chef d'escadrons de Hussards : 1794-1816*, 1892, p. 290

cette exécution comme impolitique et inutile : le prince de Talleyrand a bien défini cet acte, en disant : «C'est pis qu'un crime, c'est une faute.» Je suis loin, pour mon compte, de vouloir reprocher cette mort à Napoléon, en l'ordonnant, il ne fit qu'user de représailles contre une famille qui, depuis quelque temps, l'environnait d'assassins, et que cet acte de vigueur réduisit à ne plus conspirer le meurtre et l'assassinat; mais je dois dire que la mort du fils de Condé eut un grand et douloureux retentissement en Europe : chacun sait que cette mort servit de prétexte à l'empereur de Russie pour nouer cette coalition qui vint interrompre les projets de descente en Angleterre, et qui contraignit Napoléon d'aller vaincre à Austerlitz, puis à Eylau et à Friedland.[271]

This translates to:

Later, the execution of the Duke d'Enghien came in turn, increasing the number of malcontents. It is generally agreed to regard this execution as impolitic and useless: Prince Talleyrand well defined this act, saying: "It is worse than a crime, it is a sin." "I am far, on my account, from wanting to reproach this death to Napoleon, by ordering it, he did nothing but use reprisals against a family that, for some time, was surrounded by assassins, and that this act of force lessened those who would conspire murder and assassination; but I must say that the death of the son of Condé had large and painful repercussions in Europe: everyone knows that this death served as a pretext for the Emperor of Russia to bind this coalition that interrupted the invasion projects in England, and that compelled Napoleon to go to defeat in Austerlitz, then in Eylau and Friedland.

This analysis could easily replace what is in a typical College Western Civilization text book and it would serve the students well! Despite some hyperbole loosely comparing Napoleon's sacrifice at St. Helena in the name of humanity to Christ, Zenowicz is not afraid to point what he sees as errors of Napoleon, or to disagree with the opinions of Napoleon. For example, he states that he does not believe that Allies were surprised in

---

[271] Zenowicz, G., *Waterloo, déposition sur les quatre journées de la campagne de 1815*, Ledoyen, 1848, p. 10

Appendix IX – Evidence Relating To Grouchy's Recall

their cantonments, something that Napoleon repeatedly stated with pride about the 1815 campaign.

Zenowicz notes that though the Allies had good intelligence, they were also well informed by traitors within France, and while he recognizes that it would have been too late for Bourmont to have given useful information to the Prussians at the time of his defection, he states without substantiation that Bourmont must have passed information to the enemy earlier.

> *Dans plusieurs relations de la campagne de 1815, il est dit que les ennemis furent surpris dans leurs cantonnements, qu'ils ne connurent les mouvements de l'armée française que tard dans la journée du 15; je ne partage pas cette opinion : Les Anglais comme les Prussiens sont trop méthodiques, trop méticuleux sous le rapport des sûretés à garder en présence de l'ennemi pour qu'ils aient négligé les plus ordinaires précautions. Après qu'ils eurent pris toutes leurs mesures pour se mettre promptement en campagne en cas d'hostilités, ils n'avaient rien de mieux à faire que d'attendre tranquillement les mouvements de l'armée française, afin de tâcher de pénétrer le plan d'opérations de l'Empereur; et une preuve, entre autres, de la vérité de ce que j'avance, c'est que le général Ziethen, commandant l'avant garde de l'armée prussienne, à la première attaque des Français, forma à l'instant même un corps de dix à douze mille hommes. Une autre preuve péremptoire que tout était bien combiné d'avance dans l'armée des coalisés, c'est que l'Empereur trouva, sur la route de Bruxelles, un corps de quatre-vingt-quinze mille hommes qui lui barrait le chemin, ce qui renversa totalement son projet d'arriver sans coup férir dans la capitale de la Belgique. On m'objectera peut-être que l'ennemi fut prévenu par le général Bourmont; c'est probable, s'il était avec lui en rapport secret avant sa désertion, sinon il n'a pu lui faire connaître les mouvements de l'armée française que peu d'instants avant qu'ils ne fussent visibles pour tous. En effet, le général Ziethen étant attaqué à Charleroi, dans la matinée du 15, au moment de la désertion de Bourmont, dut faire prévenir immédiatement le feld-maréchal Blücher de ce qui se passait aux avant-postes. Le courrier de Ziethen, très-certainement, ne pouvait aller moins vite que le général Bourmont; dans tous les cas, la différence de temps ne peut être que minime, eu supposant que Bourmont arrivât le premier*

à Namur, quartier général de Blücher. L'armée anglo-prussienne était donc eu mesure de se mettre en défense au premier qui vive; elle savait même qu'elle allait être attaquée ; qui l'avait si bien renseignée? Si c'est le général Bourmont, ce ne peut être après sa désertion : il eût été trop tard alors, mais bien avant, par les renseignements qu'il se procura à l'aide de sa position, renseignements qu'il a pu faire passer à l'ennemi.[272]

Translated:

In several accounts of the campaign of 1815, it is said that the enemies were surprised in their quarters, that they learned of the movements of the French Army only late in the day of the 15th; I do not share this opinion: The English like the Prussians are too methodical, too meticulous in matters of security to be kept in the presence of the enemy so that they neglected the most ordinary precautions. After they had taken all their measures to quickly organize themselves in a campaign in the event of hostilities, they did not have anything more to do than wait quietly for the movements of the French Army, in order to try to infiltrate the plan of operations of the Emperor; and proof, among others, of the truth of what I suggest, it is that General Ziethen, commander of the advanced guard of the Prussian army, at the first attack of the French, formed at the same moment a corps of ten to twelve thousand men. More conclusive evidence is that all was combined in advance in the army of the allies, is that the Emperor found, on the road from Brussels, a corps of ninety-five thousand men who barred his way, totally turning his project around, to be able to arrive without a fight in the capital of Belgium. Or perhaps objecting that the enemy was warned by General Bourmont; it is likely, if he were with him in secret before his desertion, if not he could not have let him know about the movements of the French Army only a few moments before they were visible to all. Indeed, General Ziethen was attacked in Charleroi, on the morning of the 15th, at the moment of the desertion of Bourmont, had to warn Field-Marshal Blücher immediately about what occurred at the

---

272 Zenowicz, G., *Waterloo, déposition sur les quatre journées de la campagne de 1815*, Ledoyen, 1848, pp. 20-21

Appendix IX – Evidence Relating To Grouchy's Recall

outposts. The correspondence from Ziethen, certainly, could not go slower for General Bourmont; in any case, the difference in time can only be negligible, supposing that Bourmont arrived first at Namur, Blücher's headquarters. The Anglo-Prussian army thus had the capacity to defend first to succeed; they knew well that they were going to be attacked; who had informed them of this? If it is General Bourmont, it cannot be after his desertion: it had been too late then, but well before, by the information that he received to aid his position, information that he could have passed to the enemy.

Early in the campaign, Zenowicz had apparently taken correspondence to Napoleon. As was custom, an orderly would often remain with the recipient until given a response. In this case, Zenowicz claims that he ended up attached to Napoleon. As Napoleon later complained of the orderlies that were members of the Imperial and General Headquarters, maybe he wanted someone around that he recognized as a veteran. Napoleon would save his most trusted ADC's for the most sensitive missions, especially during battle.

This is Zenowicz's account of his actions on June 18, 1815:

Le 18 juin 1815, jour de la bataille de Waterloo, j'étais de service, comme officier supérieur, au quartier impérial, et j'eus l'ordre de ne pas quitter un instant Napoléon.

Vers neuf heures du matin, l'Empereur monta à cheval; je le suivis. En s'approchant vers la ligne droite de l'armée, après avoir parlé quelques moments au comte d'Erlon, il laissa sa suite en arrière, et, accompagné seulement du Major-Général (le maréchal Soult), il monta sur une petite élévation, d'où on découvrait facilement les diverses positions des deux armées. Après avoir examiné quelque temps avec sa lorgnette, sans changer de place, il adressa quelques paroles au Major-Général; puis, au moment où celui-ci descendit du plateau, l'Empereur me fit signe de monter près de lui ; j'obéis ; il m'adressa alors la parole : «Voilà le comte d'Erlon, notre droite,» me dit-il, en me montrant le corps d'armée de ce général ; puis continuant, après avoir décrit un cercle de sa main vers la droite de la ligne, il ajouta : « Grouchy marche dans cette direction, rendez-vous de suite auprès de lui, passez par Gambloux, suivez ses traces ; le

Major-Général vous donnera encore un ordre par écrit.» Je voulus faire observer à l'Empereur que la roule qu'il m'indiquait était trop longue ; mais sans me laisser le temps d'achever, il me dit : «C'est égal, vous seriez pris en suivant la route la plus courte ;» et désignant ensuite l'extrémité du flanc droit de la ligne, il dit encore : « Vous reviendrez par ici me rejoindre, quand Grouchy débouchera sur la ligne. Il me tarde qu'il soit en communication directe et en ligne de bataille avec nous. Partez, partez. »

Aussitôt cet ordre reçu, je courus après le Major-Général, qui se dirigeait en ce moment vers la ferme de Caillou, où le quartier impérial avait passé la nuit. Nous arrivâmes à dix heures à la ferme; le Major-Général se rendit dans sa chambre, et fit demander son secrétaire. La première chose que l'on fait en commençant à écrire un ordre, c'est d'y mettre la date et l'heure; il est facile de voir que celte heure ne peut être celle du départ de la dépêche : car, avant le départ, il faut du temps pour récrire ; il en faut aussi pour l'inscrire sur le registre d'ordre du Major-Général. Tout cela demande assez de temps; dans un service ordinaire, où les heures et les minutes n'ont aucun rôle à jouer, cette remarque n'est d'aucune importance ; mais dans un cas particulier, quand on compte les heures et les minutes, quand on jette un tort au porteur d'un ordre, il doit être permis de rétablir les faits tels qu'ils se sont produits. Je me répète, la date de l'ordre dont je fus porteur fut mise à dix heures ; je me retirai alors au salon de service. Après une demi-heure d'attente, je rejoignis le Major-Général. Rien encore que la date n'était écrit; le Major-Général regardait la carte, et son secrétaire s'amusait à tailler une plume.

Je retournai au salon, où je trouvai M. Regnault, ordonnateur en chef du premier corps, qui, apprenant que depuis vingt-quatre heures, ayant toujours été en course, je n'avais pu rien me procurer pour manger, voulut bien envoyer chercher dans son fourgon un morceau de pain et de l'eau-de-vie. Après mon repas, je rentrai de nouveau chez le Major-Général : il était occupé à dicter l'ordre que j'attendais ; je me rendis encore une fois au salon de service. Au bout d'une demi-heure, je fus demandé ; le maréchal Soult me répéta à peu

Appendix IX – Evidence Relating To Grouchy's Recall

près, en me donnant son ordre par écrit, ce que l'Empereur m'avait dit. Je partis de suite.

Tous les détails dans lesquels je viens d'entrer prouvent surabondamment, que les observations des écrivains sur ma mission sont inexactes. Quelques-uns de ces écrivains sont excusables cependant : ils n'ont pu connaître les particularités que je viens de citer; sur la foi des ordres publiés, ils m'ont jugé d'après l'heure mal fixée de mon départ; pour les autres, qui out sacrifié la vérité à leur haine politique, je n'ai pas à me préoccuper de leurs critiques partiales et sans autorité.

Translated:

On June 18, 1815, the day of the Battle of Waterloo, I was on duty as senior officer, in the imperial headquarters, and I had orders not to leave Napoleon for a moment.

About nine in the morning the Emperor mounted his horse; I followed him. Approaching to the straight line of the army, having spoken a few times to Count d'Erlon he left his suite behind, and accompanied only by the Major General (Marshal Soult), he ascended a small hill, from which one easily discovered the various positions of the two armies. After examining some time with his telescope, without changing place, he addressed a few words to the Major General; then, when he came down from the plateau, the Emperor beckoned me to sit beside him; I obeyed; He then spoke to me, "Here is Count d'Erlon, our right," he said, pointing to the corps of that general; then continuing, after describing a circle with his hand to the right of the line, he added, "Grouchy is marching in that direction, go immediately to him, go through Gembloux, follow in his footsteps; Major General will still give you a written order;" I wanted to point out to the Emperor that he was suggesting that I had to follow a route too long; but without giving me time to finish, he said: "Never mind, you would be caught following the shortest route;" and then pointing to the end of the right side of the line, he said: "You'll come back here and join me, when Grouchy will arrive on the line. I look forward to him being in direct communication and in the line of battle with us. Go, go."

At once the order received, I ran after the Major General, who was heading now towards the farm of Le Caillou, where the imperial headquarters had spent the night. We arrived at the farm at ten o'clock; the Major General returned to his room and asked for his secretary. The first thing one does while starting to write an order is to put the date and time; it is easy to see that this hour cannot be the time the dispatch was sent: because, before departure, it takes time to write; it also takes time to copy it into the Register of the Major General. All this requires enough time; in ordinary service where the hours and minutes have no role to play, this remark is of no importance; but in a particular case, when one counts the hours and minutes, when an accusation is made against the bearer of an order, it should be possible to restore the facts as they occurred. I repeat, the date of the order which I was carrying was set at ten o'clock; I then retired to the living room. After half an hour of waiting, I joined the General Staff. Still nothing than the date was written; the Major General looked at the map, and his secretary was amusing himself cutting a quill.

I returned to the living room, where I found Mr. Regnault, chief officer of the first corps, who, learning that for twenty-four hours I had always been on duty, and that I had been unable to eat anything, was kind enough to send for a piece of bread and some spirits from his caisson. After my meal, I went back to the Major General: he was busy dictating the order I expected; I once again went to the living room. After half an hour, I was requested; Marshal Soult repeated to me roughly, giving me his written orders, what the Emperor had said. I left immediately.

All the details that I have just entered give ample proof that the observations of the writers on my mission are inaccurate. Some of these writers are excusable though: they could not know the details that I just mentioned on the basis of orders as published; they judged me by the time wrongly fixed of my departure; for others, who sacrificed the truth to their political hatred, I do not have to worry about their biased criticisms, both partial and lacking authority.

Appendix IX – Evidence Relating To Grouchy's Recall

Colonel von Sachsen-Weimar Account

Erwin Muilwijk, whose work can be found at http://1815fieldarmy.nl/, provided the following at http://theminiaturespage.com/boards/msg.mv?id=284955&page=2.

> *A few years ago I translated an account from the former Colonel von Sachsen-Weimar for the wonderfull online collection of John Franklin's 1815 Limited. In this account von Sachsen-Weimar wrote the following on the suprise of the Prussians appearing on their right flank:*
>
> *"I would not, however, wish to end this letter without communicating to you what Général Bernard – who I met in the United States in 1825 – told me about the part he played at the battle of Waterloo as an Aide-de-camp to the Emperor Napoleon. It was towards the middle of that battle that the emperor, who had often been looking to the right, asked if there was anything to be seen of Grouchy? Having at last received the report that one could see Tirailleurs* (skirmishers) *appearing from afar, he charged Général Bernard to go and assure himself of who it could be. The general went to the extreme right of the French army where he found some Tirailleurs* (skirmishers) *positioned. Having no enemy troops confronting them, their officers confirmed that they could see in the distance columns arriving preceded by skirmishers, but they could not distinguish to which nation they belonged. Accompanied by only one servant, the general approached towards his troops, placed himself behind a bush from where he could comfortably observe, and saw that the caps the approaching troops were wearing bore a cross on the front. Enlightened by this, he returned quickly to the French Tirailleurs* (skirmishers) *and informed them of the visit they were about to receive, and then rushed back to the emperor. He got off his horse, having found the emperor walking with his hands behind his back in front of his suite. Having seen him the emperor asked in a low voice: 'What tidings general?'…'Bad ones, Sire'…'that they are Prussians?'…'Yes, Sire, I recognised them'…'I thought so. Good, messieurs', he said while turning towards his suite, 'It goes well, there is Grouchy who arrives'. Nevertheless, he called another*

Aide-de-camp to whom he told the truth, and who he dispatched to Comte de Lobau with the order to change front with his army corps towards the right wing so as to oppose the enemy troops who were about to arrive."

One of the recent arguments that has been debated at length is when did Napoleon become aware of the Prussians, or were the French utterly surprised when the Prussians first attacked. What we are focused on in this work is the continued example of Napoleon *expecting* Grouchy's arrival. While it is true that Napoleon expected Grouchy to be far closer than he was on the 18th of June, based on the conditions of the roads between the Waterloo battlefield and Grouchy's expected position, had Napoleon first issued a recall at 10 am, he would not have expected Grouchy's arrival by 4pm. This is more supporting evidence that this maneuver was ordered during the previous evening.

APPENDIX X
Essay on Grouchy, the Recall, and the Prussians

The following essay was provided by Chris Rollet. It is a detailed look at the French intelligence and correspondence relating to the Prussians on June 17th and 18th. It is far more detailed than what is contained in the narrative, and throws far more support behind the notion that the Prussians intercepted key communications between Napoleon and Grouchy.

But it also demonstrates, as Jean-Marc Largeaud says in the foreword, that the definitive history of this campaign is yet to be written. This essay documents several events which have been dismissed by the conventional Waterloo history, and reminds us all that there is still much work to do.

The campaign of 1815 is very much talked about. The discussions are not finished.

Napoleon's plan was excellent. In spite of their numeric superiority, the Allies passed as close to a resounding disaster as they did their triumph.

Having failed in the execution of his plans, did the Emperor then lie to mask errors?

Virulent criticisms come regularly, in this way, often by arguments that have little substantiation. Besides, we shall never be in the head of the protagonists.

Here is a presentation the purpose of which is to propose lines of thought on some points that have generated controversies.

Evening and night of the 17th

At 9 pm or shortly after, Napoleon was informed by a report from Milhaud that a strong Prussian column retreated to Wavre (see Gourgaud 1818 & Napoleon 1820). Napoleon was not worried because Grouchy was expected to intervene against the Prussians, if necessary. However, Napoleon never imagined that the troops of the Marshal were only around Gembloux. He thought that the Prussian army would not be able to intervene in force the next day as he was unaware that it had already massed around Wavre.

As a result of the report of Milhaud, Napoleon sent an order at 10 pm to Grouchy (see Gourgaud 1818 & Napoleon 1820). The order carried by the officer was labeled "sur Wavre, au nord de Gembloux." (Cf. Stoffel, Revue militaire générale, June and July, 1909, pp. 617-640 and 28-65, referenced in Napoléon et Waterloo by JM Largeaud).

This officer did not reach Grouchy (killed or captured by the Prussians? See Zach and Letourneur).

Not knowing Wellington's intentions, Napoleon considered two possibilities:
- Continue following the Anglo-Dutch army at daybreak had Wellington retreated into the night to meet with the Prussians.
- Order battle for the next day if Wellington remained in position. An Order of Battle was sent during the night in case of this eventuality, though its text has not survived.

Morning and Afternoon of the 18th

Before 4 am, Napoleon received the first report of Grouchy (from 10 pm). He learned Grouchy was in Gembloux. A second officer was sent to Grouchy to confirm the order sent at 10 pm the day before (see Gourgaud, Napoleon). This officer also failed to reach Grouchy (killed, captured? see Zach).

Around 5 or 6 in the morning (it was light and the rain had stopped), Wellington was still in position. Napoleon renews the order of battle given the previous night. The following order is the one Soult sent on the 18th, around 5 or 6 am (see *Documents Inédits* pp. 52-53, published by the son of Ney, 1840):

Appendix X – Essay on Grouchy, the Recall, and the Prussians

To Marshal Ney, Prince de la Moskowa

The Emperor orders that the army be positioned to attack the enemy at 9 o'clock in the morning; General Officers commanding Army Corps will rally their troops, will have their arms ready, and will allow the soldiers to make soup; they will also have the soldiers eat so that at precisely 9 am everyone is ready with artillery and ambulances, in the battle position that the Emperor indicated by his overnight order.

The Lieutenant-Generals, commanding the both the Infantry and Cavalry Corps will immediately send officers to the Major General to indicate their position and bring back future orders.

Given at the Imperial Headquarters, June 18, 1815.
Marshal of the Empire, Major General,
Duke of Dalmatia

Levavasseur, an aide de camp of Ney, wrote in his memoirs:

At daybreak, the Marshal had given me the mission to recognize the field and the movements of the enemy. I departed by beginning my recognition on the extreme left; I had conferred successively with all the vedettes (cavalry sentinels) who taught me nothing. However, when I arrived on the extreme right, the vedette made me observe that detachments came and went on this flank; that isolated officers rushed in this direction. I stayed one hour on the field, and, having made sure of the truth of this observation, convinced that the enemy maneuvered on our right, I joined the Marshal.

The Marshal had gone with the Emperor; I ran towards him and I announced the result of my mission and my conjectures.

Addressing the Emperor, he says: "Sire, my aide de camp, who comes from reconnaissance, declares to me that the enemy seems to maneuver on our right." – "All right, it is enough," answered the Emperor."

Napoleon might not have thought of the Prussians at this moment, but he knew by Milhaud and the first report of Grouchy that some Prussians were on the right wing, near Wavre.

Around 8 am (see Napoleon 1820), the Emperor took his lunch. Marchand says 9 am but I think this schedule is one to which Napoleon left for the field (see Zenowicz). Officers just told the Emperor that the artillery would soon be able to operate on the ground. Napoleon rode around 9 am and went to the line.

Between 9 and 9:45, Napoleon was with Soult in the field. At that time, he then had at least three - maybe four - pieces of information that enabled him to think the Prussians were near:

- Information during the evening that a strong column was in retreat to Wavre (Milhaud)
- Grouchy report of 10 pm indicating the possibility that some Prussians marched in the direction of Wavre possibly to join Wellington,
- Report of Levavasseur,
- Optionally, the second report of Grouchy.

A few words about this second report. In publications of the Grouchy family, it was given with a schedule of 2 or 3 am. The letter from Soult at 1 pm, as produced by Houssaye, shows a schedule of 6 am. There is speculation that Grouchy possibly wrote it at 2 or 3 am (note that the Marshal also wrote to Pajol at the latter time) but sent it only at 6 am. If the start was about 2:30 and 3:30 am depending on the time of writing, Napoleon was informed from 6 to 7 am (Napoleon 1820 & Gourgaud 1818 indicate about 5 am). If Grouchy sent around 6:30 am, Napoleon probably received around 10 am at the latest.

Soult was off again at 9:45 am to Le Caillou. Napoleon then gave instructions to Zenowicz and indicated that he would be captured by heading in a direct line east to Wavre (see Zenowicz).

Zenowicz joined Soult at Le Caillou. The order for the 10-hour schedule was presented to him by Soult at 11:15. Zenowicz indicated "around noon" for his departure; in my opinion that is too late, as the cannonade and the shooting began shortly after 11:30 am and Zenowicz says he heard the sounds after a few minutes of running.

APPENDIX X – ESSAY ON GROUCHY, THE RECALL, AND THE PRUSSIANS

An element confirms this: an order of Soult included in the "Documents Inédits" published by the son of Ney. In this order, Ney added:

> *Count d'Erlon understands that it is by the left that the attack will begin, instead of the right.*
> *Communicate this new provision with General in Chief Reille.*
> (On the back) *Orders dictated by the Emperor, on the battlefield of Mount-St-Jean, on the 18th, around eleven o'clock in the morning, and written by Marshal Duke of Dalmatia, Major General.*
> *Paris, June 21, 1815.*

This indication "around eleven o'clock in the morning " implies Soult had returned from Le Caillou before the attack on Hougoumont, so I set this between 11:15 and 11:30.

Levavasseur (aide de camp of Ney):

> *Little before noon, the Emperor dictates the order which Soult writes on its notebook, then the major general tears out the sheet and gives it to marshal Ney, who, before to hand it to me to communicate it to the leading generals, writes in margin with pencil:*
> *"The Count d'Erlon will understand that it is him who has to begin the attack."*

Now, see the anecdote reported by Mauduit:

> *Here again we have to report a fact of utmost gravity, but we do not know who is accountable for it.*
> *From 11 o'clock in the MORNING, thanks to the zeal and dedication of Colonel Bro, we had already learned on our far right of the arrival of the riders of the Prussian army. Here's how: the Colonel Bro, being placed with his lancers at the end of our right wing had, as a vigilant and experienced soldier, detached foremost a reconnaissance of smart NCOs, having agreed on the telegraphic signals they would do with their spears. These NCOs were being staggered in the direction, from where the Prussian army could arrive, the two most advanced were quick to recognize a cavalry column. It was a squadron of Prussian Uhlans, with their yellow*

> *and black flame. Informed, at once, of this serious news, the Colonel Bro hastened to report this to his general. It was 11 am.*
>
> *How to explain a fact of this importance had not been brought immediately to the attention of the Emperor? ... Who was the general or officer who had failed in his duty? ... Was it the Brigadier or Major General; was it one of their aides? The first two are still living, and both are interested in explaining this puzzle, and to say to the whole of France, why they kept to themselves such a warning. If they disclaim responsibility, then they would have to explain how this warning, which the salvation of the army depended on, had been stopped in the path of our right to the point where Napoleon was; he himself was aware, as we have just seen, and only by chance, TWO HOURS LATER, of the appearance of the Prussians... There is a culprit: who is it? We do not know; but history should search its name to reproach him or his negligence or his odious betrayal, because it was the cause of our disasters, and what's more of the humiliation of France!*

In his memoirs, Bro dealt only briefly on June 18 and limited his account to the D'Erlon attack and the moment he was committed against the British cavalry (he was wounded at that time and withdrew from the battlefield). He does not refer to that to what Mauduit wrote.

There is also a letter from Captain Taylor, the 10th Hussars (Vivian brigade). In position near Papelotte he saw in the morning a strong French heavy cavalry patrol eastward. He thought it was probably looking for the Prussians (see in Siborne).

This may involve the patrol sent by Bro. His Lancers were not heavy cavalry, but Taylor has seen them from a distance and could be wrong. He also wrote the letter in 1829, his memory dated some 14 years. It is possible it was another French cavalry unit.

I believe that the information was raised to Napoleon (see O'Meara, 03/26/17):

> *I learned the arrival of Bulow at eleven, but I paid it no attention.*

Appendix X – Essay on Grouchy, the Recall, and the Prussians

This does not mean that the Emperor knew at 11 am that the detected Prussians actually belonged to the corps of Bülow; he was able to generalize about it, in 1817. But the schedule is specified. Napoleon did not think it was a serious threat at the moment, but maybe it's why the plan of attack was changed before 11:30 - see order of Soult with notes of Ney.

In my opinion, this is then – about 11 am - that Ney signed the following written order (Erwin Muilwijk, http://www.russborough.com/omnium_g/manuscripts/ney-waterloo-dispatch.html) in the absence of Soult who returned from Caillou between 11:15 and 11:30.

> *The English are amassed on Mont-Saint-Jean, that is in front of the forest of Soignes. If the Prussians retreat behind the forest of Soignes you must send a thousand cavalry behind them, and come with your troops to join us. If one finds they intend to come in front of the forest at Mont Saint-Jean, then make a screen and bar the route.*
> *Ney*

The question of the authenticity of this order remains open. I think it is genuine.

Was it written from Napoleon's instruction, or not? No answer at this stage.

Who is it for? Very probably Lobau, but was he notified of the order? According to Waresquiel ("Lettres d'un lion"), Lobau left no explanation if the sixth corps was or was not intended to oppose Bülow.

The writing and the content of the text show that it was written hastily. I think the announcement – or confirmation – of the discovery of the Prussians was the cause.

In his letter to Grouchy (1830), Marbot says:

> *...At the beginning of the action, about eleven o'clock, I was detached from my regiment and division with an infantry battalion under my command. These troops were put with one flank at right angle to the main body on the far right, behind Frichemont, facing the Dyle.*
> *Specific instructions were given to me by the Emperor, by his aide de camp Labedoyere and an orderly officer whom I do not remember the name. They enjoined to leave the bulk of my forces always in*

view from the battlefield, to send 200 infantrymen in the wood of Frichemont, a squadron in Lasne, pushing on to Saint-Lambert; another squadron with half in Couture, half in Beaumont, sending reconnaissance onto the Dyle, to the bridges of Moustier and Ottignies…"

General Bruno commanded a brigade of cavalry (included in Jacquinot's division, corps of d'Erlon) to which belonged the regiment of Marbot (7th hussars). In a letter published (1838) in "La Sentinelle de l'Armée", Bruno wrote:

> *…I had detached in the morning the 7th hussars to make communications with general Domont…*

This implies that the Domon division was sent eastward at about 11 am, according with the contents of the order signed by Ney.

The mission entrusted to Marbot broadly corresponds to what is stated in the order of Ney, in a "light" organization, to complete the reconnaissance of Domon. However, Marbot was not informed of the presence of the Prussians, which is not surprising. This is corroborated by this excerpt from the testimony of Dupuy, squadron leader in the regiment of Marbot:

> *Until about four hours we remained quiet spectators of the battle. In this moment General Domon came to me; English fire was almost ceased; he said that the case was won, that the enemy was retreating, we were there to link up with the corps of Grouchy and that we would be in the evening in Brussels; he departed.*
>
> *Few moments later, instead of a junction with the troops of Marshal Grouchy as we expected, we received the attack of a Prussian Uhlans Regiment.*

The Emperor believed that the Prussian troops were relatively weak and not able to quickly intervene. In the Bulletin of June 21, it stated: "*…it was assumed that the Prussian corps, which could be present towards evening, could be fifteen thousand.*"

Appendix X – Essay on Grouchy, the Recall, and the Prussians

This was consistent with the report of Milhaud the day before, indicating a strong column retreating on Wavre, and with the reports of Grouchy, indicating that the Prussian corps passed through this city.

And maybe, it's why the attack was ordered by the left instead of the right (see the Soult's order with notes of Ney).

Around 11 / 11:30 am the bulk of the army was deployed on the battle line; some units, however, are still to be deployed (on the night of 17 to 18, the troops of the 6th corps bivouacked between Plancenoit and Genappe -see Tromelin and Marq). Lobau regiments gathered around Rossomme before going to position southwest of Belle Alliance.

I will now address the case of Colonel Alphonse de Grouchy, who commanded the 12th Chasseurs (Domon division). In his memoirs (in August 1836), the Baron Mounier related this anecdote:

> *At Waterloo, Mr. Grouchy commanded a brigade of light cavalry. At Ligny, serendipity had delivered him seven Prussian guns. Only eleven were taken: this action therefore was a brilliant feat. Here is how. A maréchal-des-logis of the 12th Chasseurs, that he commanded, was drunk, had departed and returned by announcing a Prussian battery, placed at the end of their line, was without support and that it would be easy to seize. Mr. Grouchy went to recognize it. An infantry battalion, which protected the battery, had piled arms. A squadron was unbridled. Then M. de Grouchy went with his regiment, and then swept down on the guns and carried them away. The Emperor made him a maréchal de camp.*
>
> *So at Waterloo, he had a brigade, responsible for covering the extreme right of the army and to try to link with Marshal Grouchy. An officer, he had sent in the morning to request food, etc., in the villages came to tell him he had found the Prussians who had prevented him from moving forward. Mr. Grouchy concluded that troops of Blücher were marching to join Wellington, and the thing seemed so serious that he spurred on to go to the Emperor. He found him, in the positions, with Soult, to whom he related his case. Soult advised him to inform the Emperor himself. He listened and then said, "Who is the stupid officer who made this report? The Prussians are far from there!"*

> *Mr. Grouchy returned to his brigade and, reporting to the officer what was the imperial thinking, he told him he had to go take prisoners. The officer went with a few volunteers, and Mr. Grouchy marched to support him. Soon they took two infantrymen and a hussar. Mr. Grouchy hastened to lead them to the Major général. The Emperor questioned them, and it is according to their statements that they belonged to the brigades of Ziethen and Schmidt that, presumably, the Emperor ordered to Mouton [Lobau] to walk to protect his right. It was then about two hours.*

The episode between A. de Grouchy, Soult and Napoleon, was able to take place after Soult came back from Le Caillou, shortly after 11:15 am.

A couple factors seem to confirm this:
- An indication that prisoners were captured "soon" after the departure of A. Grouchy,
- Interrogation of the prisoners and the order given to Lobau to go cover the right. The order to Lobau was indeed given at 2:30 pm or a little later, so the indication "It was then about two hours" is consistent.

Concerning units of prisoners: Ziethen commanded the 1st Prussian corps. But there was no brigade commanded by a Schmidt (see state of the Prussian army before the campaign, in de Bas & T'Serclaes). There was a Major von Schmidt, commanding the "Colbergisches Infantry Regiment" von Krafft Brigade, 2nd Prussian corps.

These two corps were the most shaken in the Battle of Ligny, and hundreds or thousands of men were scattered during or after the battle. It is possible that these prisoners were part of the "scattered".

Another assumption: the discussion between A. de Grouchy, Soult and Napoleon may have occurred shortly after 9:30 am. This could explain why Napoleon told Zenowicz, near 10 am, that he would be taken if he went to the east. If not, then Napoleon probably knew the information from Levavasseur, at that moment.

In his publication *"Grouchy, du 16 au 19 juin"*, Alphonse de Grouchy wrote this note:

Appendix X – Essay on Grouchy, the Recall, and the Prussians

I may certify the fact as for M. Zenowicz departure time. I was near him when he left, he tells me that he goes to my father, I pulled my watch, its indicated noon."

The year of publication was 1864. At this time, Zenowicz had been dead for 10 years as well as many actors. I think A. de Grouchy wanted to voluntarily confirm this schedule to confirm what Zenowicz had written.

And maybe A. de Grouchy saw Zenowiz on the field not at noon, but before 10 am, if he met Soult and Napoléon near 9:30 am.

As for the response of Napoleon, "Who is the stupid officer who made this report? The Prussians are far from there!" Either A. de Grouchy exaggerated the line (or more) or Napoleon said this because he did not want to reveal what he knew about the Prussians. But if the scene happened around 9:30 am, it is possible that was what Napoleon really thought.

For the schedule of 11 am, Napoleon knew then by the reports of Grouchy, at least two or three Corps of the Prussian army were massed near Wavre the night before. This completed the Milhaud report of 9 pm on the 17th, and the information returned by the Colonel Bro.

Shortly before 1 pm, Soult saw troops on the heights of Saint-Lambert and notified Napoleon (see Baudus). According to Napoleon, it was he who saw what appeared to be the troops towards Saint-Lambert. This episode was narrated by Rogniat too.

At 1 pm, Soult began writing the letter to Grouchy. Shortly after, at 1:15 pm, the Prussian prisoners were brought forth:
- According Gourgaud (1818), *"But fifteen minutes later, some hussars brought a Prussian orderly, carrying a dispatch, which informed us that the troops that could be seen were the vanguard of the corps's Bulow..."* In this case, the hussars bringing the prisoner can only be those of Marbot. Extract from the Marbot letter in 1830: *"One of my platoons, having advanced to a mile beyond Saint-Lambert, met a platoon of Prussian hussars, from which it took several men, including an officer. I warned the Emperor of this strange capture, and sent him prisoners..."*
- According Napoleon (1820), *"...a Chasseur officer brought a Prussian black hussar who had been taken prisoner by the riders of a flying column of three hundred Chasseurs, beating the platform between Wavre and Planchenoit..."* In this case, the Chasseurs officer is possibly A.

de Grouchy (see Mounier). Mounier extract after A. de Grouchy, *"Soon they took two infantrymen and a hussar..."*

I think in the relations of Napoleon and Gourgaud, only the Hussar was mentioned because he, and not others, was questioned in full.

There are several hypotheses for this capture:
- The prisoners taken by the patrol sent to Lasne/Saint-Lambert are brought back to Marbot then sent to Napoleon. They pass among men Domon placed behind Marbot. A. de Grouchy took the opportunity and accompanying hussars of Marbot and the prisoners and he informs Napoleon. This would explain why Gourgaud evokes hussars bringing a prisoner, when Napoleon evokes a Chasseur officer.
- Also possible that there were prisoners taken by both men of Marbot (who refers only to hussars) and those of A. de Grouchy (a hussar and 2 infantrymen).

Following information obtained from the prisoner(s), Subervie was sent as reinforcement to the east. Napoleon knew that the corps of Bülow was approaching.

A postscript was added to the letter to Grouchy of 1 pm; between 1:45/2:30 pm, the officer carrying this order departed for Grouchy. The dispatch of the Prussian Hussar was also given to him, but Grouchy did not receive it. He said the second messenger was in an advanced state of drunkenness. Maybe he was not handed the dispatch, or maybe this was never sent to Grouchy.

Around 2:15 to 2:30 pm, Lafresnaye arrived at the Emperor. He brought the report written by Grouchy at 11 am. Lafresnaye had left the Marshal shortly after 11:30 am, the gunfire heard at the time of his departure. He rode to the sound of cannon, thus without going through Quatre Bras. (See Lafresnaye in Grouchy).

Napoleon then knew that the Marshal had lagged far behind in his progress and was not before Wavre by the late morning. However, he may have hoped that Zenowicz would have joined Grouchy by that time, or would soon join him. Grouchy's troops, who since Lafresnaye's departure, had marched on Wavre, would be able to turn off towards Saint-Lambert to take Bülow in the rear by the late afternoon or early evening.

Appendix X – Essay on Grouchy, the Recall, and the Prussians

However, it was necessary to guard against the threat posed by the troops of Bülow.

As a result, around 2:45 pm, Napoleon sent Lobau's infantry to the east (see Tromelin, quoted in the biography devoted to him by Lachouque). The Domon and Subervie divisions were already on the right of the army.

It was also at 2:30 pm that the postscript was added to the letter Soult sent to Davout (see register Soult in Grouchy). The letter bears the schedule from 1:15, the postscript is as follows:

> *It is half past two; the cannonade has begun on the whole battle line; the English are in the center, the Dutch and the Belgians to the right of German troops, the Prussians are to the left; the battle is general; four hundred cannon are thundering at the moment."*

By 3 pm, the 6th corps left its position south of Belle Alliance and came to take place behind the right of d'Erlon and near the divisions Domon and Subervie.

Tromelin, according to Lachouque :

> *... at 3 pm, he* (Tromelin) *writes, the Jeanin division, following the Simmer division, crosses the road at 200 meters in south of Belle-Alliance, passes behind the corps of Milhaud's cuirassiers, leaves Plancenoit on its right and comes to deploy at one kilometer of the north-east of this latter village. The three regiments of the division are divided into two groups: the 10th line and the Cuppé battalion of the 107th were under my orders and occupied a small wood. In front of us, both batteries of the divisions of cavalry already fired at the Prussian columns which emerged from the woods...*

And for Marq, in "description des campagnes de guerre faites par moi", wrote in 1817, yet published 1901:

> *After 10 o'clock in the morning (on June 18th, 1815) the regiment went out of its camp to go on Waterloo, where the battle was already livened up, the regiments which were a part of our army corps (6th) met, and they walked in column up to the neighborhood of the battle, where we were made to hold in this position till three hours, and*

> *having been exposed for a long time to the cannonballs which fell in our ranks, they made us walk in closed columns up to the middle of the battlefield; when walking to arrive at this place several men were killed in our ranks, and having arrived, they formed us in square by regiment because the English cavalry was near us which fought with French cuirassiers, it came several times to force our squares; but it gained no success, balls and grapeshot fell in our squares as the hail, we were there with order not to fire a gunshot and with crossed bayonets, many men were killed in this position. After a few hours of position in square, the majors received the order to send their voltigeurs in skirmishing position, I was sergeant-major of the 3rd company, and immediately after this order was given, our officers lead us there, and, having arrived near the enemy we were positioned here and there near a wood situated on the right of the road of Brussels, being in good spirit, and supported by columns of cavalry which were behind us we forced the enemy to withdraw...*

At that time, Bülow was not able to seriously attack the French right wing.

Previously, Napoleon had sent General Bernard in reconnaissance eastward. Van Loben Sels reported:

> *The general, removing his hat, began to walk to the Emperor, who perceiving him asked softly, "What are the news, General?"- "Bad, sire." – "Is it not that they are the Prussians?" – "Yes, Sire, I have recognized them." – "I suspected this; Well! Gentlemen" said Napoleon, turning to his suite, "All is well. That's Grouchy who arrives towards us."*
>
> *Yet he called another aide-de-camp and he told the truth, and he hurried to Count Lobau with orders to effect a change of front with his corps on the right wing, in order to oppose strong resistance to the enemy troops, which would debouch.*

Bernard was to gather clues about the progress of Grouchy. He met French infantry (possibly the battalion placed under the command of Marbot) that were in observation. He then identified the Prussian soldiers, and

Appendix X – Essay on Grouchy, the Recall, and the Prussians

returned to inform Napoleon. The remark of the latter, made to his entourage, demonstrated that Napoleon still wanted to hide the presence of the Prussians from his staff.

Around 4:30 pm, Bülow employed his first 2 brigades on the French right flank to relieve Wellington who was then attacked by Ney's mass cavalry charges. The Prussians pushed back Subervie and Domon and were then committed against Lobau who was forced to retreat.

What about the "surprise" mentioned in the testimonies of Janin and Combes-Brassard (deputy chiefs of the 6th corps), concerning the attack of Bülow?

An excerpt of Combes-Brassard's text published in 1899 in *"Recueil de l'Académie des sciences, belles lettres et arts du Tarn-et-Garonne, Montauban"*:

> *... It was half past three, a terrible fire extended over all the line of both armies. The 6th corps finished deploying in reserve on the whole right of the army, when I went to the far end of our right, I recognized tops of column which debouched from Vavres, by Ohain and Saint-Lambert.*
>
> *These columns were Prussian. Their arrival occurred without the Emperor having given any order. Our flank was turned ...*

An excerpt of Janin ("Campagne de Waterloo etc." published in 1820):

> *The 6th corps goes forward to support the attack of the center: as soon as it reaches the crest which separates both armies that its chief of staff, general Durrieux, who was ahead, is wounded and falls back, and announces that the enemy skirmishers are extending their line over our right side: the count of Lobau advances with general Jacquinot and me to recognize them, and soon we see two columns debouching, ten thousand men each: it was the Prussian corps of Bülow. The destination of the 6th corps was changed by this incident: it was not anymore a question of renewing the attack against the English but of repelling the Prussians: in brief by the force of circumstance we were reduced to the most unfavorable defense which outcome was not doubtful any more...*

They clearly did not expect the attack. This is not surprising, as with the case of Marbot, they had not been notified of a Prussian presence. Above them, there was Lobau (and Durrieu, as chief of staff of the 6th corps). As it has not be proven that Lobau was aware, why would Janin and Combes-Brassard have been aware?

Bourdon de Vatry was appointed aide de camp of Lobau, by Napoleon, on his return from Elba. He related this anecdote:

> ... later, the Count of Lobau, commanding the right to Waterloo, sent word to the Emperor that he was attacked by the Prussians. Napoleon would not at first admit that the thing was possible. Lobau told M. de Canonne, one of his officers: "Take a prisoner and bring it to him, maybe he will be convinced." About two o'clock the order to Grouchy that he had to debouch/arrive by Saint-Lambert had been sent, but it was too late, and even if he would have arrived right after Ziethen and Thielmann, he could not have changed the face things...

From this we have to infer that Lobau was not informed of the Prussian threat. Bourdon de Vatry was with Jerôme during the campaign, not with Lobau. The story also contains errors, in addition to the mention of Thielmann, who was obviously not in Waterloo, Bourdon de Vatry wrote that Lobau was captured under a gun at Waterloo. But Lobau himself in two letters to his wife, 20 and 21 of June, says he was captured on 19, Gosselies, around 7am (in Waresquiel, "lettres d'un lion").

There is another possibility: Lobau had been informed, but he has not told his officers. Among his troops there were officers whom he probably distrusted. Lachouque, in the biography of Tromelin, told an anecdote between Lobau and Tromelin that followed the desertion of Bourmont. The 6th corps had the 10th line, whose role with the Duke of Angoulême, during the flight of the Eagle, had earned it the wrath of Napoleon; thus Napoleon had purged its ranks.

Distrust was a feature of the 1815 military.

Conclusion: I think Napoleon was aware of the Prussian presence at Waterloo by 11 am at the latest. But, at that time, they could retreat back to

Appendix X – Essay on Grouchy, the Recall, and the Prussians

the forest or advance in support of Wellington's left wing. Napoleon adapted his dispositions on the right as information was made available to him.

As for the criticism that Lobau could have better held off the Prussians had he met them farther to the east where the terrain was more favorable to the defense, at the time of the battle Napoleon was not aware of the magnitude of the Prussian forces closing in on the French right. Later, Napoleon would say (Gourgaud, St. Helena Diary, 02.25.17):

> *I might have had, seeing the immense superiority of the Prussians, ordered an earlier retreat. Then I would have lost fifty or sixty pieces of cannon. My plan was successful: I had surprised the Prussians and the English, but what do you expect? A great battle is always a serious matter....*

THE ORDERS SENT TO GROUCHY

1) Gourgaud, 1818 *History*:

> *At ten o'clock, the emperor sent an officer to Marshal Grouchy ... The emperor sent him on the spot a duplicate of the order already shipped the previous day, at ten o'clock in the evening ... The officer bearing this dispatch left before three am...*

2) Napoleon - 1820 *Memoirs*:

> *At ten o'clock, the emperor sent an officer to Marshal Grouchy ... A second officer was sent to him at four in the morning to reiterate the order which had been sent to him at ten o'clock in the evening...*

Similar to that in Gourgaud's 1818 History, but with a slight difference in the start time of the second officer.

3) Gourgaud - St. Helena Diary, 13 June 1816 Quoting Napoleon:

> *...I sent in the night of 17 three orders to Grouchy, and he said in his report that he received at eight o'clock the order to march on Saint-Lambert.. "*

Napoleon, at this time, mentions three rather than two officers. Confused memories, voluntary error or not, transcription error of Gourgaud or upon publication of the diary, all are possible hypothesis. As for the time of "eight o'clock" Grouchy's report indicates "Only around seven in the evening on June 18, I received the letter from the Duke of Dalmatia, which required me to walk on Saint-Lambert, and attack the general Bülow."

Napoleon was therefore wrong about the hour – on purpose or not, it does not change matters. As for Grouchy, he knew from Zenowicz by 4 pm at the latest, that his action towards the battle was expected by Napoleon. In his report of June 20, Grouchy recovery begins with the phrase above, which therefore concerns the letter of 1 pm. He does not evoke the order of 10 am and its contents.

4) O'Meara 02.17.17 :

> *Napoleon said he had found The Ambigu from Pelletier very interesting, though including many falsehoods and nonsense.*
>
> *"I have read," he continued, "the story of the Battle of Waterloo; it is almost exact. I tried to guess who could be the author. It has to be someone who was then with me. I would have won that battle without the imbecility of Grouchy."*
>
> *I asked if he thought Grouchy had intended to betray him.*
>
> *"No," he replied, "but there was lack of energy on his part. There was also betrayal in the staff. I think some of the staff officers I had sent Grouchy betrayed, and passed to the enemy; however I am not sure, never having seen Grouchy later."*

Evocation of orders not arrived by eventual betrayal of the messengers, without any certainty.

Appendix X – Essay on Grouchy, the Recall, and the Prussians

5) O'Meara 03.26.17 :

The loss of the battle first lies mainly of the great lethargy of Grouchy, and his failure to execute my orders.

Evocation underlying non-execution of orders, including in particular those sent but which had not reached Grouchy.

6) Bertrand Journal 5.24.19 :
The Emperor has read the battle of Gourgaud:

He was wrong to speak of Grouchy's blunders as he did. It was a first dictation and was not meant to be known. Because he says Vandamme does not fight, he casts heavy doubts on Soult saying that his orders did not arrive.

It is true I have said sometimes, about Soult, that a few of his officers were not as good as him, and it is said here that two of his officers who carried orders to Grouchy have not arrived and moved over to the English. It is likely that there wickedness from Gourgaud who did not like Soult, knowing the words that he had said to the King, at the time of the island of Elba and that Soult had reported back to the Emperor.

Napoleon certainly found a connection with the two staff members who were captured: Cambacérès (nephew of the archichancelier) and Dumoulin. During the return of Napoleon from Elba, Dumoulin played a role in Grenoble in favour of Napoleon, who therefore included him on his staff.

According to Gourgaud, they were captured on the 16th (see Gourgaud in "Nouvelle revue retrospective", 1896). For me, it's not certain. It's indicated that while carrying orders to Ney these two officers were taken.

In the French military archives in Vincennes, where the personal files of Cambacérès and Dumoulin are kept, there are no details about their capture.
Cambacérès:
Nothing concerning the Waterloo's campaign. Maybe the file was expurgated. In his memoirs, Marchand wrote Cambacérès was taken on the 18th.
Dumoulin:

There is a letter sent by Dumoulin to Soult (then minister of the War) in 1831, where he protested to obtain the rank granted by the Emperor three days after Waterloo. Dumoulin wrote: "…I was taken prisoner at Waterloo…"
This letter was approved by:
- Count de Turenne
- Duke de Bassano
- General Bertrand
- Gourgaud himself.

But "at Waterloo" can also mean during the campaign of Waterloo, not specially the 18th.
In the file of the Legion of Honour, there is a document, dated 1852, on which Dumoulin dedicated "…June 18th, wounded and taken prisoner at Waterloo…"
This time, the 18th is mentioned.

Did Gourgaud make a mistake in the date for Cambacérès and Dumoulin? Or Marchand, for Cambacérès? And did Dumoulin lie in 1852, for the 18th?
Are the answers in British or German archives? While it is not known how many or which members of the headquarters staff were captured on the 17th or 18th, the above does provide possible candidates.

7) Grouchy, *Relation Succinte*:
In the sixth series, was included a "Declaration of the Duke of Wellington on the events of 1815, noting that the orders of the Emperor has given me June 18, at four in the afternoon, did not reach me, and they fell at the hands of Blücher. "
The paper was never published. This endorsement by Grouchy induces a confirmation that officers were captured.
But considering the schedule of "four in the afternoon", is it the schedule when Wellington seen officer(s) taken, by example (or know that officer(s) taken if he hadn't seen?). If one or two officers were taken by Prussians before (during the night or at the beginning of the day), they were able to be taken by the Prussians towards Waterloo battlefield and Wellington in the afternoon.
Not a certainty, just a possibility.

APPENDIX X – ESSAY ON GROUCHY, THE RECALL, AND THE PRUSSIANS

8) Letter from Letourneur, written in 1840 Grouchy.

Caen, August 27, 1840
In 1815, during the stay of the Prussian troops at Caen under the orders of Marshal Blücher, the municipal administration sent home with a billet, a nephew of the old general, called Lanken; He was cavalry NCO in the Hussars, I believe, and could be 20 to 22 years old.

A son of the Marshal, attached to the staff of his father, came very often to visit his parent, in the company of another officer named de Vousseaux, young man also well raised, appearing as the other two, having received a distinguished education... These gentlemen spoke French perfectly, the last two, especially, infinitely better than the young Lanken.

One day, I had invited them to take the punch, and we talked of events that had led the Prussian army in France, and of the disasters of the day of Waterloo particularly: the son of the old Marshal tells me these words that I transcribed the same evening on an album:

"The loss of the battle of Waterloo is generally attributed to the fact that Mr. Marshal Grouchy would not execute the orders of the emperor...It is a great mistake! and this is what has happened under my eyes, at the headquarters of Marshal Blücher: A staff officer of the imperial general headquarters was brought to Marshal Blücher...Was he made prisoner, had he betrayed? This is what I don't know, but he is one who was carrying an order, written in pencil, to Marshal Grouchy, saying that the Marshal had to walk on the point where the Emperor stood and let six thousand men in the front of the Prussian army, to hide his movement and keep it in check while he would move. That Marshal Blücher, with this document, had done exactly the same maneuver... This is why the Emperor kept repeating, seeing off a corps from the side where it was waiting for Mr. Marshal Grouchy: it is Grouchy! It is Grouchy!"

It is permissible to think that one would encounter in Berlin some members of the family of the old Marshal Blücher, which would

easily indicate where you would find today Mr Blücher, de Vousseaux and Lanken.[273]

Blücher having left his HQ in Wavre around 11 am on the 18th, the officer led to the Prussian HQ would have been arrived before this time. This is plausible in terms of chronology, with one of the two orders having been sent the night. No certainty but a possibility.

Grouchy wrote to the ambassador of France in Berlin about the letter saying he wanted to "*be able to assess the degree of faith that it deserves.*" The ambassador answered later that he had been unable to get anything certain about the case. Which confirms nor denies anything.

The son of Blücher is listed as cavalry captain –as a volunteer- in the Prussian staff, and so is von Wussow that Letourneur translated phonetically "Vousseaux" in his letter. The translation of german "von" is "de".

I could not identify Lanken, but he should be seen in the German archives if they have not been destroyed. It also remains to be determined, if possible, Blücher's family genealogy and if he did have a relationship with Lanken.

9) Major Zach, member of the Baden General Staff, is mentioned by Grouchy in the preamble to his *Relation Succinte*. Zach's study of Waterloo was published in an Austrian military review in 1835 and translated into French in 1840. There is the following quotation:

> *It should also be attributed to fatality that orders to march towards Saint-Lambert which had been dispatched to him by Napoleon at 10 pm and at three in the morning were not received. The officer carrying the first dispatch, who rode towards Wavre, fell into the hands of the Prussians, and the one in charge of the second dispatch was probably killed on the way.*

Zach has clearly gathered information allowing him to write that the officer who went towards Wavre fell into the hands of the Prussians. Of course it is also possible that he has invented or has collected unreliable information.

---

273 Jacques Champagne likewise asks the question why this story has never been pursued while quoting the letter in *Waterloo: Battle of Three Armies*, Sidgwick and Jackson, 1979, p. 203

Appendix X – Essay on Grouchy, the Recall, and the Prussians

10) Colonel Stoffel's account (see *"Revue militaire générale"*, 1909, quoted in JM Largeaud):

> *After this reconnaissance which had lasted an hour, he mounted on his horse and went to Le Caillou, where he arrived around 9:30 in the evening. He immediately sent to corps commanders an order which required them to get under way at daybreak and indicating the locations they would have to take if there was a battle.*
>
> *It was important that Marshal Grouchy knew the situation. Napoleon, who had demanded no help from his right in case he could have challenged Wellington on the 17th, wanted on the contrary its cooperation for the battle he hoped to deliver on the 18th. Accordingly, he ordered Major General to send to Marshal Grouchy an order to send at daybreak a division of 7000 men of all arms and sixteen guns to Chapelle-Saint-Lambert to outflank the left of the English army, join the right of the main army and operate with it. Considering the case that Blücher would have withdrawn to Wavre, Napoleon ordered in addition to Marshal Grouchy, that as soon as the Prussians would have evacuated this city to withdraw either towards Brussels or Liège, he had to go with most of his troops to support the detachment he would have sent to Chapelle-Saint-Lambert.*
>
> *Marshal Soult and his General Staff had to wonder where this dispatch was to be addressed because, at 10 pm, there was no news from the right wing. We only knew that Marshal Grouchy had been to Gembloux with all his strength, and that his instructions directed him to pursue the Prussians while remaining in constant communication with the main army, it was concluded that he had taken the direction to Wavre and that he was camped near the city, having before him or on his right the Prussian army in retreat. We were confirmed in this belief by two reports coming from two different sources: one was saying that flankers of the right of the army were in communication with those of the right wing, which had pursued the Prussians all day; another, sent by General Milhaud, reported at 9 pm, that a cavalry column had retreated hastily from Tilly to Wavre. Therefore, the dispatch for Marshal Grouchy, dated from Le Caillou, 10 o'clock came to him with the address: "on Wavre, in the north of Gembloux". It was calculated that the officer to whom it was*

entrusted only needed three or four hours to reach his destination; Marshal Grouchy could thus receive it around 2 am, in time to carry out the orders given to him.

The dispatch in question was too important not to be sent in duplicate or triplicate, and that was all the more necessary in the present circumstances because it was addressed not "at Wavre" but "on Wavre", that the officer who was carrying it had to take bad ways in a country he did not know. But it was dark, the rain, which did not stop falling in torrents from 2:00 of the afternoon was still going and all the roads were rutted. But Marshal Soult sent only one officer to Marshal Grouchy. This fatal negligence can be explained by the confusion which reigned at that time at the farm of Le Caillou where Napoleon's personal Staff and General Staff, with a hundred officers of all ranks and several hundred horses, escorts, orderlies, luggage, were trying to establish. For lack of space, on duty officers of the General Staff had to settle in a not very spacious shed of the farm and at Maison-du-Roi. The dispatch for Marshal Grouchy, hastily written in pencil, was delivered by General Bailly de Monthion to the duty officer whose turn it was to be dispatched...

Stoffel gives a precision on the order of 10 pm, which he thinks wore the mentioned address and adds it was Bailly de Monthion who gave it to the officer.

Conclusion: From the elements contained in these sources, it is quite plausible that Napoleon sent Grouchy other orders than the two known on the 18th.

APPENDIX XI
Select Correspondence

AN ATTEMPT HAS BEEN MADE to collect as much correspondence relevant to the narrative as possible. Some pieces, such as Napoleon's proclamation to the army on June 14th, the anniversary of the battle of Marengo, were filtered out as it is both readily available and adds nothing to the narrative.

The correspondance was collected from these sources with a preceding abreviated name for referencing:

Porte-feuille - *Porte-feuille de Buonaparte: pris à Charleroi le 18 juin 1815*, The Hague, 1815. http://books.google.com/books?id=eqZJAAAAcAAJ

Documents Inédits - *Documents inédits sur la campagne de 1815*, M. L. Ney, 1840. http://books.google.com/books?id=noQFAAAAIAAJ

Register of the Major-Général – from *Relation succincte de la campagne de 1815 en Belgique*, Emmanuel Grouchy, 1843. This is a copy of the Major-Général's Register of orders and correspondence that passed from Soult to Grouchy, It starts on June 13th and goes through June 26th when Grouchy assumed command of the *Armée du Nord*. http://books.google.com/books?id=aowUAAAAYAAJ

Relation succincte – From the Grouchy book above, but a different appendix

Mauduit - *Histoire des derniers jours de la Grande armée, ou souvenirs, documents et correspondance inédite de Napoléon en 1815*, Hippolyte de Mauduit, 1847.
Volume 1 : http://books.google.com/books?id=8BA3AQAAMAAJ
Volume 2 : http://books.google.com/books?id=_UlBAAAAYAAJ

Pontécoulant - *Napoléon a Waterloo*, G. Pontécoulant, 1866. http://books.google.com/books?id=MUiBAAAAIAAJ

Correspondance - *Correspondance de Napoléon Ier*, Volume 28, 1869. https://archive.org/details/correspondancede28napouoft

Houssaye - *1815*, Henry Houssaye, 1900. http://books.google.com/books?id=xWBAAAAAYAAJ

Lettow-Vorbeck - *Napoleons untergang 1815*, Oscar von Lettow-Vorbeck, 1906. http://books.google.com/books?id=D_Y8AQAAIAAJ

Ordres et Apostilles - *Ordres et apostilles de Napoléon (1799-1815)*, Arthur Chuquet, 4 Volumes 1911-1912. http://catalog.hathitrust.org/api/volumes/oclc/6785054.html

Inédits Napoléoniens - *Inédits Napoléoniens*, Arthur Chuquet, 2 Volumes 1913-1919

Volume 1 : http://gallica.bnf.fr/ark:/12148/bpt6k201534r

Volume 2: http://gallica.bnf.fr/ark:/12148/bpt6k2015354

SHD - *Service historique de la défense* (Previously the *Service historique de l'armée de terre* or SHAT in many sources*)*, located in *Château de Vincennes* in Paris. These are the archives of the French Ministry of Defense that contain the records for this period. When an item is sourced from the archives, I almost always found the text in Pierre de Wit's work at his website previously mentioned. When an item could be found in one of the above sources, I chose to utilize it so that readers could for themselves find and see exactly what I had. These are often slightly different, especially where books have edited out salutations. I did not find any differences I felt impacted the narrative.

May 9, 1815

Napoleon's appointment of Soult as *Major-Général*

Ordres et Apostilles, Volume 4, page 577, no.6747[274] :

> *Paris, 9 mai 1815.*
> *Notre cousin, le maréchal Soult, duc de Dalmatie, est nommé notre major général.*

---

274 http://hdl.handle.net/2027/uc1.b4570013?urlappend=%3Bseq=583

Appendix XI – Select Correspondence

June 1, 1815

Soult's Order of the Day

Mauduit, Volume 1, pages 466-468

> La plus auguste cérémonie vient de consacrer nos institutions. L'Empereur a reçu des mandataires du peuple et des députations de tous les corps d'armée, l'expression des vœux de la nation entière sur l'acte additionnel aux Constitutions de l'Empire, qui avait été envoyé à son acceptation, et un nouveau serment unit la France et l'Empereur; ainsi, les destinées s'accomplissent, et tous les efforts d'une ligue impie ne pourront plus séparer les intérêts d'un grand peuple DU HÉROS QUE LES PLUS BRILLANTS TRIOMPHES ONT FAIT ADMIRER DE L'UNIVERS.
>
> C'est au moment où la volonté nationale se manifeste avec autant d'énergie, que des cris de guerre se font entendre ; c'est au moment où toute la France est en paix avec toute l'Europe, que des armées étrangères avancent sur nos frontières : Quel est l'espoir de cette nouvelle coalition ? Veut-elle ôter la France du rang des nations? Veut-elle plonger dans la servitude vingt-huit millions de Français ! A-t-elle oublié que la première ligue qui fut formée contre notre indépendance servit à notre indépendance et à notre gloire ! Cent victoires éclatantes, que des revers momentanés et des circonstances malheureuses n'ont pu effacer, lui rappellent qu'une nation libre, conduite par UN GRAND HOMME, est invincible.
>
> Tout est soldat en France quand il s'agit de l'honneur national et de la liberté : un intérêt commun unit aujourd'hui tous les Français. Les engagements que la violence nous avait arrachés sont détruits par la fuite des Bourbons du territoire français, par l'appel qu'ils ont fait aux armées étrangères pour remonter sur le trône qu'ils ont abandonné, et par le vœu unanime de la nation, qui, en reprenant le libre exercice de ses droits, a solennellement désavoué tout ce qui a été fait sans sa participation.
>
> Les Français ne peuvent recevoir de lois de l'Étranger ; ceux même qui sont allés y mendier un secours parricide ne tarderont pas à reconnaître et à éprouver, ainsi que leurs prédécesseurs, que le mépris

et l'infâmie suivent leurs pas, et qu'ils ne peuvent laver l'opprobre dont ils se couvrent qu'en rentrant dans nos rangs.

Mais une nouvelle carrière de gloire s'ouvre devant l'armée; l'histoire consacrera le souvenir des faits militaires qui auront illustré les défenseurs de la patrie et de l'honneur national ! Les ennemis sont nombreux, dit-on ; que nous importe ! Il sera plus glorieux de les vaincre, et leur défaite aura d'autant plus d'éclat : la lutte qui va s'engager n'est pas au-dessus du génie de Napoléon, ni au-dessus de nos forces ; ne voit-on pas tous les départements, rivalisant d'enthousiasme et de dévoûment, former, comme par enchantement, cinq cents superbes bataillons de gardes nationales, qui déjà sont venus doubler nos rangs, défendre nos places et s'associer à la gloire de l'armée ? C'est l'élan d'un peuple généreux qu'aucune puissance ne peut vaincre et que la postérité admirera. Aux armes ! ! !...

Bientôt le signal sera donné : que chacun soit à son devoir ; du nombre de nos ennemis nos phalanges victorieuses vont tirer un nouvel éclat. Soldats ! Napoléon guidera nos pas, nous combattrons pour l'indépendance de notre belle patrie ; nous sommes invincibles !

Le maréchal d'Empire, major-général,
Duc de Dalmatie.

June 3, 1815

Napoleon to Davout at Paris

Inédits Napoléoniens, Volume 1, No. 1623 :

Donnez ordre au comte de Lobau de remettre après-demain lundi le commandement de la 1re division militaire à un lieutenant général.
Proposez-moi à cet effet l'officier général qu'on charger de ce commandement; il serait convenable qu'il fut l'ancien des généraux Darricau et Durosnel, afin qu'il n'y eut aucun embarras de service. Vous étendrez son commandement sur toute la 1re division et vous y comprendrez Soissons, Château-Thierry, Arcis-sur-Aube, Nogent, Montereau et Sens.

> *Donnez ordre au comte de Lobau de partir avec son état-major le 5 pour être rendu à Laon au plus tard le 6, y passer en revue et y organiser son corps.*
>
> *Donnez ordre également que tous les bureaux du major général, de l'intendant général, et que la gendarmerie de l'armée du Nord soient rendues le 6 à Laon.*
>
> *Donnez ordre à l'état-major général de la garde de réunir toute la garde à Soissons; je lui donnerai directement le détail du mouvement.*

Napoleon to Soult at Paris

Correspondance, Vol. 28, No. 22005

> *Remettez-moi un projet de mouvement pour le corps du général Gérard ou de la Moselle, en le masquant le plus possible à l'ennemi, pour que ce corps se porte sur Philippeville. Il faudrait qu'il y fût rendu le 12, en marchant le plus vite possible. Vous me ferez connaître qui commandera alors à Metz et à Nancy. Vous donnerez sur-le-champ l'ordre d'interrompre les communications, et l'on renforcera tous les postes, Thionville, Longwy, Metz etc.*
>
> *Faites-moi connaître la situation de la garde nationale de Nancy, et si cette division est dans le cas de marcher pour couvrir Metz et remplacer la division de la Moselle. L'ennemi nous menaçant sérieusement du côté de Metz, cette division s'appuierait sur les Vosges, qui appuieraient la gauche du général Rapp.*
>
> *Ma Garde sera toute rendue à Soissons le 10, et peut-être le 13 à Avesnes; il faut donc que le 6e corps parte le 9 pour se porter sur Avesnes. Remettez-moi un croquis où la marche des colonnes soit tracée, et qui marque les jours où le 1er, le 2e, le 3e, le 6e corps et celui de la Moselle se mettront en mouvement, et les positions que, le 13, ces corps, ainsi que la Garde et la réserve de cavalerie, devront occuper, et la force que j'aurais en infanterie, cavalerie et artillerie.*
>
> *Remettez-moi un état général de la situation des corps d'armée du Nord, de la Moselle, du Rhin et du Jura, ainsi que l'organisation de toutes les divisions de réserve de la garde nationale, et la composition de toutes les garnisons.*

Partial translation of above:

Make me a movement plan for the corps of General Gérard or of the Moselle, aimed at concealing it as much as possible from the enemy, for it to march on Philippeville. It must be there by the 12th, marching as fast as possible...

My Garde will be in its entirety at Soissons on the 10th, and perhaps at Avesnes by the 13th; thus it is necessary that the 6th corps leave on the 9th for Avesnes. Give me a sketch showing the march of the columns, marking the days when the 1st, 2nd, 3rd and 6th corps and that from the Moselle will move, and the positions these corps as well as the Garde and the reserve cavalry must be at on the 13th.[275]

Napoleon's Order to Drouot at Paris

Correspondance, Vol. 28, No. 22006

Vous ferez partir demain 4, et au plus tard, pour tout délai, après demain 5 au matin, les quatre batteries de la vieille Garde, les batteries de la jeune Garde, tout ce qui reste des équipages militaires, les administrations de la Garde, la compagnie des sapeurs, la compagnie des marins, les quatre compagnies d'ouvriers de la marine, la compagnie des boulangers et les autres ouvriers de la Garde, lesquels se rendront à Soissons par Dammartin.

Vous donnerez ordre à tout ce qu'il y a de la Garde à Compiègne, jeune Garde, artillerie, cavalerie, de se rendre également à Soissons.

Vous ferez partir aussi, lundi 5, pour se rendre à Soissons : le 1er régiment de lanciers, fort de quatre escadrons et faisant au moins 400 chevaux, le 1er et le 2e régiment de chasseurs, chacun fort de 400 chevaux, ce qui fera le fond de la 1er division; le 1er régiment de dragons et le 1er régiment de grenadiers à cheval, chacun de quatre escadrons; total de cette première colonne, cinq régiments ou 2,000 chevaux.

Vous ferez partir aussi 60 gendarmes, de manière à compléter, avec les 40 qui sont à l'armée, le nombre de 100.

---

275 de Callatay, Philippe, "The Concentration of the French Army for the Campaign of June 1815", *First Empire*, #102, English translation by John Hussey, pp. 23-24

Appendix XI – Select Correspondence

Vous ferez partir, mardi 6, le 2ᵉ régiment de lanciers rouges, le 3ᵉ de chasseurs, 2ᵉ de dragons et le 2ᵉ de grenadiers, ce qui fera 1,600 chevaux qui se rendront également à Soissons. Ces colonnes iront à Soissons en trois jours, de manière à y être le 8 ou le 9.

Vous donnerez ordre également que les trois régiments de lanciers el les 1er et 2e de chasseurs, chacun fort de 400 hommes, partent le plus tôt possible; et vous vous assurerez que des mesures sont prises pour que cela ne puisse pas tarder.

Tous ces détachements de la Garde prendront la route de Dammartin.

Vous ferez partir, également lundi, les 3e et 4e de chasseurs à pied; mardi, les 3e et 4e de grenadiers à pied; mercredi, les deux 4es régiments de grenadiers et chasseurs avec les deux 3es régiments de voltigeurs et tirailleurs, et vous prendrez mes ordres mercredi pour le départ, jeudi, des deux 1ers régiments de grenadiers et de chasseurs, de sorte que, le 10, toute la Garde, artillerie, infanterie, cavalerie, équipages militaires, génie et administrations, se trouve réunie à Soissons.

Vous donnerez des ordres pour que, le 10, toute la Garde ait quatre jours de pain biscuité, et que ses caissons ordinaires et auxiliaires soient chargés de pain; enfin qu'à cette époque elle présente un corps formé de trois divisions d'infanterie, de deux divisions de cavalerie et d'une réserve d'artillerie. Toutes les ambulances, toute l'artillerie et les différents détachements seront à leurs postes.

Vous demanderez à l'artillerie une compagnie de pontonniers pour l'attacher aux marins et aux sapeurs de la Garde. Ayez un bon officier de pontonniers.

On 3 June the Emperor gave precise instructions to Drouot concerning the departure of each unit of the Guard still at Paris "so that on the 10th, the entire Garde, artillery, infantry, cavalry, military equipments, engineers and administrative troops, shall be together at Soissons. And on 10 June all the Garde was at Soissons, except for the 1st Grenadiers and 1st Chasseurs which only left Paris on the 8th."[276]

---

[276] de Callatay, Philippe, "The Concentration of the French Army for the Campaign of June 1815", *First Empire*, #102, English translation by John Hussey, p. 26

June 5, 1815

Soult's orders to Gérard

June 7, 1815

Napoleon's Order to Soult at Paris to tour the North

Correspondance, Vol. 28, No. 22028

> *Je pense qu'il serait convenable que vous partissiez demain soir. Vous vous rendrez droit à Lille et le plus incognito possible, afin de faire toutes les dispositions pour que les places de première ligne soient assurées, et faire sortir ce qui reste encore de troupes de ligne à Calais. Vous pourrez faire faire les versements qu'exigent les circonstances, soit en hommes, soit en armes, et vous verrez à donner une destination aux bataillons qui doivent arriver d'ici au 13. Il sera convenable que vous preniez bien au bureau de la guerre tous les départs des bataillons pour le Nord. Assurerez-vous bien surtout de leur habillement et armement. Cela vous prendra le 10. Voyez s'il y a suffisamment de commandants généraux et s'il y a un bon commandant de citadelle. Enfin prescrivez au général Lapoype tout ce qui est nécessaire. Le 11 vous pourrez vous rendre à Maubeuge at à Avesnes.*
>
> *Vous viendrez à ma rencontre sur la route de Laon, où il est probable que je serai le 12. Vous prendrez tous les derniers renseignements sur la position de l'ennemi; vous tâcherez de monter un bureau d'espionnage à Lille, et une compagnie d'hommes qui connaissent bien les chemins de la Belgique. Il y a des gardes forestiers des Ardennes qui communiquent par les forêts jusque derrière Bruxelles. Procurez-vous un officier intelligent qui nous procure des hommes qui puissent nous servir.*

Napoleon's order to Soult at Paris for Lobau to evacuate

Appendix XI – Select Correspondence

Laon in preparation for arrive of the *Garde*.

Correspondance, Vol. 28, No. 22029

> *Donnez ordre au comte Lobau de porter, le 9, son quartier général à Marle ou à Vervins, et d'évacuer entièrement Laon et les environs, parce que, le 9 et le 10, toute la Garde arrive à Laon.*

Napoleon's order to Bertrand to prepare the imperial head-quarters

Correspondance, Vol. 28, No. 22030

> *Donnez ordre que toute ma Maison qui se trouve à Compiègne se rende demain à Soissons, ou sera mon quartier général.*
>
> *Concertez-vous avec le grand écuyer et le maitre de ma garde-robe, afin que, s'il me manqué quelque chose, on le fasse partir. Comme je camperai souvent, il est important que j'aie mes lits de fer et mes tentes. Veillez à ce que mes lunettes soient en état.*
>
> *Il est nécessaire que le grand écuyer me fasse connaitre quel est l'écuyer qui sera de service auprès de moi lorsqu'il sera absent comme ministre des relations extérieures. Il est nécessaire aussi que les voitures de voyage soient prêtes sans qu'on le sache, afin que je puisse partir deux heures après en avoir donné l'ordre. Il est probable que je me rendrai en droite ligne à Soissons.*
>
> *Donnez ordre que tous mes aides de camp, mes officiers d'ordonnance, les aides de camp de mes aides de camp fassent partir leurs chevaux pour Soissons. Il est indispensable qu'ils soient partis demain.*

Napoleon's order to Drouot at Paris

Correspondance, Vol. 28, No. 22031

> *Faites partir demain à la pointe du jour, de manière à arriver le 10 de bonne heure à Soissons, les deux régiments de la Garde. S'ils peuvent aller en deux jours à Soissons, qu'ils y aillent; ils y seraient le 9; sans quoi, qu'ils approchent de manière à aller le 10, s'ils en reçoivent l'ordre, entre Soissons et Laon. Toute la Garde doit être*

arrive le 9 au soir à Soissons, hormis les deux régiments qui partent demain. Remettez-moi demain matin un petit état à colonnes qui me fasse connaître le jour du départ de chaque colonne et de son arrive à Soissons, et proposez-moi de faire partir le 9 au matin tout ce qui serait en séjour à Soissons, pour se rendre à Laon, et le 10 au matin tout ce qui serait arrivé le 9; de manière que le 10 au soir toute ma Garde serait entre Laon et Avesnes, hormis les deux régiments qui partent demain, qui auront dépassé Soissons. En faisant partir les 1ers bataillons de chasseurs et de grenadiers demain, retenez 100 hommes par bataillon (ce qui fera 400 hommes ici, à Paris; cela fera 25 hommes par compagnie), en prenant les plus jeunes et les plus dispos pour former un bataillon provisoire, qui sera charge de fournir ma Garde.

Vous donnerez ordre que, le 12, les deux 4es de voltigeurs et tirailleurs, avec le général de brigade qui doit les commander, partent pour Laon, ou ils arriveront le 15 au soir. Cette brigade appartiendra à la 2ᵉ division, que le général Barrois commandera.

J'ai vu avec peine que les deux régiments qui étaient partis ce matin n'avaient qu'une paire de souliers; il y en a en magasin; il faut leur en procurer deux dans le sac et une aux pieds.

June 10, 1815

Napoleon's Order of the Day

Ordres et Apostilles, no. 3001

Paris, 10 Juin 1815.

Position de l'armée au 13.

Grand quartier général et garde impériale à Avesnes.
  Les parcs d'artillerie et équipages de ponts en avant d'Avesnes sur les glacis.
    Réserve de cavalerie 1ᵉʳ et 2ᵉ corps à Beaumont.
    3ᵉ et 4ᵉ corps entre Avesnes et Beaumont.

6ᵉ corps à Beaumont. Le quartier général en arrière. Si le 6ᵉ corps voyait de l'inconvénient à arriver à Beaumont, il pourrait arriver à mi-chemin.

1ᵉʳ corps à Pont sur Sambre. Ce corps fera son mouvement sans passer par Bavay. Il passera par Le Quesnoy, afin de s'éloigner de l'ennemi. Il ne démasque son mouvement que le plus tard possible. Comme on ne suppose pas qu'il lui faille plus d'un jour étant à Valenciennes, ce ne sera que le 13 qu'il fera son mouvement pour arriver sur la Sambre.

2ᵉ corps en arrière de Maubeuge en colonne sur le chemin de Thuin, sans dépasser la frontière, et tachant de se faire voir le moins possible.

3ᵉ corps à Philippeville.

Armée de la Moselle à Mariembourg.

Toutes les communications sur la frontière seront interceptées.

Les soldats auront quatre jours de pain sur le dos, demi-livre de riz, cinquante cartouches.

Les batteries seront avec les divisions: les batteries de réserve avec leurs corps d'armée.

La cavalerie légère de chaque corps d'armée sera en avant du corps.

Chaque ambulance à sa division.

Chaque division aura sur les charriots auxiliaires ou militaires huit jours de pain, biscuits et un parc de bestiaux pour huit jours.

On ne fera aucun changement sur la frontière, on ne la dépassera sur aucun point. On ne tirera aucun coup de canon. On ne fera rien qui puisse éveiller l'ennemi.

Le présent ordre restera secret.

June 11, 1815

Bertrand to Reille

Inédits Napoléoniens, Vol. 1, no. 1684

Paris, 11 Juin 1815.

> *L'intention de l'Empereur est que le quartier général soit transporté le 12 a Avesnes; que la garde impériale y soit le 12; qu'Avesnes soit évacué par votre corps que vous porterez derrière Maubeuge, et que cependant vous y restiez de votre personne pour donner des renseignements, l'Empereur devant y arriver le 13 à 2 heures du matin. Il est très important que vous placiez votre corps d'armée derrière Maubeuge sans que l'ennemi s'aperçoive de rien. Interdisez très sévèrement toute communication.*

Napoleon's order to Davout in reference to the start of hostilities

Correspondance, Vol. 28, No. 22040

> *Mon Cousin, vous ferez connaitre, par estafette et par le télégraphe, au maréchal Suchet, que les hostilités commenceront le 14, et que de ce jour il peut s'emparer de Montmélian. S'il est indispensable qu'il le fasse avant ce temps, à cause des mouvements de l'ennemi, il y est autorisé. Cependant il serait à désirer qu'il ne le fît pas avant le 15.*

Napoleon's invitation to Ney to join the campaign

Correspondance, Vol. 28, No. 22042

> *Mon Cousin, faites appeler le maréchal Ney; s'il désire se trouver aux premières batailles qui auront lieu, dites-lui qu'il soit rendu le 14 à Avesnes, où sera mon quartier général.*

JUNE 12, 1815

Soult's report to Napoleon

Inédits Napoléoniens, Vol. 2, no. 3403

> *Avesnes, 12 juin 1815.*

Appendix XI – Select Correspondence

En exécution de l'ordre que Votre Majesté a donné le 10 de ce mois, j'ai prescrit les dispositions suivantes sur l'emplacement que les divers corps de l'armée devront occuper le 13:

Le 2ᵉ corps sur la Sambre, au-dessous de Maubeuge jusqu'à Solre-sur-Sambre, occupant les villages de Hantay, Montigny, Bousignies, Bersillies, Colleret, Cerfontaine et Ferrière-la-Grande.

Le 1ᵉʳ corps entre Pont-sur-Sambre et Maubeuge, se tenant prêt à déboucher sur l'une ou l'autre rive de la Sambre, ainsi que Votre Majesté l'ordonnera.

Le 3ᵉ corps à Beaumont.

Le 6ᵉ corps à Beaufort ou sera la quartier-général, Fontaine, Limont, Eclaibes, Dimont, Dimechaux, Wattignies, Choisies, Damousies, Obrechies et Ferrier-la-Petite.

Les 1ᵉʳ, 2ᵉ, 3ᵉ et 4ᵉ corps de cavalerie, sous les ordres de M. le maréchal Grouchy, à Solre-le-Château et dans les villages de Sars, Lez-Fontaine, Offies, L'Epine, Charnoul, Clairfayts, Epinoy, Beaurieux, Grandrieu, Hestrud, Leugnies, Cousolre, Aibes, Quiévelon, Solrinnes, Eccles.

Les parcs de l'artillerie et l'équipage de pont seront placés en avant d'Avesnes; on a laissé quelques villages vacant pour qu'ils puissant y établir des chevaux.

La ville d'Avesnes est laissée à la disposition de la garde de Votre Majesté, ainsi que les villages en arrière et ceux de la vallée de la Helpe à droite et à gauche d'Avesnes.

Portion pertaining to Gérard:
Lettow-Vorbeck, Footnote on pages 223-224

Gemass der vom Graf Gérard erhaltenen Berichte sollen die erste Division der Mosel armee am 13. in Rocroi, die zweite am 14., die dritte am 15., die Cavallerie division und der Artilleriepark am 15. dort eintreffen. Ich habe ihm sosort geschrieben, Ew. Majestat hatten bestimmt, er solle am 13. bei Rocroi vollig versammelt sein, und dass ich ihm dementsprechend die Befehle gegeben hatte. Ich habe ihm serner den Befehl wiederholt, den Marsch seiner Truppen derart zu beschleunigen, dass sie die verlorene Zeit wiedergewinnen, er muffe die Bewegung der Armee fortsessen und habe sie uber Chimay auf Beaumont zu dirigieren, wo er die zweite Linie des III.Corps bilden und diesem aus seinem Marsch nach der Sambre folgen solle, sobald dieses vorgehe.

General Delort, Commandeur der 13. Cavallerie division, hat mir am 9. aus Metz geschrieben, dass seine Division am 13. in Mézières ankommen werde und seinen Bestimmungsort Hirson erst am 15. erreichen konne.

Ich habe ihm den Besehl gesandt, sie von Mézières uber Rocroi und Chimay aus Beaumont zu dirigieren, wo sie am 15. ankommen konne und sich in gleicher Linie mit dem Rest der Cavallerie befinden wurde. Ich habe den Marschall Grouchy hiervon benachrichtigt.

Soult to Vandamme

SHD, C17/193

Avesnes, le 12 juin 1815

L'intention de l'Empereur, monsieur le comte, est que Votre Corps d'armée soit rendu demain 13 à Beaumont. Vous le concentrerez sur ce point; ainsi vous vous trouverez former la droite de l'armée et vous soutiendrez près a déboucher le 14 au matin pour la direction qui vous era donnée.

Monsieur le général comte Gérard, qui avait reçu ordre de se rendre à Rocroi, continuera sa marche sur Chimay et Beaumont ou il rejoindra votre corps d'armée; il devra prendre position un peu en arrière de la vôtre et si à son arrivée a Beaumont vous vous étiez porte en avant, il suivrait votre mouvement de manière a vous joindre le plutôt et à former une deuxième ligne derrière vous.

Aussitôt que vous avez pris la position qui vous est indiquée, vous m'enverrez un officier pour m'en rendre compte. Je vous préviens que la droite du 2ᵉ corps sera à Montignies et la tête de la réserve de cavalerie à Leugnies et Cousolre.

Le maréchal d'empire, major général, duc de Dalmatie[277]

---

[277] DeWit, Pierre, *Preparations for war : Napoleon, Part 1*, page 9 http://www.waterloo-campaign.nl/bestanden/files/preambles/adn.1.pdf

Appendix XI – Select Correspondence

Soult to Grouchy

SHD, C15/5

Monsieur le maréchal, j'ai l'honneur de vous adresser copie de l'ordre de l'Empereur en date du 10, relatif à la position de l'armée au 13. L'empereur ordonne que vous mettiez en marche les 1er, 2ᵉ, 3ᵉ et 4ᵉ corps de cavalerie et que vous les dirigiez sur Avesnes, d'où ils continueront leur route pour aller s'établir, les 1er et 2ᵉ corps en avant de Solre-le-Château, occupant les villages de Coursolre, Leugnies, Grandrieu, Hestrud, Eccles, Solrinnes, Quierelont et leurs dépendances.

Les 3ᵉ et 4ᵉ corps à Solre-le-Château, en occupant Borieu, l'Epinoy, Harnault les Fontaines, Sartz et Offies. Vous devrez, Monsieur le maréchal, vous établir de votre personne à Solre et faire toutes les dispositions pour que le mouvement de ces quatre corps de cavalerie soit terminé le 13 au soir. Je vous prie, Monsieur le maréchal, de me rendre compte de l'exécution de cet ordre. Recevez etc.[278]

Soult to Grouchy

SHD, C15/5

Monsieur le maréchal, je recois de M. le général Delort copie de l'itinéraire que suit la 14e division de cavalerie, qu'il commande, d'où il résulte qu'il arrive le 13 de ce mois à Mézières. Je lui donne l'ordre d'en partir le 14, avec tout ce qui appartient à sa division, pour se rendre à Rocroy, d'où il continuera sa route par Chimay à Beaumont, où il joindra l'armée et se réunira au 4ᵉ corps de cavalerie, dont il fait partie. Je lui mande qu'il est nécessaire qu'il puisse arriver le 15 à Beaumont ou du moins en être très rapproché.

---

[278] DeWit, Pierre, *Preparations for war : Napoleon, Part 1*, page 10
http://www.waterloo-campaign.nl/bestanden/files/preambles/adn.1.pdf

Je vous prie, monsieur le maréchal, de vous assurer de la marche de cette division et de m'informer de sa réunion au 4e corps de cavalerie. Recevez etc.[279]

June 13, 1815

Soult's order to Gazan

Inédits Napoléoniens, no. 1687

L'Empereur pense que le corps que vous aurez formé en tirant des garnisons une partie des troupes, vous mettrait à même de vous porter en avant et d'entrer dans le pays ennemi, en ayant soin d'agir avec toute la prudence et les précautions nécessaires. Il y a un corps de partisans à Cassel; vous pouvez le jeter en Belgique lorsque vous le jugerez convenable, l'intention de Sa Majesté étant de disposer en temps et lieu d'une partie des garnisons pour former le blocus des places de la Belgique et y tenir campagne.

Soult's Corrective order to Vandamme

SHD, C15/5

Note the absence of this order in copy of the *Registre du Major-Général* as provided by Grouchy. *Was it possible this was sent late on the 12th?*

L'intention de l'Empereur, Monsieur le General, est que vous formiez votre corps d'armée en avant de Philippeville afin d'être prêt à déboucher demain sur Charleroy, si des ordres vous sont envoyés à ce sujet.

L'armée de la Moselle se dirigera sur Philippeville & suivra votre mouvement; j'envoye des ordres en conséquence à Mr. le Lt. Gal. Gérard.

D'après les ordres que je vous ai envoyé hier, vous deviez réunir votre corps d'armée à Beaumont. Mais l'Empereur a de nouveau

---

[279] DeWit, Pierre, *Preparations for war : Napoleon, Part 1*, page 10 http://www.waterloo-campaign.nl/bestanden/files/preambles/adn.1.pdf

APPENDIX XI – SELECT CORRESPONDENCE

ordonne l'exécution de l'ordre du jour du 10 dont je vous ai envoyé ampliation, d'après lequel vous deviez vous former dans la journée du 13 en avant de Philippeville, ainsi [..] la disposition de l'ordre donné par l'Empereur le 10, que vous devez suivre.

Si cependant lorsque ma lettre vous parviendra vos troupes se trouvaient entre Philippeville & Beaumont vous les y laisserez et vous les disposeriez de manière à pouvoir demain déboucher sur Charleroy, en prenant votre ligne d'opérations sur Philippeville. Donnez des ordres pour qu'on cuise beaucoup de pain à Philippeville et pour que l'ordonnateur de votre corps y fasse arriver beaucoup de subsistances.

Instruisez moi de suite de l'emplacement de vos troupes et des dispositions que vous ferez pour l'exécution de ces ordres.

Vous aurez soin, général, d'envoyer un officier au devant du général Gérard pour l'informer de ces dispositions.

Le Marechal d'Empire, major général. Due dc Dalmatie[280]

Napoleon's Countermand to Soult's Corrective Order

Porte-feuille, pg. 98

Au quartier général d'Avesnes, le 13 Juin

Au Major-Général

Puisque le Général Van Damme est arrivé à Beaumont, je ne pense pas qu'il faille le faire retourner à Philippeville, ce qui fatiguerait sa troupe. Je préfère que ce Général campe en I.ere ligne à une et demi lieue de Beaumont; j'en passerai la revue demain.
Le 6ᵉ corps sera alors placé à un quart de lieue derrière.
Dans ce cas, l'armée de la Moselle se réunira demain sur Philippeville avec le détachement de Cuirassiers qui vient d'Alsace. Faites ce changement a l'ordre général.

---

280 DeWit, Pierre, *Preparations for war : Napoleon, Part 1*, page 11
http://www.waterloo-campaign.nl/bestanden/files/preambles/adn.1.pdf

Napoleon to Drouot

Porte-feuille, pg. 99

> *Au Général DROUOT.*
>
> *Donnez ordre que la division composée des Chasseurs et des Lanciers rouges se rende ce soir en avant de Solre, que toutes les divisions de Chasseurs se rendent également à Solre ;*
> *Tous les Grenadiers à Avesnes ; les Grenadiers à cheval et les Dragons en avant d'Avesnes ; chaque corps aura avec lui son artillerie. L'artillerie de réserve en avant d'Avesnes.*

Order of the Day

Register of the Major-Général

> *Avesnes, le 13 Juin 1815.*
> *Position de l'Armée le 14.*
>
> *Le grand Quartier-Général, à Beaumont.*
> *L'Infanterie de la garde impériale sera bivouaquée à un quart de lieue en avant de Beaumont et formera trois lignes : la jeune garde, les chasseurs et les grenadiers. M. le duc de Trévise reconnaitra l'emplacement de ce camp. Il aura soin que tout soit à sa place, artillerie, ambulances, équipages, etc.*
> *Le 1er régiment de grenadiers à pied se rendra à Beaumont.*
> *La cavalerie de la garde impériale sera place en arrière de Beaumont, mais les corps les plus éloignés n'en doivent pas être à une lieue.*
> *Le 2e corps prendra position à Laire c'est-à-dire le plus près possible de la frontière, sans la dépasser. Les quatre divisions de ce corps d'armée seront réunies et bivouaqueront sur deux ou quatre lignes : le quartier-général au milieu, la cavalerie en avant, éclairant tous le débouchés, mais aussi sans dépasser la frontière et la faisant respecter par les partisans ennemis qui voudraient la violer.*

Appendix XI – Select Correspondence

Les bivouacs seront placés de manière que les feux ne puissant être aperçus de l'ennemi; les généraux empêcheront que personne ne s'écarte du camp; ils s'assureront que la troupe est pourvue de 50 cartouches par hommee, quatre jours de pain et une demi-livre de viande; que l'artillerie et les ambulances sont en bon état, et les feront placer à leur ordre de bataille. Ainsi le 2e corps sera disposé à se mettre en marche le 15, a trois heures du matin, si l'ordre en est donné, pour se porter sur Charleroi et y arriver avant neuf heures.

Le 1er corps prendra position à Solre-sur-Sambre, et il bivouaquera aussi sur plusieurs lignes; observant, ainsi que le 2e corps, que ses feux ne puissant être aperçus de l'ennemi, que personne ne s'écarte du camp, et que les généraux s'assurent de l'état des munitions, des vivres de la troupe, et que l'artillerie et les ambulances soient places à leur ordre de bataille.

Le 1er Corps se tiendra également prêt à partir le 15, à trois heures du matin, pour suivre le mouvement du 2e corps, de manière que, dans la journée d'après-demain, ces deux corps manœuvrent dans la même direction et se protègent.

Le 3e corps prendra demain position à une lieue en avant de Beaumont, le plus près possible de la frontière, sans cependant la dépasser, ni souffrir qu'elle soit violée par aucun parti ennemi. Le général Vandamme tiendra tout le monde à son poste, recommandera que les feux soient cachés et qu'ils ne puissant être aperçus de l'ennemi. Il se conformera d'ailleurs à ce qui est prescrit au 2e corps pour les munitions, les vivres, l'artillerie et les ambulances, et pour être prêt à se mettre en mouvement le 15, à trios heures du matin.

Le 6e corps se porter an avant de Beaumont, et sera bivouaqué sur deux lignes, à un quart de lieue du 3e corps. M. le comte de Lobau choisira l'emplacement, et il fera observer les dispositions générales qui sont prescrites par le présent ordre.

M. le maréchal Grouchy portera les 1er, 2e, 3e et 4e corps de cavalerie en avant de Beaumont, et les établira au bivouac entre cette ville et Walcourt, faisant également respecter la frontière, empêchant que personne ne la dépasse et qu'on se laisse voir, ni que les feux puissant être aperçus de l'ennemi; et il se tiendra prêt à partir après-demain, à trios heures du matin, s'il en reçoit l'ordre, pour se porter sur Charleroi et faire l'avant-garde de l'armée.

Il recommandera aux généraux de s'assurer si tous les cavaliers sont pourvus de cartouches, si leurs armes sont en bon état, s'ils ont les quatre jours de pain et la demi-livre de riz qui ont été ordonnés.

L'équipage de ponts sera bivouaqué derrière le 6e corps et en avant de l'infanterie de la Garde impérial. Le parc centra d'artillerie sera en arrière de Beaumont.

L'armée de la Moselle prendra demain position en avant de Philippeville. M. le comte Gérard la disposera de manière a pouvoir partir après-demain 15, à trios heures du matin, pour y joindre le 3e corps et appuyer son mouvement sur Charleroi, suivant le nouvel ordre qui lui sera donné ; mais le général Gérard aura soin de bien garder son flanc droit et en avant de lui sur toutes les directions de Charleroi et de Namur.

Si l'armée de la Moselle a des pontons à sa suite, le général Gérard les fera avancer le plus possible, afin d'en disposer.

Tous les corps d'armées feront marcher en tête les sapeurs et les moyens de passage que les généraux auront réunis.

Les sapeurs de la Garde impériale, les ouvriers de la marine et les sapeurs de la réserve marcheront après le 6e corps et en tête de la garde.

Tous les corps marcheront dans le plus grand ordre et serrés. Dans le mouvement sur Charleroi, on sera disposé à profiter de tous les passages, pour écraser les corps ennemis qui voudraient attaquer l'armée ou qui manœuvreraient contre elle.

Il n'y aura à Beaumont que le grand quartier général; aucun autre ne devra y être établi, et la ville sera dégagée de tout embarras.

Les anciens règlements sur le quartier général et les équipages, sur l'ordre des marches, la police des voitures et bagages et sur les blanchisseuses et vivandières, seront remis en vigueur. Il sera fait à ce sujet un ordre général. Mais, en attendant, MM. les généraux commandant les corps d'armée prendront des dispositions en conséquence, et le grand prévôt de l'armée fera exécuter ces règlements.

L'Empereur ordonne que toutes les dispositions contenues dans le présent ordre soient tenues secrètes par MM. les généraux.

Par ordre de l'Empereur,
Le maréchal de l'Empire, major général,

APPENDIX XI – SELECT CORRESPONDENCE

Duc de Dalmatie.[281]

JUNE 14, 1815

Napoleon to Josepth, Morning

Correspondance, Vol. 28, no. 22050

> *Avesnes, 14 Juin 1815, au matin*
>
> *Mon frère, je porte ce soir mon quartier impérial à Beaumont. Demain 15, je me porterai sur Charleroi, où est l'armée Prussienne; ce qui donnera lieu à une bataille ou à la retraite de l'ennemi. L'armée est belle et le temps assez beau; le pays parfaitement disposé.*
> *J'écrirai ce soir si l'on doit faire les communications le 16. En attendant, il faut que l'on se prépare.*
> *Adieu*

Napoleon's Order of Movement, Evening

Register of the Major-Général

> *Ramorino carried to d'Erlon*
> *Macarty carried to Reille*
> *Faviers carried to Vandamme*
> *Poirot carried to Lobau*
> *Bénard carried to Gérard*
> *Gentet carried to Drouot and Mortier, Duc de Trévise*
> *Vaucher carried to Grouchy*
> *Lefébure carried to Ruty and Rogniat*
> *Ricou carred to M. Daure*
>
> *Beaumont, le 14 Juin 1815*

---

281 See variation in *Correspondance Tome 28*, No 22049

Demain 15, à deux heures et demie du matin, la division de cavalerie légère du général Vandamme montera à cheval et se portera sur la route de Charleroi. *Elle enverra des partis dans toutes les directions pour éclairer le pays et enlever les postes ennemis; mais chacun de ces partis sera au moins de 50 hommes. Avant de mettre en marche la division, le général Vandamme s'assurera qu'elle est pourvue de cartouches.*

A la même heure, le lieutenant général Pajol réunira le 1er corps de cavalerie et suivra le mouvement de la division du général Domon, qui sera sous les ordres du général Pajol. Les divisions du 1er corps de cavalerie ne fourniront point de détachements; ils seront pris dans la 3ᵉ division. Le général Domon laissera sa batterie d'artillerie pour marcher après le 1er bataillon du 3ᵉ corps d'infanterie; le lieutenant général Vandamme lui donnera des ordres en conséquence.

Le lieutenant général Vandamme fera battre la diane à deux heures et demie du matin; à trois heures il mettra en marche son corps d'armée et le dirigera sur Charleroi. *La totalité de ses bagages et embarras seront parqués en arrière, et ne se mettront en marche qu'après le 6ᵉ corps et la garde impériale auront passé. Ils seront sous les ordres du vaguemestre général, qui les réunira à ceux du 6ᵉ corps, de la Garde Impériale et du grand quartier général, et leur donnera des ordres de mouvement.*

Chaque division du 3ᵉ corps d'armée aura avec elle sa batterie et ses ambulances; toute autre voiture qui serait dans les rangs, sera brulée.

M. le comte Lobau fera battre la diane à trois heures et demie, et il mettra en marche le 6ᵉ corps d'armée à quatre heures pour suivre le mouvement du général Vandamme et l'appuyer. Il fera observer, pour les troupes, l'artillerie, les ambulances et les bagages, le même ordre de marche qui est prescrit au 3ᵉ corps. Les bagages du 6ᵉ corps seront réunis à ceux du 3ᵉ, sous les ordres du vaguemestre général, ainsi qu'il est dit.

La jeune garde battra la diane à quatre heures et demie, et se mettra en marche à cinq heures; elle suivra le mouvement du 6ᵉ corps sur la route de Charleroi.

Appendix XI – Select Correspondence

Les chasseurs à pied de la garde battront la diane à cinq heures, et se mettront en marche à cinq heures et demie, pour suivre le mouvement de la jeune garde.

Les grenadiers à pied, de la garde, battront la diane à cinq heures et demie et partiront à six heures, pour suivre le mouvement des chasseurs à pied. Le même ordre de marche pour l'artillerie, les ambulances et les bagages, prescrit pour le 3e corps d'infanterie, sera observé dans la garde impériale.

Les bagages de la garde seront réunis à ceux des 3e et 6e corps d'armée, sous les ordres du vaguemestre-général, qui les fera mettre en mouvement.

M. le maréchal Grouchy fera monter à cheval, à cinq heures et demie du matin, celui des trois autres corps de cavalerie qui sera le plus près de la route, et il lui fera suivre le mouvement sur Charleroi. *Les deux autres corps partiront successivement à une heure d'intervalle l'un de l'autre; mais M. le maréchal Grouchy aura soin de faire marcher la cavalerie sur les chemins latéraux de la route principale que la colonne d'infanterie suivra, afin d'éviter l'encombrement, et aussi pour que sa cavalerie observe un meilleur ordre. Il prescrira que la totalité des bagages reste en arrière parqués et réunis, jusqu'au moment ou le vaguemestre-général leur donnera l'ordre d'avancer.*

M. le comte Reille fera battre la diane à deux heures et demie du matin, et il mettra en marche le 2e corps à trois heures; il le dirigera sur Marchiennes-au-Pont, *où il fera en sorte d'être rendu avant neuf heures du matin. Il fera garder tous les ponts de la Sambre, afin que personne n'y passe. Les postes qu'il laissera, seront successivement relevés par le 1er corps; mais il doit tâcher de prévenir l'ennemi à ces ponts pour qu'ils ne soient pas détruits, surtout celui de Marchienne, par lequel il sera probablement dans le cas de déboucher, et qu'il faudrait faire aussitôt réparer s'il avait été endommagé.*

A Thuin *et à* Marchienne, *ainsi que dans tous les villages sur sa route, M. le comte Reille interrogera les habitants, afin d'avoir des nouvelles des positions et forces des armées ennemis. Il fera aussi prendre les lettres dans les bureaux de poste, et les dépouillera, pour faire aussitôt parvenir à l'empereur les renseignements qu'il aura obtenus.*

M. le comte d'Erlon mettra en marche le 1er corps à trois heures du matin, et le dirigera aussi sur Charleroi, *en suivant le mouvement* *du 2ᵉ corps, duquel il gagnera la gauche le plus tôt possible pour le soutenir et l'appuyer au besoin. Il tiendra une brigade de cavalerie en arrière pour se couvrir et pour maintenir par de petits détachements ses communications avec Maubeuge; il enverra des partis en avant de cette place dans les directions de* Mons *et de* Binche *jusqu'à la frontière pour avoir des nouvelles des ennemis, et en rendre compte aussitôt; ces partis auront soin de ne pas se compromettre et de ne point dépasser la frontière.*

M. le comte d'Erlon fera occuper Thuin *par une division; et, si le pont de cette ville était détruit, il le ferait aussitôt réparer, en même temps qu'il fera tracer et exécuter immédiatement une tête de pont sur la rive gauche. La division qui sera à* Thuin *gardera aussi le pont de* l'abbaye d'Alnes, *où M. le comte d'Erlon fera également construire une tête de pont sur la rive gauche.*

Le même ordre de marche prescrit au 3ᵉ corps pour l'artillerie, les ambulances et les bagages, sera observé aux 2ᵉ et 1ᵉʳ corps qui feront réunir et marcher leurs bagages et marcher à la gauche du 1ᵉʳ corps sous les ordres du vaguemestre le plus ancien.

Le 4ᵉ corps (armée de la Mozelle) a reçu l'ordre de prendre aujourd'hui position en avant de Philippeville; si son mouvement est opéré, et si les divisions qui composent ce corps d'armée sont réunies, M. le lieutenant général Gérard les mettra en marche demain à trois heures du matin et les dirigera sur Charleroi; *il aura soin de se tenir à hauteur du 3ᵉ corps avec lequel il communiquera, afin d'arriver à peu près en même temps devant* Charleroi; *mais le général Gérard fera éclairer sa droite et tous les débouchés qui vont sur* Namur, *il marchera serré en ordre de bataille et fera laisser à* Philippeville *tous ses bagages et embarras afin que son corps d'armée se trouvant plus léger, soit plus à même de manœuvrer.*

Le général Gérard donnera ordre à la 14ᵉ division de cavalerie, qui a dû aussi arriver aujourd'hui à Philippeville, de suivre le mouvement de son corps d'armée sur Charleroi, *où cette division joindra le 4ᵉ corps de cavalerie.*

Les lieutenants-généraux Reille, Vandamme, Gérard et Pajol se mettront en communication par de fréquents partis, et ils règleront leur marche de manière à arriver en masse et ensemble devant Charleroi : *ils mettront autant que possible à l'avant-garde des*

Appendix XI – Select Correspondence

officiers qui parlent flamand, pour interroger les habitants et en prendre des renseignements; mais ces officiers s'annonceront comme commandant des partis, sans dire que l'armée est en arrière.

Les lieutenants-généraux Reille, Vandamme et Gérard feront marcher tous les sapeurs de leur corps d'armée (ayant avec eux des moyens pour réparer les ponts), après le 1er régiment d'infanterie légère, et ils donneront ordre aux officiers du génie de faire réparer les mauvais passages, ouvrir des communications latérales, et placer des ponts sur les courants d'eau où l'infanterie devrait se mouiller pour les franchir.

Les marins, les sapeurs de la garde et les sapeurs de la réserve marcheront après le 1er régiment du 3e corps. Les lieutenants généraux Rogniat et Haxo seront à leur tête; ils n'emmèneront avec eux que deux ou trois voitures; le surplus du parc du génie marchera à la gauche du 3e corps. Si on rencontre l'ennemi, ces troupes ne seront point engagées ; mais les généraux Rogniat en Haxo les emploieront aux travaux de passages de rivières, de têtes de ponts, de réparations de chemins et d'ouvertures de communications etc.

La cavalerie de la garde suivra le mouvement sur Charleroi *et partira à huit heures.*

L'empereur sera à l'avant-garde, sur la route de Charleroi. *MM. les lieutenants-généraux auront soin d'envoyer à S. M. de fréquents rapports sur leurs mouvements et les renseignements qu'ils auront recueillis : ils sont prévenus que l'intention de S. M. est d'avoir passé la Sambre avant midi, et de porter l'armée à la rive gauche de cette rivière.*

L'équipage de ponts sera divisé en deux sections; la 1er section se subdivisera en trois parties, chacune de cinq pontons et cinq bateaux d'avant-garde, pour jeter trois ponts sur la Sambre ; il y aura à chacune de ces subdivisions une compagnie de pontonniers ; la 1er section marchera à la suite du parc du génie après le 3e corps.

La 2e section restera avec le parc de réserve d'artillerie à la colonne des bagages; elle aura avec elle la 4e compagnie de pontonniers. Les équipages de l'empereur et les bagages du grand quartier général seront réunis et se mettront en marche à dix heures ; aussitôt qu'ils seront passés, le vaguemestre-général fera partir les équipages de la garde impériale, du 3e corps et du 6e corps, en même temps il enverra *ordre à la colonne d'équipages de la réserve de cavalerie, de se mettre en marche et de suivre la direction que la cavalerie aura prise.*

Les ambulances de l'armée suivront le quartier-général et marcheront en tête des bagages; mais, dans aucun cas, ces bagages, ainsi que les parcs de réserve de l'artillerie et la 2ᵉ section de l'équipage de ponts, ne s'approcheront à plus de trois lieues de l'armée, à moins d'ordres du major général, et ils ne passeront la Sambre aussi que par ordre.

Le vaguemestre-général formera des divisions de ces bagages, et il y mettra des officiers pour les commander, afin de pouvoir en détacher ce qui sera ensuite appelé au quartier-général ou pour le service des officiers.

L'intendant-général fera réunir à cette colonne d'équipages, la totalité des bagages et transports de l'administration auxquels il sera assigné un rang dans la colonne.

Les voitures qui seront en retard prendront la gauche et ne pourront sortir du rang qui leur sera donné que par ordre du vaguemestre-général.

L'empereur ordonne que toutes les voitures d'équipages qui seront trouvées dans les colonnes d'infanterie, de cavalerie ou d'artillerie, soient brulées, ainsi que les voitures de la colonne des équipages qui quitteront leur rang, ou intervertiront l'ordre de marche sans la permission expresse du vaguemestre général.

A cet effet, il sera mis un détachement de cinquante grenadiers à la disposition du vaguemestre-général, qui est responsable, ainsi que tous les officiers de la gendarmerie et les gendarmes, de l'exécution de ces dispositions, desquelles le succès de la campagne peut dépendre.

Par ordre de l'Empereur:
Le maréchal de l'Empire, major-général, Duc de Dalmatie[282]

Soult to Vandamme

Register of the Major-Général

Beaumont, le 14 Juin.

---

282 See variation in *Correspondance*, Vol. 28, 22053

APPENDIX XI – SELECT CORRESPONDENCE

J'ai reçu, M. le lieutenant-général, votre lettre de ce jour où vous tracez un itinéraire sur Charleroi. Vous verrez, par l'ordre du mouvement que l'Empereur a donné et que je vous envoie, que les 2ᵉ, et 1ᵉ. corps doivent déboucher par Marchienne-au-Pont. *Il ne faut donc pas que votre colonne aille aboutir à Marchienne car il y aurait confusion, mais vous pourrez passer l'Eure à Ham, à Jamignon ou à Bomerée où existent des ponts suivant la bonté de la route, et vous en préviendrez les généraux Pajol et Domon qui doivent vous précéder.*

Je vous préviens qu'il vient de m'être rendu compte qu'il existe à Jamignon un corps prussien de 6,000 hommes avec du canon qu'il faut faire en sorte d'enlever. J'en préviens aussi M. le maréchal Grouchy qui doit passer avec les 2ᵉ, 3ᵉ. et 4ᵉ. corps de cavalerie par Stenrieux et Yves, *où il prendra la route de Philippeville à Charleroi afin qu'il règle ses mouvements en conséquence. Aussitôt que vous aurez des renseignements sur les ennemis, envoyez à l'Empereur des officiers pour rendre compte à S. M. de ce que vous aurez appris.*

Soult to Grouchy

Register of the Major-Général

Beaumont, le 14 Juin 1815.

Je vous envoie monsieur le maréchal, l'ordre de mouvement pour demain que l'Empereur vient de donner. Conformez-vous à ce qui vous est prescrit dans cet ordre.
 Plusieurs routes mènent à Charleroi en partant de Beaumont. Celle de droite passe à Bossus, Fleurieux, Vaugenée et Yves ou elle joint la grand route de Philippeville à Charleroi; c'est cette route que vous devez prendre afin de ne pas tomber dans les autres colonnes; mais auparavant faites la bien reconnaître et réglez votre mouvement de manière à être toujours à hauteur de la colonne de gauche, à la tête de laquelle le général Pajol doit marcher.
 Je préviens de la direction que vous prenez M. le lieutenant-général Gérard, dont le corps est formé en avant de Philippeville et qui doit aussi se porter sur Charleroi par la même direction.

Je dois vous prévenir qu'il vient de m'être rendu compte qu'un corps de 6,000 prussiens, infanterie, est établi à Jamignon. Si cela est vrai, l'empereur veut que le corps soit enlevé, ainsi vous manœuvrerez en conséquence; j'écris dans le même sens aux lieutenants-généraux Vandamme et Gérard. Envoyez moi un officier au moment ou vous vous mettrez en marche, et ensuite toutes les heures pendant le mouvement.

Grouchy to Soult at 2pm

??

Beaumont, le 14 juin 1815, à 2 heures après-midi

Monsieur le Maréchal,

Je m'empresse de vous prévenir que les hommes du train des batteries d'artillerie attachées aux 4e et 5e divisions formant le premier corps de cavalerie, sont dans une déplorable situation, quant à l'habillement et au personnel.
 Ces hommes sont pour la plupart des enfants; ils n'ont point de capotes, peu de bons vêtements, point de bottes. Si le temps froid et pluvieux continue, ils tomberont malades au bivouac ou déserteront. On me rend même compte que plusieurs ont déjà disparu.
 J'ai l'honneur de vous prier, Monsieur le Maréchal, de faire changer dès que possible les soldats du train de ces deux batteries, ou du moins de leur faire donner des vêtements. La chose est d'autant plus nécessaire, que ce sont précisément les batteries attachées au 1er corps uniquement composé de cavalerie légère et destiné à former l'avant-garde, qui se trouvent les moins partagés.
 Il n'y a point de caisson d'infanterie attaché aux batteries du 1er corps de cavalerie. Il est indispensable qu'il y en soit envoyé sans délai, et je vous prie d'en donner l'ordre.
 Quoique le général commandant l'artillerie du 1er corps de cavalerie écrive, pour les mêmes objets dont je vous entretiens dans cette lettre, au lieutenant-général Ruty, j'ai cru devoir aussi vous en parler, à raison de l'intérêt majeur dont ils sont.

Recevez, Monsieur le maréchal, les assurances de ma haute considération.

Signé Le Maréchal Grouchy.

Soult to Gérard

Register of the Major-Général

Beaumont, le 14 Juin, 1815.

On l'a prévenu de la direction du maréchal Grouchy ; il lui a écrit dans le même sens au sujet du corps prussien de Jamignon, pour qu'il se règle en conséquence et qu'il s'éclaire toujours bien sur sa droite.

D'Erlon's Order of the Day

Pontécoulant, page 53

Ordre du jour du 1er corps pour la journée du 15.

Solre-sur-Sambre, 14 juin 1815 (au soir).

La diane battra à quatre heures précises; l'ordre du jour de l'armée, daté du 14, sera lu aux troupes.

Signé : le lieutenant général commandant en chef,
comte d'Erlon.

P. S. Les ponts sur la Sambre vont être coupés. Si vous avez des troupes sur la rive gauche, veuillez les faire retirer au jour.

Pour copie conforme :
L'adjudant commandant, chef d'état-major de la 3e division,
Ch. d'Arsonval.

Grouchy to Soult

??

Bossus, le 14 juin 1815.

Monsieur Le Maréchal

J'ai l'honneur de vous rendre compte que le 1er corps de cavalerie a bivouaqué à Fontenelle et Valcourt, le 2e corps à Bossus et les 3 et 4e corps à la lisière des bois de Gayolle.
    Je vous envoie un de mes officiers de Bossus, où j'ai établi mon quartier-général pour recevoir vos ordres pour demain.
    Je vous transmettrai sous une couple d'heures, un rapport que j'attends de l'un des douaniers de cette partie de la frontière, qui promet de m'instruire de ce qui se passe en face de nous.
    Le bruit que nous devons attaquer demain 15, y est général depuis plusieurs jours.

Recevez, Monsieur le Maréchal, etc.
Signé Le Maréchal Grouchy.

June 15, 1815

Napoleon to Joseph at 3 am

Correspondance, Vol. 28, no. 22054

Beaumont, le 15 Juin 1815, trois heures du matin.

Mon frère, l'ennemi faisant des mouvements pour nous attaquer, je marche à sa rencontre. Les hostilités vont donc commencer aujourd'hui : ainsi je desire que l'on fasse les communications qui ont été préparées. Informez-en le duc Vicence.

NAPOLÉON

Appendix XI – Select Correspondence

Gérard to Soult

SHD, C15/5

Au quartier général à Philippeville, le quinze juin 1815

à son Excellence le major général, à Beaumont,

Monseigneur,

M. le lieutenant général Bourmont, commandant la 14e division d'infanterie est passé, ce matin, à l'ennemi aves ses aides de camps l'adjudant commandant Clouet, son chef d'état-major; il parait même qu'il a emmené les adjoints qui sont le chef d'escadron Villoutreis et le capitaine Sourdat.
 Je m'empresse d'adresser à Votre Excellence les lettres que m'ont écrit, au moment de leur départ, M.M. Bourmont et Clouet. Ce général n'avait pas encore recu l'ordre de mouvement d'aujourd'hui, ni la série de [..]. d'ordre. Jusqu'à ce jour, il n'était rien venu à ma connaissance, qui put me le faire soupconner capable de trahison.
 Le maréchal de camp Hulot prend provisoirement le commandement de la 14e division. Je prie Votre Excellence de vouloir bien y envoyer le plutot possible un lieutenant-général et des officiers d'état-major.

Agréez, Monseigneur, l'hommage de mon respect,
Le général en chef, pair de France,
Cte. Gérard[283]

Soult to Reille at 8:30 am

Documents inédits, pages 22-23

Monsieur le comte Reille, l'empereur m'ordonne de vous écrire de passer la Sambre, si vous n'avez pas de forces devant vous, et de

---

[283] DeWit, Pierre, *The 4th corps and the division of Delort*, pages 2 and 3 http://www.waterloo-campaign.nl/bestanden/files/june15/Gérard.pdf

vous former sur plusieurs lignes, A UNE OU DEUX LIEUES EN AVANT, de manière à être à cheval sur la grande route de Bruxelles, en vous éclairant fortement dans la direction de Fleurus. M. le comte d'Erlon passera à Marchienne et se formera en bataille sur la route de Mons à Charleroi, où il sera à portée de vous soutenir au besoin.

Si vous étiez encore à Marchienne lorsque le présent ordre vous parviendra, et que le mouvement par Charleroi ne pût avoir lieu, vous l'opéreriez toujours par Marchienne, mais toujours pour remplir les dispositions ci-dessus.

L'empereur se rend devant Charleroi. Rendez compte immédiatement à Sa Majesté de vos opérations et de ce qui se passe devant vous.

Le maréchal d'empire, major général,
Duc De Dalmatie.

Au Bivouac de Jumignon, le
15 juin 1815, à 8 heures et
demie du matin.

Pour Copie Conforme : Comte Reille

Soult to Reille at 10 am

Register of the Major-Général

This order is a slightly modified copy of the above order of 8:30am. The above was based on an original from the collection of Reille, while the following is what was apparently copied into the order book. While minor differences are not surprising, the time difference is very puzzling. They should be identical.

Au Biwouac de Jamignon, 15 Juin, à dix heures du matin.

M. le comte Reille, l'Empereur m'ordonne de vous écrire de passer la Sambre, si vous n'avez pas de forces devant vous, et de vous former sur plusieurs lignes, à une ou deux lieues en avant, de manière à être à cheval sur la grande route de Bruxelles, en vous éclairant fortement dans la direction de Fleurus.

M. le comte d'Erlon passera à Marchienne et se formera en bataille sur la route de Mons à Charleroi, où il sera à portée de vous soutenir au besoin par Charleroi. Si vous étiez encore à Marchienne lorsque le présent ordre vous parviendra, vous opéreriez votre mouvement par Marchienne, mais toujours pour remplir les dispositions cidessus. L'Empereur se porte en avant de Charleroi ; rendez compte à S. M. de vos opérations et de ce qui se passe devant vous.

Soult to d'Erlon at 10 am

Register of the Major-Général

Au biwouac de Jamignon, le 15 juin, à dix heures du matin.

M. le comte, l'Empereur m'ordonne de vous écrire que M. le comte Reille reçoit ordre de passer la Sambre à Charleroi, et de se former sur plusieurs lignes à une ou deux lieues en avant, à cheval sur la grand'route de Bruxelles.
L'intention de S. M. est aussi que vous passiez la Sambre à Marchienne ou à Ham, pour vous porter sur la grand'route de Mons à Charleroi, où vous vous formerez sur plusieurs lignes, et prendre des positions qui vous rapprocheront de M. le comte Reille, liant vos communications et envoyant des partis dans toutes les directions, Mons, Nivelles, etc. Ce mouvement aurait également lieu si M. le comte Reille était obligé d'effectuer son passage par Marchienne. Rendez-moi compte de suite de vos opérations et de ce qui se passe devant vous. L'Empereur sera devant Charleroi.

Soult to d'Erlon at 3 pm

Register of the Major-Général

En avant de Charleroi, à trois heures du soir, 15 Juin 1815.

Monsieur le comte d'Erlon, l'Empereur ordonne à M. le comte Reille de marcher sur Gosselies et d'y attaquer un corps ennemi qui paraissait s'y arrêter. L'intention de l'Empereur est que vous marchiez aussi sur Gosselies, pour appuyer le comte Reille et le seconder dans ses opérations. Cependant vous devrez toujours faire garder Marchienne et vous enverrez une brigade sur les routes de Mons, lui recommandant de se garder très - militairement.

Soult to Gérard at 3:30 pm

Register of the Major-Général

Même date, à 3 heures ½.

M. le comte Gérard, l'empereur me charge de vous donner l'ordre de vous diriger avec votre corps d'armée sur Chatelet où vous passerez la Sambre et vous porterez en avant en suivant la route de Fleurus, direction que l'Empereur fait prendre en ce moment à une partie de l'armée, dans l'objet d'attaquer un corps ennemi qui s'y est arrêté en tête du bois de Jambufart. Si ce corps tenait encore après que vous aurez passé la Sambre, vous l'attaqueriez également. Rendez-moi compte de vos dispositions, et informez-moi si la 14ᵉ division de cavalerie est à votre suite; dans ce cas vous la feriez aussi avancer.

Soult to Delort

Register of the Major-Général

Charleroi, 15 Juin 1815.

Ordre au général Delort de prendre position en arrière de la ville.

D'Erlon to Soult at 4:30 pm

SHD, C15/5

Marchienne-au-Pont, le 15 juin 1815 à 4 heures 1/2 du soir

Monseigneur,

Appendix XI – Select Correspondence

J'ai recu les deux lettres que votre Excellence m'a fait l'honneur [?] de m'écrire aujourd'hui. La prémière m'a été remise à Montigny le Tigneux et je viens recevoir l'autre à Marchienne. Conformément à l'ordre général d'hier j'ai laissé une brigade de cavalerie à Solre et Bienne sous Thuin, et ma division d'infanterie à Thuin, Lobbes et l'abbaye d'Aulnes.

Mes autres troupes commencent à arriver à Marchienne, aussitôt que la queue du 2e corps aura filée, je leur ferai passer la Sambre, je porterai une brigade sur la route de Mons, une autre brigade restera en avant de Marchienne et avec les deux autres divisions d'infanterie je me porterai sur Gosselies.

J'ai vu la position de Thuin; elle est très forte par elle même, mais vu les localités on ne peut pas y établir de tête de pont.

Je prie Votre Excellence de me faire connaitre si je dois laisser encore des troupes à Thuin, Solre et environ.

Daignez, Monseigneur, agréer l'hommage de mon profond respect,

le lieutenant général commandant en chef du 1er corps comte D'Erlon[284]

Lobau to Soult at 8 pm

SHD, C15/5

Au quartier général sur le plateau à une lieue en arrière de Charleroi entre Jamignon et le bois du prince de Liège le 15 juin 1815 à 8 heures du soir.

Monsieur le maréchal,

Le 6e corps, d'après l'ordre général de mouvement reçu la nuit dernière, a pris les armes ce matin à 3 1/2 heures et s'est mis en marche à quatre heures.

---

284 DeWit, Pierre, *The 1st corps*, pages 2 and 3
http://www.waterloo-campaign.nl/bestanden/files/june15/derlon.pdf

J'ai bientôt joint la gauche du 3e corps, où j'ai fait halte jusqu'à sept heurres parce que ce n'est que vers six heures que ce corps d'armée a commencé son mouvement. J'ai laissé passer devant moi le parc du génie et une partie de l'équipage de pont. J'ai suivi la direction du 3e corps, et j'ai passé par Clermont, par Donstienne, Marbais, Ham sur Eure, les Hayes de Nalines.

Notre marche a été très lente, à cause des défilés et des mauvais chemins. Il est huit heures et j'arrive seulement sur le plateau que j'occupe, quoique je n'aie fait tout au plus que six lieues dans la journée.

La troupe est très fatiguée, mais les chevaux d'artillerie encore plus. Ne recevant point d'instructions, j'ai pris sur moi d'établir mon camp, et d'attendre vos ordres.

Je n'ai pas des nouvelles des équipages du corps d'armée. Je pense qu'ils nous joindront demain; ....j'en ai vu d'autres devant moi. J'ai l'honneur d'être de Votre Excellence le très humble et très obéissant serviteur, le lieutenant général aide-de-camp de l'empereur, commandant le 6e corps,

Cte.Lobau

P.S. Ci-joint le croquis de ma position fait par Mr.Guibert. Mon chef d'état-major vous a envoyé une situation le 11, de la Capelle, il vous [..] cette nuit.[285]

D'Erlon to Soult around 8 pm

SHD, C15/5

Jumay, le 15 juin 1815

Monseigneur,

Conformément à l'ordre de V.E. en date de ce jour, 3 heures du soir, je m'étais dirigé sur Gosselies. J'y ai trouvé le 2e corps établi; en conséquence j'ai placé ma quatrième division en arrière de ce village,

---

285 DeWit, Pierre, *The 6th corps*, page 1
http://www.waterloo-campaign.nl/bestanden/files/june15/lobau.pdf

et ma seconde en avant de Jumay, la brigade de cavalerie se trouve dans ce dernier endroit. La 3e division est restée à Marchienne et la 1er à Thuin, mon autre brigade de cavalerie est à Solre et Bienne-sous-Thuin, ce qui dissémine beaucoup mes troupes; je prie V.E. de vouloir bien me faire savoir si je dois rappeler celles que j'ai laissées en arrière. La reconnaissance que j'ai fait pousser sur Fontaine-l'Eveque a appris que 1500 prussiens, qui s'y trouvaient ce matin avec trois pièces d'artillerie en sont partis à midi se dirigeant sur Marchele-le-Chateau; ils ont emmené avec eux beaucoup de bestiaux. J'attends l'ordre de demain par l'officier qui aura l'honneur de remettre cette lettre à V.E. Je la prie d'agréer l'hommage de mon profond respect.

(Signé) Comte d'Erlon[286]

D'Erlon to Ney after 8 pm

In his 11 pm correspondence to Soult, Ney indicated he had received d'Erlon's dispositions.

Lefebvre-Desnouettes to Ney at 9 pm

SHD, C15/5

Frasnes, le 15 juin 9 heures du soir

Monseigneur,

En arrivant à Frasne suivant vos ordres nous l'avons trouvé occupé par un régiment de Nassau infanterie d'environ 1500 hommes et 8 pièces d'artillerie. Comme ils se sont apercus que nous manoeuvrions pour les tourner, ils sont sortis du village ; là nous les avons, en effet, enveloppés de nos escadrons. Le général Colbert a même été à une portée de fusil des 4 Bras sur la grande-route; mais comme le terrain était difficile et que l'ennemi s'est appuyé au bois de Bossu et qu'il a fait un feu très vif de ses 8 pièces de canon, il nous a été impossible

---

286 DeWit, Pierre, *The 1st corps*, page 3
http://www.waterloo-campaign.nl/bestanden/files/june15/derlon.pdf

de l'entamer. Cette troupe que nous avons trouvée à Frasne ne s'est pas portée ce matin en avant et ne s'est pas battue à Gosselies; elle est sous les ordres de Lord Wellington et semble vouloir se retirer vers Nivelles; ils ont allumé un fanal aux Quatre Bras et ont beaucoup tiré de leur canon. Aucunes des troupes qui se sont battues ce matin à Gosselies n'ont passé par ici; elles ont marché vers Fleurus. Les paysans ne peuvent pas me donner de renseignements sur un grand rassemblement de troupes dans ces environs, seulement, il y a un parc d'artillerie à Tubise composé de 100 caissons et 12 pièces d'artillerie. On dit que l'armée Belge est dans les environs de Mons et que le quartier général du jeune prince Frédéric d'Orange est à Brenne-le-Comte. [sic] Nous avons fait une quinzaine de prisonniers et nous avons eu une dizaine d'hommes tués ou blessés.

Demain à la pointe du jour j'enverrai aux Quatre Bras une reconnaissance qui l'occupera s'il est possible, car je pense que les troupes de Nassau sont parties.

Il vient de m'arriver un bataillon d'infanterie que j'ai placé en avant du village. Mon artillerie ne m'ayant pas rejoint, je lui ai envoyé l'ordre de bivouaquer avec la division Bachelu; elle me rejoindra demain matin. Je n'écris pas à l'empereur n'ayant pas de choses plus importantes à lui dire que ce que je dis à votre Excellence.

J'ai l'honneur d'être avec respect, Monseigneur, votre très humble et très dévoué serviteur,

Lefebvre Desnouettes

Je vous envoie un maréchal-des-logis qui prendra les ordres de Votre Excellence. J'ai l'honneur d'observer à Votre Excellence que l'ennemi n'a point montré de cavalerie devant nous, mais l'artillerie et de l'artillerie légère.[287]

Reille to Soult at 9 pm

SHD, C15/22

---

287 DeWit, Pierre, *The action at Frasnes*, pages 2 and 3
http://www.waterloo-campaign.nl/bestanden/files/june15/frasnes.pdf

Appendix XI – Select Correspondence

à Gosselie le 15 juin 1815 à 9 heures du soir

Son Excellence le maréchal duc de Dalmatie major général,

Monsieur le maréchal,

D'après l'ordre de l'armée je suis parti de Lair Fauster avec le 2e corps à trois heures du matin, en avant de Thuin j'ai rencontré un avantgarde ennemi de cavalerie et d'infanterie et dans ce village environ 800 hommes; après quelque coups de canon et une fusillade assez vive, nous les avons chassé de cette position, qui est d'un accès très difficile. L'ennemi a laissé du monde; des blessés et quelques prisonniers parmi lesquels deux officiers. Les ponts de Lobbes, de Thuin et d'Aulne sont restés en bon état. Nous avons rencontré encore l'ennemi dans le Bois de Montigny le Tigneux; une fusillade très vive a été engagée; nous l'avons chassé du village et il a cherché ensuite à faire sa retraite sur Marchienne; mais étant serré de près par notre infanterie, j'ai fait déboucher les généraux Piré et Hubert avec le 1er de chasseurs qui les a chargé avec beaucoup de vigueur; une centaine ont été sabrés et plus de 200 ont été faits prisonniers.

Après avoir passé le pont de Marchienne j'ai dirigé la cavalerie en laissant à gauche le Bois de Monceaux et je l'ai traversé avec la colonne d'infanterie; arrivé près de Jumay, le général Bachelu est tombé sur la colonne ennemie, qui avait forcé le 1er de chasseurs à la retraite; lui a tué des hommes et fait quelques prisonniers. Le 2e corps s'est ensuite porté en avant et a pris position; les 5e et 9e division d'infanterie ainsi que la cavalerie à droite et à gauche de Gosselies et la 6e division en arrière du Bois de Lombuc. La 7e, qui était en seconde ligne de la 6e, a recu une heure avant la nuit l'ordre d'après celui de Sa Majesté de prendre la route de Jumay à Fleurus et de pousser des tirailleurs jusqu'à ce village.

Le 2e d'infanterie légère, qui a tenu toute la journée la tête de la colonne, a montré la plus grande vigueur, il a eu environ 80 hommes tués ou blessés, le 1er de chasseurs en a eu 20 à 25; le nombre des prisonniers envoyé à l'état major général est de 255 et 5 officiers.

Je prie Votre Excellence d'agréer mon hommage respectueux, le général commandant le 2e corps Comte Reille[288]

Gérard to Soult, late evening

SHD C15/11

Armée de la Moselle
Au quartier général à Chatelet, le 15 juin 1815

A son Excellence, le Major-Général à Charleroy

Monseigneur,

J'avais déjà dépassé les haies à Nalinnes dans la direction de Charleroy, lorsque j'ai recu l'ordre de Votre Excellence de me diriger sur <u>Chatelet</u> et d'y passer la Sambre.
 Les trois divisions d'infanterie avec leur artillerie, sont arrivées à Chatelet, la quatorzième division d'infanterie, commandée par le maréchal de camp Hulot, a passé la Sambre et occupe Chatelineau.
 Les deux autres divisions d'infanterie sont à Chatelet. Je fais pousser des reconnaissances sur les deux rives de la Sambre et observer les communications sur Namur et Dinant.
 Le sixième division de cavalerie commandée par le lieutenant-général Maurin n'a pu arriver qu'à Bouflieu.
 La division de cuirassiers du général Delort est encore en arrière sur la route de Philippeville; je lui ai envoyé succesivement trois officiers, pour lui faire prendre la direction de Chatelet.
 Partout où l'Armee de la Moselle a passé aujourd'hui, les habitants de la Belgique l'ont accueillie aux acclamations de <u>Vive l'empereur</u>.
 L'officier porteur de cette dépêche est, en mêm tems, chargé de conduire à votre Excellence, un capitaine du 28ᵉ régt. d'infanterie prussienne, nommé Neuhaus, qui a été fait prisonnier aujourd'hui par des dragons.

---

288 DeWit, Pierre, *The French positions on the evening of the 15ᵗʰ June*, page 7 http://www.waterloo-campaign.nl/bestanden/files/june15/fr.avond.pdf

Appendix XI – Select Correspondence

Je prie Votre Excellence d'agréer l'hommage de mon respect,

Le général en chef,
Pair de France
Cte. Gérard[289]

Vandamme to Napoleon around 10 pm

SHD, C15/5

à la cense de Fontenelle, 15 juin 1815 10 heures du soir

Sire,

J'ai l'honneur de rendre compte à Votre Majesté que les lieutenants généraux Burth et Cardinal commandent ce qui est devant nous. Je pense que l'ennemi n'a que 12 à 15.000 hommes. Le maréchal Grouchy croit qu'il y a 30.000 hommes.
   L'ennemi n'a démasqué que 10 à 12 pièces de canon.
   L'ennemi est maintenant en arrière de Fleurus entièrement en retraite. Il n'a laissé que quelques postes de cavalerie légère dans Fleurus. Je suis entièrement réuni; la droite en avant de Winage sur la droite de la route de Namur. C'est la 8e division.
   J'ai mon quartier général à la Cense de Fontenelle. De cette Cense à la droite de Namur se trouve la 3e division de cavalerie légère qui a ses postes sur Lambussart.
   De la droite de la Cense à la route de Fleurus se trouve la 10e division.
   La 11e division est au Camp d'Andois.
   Une partie de ma réserve d'artillerie ici m'arrive à l'instant.
   J'ai l'honneur d'être, Sire, du votre Majesté impériale, le très humble et très obéissant serviteur et fidèle sujet,

---

289 DeWit, Pierre, *The 4th corps and the division of Delort*, pages 5 and 6
http://www.waterloo-campaign.nl/bestanden/files/june15/Gérard.pdf

Vandamme[290]

Grouchy to Napoleon around 10 pm

SHD, C15/5

au village de Campinaire, le 15 juin à 10 heures du soir

Sire, j'ai l'honneur de rendre compte à Votre Majesté que le corps du général Exelmans, destiné à déborder la position que l'ennemi occupait au delà du village de Gilly, ayant traversé le ravin qui l'en séparait, l'a chargé dans la plaine au dessus de Chatelineau; l'a poussé jusque pas delà Ronchamps, et ayant rejeté au loin sa cavalerie, est tombé sur des carrés d'infanterie; les a enfoncés et a fait plus de 400 prisonniers.

L'ennemi, essayant de tenir dans le bois, est même de redeboucher sous la protection du feu de son infanterie, quelques compagnies de dragons ont mis pied à terre, ont contenu par leur feu l'infanterie prussienne et donné le temps à l'infanterie du général Vandamme d'arriver.

Celle-ci, marchant sur la route qui traverse le bois a été soutenue de nouveau par les dragons qui ont poursuivi les prussiens jusqu'au delà du village de Lambusart dont le général Chastel les a encore chassé. Il est impossible de montrer plus d'intrépidité que n'a fait le corps du général Exelmans et notamment la brigade du général Vincent, composée du 15e et 20e régiments de dragons. Le chef d'escadron Guibourg, de 15e régiment, a enfoncé un carré et fait 300 prisonniers. Je le recommande aux bontés de Votre Majesté. Le général Pajol, à la tête du 1er corps, a chassé l'ennemi de la route directe de Gilly à Fleurus, lui a fait plusieurs centaines de prisonniers et s'est non moins distingué que le général Exelmans, dont je ne puis assez faire d'éloge à Votre Majesté. C'est constamment aux cris de «Vive l'empereur» et avec un enthousiasme difficile à décrire que les troupes ont partout abordé l'ennemi.

---

290 DeWit, Pierre, *The French positions on the evening of the 15th June*, page 2 http://www.waterloo-campaign.nl/bestanden/files/june15/fr.avond.pdf

APPENDIX XI – SELECT CORRESPONDENCE

Je suis avec respect, Sire,

signé Maréchal Grouchy[291]

Ney to d'Erlon before 11 pm

In his 11 pm correspondence to Soult, Ney indicates he has just sent orders to d'Erlon.

Ney to Soult around 11 pm

SHD, C15/5

Gosselies, 15 juin, 11 heures du soir

Monsieur le maréchal, j'ai l'honneur de rendre compte à Votre Excellence que, conformément aux ordres de l'Empereur, je me suis rendu cet après-midi sur Gosselies pour en déloger l'ennemi avec la cavalerie du général Piré et l'infanterie du général Bachelu. La résistance de l'ennemi a été peu opiniâtre; on a échangé de part et d'autre 25 à 30 coups de canon; il s'est replié par Heppignies sur Fleurus.

Nous avons fait 5 à 600 prisonniers prussiens du corps du général Zieten.

Voici l'emplacement des troupes:
Le général Lefebvre Desnouettes avec les lanciers et les chasseurs de la garde à Frasne.
Le général Bachelu avec la 5e division à Mellet.
Le général Foy avec la 9e division à Gosselies.
La cavalerie légère du général Piré à Heppignies.
Je ne sais où se trouve le général en chef Reille.
Le général comte d'Erlon me mande qu'il est à Jumet avec la plus grande partie de son corps d'armée. Je viens de lui transmettre les dispositions prescrites par la lettre de Votre Excellence en date de ce jour.
Je joins à ma lettre un rapport du général Lefebvre-Desnouettes.

---

291 DeWit, Pierre, *The French positions on the evening of the 15th June*, pages 2 and 3 http://www.waterloo-campaign.nl/bestanden/files/june15/fr.avond.pdf

Agréez, Monsieur le maréchal, l'assurance de ma haute considération,

Le maréchal Prince de la Moskowa, Ney[292]

Soult to d'Erlon before midnight, or 9:30 pm

Documents inédits, pages 25-26
Note how this particular order so revealing on the status of the left wing during the evening of the 15th of June was *not* copied into the order book.

A M. le comte d'Erlon, commandant le 1er corps

Charleroi, le 15 juin 1815

Monsieur le comte, l'intention de l'empereur est que vous ralliez votre corps sur la rive gauche de la Sambre, pour joindre le 2ᵉ corps à Gosselies, d'après les ordres que vous donnera à ce sujet M. le Maréchal prince de la Moskowa.
Ainsi, vous rappellerez les troupes que vous avez laissées à Thuin, Sobre et environs; vous devrez cependant avoir toujours de nombreux partis sur votre gauche pour éclairer la route de Mons.

Le maréchal d'empire, Major-Général,

Duc de Dalmatie

Army Bulletin

Correspondance, Vol. 28, 22056

Charleroi 15 juin 1815, au soir.

Le 14, l'armée était placée de la manière suivante:
Le quartier impérial à Beaumont.

---

[292] DeWit, Pierre, *The action at Frasnes*, page 3
http://www.waterloo-campaign.nl/bestanden/files/june15/frasnes.pdf

Le 1er corps, commandé par le général d'Erlon, était à Solre, sur la Sambre.

Le 2e corps, commandé par le général Reille, était à Ham-sur-Heure.

Le 3e corps, commandé par le général Vandamme, était sur la droite de Beaumont.

Le 4e corps, commandé par le général Gérard, arrivait à Philippeville.

Le 15, à trois heures du matin, le général Reille attaqua l'ennemi et se porta sur Marchienne-au-Pont, Il eut différents engagements dans lesquels sa cavalerie chargea un bataillon prussien et fit 300 prisonniers.

A une heure du matin, l'Empereur était à Jamioulx-sur-Heure.

La division de cavalerie légère du général Domon sabra deux bataillons prussiens et fit 400 prisonniers.

Le général Pajol entra à Charleroi à midi. Les sapeurs et les marins de la Garde étaient à l'avant-garde pour réparer les ponts; ils pénétrèrent les premiers en tirailleurs dans la ville, Le général Reille avec le 1er de hussards, se porta sur Gosselies, sur la route de Bruxelles, et le général Pajol sur Gilly, sur la route de Namur.

A trois heures après midi, le général Vandamme déboucha avec son corps sur Gilly.

Le maréchal Grouchy arrive avec la cavalerie du général Exelmans.

L'ennemi occupait la gauche de la position de Fleurus. A cinq heures après midi, l'Empereur ordonna l'attaque. La position fut tournée et enlevée. Les quatre escadrons de service de la Garde, commandés par le général Letort, aide de camp de l'Empereur, enfoncèrent trois carrés : les 26e, 27e et 28e régiments prussiens furent mis en déroute. Nos escadrons sabrèrent 4 ou 500 hommes et firent 1,500 prisonniers.

Pendant ce temps, le général Reille passait la Sambre à Marchienne-eau-Pont, pour se porter sur Gosselies avec les divisions du Prince Jérôme et du général Bachelu, attaquait l'ennemi, lui faisait 250 prisonniers et le poursuivait sur la route de Bruxelles.

Nous devînmes ainsi maîtres de toute la position de Fleurus.

A huit heures du soir, l'Empereur rentra à son quartier général Charleroi.

Cette journée coûte à l'ennemi cinq pièces de canon et 2,000 hommes, dont 1,000 prisonniers. Notre perte est de 10 hommes tués et de 80 blessés, la plupart, des escadrons de service, qui ont fait les charges, et des trois escadrons du 20e de dragons, qui ont aussi chargé un carré avec la plus grande intrépidité. Notre perte, légère quant au nombre, a été sensible à l'Empereur, par la blessure grave qu'a reçue le général Letort, son aide de camp, en chargeant à la tête des escadrons de service. Cet officier est de la plus grande distinction. Il a été frappé d'une belle au bas-ventre, et le chirurgien fait craindre que sa blessure ne soit mortelle.

Nous avons trouvé à Charleroi quelques magasins. La joie des Belges ne saurait se décrire. Il y a des villages qui, à la vue de leurs libérateurs, ont formé des danses, et partout c'est un élan qui part du coeur.

Dans le rapport de l'état-major général, on insérera les noms des officiers et soldats qui se sont distingués.

L'Empereur a donné le commandement de la gauche au prince de la Moskova, qui a eu le soir son quartier général aux Quatre-Chemins, sur la route de Bruxelles.

Le duc de Trévise, à qui l'Empereur avait donné le commandement de la jeune Garde, est resté à Beaumont, malade d'une sciatique qui l'a forcé de se mettre au lit.

Le 4e corps, commandé par le général Gérard, arrive ce soir à Châtelet. Le général Gérard a rendu compte que le lieutenant général Bourmont, le colonel Clouet et le chef d'escadron Villoutreys ont passé à l'ennemi. Un lieutenant du 11e de chasseurs a également passé à l'ennemi. Le major général a ordonné que ces déserteurs fussent sur-le-champ jugés conformément aux lois.

Rien ne peut peindre le bon esprit et l'ardeur de l'armée. Elle regarde comme un événement heureux la désertion de ce petit nombre de traîtres, qui se démasquent ainsi.

June 16, 1815

Soult to Napoleon

Porte-feuille, page 125

> *Charleroi le 16 Juin 1815.*
>
> SIRE,
>
> *Le service actif que font chaque jour, les officiers d'Etat-Major, nécessite un plus grand nombre de chevaux, que la plupart est dans l'impossibilité de se procurer, faute de moyens pécuniaires.*
>   *J'ai donc l'honneur de proposer à Votre Majesté d'accorder à titre de gratification extraordinaire aux Adjudants, Commandants et Officiers d'Etat-Major portés dans l'état ci-joint, la somme de huit cents francs pour les Adjudants-Commandants et celle de six cents francs pour les officiers d'Etat-Major.*
>   *Je prie Votre Majesté de me faire connaitre sa décision à ce sujet,*
>
> *Le Major-Général*
> *Duc de Dalmatie*

D'Arsonval to General Nogues at 3am

Pontécoulant – page 144

> *Quartier général a Marchienne-au-Pont,*
>
> *D'après l'intention du général eu chef, le lieutenant général me charge de vous inviter à faire partir de suite votre brigade pour être rendue à six heures du matin, et plus tôt s'il était possible, à Gosselies.*
>
> *L'adjudant commandant, chef d'état-major.*
> *Ch. d'Arsonval.*

P. S. La 2e brigade reste ici jusqu'à l'arrivée de la première division, pour se rendre ensemble à la même destination.

Napoleon to Joseph

Correspondance, Vol. 28, no. 22057

Charleroi, 16 juin 1815

Mon Frère, le bulletin vous fera connaitre ce qui s'est passé. Je porte mon quartier général à Fleurus. Nous sommes en grand mouvement. Je regrette beaucoup la perte du général Letort. La perte de la journée d'hier est peu considérable et porte presque toute sur les quatre escadrons de service.

La confiscation des biens des traîtres qui forment des rassemblements à Gand est nécessaire.

Napoléon

Grouchy to Soult at 5 am

SHD, C15/5

Campinaire, le 16 juin 1815 à 5 heures du matin

Monsieur le maréchal,

Les quatre corps de cavalerie sont placés de la manière suivante:
Le 1er a une de ses divisions à Lambusart, et la seconde sur la route de Gilly à Fleurus en avant de l'embranchement de Capinaire. Le 2e corps a une de ses divisions à Lambusart et l'autre en arrière du défilé de Ronchamp.
Le 4e corps a raillé sa seconde division et est au village de St. Francois et censes environnantes.
Le 3e corps doit se trouver entre Charleroi et le point où nous avons chargé les carrés de l'infanterie prussienne. Le général

APPENDIX XI – SELECT CORRESPONDENCE

Kellermann ne m'a point envoyé de Charleroi, son emplacement; mais il est de ce coté-ci.

Je n'ai point encore le rapport des pertes qu'on fait les 1er et 2e corps dans la journée d'aujourd'hui. Je l'ai demandé et le remettrai d'en qu'il me sera parvenu. Ci-joint copie de celui que j'adressai hier à l'Empereur.

Le total des prisonniers faits par la cavalerie dans la journée d'hier est de huit à neuf cents hommes.

Agréez, Monsieur le maréchal, l'assurance de ma haute considération.

Le maréchal commandant la cavalerie
Comte de Grouchy

P.S. Le premier hussards fesant parti du 1er corps en a été détaché par Vos Ordres, et je désire que vous lui fesiez rallier la division Soult, d'en qu'il sera possible[293]

Soult to the Army

Register of the Major-Général

Charleroi, le 16 Juin 1815.
Ordre de ne point render d'honneurs à l'Empereur quand il se trouve aux avant-postes.

Soult to Ney around 5 am

Register of the Major-Général

Charleroi, le 16 Juin 1815.

Prévenu que l'Empereur vient de donner l'ordre au comte de Valmy de réunir son corps et de le diriger sur Gosselies où il sera à la disposition

---

293 DeWit, Pierre, *The right wing*, pages 1 and 2
http://www.waterloo-campaign.nl/bestanden/files/june16/frrechtervleugel.pdf

du maréchal Ney. Que l'intention de l'Empereur est que la cavalerie de sa garde qui a été portée sur la route de Bruxelles reste en arriére et rejoigne de restant de la garde impériale ; mais pour qu'elle ne fasse pas de mouvement retrograde, il pourra, après l'avoir remplacée sur la ligne, la laisser un peu en arriére où il lui sera envoyé des ordres dans le mouvement de la journée ; que le général Lefèvre-Desnouettes enverra à cet effet un officier pour prendre des ordres. On lui demande si le premier corps a opéré son mouvement, et quelle est ce matin la position exacte des 1ᵉʳ et 2ᵉ corps, et des divisions de cavalerie qui y sont attachées, en faisant connaitre ce qu'il y a devant vous et ce qu'on a appris.

Ney to Soult at 7 am

Houssaye, pages 344 and 346

According to Pierre De Wit, this report is not to be found in the papers of Baron Gourgaud.[294] Houssaye apparently saw the 7 am report, and quoted from it to confirm the undiscovered report of Ney to Soult from the previous evening.

Soult to Comte de Valmy

Register of Major-Général

Charleroi, le 16 Juin 1815.

Ordre au comte de Valmy de réunir et diriger le 3ᵉ corps de cavalerie sur Gosselies où il sera à la disposition du maréchal Ney.

Soult to Lobau before 8 am

Register of Major-Général

Porté par M. Poirau.

---

294 From http://www.waterloo-campaign.nl/bestanden/files/june16/frlinkervleugel.pdf

Appendix XI – Select Correspondence

Charleroi, le 16 juin 1815

M. le comte, l'Empereur ordonne que vous mettiez en marche le 6ᵉ corps pour lui faire prendre position à mi-chemin de Charleroi à Fleurus, et que vous fassiez en même-temps garder Charleroi où vous nommerez provisoirement un commandant. J'ai ordonné que tous les prisonniers ainsi que tous les blessés ennemis et francais fussent dirigés sur Avesnes. Je vous prie de veiller à l'exécution de cet ordre.

Soult to Drouot before 8 am

Register of Major-Général

Charleroi, le 16 juin 1815

M. le comte, l'Empereur ordonne que la garde impériale, infanterie, cavalerie et artillerie se mette immédiatement en marche pour Fleurus; veuillez lui donner des ordres en conséquence; la division du général Lefebvre-Desnouettes, étant détachée, en recevra directement.

Soult to Gérard before 8 am

Register of Major-Général

Porté par M. Crava.

Même date.

M. le comte, l'empereur ordonne que vous mettiez en marche le 4ᵉ corps d'armée et que vous le dirigiez sur **Sombref**, *en laissant Fleurus à gauche, afin d'éviter l'encombrement.*
   Je vous préviens que l'intention de Sa Majesté est que vous preniez les ordres de M. le maréchal Grouchy comme commandant d'Aile, ainsi vous l'instruirez de votre mouvement. Vous enverrez sur le champ près de lui un officier pour lui demander des ordres, sans cependant retarder votre marche. M. le maréchal Grouchy doit se trouver en ce moment du côté de Fleurus. Vous ne recevrez des ordres

directs de l'Empereur que lorsque S. M. sera présente; mais vous continuerez à m'adresser vos rapports et états ainsi qu'il est établi.

Soult to Vandamme before 8 am

Register of Major-Général

Porté par M. Guyardin.

Charleroy, le 16 juin 1815

M. le général, l'Empereur ordonne que vous vous mettiez en marche avec le 3ᵉ corps, pour vous diriger sur Sombref où le 4ᵉ corps et les corps de réserve de cavalerie vont se rendre également. S. M. ordonne aussi que vous preniez les ordres de M. le maréchal Grouchy comme commandant d'une aile de l'armée. Ainsi vous l'instruirez de votre mouvement et vous lui enverrez sur le champ un officier pour lui demander ses ordres, sans cependant retarder votre marche. M. le comte Grouchy doit être en ce moment du côté de Fleurus, vous ne recevrez des ordres directs de l'Empereur que lorsque S. M. sera présente; mais vous continuerez à m'adresser vos rapports et états ainsi qu'il a été établi.

Soult to Grouchy around 8 am

Register of the Major-Général

Porté par M. Liom.

Même date.

M. le maréchal, l'Empereur ordonne que vous vous mettiez en marche avec les 1ᵉʳ, 2ᵉ et 4ᵉ corps de cavalerie, et que vous les dirigiez sur Sombref où vous pendrez position. Je donne pareil ordre à M. le lieutenant-général Vandamme pour le 3ᵉ corps d'infanterie, et à M. le lieutenant- général Gérard pour le 4ᵉ corps, et je préviens ces deux généraux qu'ils sont sous vos ordres et qu'ils doivent vous envoyer immédiatement des officiers pour vous instruire de leur marche et prendre vos instructions. Je leur dis cependant que lorsque S. M. sera présente, ils pourront recevoir d'elle des ordres directs, et qu'ils devront continuer à m'envoyer des rapports de service et états qu'ils ont coutume de fournir.

Je préviens aussi M. le général Gérard que dans son mouvement sur Sombref il doit laisser la ville de Fleurus à gauche, afin d'éviter l'encombrement ; ainsi vous lui donnerez une direction pour qu'il marche d'ailleurs bien réuni et à portée du 3e corps, et soit en mesure de concourir à l'attaque de Sombref si l'ennemi fait résistance.

Vous donnerez aussi des instructions en conséquence à M. le général comte Vandamme.

J'ai l'honneur de vous prévenir que M. le comte de Valmy a reçu ordre de se rendre à Gosselies, avec le 3e corps de cavalerie où il sera à la disposition de M. le maréchal prince de la Moskowa.

Le 1er régiment de hussards rentrera au 1er corps de cavalerie dans la journée, je prendrai à ce sujet les ordres de l'Empereur.

J'ai l'honneur de vous prévenir que M. le maréchal prince de la Moskowa reçoit l'ordre de se porter avec le 1er et le 2e corps d'infanterie et le 3e de cavalerie, à l'intersection des chemins dits les trois Bras, *sur la route de Bruxelles, et qu'il détachera un fort corps à* Marbais *pour se lier avec vous sur Sombref et seconder au besoin vos opérations.*

Aussitôt que vous vous serez rendu maître de Sombref, il faudra envoyer une avant-garde à Gembloux *et faire reconnaitre toutes les directions qui aboutissent à Sombref, particulièrement la grande route de Namur, en même temps que vous établirez vos communications avec M. le Maréchal Ney.*

La garde impériale se dirige sur Fleurus.

Soult to Ney before 8 am

Register of the Major General

Porté par M. Leroux

Charleroy, le 16 juin 1815

M. le maréchal, l'Empereur ordonne que vous mettiez en marche les 1ᵉʳ et 2ᵉ corps d'armée, ainsi que le 3ᵉ corps de cavalerie qui a été mis à votre disposition pour les diriger sur l'intersection des chemins dits les Trois-Bras *(route de Bruxelles), où vous leur ferez prendre position. Et vous porterez en même temps des reconnaissances aussi avant que possible sur la route de Bruxelles et sur* Nivelles, *d'où probablement l'ennemi s'est retiré. S. M. désire que, s'il n'y a pas d'inconvénient, vous établissiez une division avec de la cavalerie à Jenapes, et elle ordonne que vous portiez une autre division du côté de* Marbais *pour couvrir l'espace entre* Sombref *et les Trois Bras. Vous placerez, près de cette division, la division de cavalerie de la garde impériale commandée par le général Lefebvre-Desnouettes, ainsi que le 1ᵉʳ régiment de hussards qui a été détaché hier vers* Gosselies.

Le corps qui sera à Marbais *aura aussi pour objet d'appuyer les mouvements de M. le maréchal Grouchy sur Sombref, et de vous soutenir à la position* des Trois Bras, *si cela devenait nécessaire. Vous recommanderez au général qui sera à Marbais, de bien s'éclairer sur toutes les directions, particulièrement sur celles de* Gembloux *et de Vavres.*

Si cependant la division du général Lefebvre-Desnouettes était trop engagée sur la route de Bruxelles, vous la laisseriez, et vous la remplaceriez au corps qui sera à Marbais, par le 3ᵉ corps de cavalerie, qui sera aux ordres de M. le comte de Valmy et par le 1ᵉʳ régiment de hussards.

J'ai l'honneur de vous prévenir que l'Empereur va se porter sur Sombref, où, d'après les ordres de S. M., M. le maréchal Grouchy doit se diriger avec les 3ᵉ et 4ᵉ corps d'infanterie, et les 1ᵉʳ, 2ᵉ et 4ᵉ corps de cavalerie. M. le maréchal Grouchy fera occuper Gembloux.

Je vous prie de me mettre de suite à même de rendre compte à l'Empereur de vos dispositions, pour exécuter l'ordre que je vous envoie ainsi que de tout ce que vous aurez appris sur l'ennemi.

S. M. me charge de vous recommander de prescrire aux généraux commandants les corps d'armée, de faire réunir leur monde et faire rentrer les hommes isolés, de maintenir l'ordre le plus parfait dans la troupe et de rallier toutes les voitures d'artillerie et d'ambulances qu'ils auraient pu laisser en arrière.

Appendix XI – Select Correspondence

Napoleon to Ney before 9 am

Correspondance, Vol. 28, 22058

Charleroi, 16 juin 1815.

Mon cousin, je vous envoie mon aide de camp le général Flahaut, qui vous porte la présente lettre, Le major général a dû vous donner des ordres mais vous recevrez les miens plus tot, parce que mes officiers vont plus vite que les siens, Vous recevrez l'ordre de mouvement du jour, mais je veux vous en écrire en détail, parce que c'est de la plus haute importance.

Je porte le maréchal Grouchy avec les 3e et 4e corps d'infanterie sur Sombreffe; je porte ma Garde à Fleurus, et j'y serai de ma personne avant midi, J'y attaquerai l'ennemi si je le rencontre, et j'éclairerai la route jusqu'à Gembloux. Là, d'après ce qui se passera, je prendrai mon parti peut-etre à trois heures après midi, peut-être ce soir. Mon intention est que, immédiatement après que j'aurai pris mon parti, vous soyez prêt à marcher sur Bruxelles, Je vous appuierai avec la Garde, qui sera à Fleurus ou à Sombreffe, et je désirerais arriver à Bruxelles demain matin, Vous vous mettriez en marche ce soir même , si je prends mon parti d'assez bonne heure pour que vous puissiez en être informé de jour et faire ce soir trois ou quatre lieues et être demain à sept heures du matin à Bruxelles.

Vous pouvez donc disposer vos troupes de la manière suivante: Première division, à deux lieues en avant des Quatre-Chemins, s'il n'y a pas d'inconvénient; six divisions d'infanterie autour des Quatre-Chemins, et une division à Marbais, afin que je puisse l'attirer à moi à Sombreffe, si j'en avais besoin; elle ne retarderait d'ailleurs pas votre marche;

Le corps du comte de Valmy, qui a 3,000 cuirassiers d'élite, à l'intersection du chemin des Romains et de celui de Bruxelles, afin que je puisse l'attirer à moi si j'en avais besoin, Aussitôt que mon parti sera pris, vous lui enverrez l'ordre de venir vous rejoindre.

Je désirerais avoir avec moi la division de la Garde que commande le général Lefebvre-Desnoëttes, et je vous envoie les deux divisions du corps du comte de Valmy pour la remplacer, Mais, dans mon projet actuel, je préfère placer le comte de Valmy de manière à le rappeler si j'en avais besoin, et ne point faire faire de fausses marches au général Lefebvre-Desnoëttes, puisqu'il est probable que je me déciderai ce soir à marcher sur Bruxelles avec la Garde. Cependant couvrez la division Lefebvre par les divisions de cavalerie d'Erlon et de Reille, afin de ménager la Garde: s'il y avait quelque échauffourée avec les Anglais, il est préférable que ce soit sur la ligne que sur la Garde.

J'ai adopté comme principe général, pendant cette campagne, de diviser mon armée en deux ailes et une réserve. Votre aile sera composée des quatre divisions du 1er corps, des quatre divisions du 2e corps, de deux divisions de cavalerie légère et de deux divisions du corps du comte de Valmy. Cela ne doit pas être loin de 45 à 50,000 hommes.

Le maréchal Grouchy aura à peu près la même force et commandera l'aile droite.

La Garde formera la reserve, et je me porterai sur l'une ou l'autre aile, selon les circonstances. Le major général donne les ordres les plus précis pour qu'il n'y ait aucune difficulté sur l'obéissance à vos ordres lorsque vous serez détaché, les commandants de corps devant prendre mes ordres directement quand je me trouve présent.

Selon les circonstances, j'affaiblirai l'une ou l'autre aile, en augmentant ma réserve.

Vous sentez assez l'importance attachée à la prise de Bruxelles. Cela pourra d'ailleurs donner lieu à des incidents, car un mouvement aussi prompt et aussi brusque isolera l'armée anglaise de Mons, Ostende, etc, Je désire que vos dispositions soient bien faites, pour qu'au premier ordre vos huit divisions puissent marcher rapidement et sans; obstacle sur Bruxelles.

Napoléon.

Napoleon to Grouchy before 9 am

Correspondance, Vol 28, 22059

Charleroi, le 16 juin 1815.

Appendix XI – Select Correspondence

Mon Cousin, je vous envoie Labédoyère, mon aide de camp, pour vous porter la présente lettre. Le major général a du vous faire connaitre mes intentions; mais, comme il a des officiers mal montés, mon aide de camp arrivera peut-être avant.

Mon intention est que, comme commandant l'aile droite, vous preniez le commandement du 3ᵉ corps que commande le général Vandamme, du 4ᵉ corps que commande le général Gérard, les corps de cavalerie que commandent les généraux Pajol, Milhaud, Exelmans; ce qui ne doit pas faire loin de 50.000 hommes. Rendez-vous avec cette aile droite à Sombref. Faites partir en conséquence de suite les corps des généraux Pajol, Milhaud, Exelmans et Vandamme, et, sans vous arrêter, continuez votre mouvement sur Sombref. Le 4e corps, qui est à Châtelet, recoit directement l'ordre de se rendre à Sombref sans passer par Fleurus. Cette observation est importante parce que je porte mon quartier général à Fleurus et qu'il faut éviter les encombrements. Envoyez de suite un officier au général Gérard pour lui faire connaitre votre mouvement et qu'il exécute le sien de suite.

Mon intention est que tous les généraux prennent directement vos ordres; ils ne prendront les miens que lorsque je serai présent. Je serai entre dix et onze heures à Fleurus; je me rendrai à Sombref laissant ma garde, infanterie et cavalerie, à Fleurus. Je ne la conduirais à Sombref qu'en cas qu'elle fut nécessaire. Si l'ennemi est à Sombref, je veux l'attaquer; je veux même l'attaquer à Gembloux et m'emparer aussi de cette position, mon intention étant, après avoir connu ces deux positions, de partir cette nuit, et d'opérer avec mon aile gauche, que commande le maréchal Ney, sur les Anglais. Ne perdez donc point un moment, parce que plus vite je prendrai mon parti, mieux cela vaudra pour la suite de mes opérations. Je suppose que vous êtes à Fleurus. Communiquez constamment avec le général Gérard, afin qu'il puisse vous aider pour attaquer Sombref, s'il était nécessaire.

La division Girard est à portée de Fleurus; n'en disposez point à moins de nécessité absolue, parce qu'elle doit marcher toute la nuit. Laissez aussi ma Jeune Garde et toute son artillerie à Fleurus.

Le comte de Valmy, avec ses deux divisions de cuirassiers, marche sur la route de Bruxelles; il se lie avec le maréchal Ney, pour contribuer à l'opération de ce soir, à l'aile gauche.

Comme je vous l'ai dit, je serai de dix à onze heures à Fleurus. Envoyez-moi des rapports sur tout ce que vous apprendrez. Veillez à ce que la route de Fleurus soit libre. Toutes les données que j'ai sont que les Prussiens ne peuvent point nous opposer plus de 40.000 hommes.

Napoléon

Sout to Ney before 10 am

Register of the Major-Général

Porté par M. Waleski

Charleroi, le 16 juin 1815.

M. le maréchal, un officier de lanciers vient de dire à l'Empereur que l'ennemi présentait des masses du côté des Quatre-Bras ; réunissez-les corps des comtes Reille et d'Erlon et celui du comte de Valmy qui se met en ce moment en route pour vous rejoindre; avec ces forces vous devrez battre et détruire tous les corps ennemis qui peuvent se présenter ; Blücher était hier à Namur et il n'est pas vraisemblable qu'il ait porté des troupes vers les Quatre-Bras, ainsi vous n'avez à faire qu'à ce qui vient de Bruxelles.
  Le maréchal Grouchy va faire le mouvement sur Sombref que je vous ai annoncé, et l'Empereur va se rendre à Fleurus; c'est là que vous adresserez vos nouveaux rapports à S. M.

Reille to Ney at 10 am

Documents inédits, pages 37 and 38

Gosselies, le 16 juin 1815, 10 heures et quart du matin

Monsieur le maréchal,

J'ai l'honneur d'informer Votre Excellence du rapport que me fait faire verbalement le général Girard par un des ses officiers.

Appendix XI – Select Correspondence

L'ennemi continue à occuper Fleurus par de la cavalerie légère qui a des vedettes en avant; l'on apercoit deux masses ennemis venant par la route de Namur et dont la tête est à la hauteur de Saint-Amand. Elles se sont formées peu à peu, et ont gagné quelque terrain à mesure qu'il leur arrivait du monde: on n'a pu guère juger de leur force à cause de l'éloignement: cependant ce général pense que chacune pouvait d'être de six bataillons en colonne par bataillon. On apercevait des mouvements de troupes derrière.

M. le lieutenant-général Flahaut m'a fait part des ordres qu'il portait à Votre Excellence; j'en ai prévenu M.le comte d'Erlon, afin qu'il puisse suivre mon mouvement. J'aurais commencé le mien sur Frasnes aussitot que les divisions auraient été sous les armes; mais d'après le rapport du général Girard, je tiendrai les troupes prêtes à marcher en attendant les ordres de Votre Excellence, et comme ils pourront me parvenir très vite, il n'y aura que très peu de temps de perdu.

J'ai envoyé à l'empereur l'officier qui m'a fait le rapport du général Girard.

Je renouvelle à Votre Excellence les assurances de mon respectueux dévouement.

Le général en chef du 2ᵉ corps
Comte Reille

Reille to d'Erlon

Per above, Reille communicated the intentions of Flahaut to d'Erlon, possibly verbally.

Note however, due to report of Girard of massing Prussians, Reille did not commence execution until hearing from Ney. This extenuates the delays.

Ney to d'Erlon before 11 am

There is no record of this, but d'Erlon and staff from his divisions write that they received orders to march anywhere from 10 am to noon. As II Corps was in the way still, there was a delay in execution.

Ney to Reille at 11 am

Documents Inédits – pages 38 and 39

A M. le Comte Reille,
Commandant le 2ᵉ corps d'armée.

Frasnes, le 16 juin 1815.

ORDRE DE MOUVEMENT.

Conformément aux instructions de l'empereur, le 2ᵉ corps se mettra en marche de suite pour aller prendre position, la cinquième division en arrière de Genappes, *sur les hauteurs qui dominent cette ville, la gauche appuyée à la grande route. Un bataillon ou deux couvriront tous les débouchés en avant sur la route de Bruxelles. Le parc de réserve et les équipages de cette division resteront avec la seconde ligne.*
   La neuvième division suivra le mouvement de la cinquième, et viendra prendre position en seconde ligne sur les hauteurs à droite et à gauche du village de Banterlet.
   Les sixième et septième divisions à l'embranchement des Quatre-Bras, où sera votre quartier général. Les trois premières divisions du comte d'Erlon viendront prendre position à Frasnes; *la division de droite s'établira à* Marbais *avec la deuxième division de cavalerie légère du général Piré; la 1er couvrira votre marche, et vous éclairera sur Bruxelles et sur vos deux flancs. Mon quartier à* Frasnes.

Pour le Maréchal prince de la Moskowa,
Le Colonel, premier aide de camp,
HEYMÈS

   Deux divisions du comte de Valmy, s'établiront à Frasnes *et à* Liberchies.
   Les divisions de la garde des généraux Lefebvre Desnouettes et Colbert resteront dans leur position actuelle de Frasnes.

Appendix XI – Select Correspondence

Pour copie conforme :
Comte Reille

Ney to Soult at 11 am

SHD, C15/5

Frasne, le 16 juin 1815 à 11 heures du matin.

à Son Excellence le Maréchal Duc de Dalmatie, major général,

Je recois à l'instant vos instructions sur le mouvement des 1er et 2e corps d'infanterie, de la division de cavalerie légère du général Piré et des 2 divisions de cavalerie du 3e corps.
    Celles de l'Empereur m'étaient déjà parvenues. Voici les dispositions que je viens d'expédier:
    Le 2e corps, général Reille, aura une division en arrière de Genappe, une autre à Banterlet, les 2 autres à l'embranchement des Quatre Bras.
    Une division de cavalerie légère du général Piré couvrira la marche du 2e corps.
    Le 1er corps s'établira savoir: une division à Marbais, les 2 autres à Frasne, une division de cavalerie légère à Marbais, les 2 divisions du Comte de Valmy à Frasne et Liberchies.
    Les 2 divisions de cavalerie légère de la garde resteront à Frasne où j'établis mon quartier général.
    Tous les renseignements portent qu'il y a environ 3000 hommes d'infanterie ennemie aux Quatre Bras et fort peu de cavalerie. Je pense que les dispositions de l'Empereur pour la marche ultérieure sur Bruxelles s'exécuteront sans grands obstacles.

Le maréchal Prince de la Moskowa,

Ney[295]

---

295 DeWit, Pierre, *The French left wing*, Pages 2 and 3
http://www.waterloo-campaign.nl/bestanden/files/june16/frlinkervleugel.pdf

Delcambre, Chief of Staff of I Corps to Donzelot after Noon

Revue des études napoléniennes, 1932/07, page 361
http://gallica.bnf.fr/ark:/12148/bpt6k15511d

> *Au Quartier Général, le 16 juin 1815.*
>
> Mon Général,
>
> *Donnez, je vous prie, ordre à votre division de prendre les armes sur le champ. L'armée va marcher.*
> *L'Empereur ne veut pas que l'on lui rende d'honneurs lorsqu'il se trouve aux avant-postes, car c'est faire voir que S. M. s'y trouve et celà peut avoir de l'inconvénient.*
> *Donnez, je vous prie, vos ordres en conséquence.*
>
> *Le Maréchal de Camp,*
> *Chef d l'Etat-Major du 1ᵉʳ Corps,*
> *Bᵒⁿ DELCAMBRE.*[296]

Lobau to Napoleon around 1 pm

SHD, C15/5

> Sire,
>
> *En conformité des ordres de Votre Majesté, j'ai envoyé l'adjudant commandant Jeanin au corps commandé par M.le maréchal Prince de la Moskowa. Cet officier a trouvé ces troupes échelonnées depuis les environs de Gosselies jusqu'au-delà du village de Frasnes. Il a beaucoup d'habitude de la guerre et croit que l'ennemi n'est pas en très grande force; mais il est difficile, en raison des forêts, de juger avec précision.*
> *Le colonel précité a causé avec plusieurs officiers supérieurs, et il a enfin interrogé des déserteurs, et aucun des individus questionnés*

---

[296] Cited by: DeWit, Pierre, *The French left wing*, Page 5
http://www.waterloo-campaign.nl/bestanden/files/june16/frlinkervleugel.pdf

n'a porté le nombre de l'ennemi au-delà de vingt-mille hommes; quand cet officier a quitté le terrain, il n'y avait que des tirailleurs engagés, même en assez petit nombre.

Je suis toujours en position en avant de Charleroi ou je resterai jusqu'à nouvel ordre. Il serait bon que Votre Majesté voulut bien faire remplacer le bataillon que j'ai en ville pour la police et pour un assez grand nombre de bagages; protéger les blessés etc.; ce point ne pouvant, ce me semble, rester totalement dégarni des troupes.

Charleroi, le 16 juin 1815

Le lieutenant général, l'aide de camp de l'Empereur, commandant en chef du 6e corps

Lobau

P.S. Le colonel Jeanin rapporte que le colonel Tancarville, chef d'état-major du Cte de Valmy, lui a dit que des émissaires venus au Cte D'Erlon lui auraient déclaré que l'ennemi devait aujourd'hui marcher de Mons sur Charleroi. Votre Majesté sera surement à portée d'apprécier cet avis.[297]

D'Erlon to Soult between 1 pm and 3 pm

Houssaye, page 117 and Footnote 41 on page 362

There [Gosselies] d'Erlon halted his troops, until the return of a strong reconnaissance which he had sent from Jumet, in the direction of Chapelle-Herlaymont. A false account given by the peasants led him to believe he would find a corps of Anglo-Belgians threatening his left at the latter village.[41] *... Be this as it may, it was three o'clock when he started on his march again.*

41. Letter from d'Erlon to Soult, Gosselies, 16th June (without any reference to time, between one and three o'clock), (General G.'s papers).

---

297 DeWit, Pierre, *The battle. Part 3*, Pages 4 and 5
http://www.waterloo-campaign.nl/bestanden/files/june16/ligny.3.pdf

Soult to Ney at 2 pm

Register of the Major-Général

En avant de Fleurus, le 16 Juin, à deux heures.

M. le maréchal, l'Empereur me charge de vous prévenir que l'ennemi a réuni un corps de troupes entre Sombref *et* Bry, *et qu'à deux heures ½ M. le maréchal Grouchy avec les 3ᵉ et 4ᵉ corps l'attaquera. L'intention de Sa Majesté est que vous attaquiez ainsi ce qui est devant vous, et qu'après l'avoir vigoureusement pressé vous rabattiez sur nous pour concourir à envelopper le corps dont je viens de vous parler. Si ce corps était enfoncé auparavant, alors Sa Majesté ferait manoeuvrer dans votre direction, pour hâter également vos opérations.*

Instruisez de suite l'empereur de vos dispositions et de ce qui se passe sur votre front.

Soult to Ney at 3:15 pm

Register of the Major-Général

En avant de Fleurus, le 16, à 3 h. un quart et 3 ½

M. le maréchal, je vous ai écrit, il y a une heure, que l'Empereur ferait attaquer l'ennemi à deux heures et demie dans la position qu'il a prise entre le village de St. Amand et de Bry, en ce moment l'engagement est très-prononcé. S. M. me charge de vous dire que vous devez manoeuvrer sur le champ, de manière à envelopper la droite de l'ennemi et à tomber à bras racourci sur ses derrières. Cette armée est perdue si vous agissez vigoureusement. Le sort de la France est dans vos mains ; ainsi n'hésitez pas un instant pour faire le mouvement que l'Empereur vous ordonne et dirigez vous sur les hauteurs de St.-Amand et de Bry pour concourir à une victoire peut-être décisive, l'ennemi est pris en flagrant délit, au moment où il cherche à se réunir avec les anglais.

Appendix XI – Select Correspondence

major général, duc du Dalmatie

Soult to Ney at 3:30 pm

(Duplicate of 3:15 order)

Soult to Lobau to 3:30 pm

Register of the Major-Général

> *En avant de Fleurus, le 16, à trois heures et demie.*
>
> *Amle comte Lobau,*
>
> *Ordre au comte Lobau de se rendre à Fleurus; il laissera un bataillon à Charleroi pour conserver la place et protéger le parc.*

Ney to Soult at 10 pm

SHD C15/5

> *Frasnes, le 16 juin 1815, 10 heures du soir.*
>
> *Monsieur le maréchal ! L'attaque que j'ai dirigée contre les anglais dans la position de Quatre Bras a sûrement été de la plus grande vigueur; un mal-entendu de la part du comte d'Erlon m'a privé de l'espérance d'une belle victoire car au moment les 5e et 9e division du général Reille avaient tout culbuté le 1er corps a marché sur Saint Amand, pour appuyer la gauche de S.M., et ce qu'il y a de fatal, c'est que ce corps ayant retrogradé ensuite pour me rejoindre, n'a pu ainsi être utile à personne. La division du Prince Jérôme a donné avec une grande valeur. S.A.I. a été légèrement blessé. Il n'y a donc eu réellement d'engagé que trois divisions d'infanterie et une brigade de cuirassiers et la cavalerie du général Piré. Le comte de Valmy a fait une belle charge. Tout le monde a fait son devoir excepté le 1er corps. L'ennemi a perdu beaucoup de monde; nous avons pris du canon et un drapeau. Nous n'avons réellement perdu qu'environ*

deux mille hommes tués et quatre mille blessés. J'ai demandé les rapports des généraux comte Reille et d'Erlon et je les enverrai à Votre Excellence. Agréez, Monsieur le Maréchal, l'assurance de ma haute considération,

Le maréchal Prince de la Moskowa,

Ney[298]

June 17, 1815

Soult to Ney at 8 am

Register of the Major-Général

M. le maréchal, le général Flahaut, qui arrive à l'instant, fait connaître que vous êtes dans l'incertitude sur les résultats de la journée d'hier. Je crois cependant vous avoir prévenu de la victoire que l'Empereur a remportée. L'armée prussienne a été mise en déroute. Le général Pajol est à sa poursuite sur les routes de Namur et de Liège. Nous avons déjà plusieurs milliers de prisonniers et 30 pièces de canon. Nos troupes se sont bien conduites. Une charge de six bataillons de la garde et des escadrons de service, et la division du général Delort, ont percé la ligne ennemie, porté le plus grand désordre dans ses rangs, et enlevé la position.

L'Empereur se rend au moulin de Bry où passe la grand'route qui conduit de Namur aux Quatre-Bras, il n'est donc pas possible que l'armée anglaise puisse agir devant vous; si cela était l'Empereur marcherait directement sur elle par la route des Quatre-Bras, tandis que vous l'attaqueriez de front avec vos divisions qui à présent, doivent être réunies, et cette armée serait dans un instant détruite ; ainsi, instruisez S. M. de la position exacte des divisions et de tout ce qui se passe devant vous.

---

298 DeWit, Pierre, *The battle of Quatre Bras. The Action. Part 6,* Pages 1 and 2 http://www.waterloo-campaign.nl/bestanden/files/june16/qb.8.pdf

L'Empereur a vu avec peine qu'hier vous n'ayez pas réussi : les divisions ont agi isolément ; ainsi vous avez éprouvé des pertes. Si les corps des comtes d'Erlon et Reille avaient été ensemble, il ne réchappait pas un anglais du corps qui venu vous attaquer ; si le comte d'Erlon avait exécuté le mouvement sur Saint-Amand que l'Empereur ordonné, l'armée prussienne était totalement détruite et nous aurions fait peut-être 30 mille prisonniers. Les corps des généraux Vendamme et Gérard, la garde impériale ont toujours été réunis; l'on s'expose à des revers lorsque des détachements sont compromis.

L'Empereur espère et désire que vos sept divisions d'infanterie et la cavalerie soient bien réunies et formées, et qu'ensemble elles n'occupent pas une lieue de terrain, pour les avoir bien dans votre main et les employer au besoin.

L'intention de S. M. est que vous preniez position aux Quatre-Bras, ainsi que l'ordre vous en a été donné; mais si par impossible cela ne peut avoir lieu, rendez-en compte sur-le-champ avec détail et l'Empereur s'y portera ainsi que je vous l'ai dit ; si au contraire il n'y a qu'une arrière-garde, attaquez-la et prenez position.

La journée d'aujourd'hui est nécessaire pour terminer cette opération et pour compléter les munitions, rallier les militaires isolés et faire rentrer les détachements. Donnez des ordres en conséquence et assurez-vous que tous les blessés sont pansés et dirigés sur les derrières. L'on s'est plaint que les ambulances n'avaient pas fait leur devoir.

Le fameux partisan Lützow, qui a été pris, disait que l'armée prussienne était perdue et que Blücher avait exposé une seconde fois la monarchie prussienne.

Soult to Davout before 10 am

Register of the Major-Général

Fleurus, 17 juin.

J'ai annoncé hier du champ de bataille de Ligny à S.A.I. le prince Joseph, la victoire signalée que l'Empereur venait de remporter: je suis rentré avec S.M. à 11 heures du soir, et il a fallu passer la nuit à soigner les blessés, car les ambulances sont si mal organisés et manquent tellement soit de personnel soit d'autres objets indispensables qu'on ne peut compter sur elles.

L'Empereur remonte à cheval pour suivre les succès de la bataille de Ligny ; on s'est battu avec acharnement et le plus grand enthousiasme de la part des troupes; nous étions un contre trois. A huit heures du soir l'Empereur a marché avec sa garde; six bataillons de vieille garde, les dragons et grenadiers à cheval, et les cuirassiers du général Delort ont débouché par Ligny, et ont exécuté une charge qui a partagé la ligne ennemie. Lord Wellington et Blücher ont eu peine à se sauver, cela a été comme un effet de théatre, dans un instant le feu a cessé et l'ennemi s'est mis en déroute dans toutes les directions. Nous avons déjà plusieurs mille prisonniers et 40 pièces de canon. Le 6e et le 1er corps n'ont pas donné, le comte d'Erlon a eu de fausses directions ; car s'il eût exécuté l'ordre de mouvement que l'Empereur avait prescrit l'armée prussienne était entièrement perdue.

L'aile gauche s'est battue contre l'armée anglaise et lui a enlevé du canon et des drapeaux.

La nuit prochaine je vous donnerai d'autres détails, car à chaque instant on nous annonce des prisonniers.

Notre perte ne paraît pas énorme puisque sans la connaître je ne l'évalue pas à plus de 3000 hommes ; mais c'est le moment de nous envoyer des troupes et de faire passer la levée des 200,000 hommes. Je viens de donner ordre à dix bataillons des garnisons de la 16e division militaire de se réunir sur le champ à Avesnes, pour être employés à l'escorte des prisonniers, ou pour en disposer.

Je vous prie de donner des ordres pour faire accéler leur réunion, et de prescrire qu'on choisisse ceux qui sont le plus complet et le mieux en état, il sera nécessaire d'y mettre des généraux et des officiers supérieurs. Si on excite ces bataillons tous voudront marcher, déjà l'Empereur a recu plusieurs demandes à ce sujet ; l'on doit profiter de cet enthousiasme. En France, c'est toujours le moment qu'il faut choisir ; d'ailleurs cette augmention de moyens fera du bien et assurera de nouveaux succ, c'est toujours le moment qu'il faut choisir ; d'ailleurs cette augmention de moyens fera du bien et assurera de nouveaux succés.

Appendix XI – Select Correspondence

P.S. L'armée est formée sur la grand'route de Namur à Bruxelles où l'Empereur se rend en ce moment. Le dernier rapport du général Pajol est daté de Mazi, et la gauche dans la direction des Trois Bras.

Soult to Ney, Noon

Documents Inédits – page 44

A M. le Maréchal Prince de la Moskowa
4ᵉ corps d'armée, à Gosselies

En avant de Ligny, le 17 à midi.
Monsieur le maréchal, l'empereur vient de faire prendre position en avant de Marbais, à un corps d'infanterie et à la garde impériale; S. M. me charge de vous dire que son intention est que vous attaquiez les ennemis aux Quatre-Bras, pour les chasser de leur position, et que le corps qui est à Marbais secondera vos opérations ; S. M. va se rendre à Marbais, et elle attend vos rapports avec impatience.

Le maréchal d'Empire, Major-Général,
Duc de Dalmatie

Napoleon to Ney, after 1pm

Monsieur le prince de la Moskowa,

Je suis surpris de votre grand retard à exécuter mes ordres. Il n'y a plus de tems [sic] à perdre; attaquez avec le plus grande impétuosité tout ce que est devant vous. Le sort de la patrie est dans vos mains.

1 heure après midi

Napoleon[299]

---

299 DeWit, Pierre, *General headquarters and the redistribution of the French forces. Part 2*, page 2
http://www.waterloo-campaign.nl/bestanden/files/june17/REDISTRIBUTION.pdf

Napoleon to Grouchy after 11:30 am

Inédits Napoléoniens – 1718

> *Ligny, 17 juin 1815, aa heures et demie.*
>
> *Dicté à Bertrand, en l'absence de Soult.*
>
> *Ordonnez au général Domon de se rendre sur-le-champ à Marbais. Il y sera sous les ordres du comte de Lobau. Il dirigera des détachements sur les Quatre-Chemins, route de Bruxelles, et se réunira par la gauche avec les troupes des 1er et 2e corps, qui occupent ce matin le village de Frasne et qui doivent aussi marcher sur les Quatre-Chemins où les Anglais sont supposés être.*
> *Ordonnez au général Milhaud de se rendre à Marbais. Il aura devant lui la cavalerie légère du général Domon. Il y trouvera le corps du comte de Lobau et la garde.*

Napoleon to Grouchy at 11:45 am

Inédits Napoléoniens – 1719

> *Ligny, le 17 juin 1815, 11 heures trois quarts.*
>
> *Dicté à Bertrand, en l'absence de Soult.*
>
> *Rendez-vous à Gembloux avec le corps de cavalerie du général Pajol, la cavalerie légère du 4e corps, le corps de cavalerie du général Exelmans, la division du général Teste dont vous aurez un soin particulier, étant détachée de son corps d'armée, et les 3e et 4e corps d'infanterie. Vous vous ferez éclairer sur la direction de Namur et de Maestricht, et vous poursuivrez l'ennemi. Éclairez sa marche et instruisez-moi de ses mouvements de manière que je puisse pénétrer ce qu'il veut faire.*
> *Je porte mon quartier général aux Quatre-Chemins où ce matin étaient encore les Anglais. Notre communication sera donc directe par la route pavée de Namur. Si l'ennemi a évacué Namur, écrivez*

au général commandant la 2ᵉ division militaire à Charlemont, de faire occuper Namur par quelques bataillons de garde nationale et une battterie de canons qu'il formera à Charlemont. Il donnera ce commandement à un maréchal de camp.

Il est important de pénétrer ce que l'ennemi veut faire. Ou il se sépare des Anglais ou ils veulent se réunir encore pour couvrir Bruxelles et Liège, en tentant le sort d'une nouvelle bataille. Dans tous les cas, tenez constamment vos deux corps d'infanterie réunis dans une lieue de terrain et occupez tous les soirs une bonne position militaire, ayant plusieurs débouchés de retraite. Placez des détachements de cavalerie intermédiaire, pour communiquer avec le quartier général.

D'Erlon to Soult after 8 pm

Pontécoulant – page 235

Au bivouac, en avant de Frasne, le 17 juin 1815 (matin).

Monsieur le maréchal, conformément aux ordres de Sa Majesté, le 1ᵉʳ corps d'armée tient la première ligne à cheval sur la route de Bruxelles ; la 1ᵉʳ division de cavalerie flanque le corps d'armée et couvre son front.

J'ai l'honneur d'informer Votre Excellence, que la 1ᵉʳ division de cavalerie, a fait plusieurs charges heureuses et qu'elle a enlevé quelques voitures et un certain nombre de prisonniers.

Daignez agréer l'hommage de mon respect,
Le lieutenant général, commandant en chef de 1ᵉʳ corps,
D. Comte d'Erlon

Grouchy to Napoleon at 10 pm

Relation Succincte – 2ⁿᵈ Series, Page 3

Gembloux, le 17 juin 1815, à dix heures du soir

SIRE,

J'ai l'honneur de vous rendre compte que j'occupe Gembloux ou commence à arriver le quatrième corps ; le troisième est en avant de cette ville, et une partie de ma cavalerie à Sauvenière.

Le corps prussien, fort d'environ trente mille hommes, qui était encore ici ce matin, a effectué son mouvement de retraite dans la direction de Sauvenières. D'après divers rapports, il paraitrait qu'arrivée à Sauvenières, une partie de l'armée prussienne se serait divisée : une colonne se serait portée sur Pervès-le-Marchez, une autre aurait pris le chemin de Wawres, en passant par Sart-à-Walhain. Peut-être pourrait-on en inférer que quelques corps prussiens iraient joindre Wellington, et que d'autres se retireraient sur Liège.

Une colonne prussienne, avec de l'artillerie, a pris, en quittant le champ de bataille de Fleurus, la route de Namur. L'ennemi nous a abandonné à Gembloux un parc de quatre cents bêtes à cornes, des magasins, des bagages.

Le général Exelmans a ordre de pousser, ce soir, six escadrons sur Sart-à-Walhain, et trois escadrons sur Perwez.

Si j'apprends par des rapports qui, j'espère, me parviendront pendant la nuit, que de fortes masses prussiennes se portent sur Wavres, je les suivrai dans cette direction et les attaquerai des que je les aurai jointes.

Les généraux Thielmann et Borstell faisaient partie de l'armée que Votre Majesté a battue hier : ils étaient encore ici ce matin ont avoué que vingt mille hommes des leurs avaient été mis hors de combat. Ils ont demandé, en partant, les distances de Wavres et de Perwez.

Blücher a été légèrement blessé au bras, le 16, ce qui ne l'a pas empêché de continuer à commander, après s'être fait panser. Il n'a point passé à Gembloux.

Je suis, etc., etc.

Le maréchal Grouchy

Appendix XI – Select Correspondence

Napoleon to Army around 10 pm

Inédits Napoléoniens – 1721

> *[Ordre par lequel l'Empereur indique à chacun sa position de bataille].*

Napoleon to Grouchy at 10 pm

Napoleon's Memoirs, Page 517-518

> *At ten o'clock in the evening, I sent an officer to Marshal Grouchy whom I supposed to be at Wavres, in order to let him know that there would be a big battle next day; that the Anglo-Dutch army was in position in front of the forest of Soignes, with its left resting on the village of La Haye; that I ordered him to detach from his camp at Wavres a division of 7,000 men of all arms and sixteen guns, before daylight, to go to Saint-Lambert to join the right of the Grand Army and co-operate with it; that as soon as he was satisfied that Marshal Blücher had evacuated Wavres, whether to continue his retreat on Brussels or to go in any other direction, he was to march with the bulk of his troops to support the detachment which he had sent to Saint-Lambert.*

June 18, 1815

Grouchy to Napoleon at 3 am

Relation Succincte – 2nd Series, Page 4

> *Gembloux, le 18 juin 1815, trois heures du matin.*
>
> *Sire,*
>
> *Tous mes rapports et renseignements confirment que l'ennémi se retire sur Bruxelles, pour s'y concentrer, où livrer bataille, après s'être réuni à Wellington.*

Namur est évacué, à ce que me marque le général Pajol.

Le premier et second corps de l'armée de Blücher paraissent se diriger, le premier sur Corbais, et le deuxième sur Chaumont. Ils doivent être partis hier soir, à huit heures et demie, de Toürrines et avoir marché pendant toute la nuit; heureusement qu'elle a été si mauvaise, qu'ils n'auront pu faire beaucoup de chemin.

Je pars à l'instant pour Sart-à-Valliain, d'où je me porterai à Corbaix et Wavres. J'aurai l'honneur de vous écrire de l'une et l'autre de ces villes.

Je suis, etc., etc.

Le maréchal Grouchy

P. S. Conformément à vos ordres, j'écris au général commandant la deuxième division militaire, à Charlemont, de faire occuper Namur par quelques bataillons de gardes nationaux et quelques batteries de canon, qu'il formera à Charlemont.

Je laisse ici vingt-cinq chevaux pour assurer la correspondance avec Votre Majesté.

Les corps d'infanterie et la cavalerie que j'ai avec moi n'ont qu'un approvisionnement et demi, de sorte qu'en cas d'une affaire majeure il me paraîtrait nécessaire que Votre Majesté voulût bien faire approcher les réserves de munitions, ou m'indiquer les points ou l'artillerie pourrait aller prendre ses remplacements.

Napoleon to Grouchy at 4 am

Napoleon's Memoirs, page 518

A second officer was sent to him at four o'clock in the morning to repeat the order which had been sent to him at ten in the evening.

Soult to Army at 5 am

Documents Inédits – page 52 and 53

L'empereur ordonne que l'armée soit disposée à attaquer l'ennemi à 9 heures du matin ; MM. les commandants des corps d'armée rallieront leurs troupes, feront mettre les armes en état, et permettront que les soldats fassent la soupe; ils feront aussi manger les soldats afin qu'à 9 heures précises chacun soit prêt et puisse être en bataille avec son artillerie et ambulances, à la position de bataille que l'empereur a indiquée par son ordre d'hier soir.

MM. les lieutenants-généraux, commandant les corps d'armées d'infanterie et de cavalerie enverront sur-le-champ des officiers au major général pour faire connaitre leur position et porter des ordres.

Au quartier-général impériale, 18 juin, 1815.
Le maréchal d'Empire, major général,
Duc de Dalmatie

Soult to Grouchy at 10 am

Register of the Major-Général

Par l'adjudant Comte Lenowich.

En avant de la ferme du Caillou, le 18 juin, à 10 h. du matin.

M. le maréchal, l'Empereur a reçu votre dernier rapport daté de Gembloux, vous ne parlez à Sa Majesté que des deux colonnes prussiennes qui ont passé à Sauvenières *et* Sart à Walhain. *Cependant des rapports disent qu'une troisième colonne qui était assez forte a passé à* Géry *et* Gentinnes *se dirigeant sur* Wavres.

L'Empereur me charge de vous prévenir qu'en ce moment Sa Majesté va faire attaquer l'armée anglaise qui a pris position à Waterloo près de la forêt de Soignes ; ainsi Sa Majesté désire que vous dirigiez vos mouvements sur Wavres, *afin de vous rapprocher de nous, vous mettre en rapport d'opérations et lier les communications poussant devant vous les corps de l'armée prussienne qui ont pris cette direction, et qui auraient pu s'arrêter à* Wavres *où vous devez arriver le plus tôt possible.*

Vous ferez suivre les colonnes ennemies qui ont pris sur votre droite, par quelques corps légers afin d'observer leurs mouvements et ramasser leurs trainards.

Instruisez-moi immédiatement de vos dispositions et de votre marche ainsi que des nouvelles que vous avez sur les ennemis, et ne négligez pas de lier vos communications avec nous ; L'Empereur désire avoir très-souvent de vos nouvelles.

Soult to Ney at 11 am

Document Inédits – page 53

Une fois que toute l'armée sera rangée en bataille, à peu près à 1 heure après midi, au moment où l'Empereur en donnera l'ordre au maréchal Ney, l'attaque commencera pour s'emparer du village de Mont Saint Jean où est l'intersection des routes. A cet effet, les batteries de 12 du 2me corps et celles du 6e se réuniront à celles du 1er corps. Ces 24 bouches à feu tireront sur les troupes de Mont Saint Jean, et le comte d'Erlon commencera l'attaque, en portant en avant sa division de gauche et la soutenant, suivant les circonstances, par les divisions du 1er corps.

Le 2e corps s'avancera à mesure pour garder la hauteur du comte d'Erlon.

Les compagnies de sapeurs du 1er corps seront prêtes pour se barricader sur-le-champ à Mont Saint Jean.

(Au crayon et de l'écriture du maréchal Ney.)

Ajouté par M. le maréchal Ney :

Le comte d'Erlon comprendra que c'est par la gauche que l'attaque commencera, au lieu de la droite.

Communiquer cette nouvelle disposition au général en chef Reille.

(Au dos) Ordres dictés par l'empereur, sur le champ de bataille du Mont-St-Jean, le 18, vers onze heures du matin, et écrit par le maréchal duc de Dalmatie, major général.

Paris, le 21 juin 1815.)

Appendix XI – Select Correspondence

Le Maréchal Prince de LA MOSKOWA,
Pair de France, NEY.

Grouchy to Napoleon at 11 am

Relation Succincte – 2nd Series, Page 5

Sart-à-Valhain, le 18 juin 1815 à onze heures du matin

Sire,

Je ne perds pas un moment à vois transmettre les renseignements que je recueille ici ; je les regarde comme positifs, et afin que Votre Majesté les recoive le plus promptement possible, je les lui expédie par le major Lafresnaye, son ancien page ; il est bien monté et bon écuyer.
 Les premier, deuxième et troisième corps de Blücher marchent dans la direction de Bruxelles. Deux de ces corps ont passé à Sart-à-Valhain; ou à peu de distance, sur la droite ; ils ont défilé en trois colonnes, marchant à peu près à meme hauteur. Leur passage a duré six heures, sans interruption. Ce qui a défilé en vue de Sart-à-Valhain peut être évalué à 30,000 hommes au moins, et avait un matériel de 50 à 60 bouches à feu.
 Un corps venu de Liège a effectué sa jonction avec ceux qui ont combattu à à Fleurus (Ci-joint une réquisition qui le prouve.) Quelques-uns des Prussiense que j'ai devant moi se dirigent vers la plaine de la Chyse, située prés de la route de Louvain, et à deux lieues et demie de cette ville.
 Il semblerait que ce serait à dessein de s'y masser ou de commbattre les troupes qui les y poursuivraient, ou enfin de se réunir à Wellington, projet annoncé par leurs officiers, qui, avec leur jactance ordinaire, prétendent n'avoir quitté le champ de bataille, le 16, qu'afin d'opérer leue réunion avec l'armée anglaise, sur Bruxelles.
 Ce soir, je vais être massé à Wavres, et me trouver ainsi entre Wellington, que je présume en retraite devant Votre Majesté, et l'armée prussienne.

> *J'ai besoin d'instructions ultérieures sur ce que Votre Majesté ordonne que je fasse. Le pays entre Wavres et la plaine de la Chyse est difficile, coupé et en partie marécageux.*
>
> *Par la route de Wilworde, j'arriverai facilement à Bruxelles avant tout ce qui sera arrêté à la Chyse, si tan il y a que les Prussiens y fassent une halte.*
>
> *Daignez, Sire, me transmettre vos ordres; je puis les recevoir avant de commmencer mon mouvement de demain.*
>
> *Je suis, etc., etc.*
> *Le maréchal GROUCHY.*

Ney to Lobau

http://www.russborough.com/omnium_g/manuscripts/ney-waterloo-dispatch.html

> *Les anglais sont massés sur le mont saint jean c'est à dire en avant de la foret de Soignes. Si les pruchiens [sic] battent en retraite arrière de Brux. et Soignes bornez vous à envoyer mille cavaliers derrière eux et venez avec vos troupes vous joindre à nous. Si, au contraire, ils tentent de venir en avant de la forest à ce mont saint jean, alors faites écran et barrez leur la route.*
>
> *Ney*

Soult to Grouchy around 1 pm

Relation succincte – 1st Series, Page 21

> *Monsieur Le Maréchal,*
>
> *Vous avez écrit à l'Empereur ce matin, à trois heures, que vous marchiez sur* Sart-à- Walhain, *donc votre projet était de vous porter à* Corbaix *et à* Wavres. *Ce mouvement est conforme aux dispositions de Sa Majesté, que vous ont été communiquées. Cependant l'Empereur m'ordonne de vous dire que vous devez toujours manoeuvrer*

dans notre direction et chercher à vous raprocher de l'armée, afin que vous puissez nous joindre avant qu'aucun corps puisse se mettre entre nous. Je ne vous indique pas de direction, c'est à vous à voir où nous sommes, pour vous régler en conséquence et pour lier nos communications ainsi que pour être toujours en mesure de tomber sur quelques troupes ennemies qui chercheraient à inquiéter notre droite, et les écraser.

En ce moment la bataille est engagée sur la ligne de Waterloo, en avant de la forêt de Soignes. Le centre de l'ennemi est à Mont-Saint-Jean ; ainsi, manoeuvrez pour joindre notre droite.

Signé le maréchal Duc de Dalmatie

P.S. Une lettre qui vient d'être interceptée porte que le général Bülow doit attaquer notre flanc droit ; nous croyons apercevoir ce corps sur les hauteurs de St.Lambert. Ainsi, ne perdez un instant pour vous raprocher de nous et nous joindre, et pour écraser Bülow, que vous prendrez en flagrant délit.

Signé le maréchal Duc de Dalmatie

Soult to Davout at 2:30 pm

Register of the Major-Général

Du bivouac en avant de Caillou, le 18 juin, à 1 h. un quart

M. le maréchal nous nous battons en ce moment, l'ennemi est en position en avant de la forêt de Soignes, *son centre à Waterloo.*
Nous allons consommer beaucoup de munitions; nous en avons usé une grande quantité à la bataille de Ligny. L'Empereur ordonne que vous en fassiez diriger sur les places du nord, sur Avesnes, par des moyens accélérés. Ces munitions seront escortées d'Avesnes au moyen des bataillons qu'on a ordonné d'y établir pour l'escorte de prisonniers; la direction que vous devez leur faire donner est celle de Beaumont sur Charleroi pour rejoindre l'armée.

Vous sentirez, M. le maréchal, combien il est important que les ordres de l'Empereur soient promptement exécutés. Je vous prie de me prévenir de ceux que vous donnerez à cet égard.

P.S. Il est deux heures et demie, la canonnade est engagée sur toute la ligne; les Anglais sont au centre, les Hollandais et Belges à la droite des troupes allemandes, les Prussiens sont à la gauche, la bataille est générale; 400 bouches à feu tonnent en ce moment.

Soult to Girard in evening

Register of the Major-Général

18 juin, en avant de Caillou

Ordre au maréchal-de-camp Remond de prendre le commandement de la division Girard et de se porter aux Quatre-Bras pour y prendre position.

APPENDIX XII
TRANSLATED SELECT CORRESPONDENCE

See the original French above for sourcing on the correspondence below.

MAY 9, 1815

Napoleon's appointment of Soult as *Major-Général*

> Paris, May 9, 1815.
>
> Our cousin, Marshal Soult, Duke of Dalmatia, is named our Major General.

JUNE 1, 1815

Soult's Order of the Day

> Paris, 1 June 1815.
>
> *A most impressive ceremony has just sanctified our institutions. The Emperor received from representatives of the people and deputations of all army corps, the expression of the wishes of the whole nation on the Additional Act to the Constitutions of the Empire, which had been sent for its acceptance; and a new oath united France and the Emperor; so destinies are fulfilled, and all the efforts of an*

impious league can no longer separate the interests of a great people from the hero whose most brilliant triumphs are universally admired.

It is when the national will shows itself with as much energy, that war cries are heard; it is when France is at peace with all Europe, that foreign armies are advancing on our borders: What is the hope of this new coalition? Does it want to remove France from the existing nations? Does it want to put into the servitude twenty-eight million French! How could it have forgotten that the first league which was formed against our independence served our independence and our glory! Hundred brilliant victories, that momentary setbacks and unfortunate circumstances could not erase, remind it that a free nation, led by a great man is invincible.

Everyone is a soldier in France when it comes to national honor and freedom: a common interest today unites all French. The commitments forced upon us by violence are destroyed by the flight of the Bourbons outside the French territory, by the call they made to foreign armies to restore them to the throne they have abandoned, and by the unanimous wish of the nation which, by taking again the free exercise of its rights, solemnly repudiated everything that was done without its participation.

The French cannot receive laws from abroad, even those who went there to beg parricidal help will discover again without delay and will experience, as did their predecessors, that contempt and infamy follow their steps, and that they can erase the shame which they cover themselves only by going back into our ranks.

But a new path of glory opens before the army; history will consecrate the memory of military events that the defenders of the homeland and of national honor will have illustrated! The enemies are many, they say, it doesn't matter! It will be more glorious to prevail, and their defeat will be all the more sensational: the fight which is about to begin is not above the genius of Napoleon, nor above our strength; don't you see how all departments are competing in enthusiasm and devotion, having raised, as if by magic, five hundred superb battalions of national guards, who already came to double our ranks, defend our fortresses and join the glory of the Army? It is the impulse of a generous people that no power can overcome and that posterity will admire. To arms!

Soon they will give the signal; everyman shall do his duty, our victorious phalanxes will shine in new splendor against our enemies. Soldiers! Napoleon will guide us, we will fight for the independence of our beautiful country; we are invincible!

Marshal of the Empire, Major-General,
Duke of Dalmatia.

June 3, 1815

Napoleon to Davout at Paris

Give the order to Count Lobau that after tomorrow, Monday, he'll have to give the command of the 1st Military Division to a lieutenant general.

Suggest to me the general officer for the purpose of taking charge of this command; it would be suitable that he was of the elder of Generals Darricau and Durosnel, so that there should be no trouble in the service. You will extend his command to all of the 1st Division and you will include Soissons, Château-Thierry, Arcis-sur-Aube, Nogent, Montereau, and Sens.

Give the order to Count Lobau to leave with his staff on the 5th, in order to be at Laon no later than the 6th, and to inspect and organize his corps there.

Also give the order that all of the officers of the Major General, of the Intendant Général, *and the* Gendarmerie *of the Army of the North be in Laon on the 6th.*

Give the order to the General Staff of the Guard to gather all of the guard at Soissons; I will give him movement details directly.

Napoleon to Soult at Paris

Give me a plan of movement for the corps of General Gérard or the Moselle, concealing it as much as possible from the enemy, for this corps to march on Philippeville. It should be there on the 12th, marching as quickly as possible. Inform me then who will command at Metz and Nancy. You will give the order at once to suspend the communications, and strengthen all of the posts, Thionville, Longwy, Metz, etc.

Inform me of the situation of the National Guard from Nancy, and if this division is marching to cover Metz and replace the division of Moselle. If the enemy is seriously threatening us near Metz, this division would have to be pressed to the Vosges, which would support the left of General Rapp.

All my Guard will be in Soissons on the 10th, and perhaps on the 13th in Avesnes; it is therefore necessary that the 6th Corps march to Avesnes on the 9th. Give me a sketch tracing the march of the columns, and that marks the days when the 1st, 2nd, 3rd, 6th Corps, and that of Moselle will be moving, and the positions that, on the 13th, these Corps, as well as the Guard and the reserve cavalry, must occupy, and the force which I would have in infantry, cavalry, and artillery.

Give me a general status of the situation of the Army Corps of the North, of the Moselle, of the Rhine and the Jura, as well as the organization of all reserve divisions of the national guard, and the composition of all of the garrisons.

Napoleon's Order to Drouot at Paris

You will have to send tomorrow, the 4th, and at the latest, with any delay, in the morning on the day after tomorrow, the 5th, the four batteries of the Old Guard, the batteries of the Young Guard, all that remains of the supply trains, the administration of the Guard, the Sapper Company, the Marines company, the four Marines workers companies, the Bakers company and the other workers of the Guard, who will go to Soissons by Dammartin.

You will give orders to all of the Guard at Compiègne, Young Guard, artillery, cavalry, to also go to Soissons.

You will also prepare to send, Monday the 5th to go to Soissons: the 1st Lancers Regiment, a force of four squadrons and having at least 400 horses, the 1st and 2nd Chasseurs regiments, each one at a force of 400 horses, that will make the basis of the 1st Division; the 1st Dragoons Regiment and the 1st Grenadiers à Cheval Regiment,

Appendix XII – Translated Select Correspondence

each with four squadrons; the total of this first column, five regiments or 2,000 horses.

You will also send with 60 Gendarmes, so as to form, with the 40 who are with the army, a number of 100.

You will send, Tuesday the 6th the 2nd Lancers Regiment (Lanciers Rouges), 3rd Chasseurs, 2nd Dragoons, and 2nd Grenadiers, that will make 1,600 horses that will also go to Soissons. These columns will go to Soissons in three days, to be there on the 8th or the 9th.

You will also order that the three Regiments of Lancers and the 1st and 2nd Chasseurs, each one at a force of 400 men, leave as soon as possible; and you will make sure that steps are taken so that there can be no delay.

All of these Guard detachments will take the Dammartin route.

You will send, also on Monday, the 3rd and 4th Chasseurs à Pied; Tuesday, the 3rd and 4th Grenadiers à Pied; Wednesday, the two 4^{the} Regiments of Grenadiers and Chasseurs with the two 3rd Regiments of Voltigeurs and Tirailleurs, and you will take my orders Wednesday for the departure, on Thursday, for the two 1st Regiments of Grenadiers and Chasseurs, so that, on the 10th, all of the Guard, artillery, infantry, cavalry, military supplies, engineers, and administrations, are gathered in Soissons.

You will give the orders so that, on the 10th, all the Guard have four days of biscuit bread, and that its ordinary and auxiliary caissons are filled with bread; finally that at that time it presents a corps formed with three infantry divisions, of two cavalry divisions, and of one artillery reserve. All of the ambulances, all of the artillery, and the various detachments will be at their posts.

You will request from the artillery a company of pontoniers to support the Guard Marines and Sappers. Have a good officer from the pontonniers.

June 7, 1815

Napoleon's Order to Soult at Paris to tour the North

> *I think it would be reasonable for you to leave tomorrow evening. You will go straight to Lille and be as unrecognizable as possible, in order to make all the arrangements so that the positions of the fortresses of the first line are assured, and you'll give the order to depart to the remaining troops of the line at Calais. You will be able to make the transfers required under the circumstances, either in men, or in weapons, and you will give their destination to the battalions that must arrive here on the 13th. It will be appropriate that you note to the war office all the departures of the battalions to the North. Make sure especially of their clothing and armament. That will occupy you until the 10th. See if there are sufficient general commanders and if there is a good citadel commander. Lastly, prescribe to General Lapoype all that is necessary. On the 11th you will be able to go to Maubeuge and to Avesnes.*
>
> *You will meet me on the Laon road, where it is likely that I will be on the 12th. You will take note all of the latest information on the position of the enemy; you will try to organize an espionage office at Lille, and a company of men who know the roads of Belgium well. There are Gardes Forestiers of Ardennes who communicate through the forests until behind Brussels. Obtain an intelligent officer who can get men who can serve us.*

Napoleon's order to Soult at Paris for Lobau to evacuate Laon in preparation for arrival of the Guard.

> *Give an order to Count Lobau to march, on the 9th, his headquarters to Marle or Vervins, and to entirely evacuate Laon and the surroundings, because, on the 9th and the 10th, the full Guard arrives at Laon.*

Appendix XII – Translated Select Correspondence

Napoleon's order to Bertrand to prepare the imperial head-quarters

Give the order that all of my Household, which is in Compiègne, must go tomorrow to Soissons, where my headquarters will be.

Coordinate with the Grand Écuyer and the master of my wardrobe, so that if something is missing, make sure it leaves. As I will camp often, it is important that I have my iron bed and my tents. See that my telescopes are in good condition.

It is necessary that the Grand Écuyer informs me who will be the ecuyer that will serve me when he will be absent as Minister of Foreign Affairs. It is also necessary that the carriages are ready without anyone's knowledge, so that I can leave two hours after giving the order. It is likely that I will go straight to Soissons.

Give the order that all of my Aides-de-Camp, my Ordonnance Officiers, the Aides-de-Camp for my Aides-de-Camp have their horses leave for Soissons. It is essential that they depart tomorrow.

Napoleon's order to Drouot at Paris

The two Guard Regiments will have to leave tomorrow at daybreak, so as to arrive early on the 10th at Soissons. If they can go in two days to Soissons, so tbe it; they would be there on the 9th; otherwise they have to march in order to be there on the 10th, if they receive the order, between Soissons and Laon. All of the Guard must arrive by the evening of the 9th in Soissons, except for the two regiments which leave tomorrow. Tomorrow morning bring me a small table that will inform me about the day of departure of each column and its arrival at Soissons, and suggest departures, on the morning of the 9th, all that would be staying in Soissons, towards Laon, and in the morning of the 10th all that would have arrived on the 9th; so that on the evening of the 10th all of my Guard will be between Laon and Avesnes, except the two regiments that leave tomorrow, who will have passed Soissons. In preparing the departure of the 1st Battalions of Chasseuers and Grenadiers tomorrow, retain 100 men per battalion (which will make 400 men here, in Paris; that will make the 25 men per company), by taking the youngest and most fit to form a provisional battalion, who will be charged to furnish my Guard.

You will order that, on the 12th, both 4th Voltigeurs and Tirailleurs, with the Brigadier General who must command them, will leave for Laon, where they will arrive on the evening of the 15th. This brigade will be part of the 2nd Division that General Barrois will command.

I watched with sadness that the two regiments that left this morning had only one pair of shoes; we have a stock; it is necessary to provide for them two in the sack and one on their feet.

June 10, 1815

Napoleon's Order of the Day

Paris, June 10, 1815.

Position of the army on the 13th.

Imperial Headquarters and the Imperial Guard at Avesnes.
Artillery parks and bridge supplies on the banks before Avesnes.
Of the Reserve Cavalry 1st and 2nd Corps at Beaumont.
3rd and 4th Corps between Avesnes and Beaumont.
6th Corps at Beaumont. The headquarters to the rear. If the 6th Corps finds it troublesome to arrive at Beaumont, they could arrive halfway.
1st Corps at Pont sur Sambre. This Corps will move without passing by Bavay. They will pass by Le Quesnoy, in order to avoid the enemy. They will reveal their movement as late as possible. As we do not suppose that it is necessary to spend more than one day in Valenciennes, it will be just the 13th that they will prepare their movement to arrive on the Sambre.
The 2nd Corps behind Maubeuge in columns on the Thuin road, without passing the border, and moving as unnoticed as possible.
The 3rd Corps at Philippeville.

Armée de la Moselle at Mariembourg.

All of the communications on the border will be intercepted.

The soldiers will have four days of bread on their backs, half-pound of rice, fifty cartridges.

The batteries will be with the divisions: reserve batteries with their army corps.

The light cavalry of each army corps will be in front of the corps.

Each ambulance with its division

Each division will have on the auxiliary or military wagons eight days of bread, biscuits, and a cattle pen for eight days.

We will make no change on the border, we will not cross it at any point. We will fire no cannons. We will do nothing that could wake the enemy.

This order will remain secret.

June 11, 1815

Bertrand to Reille

Paris, June 11, 1815.

The intention of the Emperor is that the Headquarters be transported to Avesnes on the 12th; that the Imperial Guard is there on the 12th; that Avesnes is evacuated by your Corps which you will bring behind Maubeuge, however that you will remain there so that you may provide information, the Emperor will arrive on the 13th at 2 o'clock in the morning. It is very important that you place your army Corps behind Maubeuge without the enemy perceiving anything. Forbid forbid any communication very strictly.

Napoleon's order to Davout in reference to the start of hostilities

My Cousin, you will inform Marshal Suchet, by courier and telegraph, that the hostilities will begin on the 14th, and that on this day he can seize Montmélian. If it is essential that he does so before this time, because of the movements of the enemy, then it is permitted. However it would be desirable that he did not do it before the 15th.

Napoleon's invitation to Ney to join the campaign

My Cousin, call up Marshal Ney; tell him, if he wishes to be present when the first battle takes place, then he must be at Avesnes on June 14th, there he will find my headquarters.

June 12, 1815

Soult's report to Napoleon

Avesnes, 12 June 1815

In executing the order that Your Majesty gave on the 10th of this month, I have issued the following dispositions regarding the sites that the various army corps must occupy on the 13th:
The 2nd Corps on the Sambre, from below Maubeuge to Solre-sur-Sambre, occupying the villages of Hantay, Montigny, Bousignies, Bersillies, Colleret, Cerfontaine and Ferrière-la-Grande.
The 1st Corps between Pont-sur-Sambre and Maubeuge, staying ready to debouch on one or other bank of the Sambre, as your Majesty has ordered.
The 3rd Corps at Beaumont.
The 6th Corps at Beaufort where it will have its headquarters, Fontaine, Limont, Eclaibes, Dimont, Dimechaux, Wattignies, Choisies, Damousies, Obrechies, and Ferrier-la-Petite.
The 1st, 2nd, 3rd and 4th Cavalry Corps, under the command of Marshal Grouchy, at Solre-le-Château and in the villages of Sars, Lez-Fountain, Offies, L'Epine, Chamoul, Clairfayts, Epmoy, Beaurieux, Grandrieu, Hestrud, Leugmes, Cousolre, Aibes, Quiévelon, Solrimes, Eccles.
The artillery parks and bridging equipment will be placed in front of Avesnes; we have left some villages vacant so that they can stable their horses.

The town of Avesnes is left at the disposal of Your Majesty's Guard, as well as the villages behind and those in the Helpe valley on the right and left of Avesnes.

Portion from Lettow-Vorbeck, pages 223-224:

According to a report received from Count Gérard, the first division of the Armée de la Moselle will reach Rocroi on the 13th, the second on the 14th, the third on the 15th, the cavalry division and the artillery park also on the 15th. I immediately wrote that Your Majesty had ordered that he should be fully assembled at Rocroi on the 13th and that I had given him an order to this effect. I repeated the order to him to accelerate the march of his troops to make up for the time lost, and to continue the march of his army by directing it via Chimay on Beaumont, where it will form the second line behind the 3rd corps and follow it on its march towards the Sambre as soon as that begins.

General Delort, commanding the 14th cavalry division, wrote to me from Metz on the 9th that his division would arrive at Mézières on the 13th and that he could not reach his destination at Hirson until the 15th. I sent him an order to march from Mézières via Rocroi and Chimay to Beaumont to reach there by the 15th and to place himself in line with the remainder of the cavalry. I have informed Marshal Grouchy of this.[300]

Soult to Vandamme

Avesnes, June 12, 1815

The intention of the Emperor, Count, is that your Army Corps will be tomorrow, the 13th, in Beaumont. Concentrate on this point; thus you will find yourself forming the right of the army and you will be ready to debouch on the morning of the 14th in the direction you will be given.

---

300 Translation by John Hussey. I have expanded YM to Your Majesty, and I have removed the division designations which were incorrect. The first division on the march was the 14th under General Bourmont, followed by the 12th and then the 13th Divisions.

General Count Gérard, who has received orders to go to Rocroi will continue his march on Chimay and Beaumont where he will join your army corps; he will have taken a position slightly behind yours and if on his arrival at Beaumont you have marched ahead, he would follow your movement so as to join you instead and form a second line behind you.

As soon as you have taken the position which is indicated, you will send an officer to inform me of this. I inform you that the right of the 2nd Corps will be in Montignies and the head of the Cavalry Reserve at Leugnies and Cousolre.

Marshal of the Empire, Major General, Duke of Dalmatia

Soult to Grouchy

Marshal, I have the honor to address to you a copy from the Emperor dated the 10th, relating to the position of the army on the 13th. The Emperor orders that you prepare to march, the 1st, 2nd, 3rd and 4th Cavalry Corps and that you direct them on Avesnes, from where they will continue on their route to establish, the 1st and 2nd Corps in front of Solre-le-Château, occupying the villages of Coursolre, Leugnies, Grandrieu, Hestrud, Eccles, Solrinnes, Quierelont, and their dependences.

The 3rd and 4th Corps at Solre-le-Château, while occupying Borieu, Epinoy, Harnault Fountains, Sartz and Offies. You must, M. Maréchal, establish yourself at Solre and make all arrangements so that the movement of these four Cavalry Corps is finished by the evening of the 13th. I request, Marshal, that you realize the execution of this order. Receive etc.

Soult to Grouchy

Marshal, I receive from General Delort a copy of the route which the 14th Cavalry Division, that he commands, follows; from it the location he will arrive on the 13th of this month is at Mézières. I give him the order to leave on the 14th, with all that belongs to his division, to go to Rocroy, from where he will continue on his route *by Chimay to Beaumont, where he will join the army and will meet with the 4th Cavalry Corps, of which he is a part. I summon him that it is necessary that he can be on the 15th at Beaumont or at least be very near.*

I ask you, Marshal, to be sure of this division's march and inform me when he joins with the 4th Cavalry Corps. Receive etc.

June 13, 1815

Soult's order to Gazan

The Emperor thinks that the corps that you will form by taking a part of the troops from the garrisons, you should be able to march forward and enter into enemy country, taking care to act with all of the necessary prudence and precautions. There is a corps of partisans at Cassel; you can drive it in Belgium when you consider it reasonable, the intention of His Majesty is to arrange a time and place for part of the garrisons to organize the blockade of the locations in Belgium and to conduct the campaign there.

Soult's Corrective order to Vandamme

Note the absence of this order in copy of the Register of the Major-Général as provided by Grouchy. *Was it possible this was sent late on the 12th?*

The intention of the Emperor, General, is that you form your Army Corps in front of Philippeville in order to be ready to debouch tomorrow on Charleroy, if orders are sent to you on this subject.

The Armée de la Moselle will direct to Philippeville and will follow your movement; I sent orders consequently to Lt. Gal. Gérard.

According to the orders that I sent to you yesterday, you ought to assemble your Army Corps in Beaumont. But the Emperor has again ordered the execution of the order of the date of the 10th, of which I sent a copy to you, according to which you must be positioned on the date of the 13th in front of Philippeville, thus it is the disposition of the order of the 10th given by the Emperor, that you must follow.

If, however when my letter reaches you, your troops are found between Philippeville and Beaumont, you will leave them there and you will arrange them so as to be able to debouch to Charleroy tomorrow, by taking your line of operations on Philippeville. Give the orders to bake much bread at Philippeville and that the organizing officer of your corps to get much food stored.

Inform me of the progress of your troops placement and measures which you will take for the execution of these orders.

You will take care, Général, to send an officer to Général Gérard to inform him of these measures.

Marshal of the Empire, Major General, Duke of Dalmatia

Napoleon's Countermand to Soult's Corrective Order

As Général Vandamme has reached Beaumont, I no longer think he should to return to Philippeville, as it would exhaust his troops. I prefer that this General camp in the first line a league and a half from Beaumont; I will review them tomorrow.

The 6th Corps will then be located at a quarter of a league to the rear.

In this case, the Armée de la Moselle will concentrate tomorrow on Philippeville with the cuirassier detachment coming from Alsace. Make these changes by general order.

Napoleon to Drouot

To General Drouot.

Give the order that the division of the Chasseurs and Red Lancers must go this evening before Solre, that all divisions of Chasseurs also go to Solre;

All Grenadiers to Avesnes; the Grenadiers à Cheval and Dragoons before Avesnes; each corps will have its artillery with them. The reserve artillery in front of Avesnes.

Appendix XII – Translated Select Correspondence

Order of the Day

Position of the Army on the 14th.

The Imperial Headquarters in Beaumont.
The Imperial Guard Infantry will bivouac at a quarter of a league in front of Beaumont and will form three lines: Young Guard, Chasseurs and Grenadiers. M. Duc de Trévise (Mortier) will scout the location of this camp. He will take care that everything is in its place, artillery, ambulances, baggage-wagons, etc.
The 1st Régiment of Grenadiers à Pied will go to Beaumont.
The Cavalry of the Imperial Guard will be placed to the rear of Beaumont, but the most distant corps should not be beyond a league from this place.
The 2nd Corps will take a position at Leers, being as close as possible to the border, without crossing it. The four divisions of this army corps will be massed and will bivouac on two or four lines: the headquarters in the middle, the cavalry forward, scouting all of the debouches, but without crossing the border and protecting it from the enemy partisans who would wish to invade.
The bivouacs will be placed so that the fires cannot be seen by the enemy; the Generals will prevent anyone from leaving the camp; they will assure that the troops are equipped with 50 cartridges per man, four days of bread and a half pound of meat; that the artillery and the ambulances are in good condition, and they will be placed in their order of battle. Thus the 2nd Corps will be arranged so that it can begin marching on the 15th, at 3:00 o'clock in the morning, if the order is given, to march on Charleroi and to arrive there before nine o'clock.
The 1st Corps will take a position at Solre-sur-Sambre, and they will also bivouac on several lines; observing, as well as the 2nd Corps, that its fires cannot be seen by the enemy, that nobody separates from the camp, and that the Généraux assure the condition of the munitions, of the food for the troops, and that the artillery and the ambulances are placed at their order of battle.
The 1st Corps will also prepare to leave on the 15th, at 3 o'clock in the morning, to follow the movement of the 2nd Corps, so that,

during the day after tomorrow, these two corps will maneuver in the same direction and are protected.

The 3rd Corps, tomorrow, will take a position one league in front of Beaumont, as close as possible to the border, but without crossing it, nor will it allow the enemy to cross it. General Vandamme will keep everyone at their post, will direct that the fires are concealed and that they cannot be seen by the enemy. He will also comply to what is prescribed for the 2nd Corps for ammunition, food, artillery, and ambulances, and be ready to move on the 15th, at 3 o'clock in the morning.

The 6th Corps will also be in front of Beaumont, and will bivouac in two lines, within a quarter of a league of the 3rd Corps. Count Lobau will choose the site, and he will observe the general arrangements which are prescribed by this order.

Marshal Grouchy will bring the 1st, 2nd, 3rd and 4th Cavalry Corps beyond Beaumont, and will organize them in bivouac between this town and Valcourt, also respecting the border, preventing anyone from crossing it and that no one may be seen, nor the fires can be seen by the enemy; and they will be kept ready to leave on the day after tomorrow at 3 o'clock in the morning, if they receive the order for it, to move on Charleroi and form the advanced guard of the army.

He will direct the Generals to assure that all of the cavaliers are equipped with cartridges, that their weapons are in good condition, that they have four days of bread and a half pound of meat that was ordered.

The bridge crews will be bivouacked behind the 6th Corps and in front of the Imperial Guard infantry. The central artilley park will be to the rear of Beaumont.

The Armée de la Moselle will take a position in front of Philippeville tomorrow. Count Gérard will arrange to be able to leave on the day after tomorrow, the 15th, at 3 o'clock in the morning, to join the 3rd Corps and to press its movement on Charleroi, according to the new order that will be given to him; but General Gérard must especially guard his right flank and reconnoiter all the roads running to Charleroi and Namur.

If the Armée de la Moselle has pontoons along with them, General Gérard will place them near the head of his column as possible, in order to use them if the need arises.

All of the army corps will march with the Sappers and bridging material that the Generals have collected at the head of the columns.

The Sappers of the Imperial Guard, and those of the Marines and Reserve will march after the 6th Corps and at the head of the Guard.

All of the Corps will march in perfect order and closed up. In the movement on Charleroi, we will be prepared to make the most of all of the passages, crushing the enemy corps that would attack the army or would maneuverer against it.

In Beaumont there will only be the Imperial Headquarters; nothing else will be established there, and the town will be free of any obstructions.

The old regulations for the headquarters and baggage wagons in the order of march, police for the carriages and baggage, and about the launderers and sutlers, will be enforced. This will be subject to a general order. But, meanwhile, General Officers commanding the Army Corps will make arrangements accordingly, and the chief Provost-Marshal of the Army assure that these orders are carried out.

The Emperor orders that all of the dispositions detailed in this order are kept secret by the General Officers.

By the order of the Emperor,
Marshal of the Empire, Major General, Duke of Dalmatia

June 14, 1815

Napoleon to Josepth, Morning

Avesnes, June 14, 1815, morning
My brother, I move my Imperial Headquarter to Beaumont this evening. Tomorrow the 15th, I will march on Charleroi, where the Prussian army is; this will give way to a battle or the retreat of the enemy. The army is handsome and the weather fine enough; the country support us strongly.

I will write this evening if we must have communications on the 16th. In the meantime, we must prepare.
   Farewell

Napoleon's Order of Movement, Evening

Register of the Major-Général

>*Captain Ramorino carried to d'Erlon*
>*Macarty carried to Reille*
>*Captain Faviers carried to Vandamme*
>*Poirot carried to Lobau*
>*Chef de Bataillon Bénard carried to Gérard*
>*Chef de Bataillon Gentet carried to Drouot and Mortier, Duc de Trévise*
>*Vaucher carried to Grouchy*
>*Chef de Bataillon Lefébure carried to Ruty and Rogniat*

>   *Tomorrow the 15th, at two thirty in the morning, General Vandamme's Light Cavalry Division will advance along the Charleroi road. Patrols will be sent in all the directions to scout the countryside and take out the enemy advanced posts; but each one of these patrols will have at least of 50 men. Before the division starts to march, General Vandamme will make sure that the cavalry are equipped with cartridges.*
>   *At the same time, Lieutenant General Pajol will join the 1st Cavalry Corps and will follow the movement of General Domon's Division, who will take orders from General Pajol. The Divisions of the 1st Cavalry Corps will not provide detachments; they will be taken from the 3rd Division. General Domon will leave his artillery battery to march after the 1st Bataillon of the 3rd Infantry Corps; Lieutenant General Vandamme will give him orders accordingly.*
>   *Lieutenant General Vandamme will sound the diane at two thirty in the morning; at three am he will begin to march his Army Corps and direct it on* Charleroi. *The totality of his baggage and clutter will be confined behind, and will begin to march only after*

the 6*th* Corps and the Imperial Guard have passed. *They will be under the orders of the vaguemestre-général , who will have them join with the 6*th* Corps, of the Imperial Guard and the Imperial Headquarters, and will give them movement orders.*

*Each division of the 3*rd* Army Corps will have with it its battery and its ambulances; any other vehicle which would be in the column will be burned.*

*Count Lobau will sound the diane at three thirty, and will begin to march the 6*th* Army Corps at four o'clock to follow the movement of General Vandamme and to support him. He will observe, for the troops, the artillery, the ambulances and the baggage, the same marching order that is prescribed for the 3*rd* Corps. The baggage of the 6*th* Corps will be joined with those of the 3*rd*, under the orders of the vaguemestre général, as already detailed.*

*The Young Guard will sound the diane at four thirty, and will begin to march at five o'clock; they will follow the movement of the 6*th* Corps on the* Charleroi *route.*

The Chasseurs à Pied of the Guard will sound the diane at five o'clock, and will be begin to march at five thirty, to follow the movement of the Young Guard.

*The Grenadiers à Pied of the Guard will sound the diane at five o'clock, and will leave at five thirty, to follow the movement of the Chasseurs à Pied. The same order of march for the artillery, the ambulances and the baggage, prescribed for the 3*rd* Army Corps, will be observed by the Imperial Guard.*

*The Guard baggage will be joined with that of the 3*rd* and 6*th* Corps, under the orders of the vaguemestre-général, who will start them moving.*

Marshal Grouchy will mount his horse, at five thirty in the morning, along with the cavalry corps which are closer to the road, and he will have them follow the movement on Charleroi. *The two other corps will leave in succession at hourly intervals to one another; but Marshal Grouchy will assure that they march the cavalry along side of the main route that the infantry column will follow, in order to avoid obstructing, and also so that his cavalry observes a better order. He will order the whole of his baggage remains parked at the rear and grouped together, until the time when the vaguemestre-général will order their advance.*

Count Reille will sound the diane at two thirty in the morning, and will begin the 2nd Corps march at three o'clock; he will direct it on Marchiennes-au-Pont, *where he will take them before nine o'clock in the morning. He will guard all the bridges on the Sambre, so that no one passes. The posts that he will leave, will be successively relieved by the 1st Corps; but he must attempt to avert the enemy at these bridges so that they are not destroyed, especially at Marchienne, where he will likely be able to cross, and which he would immediately repair if it was damaged.*

At Thuin *and at* Marchienne, *as well as all the villages on his route, M. Comte Reille will question the inhabitants, in order to receive news of the enemy positions and forces. He will also have the letters in the post offices taken, and will go through them, to immediately forward the information that he will have obtained, to the Emperor.*

Count d'Erlon will have the 1st Corps march at three o'clock in the morning, and will also direct it on Charleroi, *following the movement of the 2nd Corps, of which he will take the left as soon as possible in order to support it as needed. He will hold a cavalry brigade to the rear to cover and maintain by small detachments his communications with Maubeuge; he will send patrols in front of this place in the directions of* Mons *and* Binche *to the border to get news of the enemy, and to report of it immediately; these patrols will be sure not to compromise themselves and are not to cross the border.*

Count d'Erlon will occupy Thuin *with a division; and, if the bridge of this town is destroyed, he would make the repairs at once, at the same time he will chart and immediately make a bridge head on the left bank. The division which will be at* Thuin *will also guard the* Abbey d'Alnes *bridge, where Count d'Erlon will also build a bridge head on the left bank.*

The same marching order given to the 3rd Corps for artillery, ambulances and baggage, will be observed by the 2nd and 1st Corps which will join and carry their baggage and march to the left of the 1st Corps under the orders of the senior vaguemestre.

Appendix XII – Translated Select Correspondence

The 4th Corps (Armée de la Moselle) received the order to take a position before Philippeville today; if his movement is carried out, and if the divisions that form this army corps are concentrated, Lieutenant General Gérard will begin their march tomorrow at three o'clock in the morning and will direct them on Charleroi; *he will be sure to stay with the 3rd Corps with which he will communicate, in order to arrive at about the same time before* Charleroi; *but General Gérard will scout to his right and all the roads leading to* Namur, *he will march in close order of battle and will leave at* Philippeville *all his baggage and clutter so that his army corps will be lighter and more maneuverable.*

General Gérard will order the 14th Cavalry Division, that also had arrived today at Philippeville, to follow the movement of his army corps on Charleroi, *where this division will join the 4th Cavalry Corps.*

Lieutenant Generals Reille, Vandamme, Gérard, and Pajol will stay in communication with frequent patrols, and they will manage their march so as to arrive in mass and assemble before Charleroi: *they will place, as much as possible, Flemish speaking officers in the advanced guard, to question the inhabitants and take their information; but these officers will announce themselves as commanders of patrols, without saying that the army is behind.*

Lieutenant General Reille, Vandamme, and Gérard will have all the Sappers of their army corps march (having with them the means to repair bridges), after the leading light infantry regiment, and they will order the engineer's officers to repair the inferior passages, open lateral communications, and place bridges on the streams where the infantry would get wet crossing them.

The marines, the Sappers of the Guard and the Sappers of the reserve will march after the leading regiment of the 3rd Corps. Lieutenant Generals Rogniat and Haxo will be at their lead; they will take along with them only two or three carriages; the remainder of the engineering park will march to the left of the 3rd Corps. If we meet the enemy, these troops will not be engaged; but Generals Rogniat and Haxo will employ them in the work of river passages, bridge heads, road repairs, and opening communications, etc.

The Cavalry of the Guard will follow the movement on Charleroi *and will leave at eight o'clock.*

The Emperor will be with the advanced guard, on the road to Charleroi. *Lieutenant-Générals will be sure to send to H.M. frequent reports of their movements and the information that they will collect: they are informed that the intention of H.M. is to have crossed the Sambre before midday, and to have the army march to the left bank of this river.*

The bridge equipment will be divided into two sections; the 1st section will be subdivided in three parts, each of five bridges and five boats for the advanced guard, to install three bridges on the Sambre; there will be with each one of these subdivisions a company of pontonniers; the 1st section will march following the engineering park after the 3rd Corps.

The 2nd section will remain with the reserve artillery park with the baggage column; it will have with it the 4th Company of Pontonniers.

The Emperor's baggage and that of the Headquarters' staff will be together and will be transported at ten o'clock; as soon as this has passed, the vaguemestre-général will have the supplies of the Imperial Guard, of the 3rd Corps and of the 6th Corps, at the same time he will send orders to the supply columns of the Cavalry Reserve, to begin marching and to follow in the direction that the cavalry has taken.

The army ambulances will follow the headquarters and will march at the head of the baggage; but, in any case, this baggage, as well as the parks of artillery reserve and the 2nd section of bridge supplies, will approach within no more than three leagues of the army, unless there are orders from the Major General, and they will cross the Sambre, also only by orders.

The vaguemestre-général will form divisions for this baggage, and he will place officers at the commands, in order to be able to detach what will then be called to the headquarters or for the service of the officers.

The Intendant Général will have this supply column join together, all of the baggage and administration transports will be assigned a place in the column.

The carriages that will be late will take the left and will not be able to leave the place given to them by the vaguemestre-général's order.

The Emperor orders that all the transport carriages that are found in the columns of infantry, cavalry, or artillery, be burned, as well as the carriages for the baggage column that leave their place, or will change the march order without the expressed permission of the Vaguemestre Général.

For this purpose, a detachment of fifty grenadiers will be placed at the disposal of the vaguemestre-général, who is held responsible, as well as all the officers of the gendarmerie and the gendarmes, for the execution of these arrangements, of whom the success of the campaign can depend.

By order of the Emperor:
Marshal of the Empire, Major General, Duke of Dalmatia

Soult to Vandamme

Beaumont, on June 14

I have received, Lieutenant-General, your letter of today where you planned a route for Charleroi. You will see, by the order of movement that the Emperor has given and that I send to you, that the 2nd, and 1st Corps must debouch by Marchienne-au-Pont. *It is therefore not necessary that your column will lead to Marchienne because there would be confusion, but you will be able to cross the Eure at Ham, Jamignon, or at Bomerée where bridges exist according to the integrity of the road, and you will inform Generals Pajol and Domon who must precede you.*

I caution you that it has just been discovered that in Jamignon, there is a Prussian Corps of 6,000 men with cannon that should be removed. I also cautioned Marshal Grouchy of this, who must pass with the 2nd, 3rd, and 4th Cavalry Corps by Stenrieux and Yves, *where he will take the Philippeville route to Charleroi, so that he can adjust his movements accordingly. As soon as you have information about the enemy, send officers to the Emperor to report to H.M. what you have learned.*

Soult to Grouchy

Beaumont, on June 14, 1815.

I send you, Marshal, movement orders for tomorrow that the Emperor has given. Follow closely with what is prescribed for you in this order.

Several roads lead to Charleroi starting from Beaumont. That on the right side passes through Bossus, Fleurieux, Vaugenée, and Yves where it meets the main road from Philippeville to Charleroi; it is this road that you must take in order not to bump into the other columns; but first scout it well and adjust your movement so as to always be at the same level of the left column, at the head of which General Pajol must march.

I inform Lieutenant-General Gérard about the direction that you take, whose corps is formed in front of Philippeville and who must also march on Charleroi by the same direction.

I must caution you that it has just been reported that a corps of 6,000 Prussians, infantry, is established in Jamignon. If that is true, the Emperor wants that corps to be removed, thus you will manoeuver accordingly; I write in the same manner to Lieutenant-Generals Vandamme and Gérard. Send an officer to me at the moment when you begin to march, and then every hour during the movement.

Grouchy to Soult at 2pm

Beaumont, on June 14, 1815, at 2 o'clock in the afternoon

Marshal,

I hasten to caution you that the men of the artillery batteries train attached to 4th and the 5th Divisions forming the 1st Corps de Cavalerie, are in a deplorable situation, as far as clothing and personnel.

These men are for the most part children; they do not have great-coats, lack good clothing and boots. If the cold and rainy weather continues, they will fall sick in the bivouac or will desert. It has been reported to me that several have already vanished.

I have the honor to ask you, Marshal, to change as soon as possible the soldiers of these two battery trains, or at least to give them clothing. Why this is all the more necessary, is that they are exactly the batteries attached to the 1st Corps composed only of light cavalry and intended to form the advanced guard, which is the least well supplied.

There is no caisson of infantry attached to the batteries of the 1st Cavalry Corps. It is essential that it is sent there without delay, and I ask you to give the order.

Though the general commanding the artillery of the 1st Cavalry Corps writes for the same objectives that I request of you in this letter, to Lieutenant-Général Ruty, I believe that I had to tell you about it because of the great interest in they represent.

Receive, Marshal, the assurances of my high regard.

Signed, Marshal Grouchy

Soult to Gérard

Beaumont, June 14, 1815.

He was informed about Marshal Grouchy's direction; he wrote to him on the same subject about the Prussian Corps at Jamignon, so that it is adjusted accordingly and that he always scouts well on his right.

D'Erlon's Order of the Day

Order of the day of the 1st Corps for the day of the 15th.

Solre-sur-Sambre, June 14, 1815 (in the evening).

The diane will sound precisely at four o'clock; the order of the day for the army, on the date of the 14th, will be read to the troops.

Signed: Lieutenant General Commander in Chief,

Count d'Erlon

P. S. The bridges on the Sambre will be closed. If you have troops on the left bank, withdraw them at first daylight.

True copy:
Adjudant Commandant, Chief of Staff of the 3rd Division,
Ch. d'Arsonval.

Grouchy to Soult

Bossus, June 14, 1815.

Marshal

    I have the honor to report to you that the 1st Cavalry Corps bivouacked in Fontenelle and Valcourt, the 2nd Corps at Bossus and the 3rd and 4th Corps at the edge of the woods of Gayolle.
    I send you one of my officers from Bossus, where I have established my headquarters, to receive your orders for tomorrow.
    I will pass on to you within a couple of hours, a report that I expect from one of the customs officers from this area of the border, who promises to inform me of what occurs opposite us.
    The rumor we must attack tomorrow, the 15th, has been widespread for several days.

Receive, Marshal, etc.
Signed, Marshal Grouchy

June 15, 1815

Napoleon to Joseph at 3 am

Beaumont, June 15, 1815, three o'clock in the morning.

Appendix XII – Translated Select Correspondence

My brother, the enemy is moving to attack us, I march to meet him. Then hostilities are going to begin today: so I want the announcements that have been prepared to be made. Inform the Duke of Vicenza (Caulaincourt).
NAPOLÉON

Gérard to Soult

To headquarters in Philippeville, June 15th, 1815

to his Excellency Major General, at Beaumont,

Your Highness,

Lieutenant General Bourmont, commanding the 14th Infantry Division has passed, this morning, to the enemy with his Aide-de-Camps Adjudant Commandant Clouet, his Chief of Staff; it even appears that he took along the adjuncts, Major Villoutreis and Captain Sourdat.
I hasten to address to Your Excellence the letters that Bourmont and Clouet wrote to me, at the time of their departure. This general had not yet received movement orders of today, nor the series of [..] of orders. Until today, nothing has come to my knowledge that could make me suspect him capable of treason.
Major General Hulot takes temporary command of the 14th Division. I request Your Excellency to please send instead if possible a Lieutenant-General and staff officers.

Accept, Monseigneur, my respect,
General in Chief, Peer of France,
Cte. Gérard

Soult to Reille at 8:30 am

Count Reille, the Emperor orders me to write to you of crossing the Sambre, if you do not have forces in front of you, and for you to form several lines, AT ONE OR TWO LEAGUES AHEAD, in order to hold both sides of the the main Brussels road, scouting out in the direction of Fleurus. Count d'Erlon will cross at Marchienne and will be in battle formation on the road from Mons to Charleroi, where he will march to support you as needed.

If you are still in Marchienne when this order reaches you, and if the movement by Charleroi could not occur, you could manouever by Marchienne, but always fulfill the measures above.

The Emperor moves before Charleroi. Report immediately to His Majesty of your operations and of what occurs before you.

*Marshal of the Empire, Major General,
Duke of Dalmatia.*

*To Bivouac in Jumignon,
June 15, 1815, at 8:30
in the morning.*

True copy: Count Reille

Soult to Reille at 10 am

This order is a slightly modified copy of the above order of 8:30am. The above was based on an original from the collection of Reille, while the following is what was apparently copied into the order book. While minor differences are not surprising, the time difference is very puzzling. They should be identical.

At Bivouac in Jamignon, June 15, at ten o'clock in the morning.

Count Reille, the Emperor orders me to write to you of crossing the Sambre, if you do not have forces in front of you, and for you to form several lines, at one or two leagues ahead, so as to hold both sides of the main Brussels road, with you watching out in the direction of Fleurus.

Count d'Erlon will cross to Marchienne and will be in battle formation on the road from Mons to Charleroi, where he will march to support you as needed at Charleroi. If you are still in Marchienne when this order reaches you, you could manouever by Marchienne, but always fulfill the measures above. The Emperor marches before Charleroi; report to H.M. of your operations and of what occurs in front of you.*

Soult to d'Erlon at 10 am

At Bivouac in Jamignon, June 15, at ten o'clock in the morning.

Count, the Emperor orders to me to write to you that Count Reille receives the order to cross the Sambre at Charleroi, and to form several lines one or two leagues ahead, so as to hold both sides of the main Brussels road.

The intention of H.M. is also that you cross the Sambre at Marchienne or at Ham, for you march on the main road from Mons to Charleroi, where you will form several lines, and to take positions which will bring you closer to Count Reille, linking your communications and sending parties in all directions, Mons, Nivelles, etc. This movement would also take place if Count Reille was obliged to carry out his crossing by Marchienne. Report to me accounts that follow your operations and of what occurs in front of you. The Emperor approaches Charleroi.

Soult to d'Erlon at 3 pm

Before Charleroi, at three o'clock in the evening, June 15, 1815.

Count d'Erlon, the Emperor orders Count Reille to march on Gosselies and to attack there an enemy corps that appeared to stop there. The intention of the Emperor is for you to march on Gosselies to support Count Reille and assist in his operations. However you must continue to guard Marchienne and you will send a brigade on the Mons road, recommending its commander to guard itself very militarily.

Soult to Gérard at 3:30 pm

Same date, at 3:30 pm

Count Gérard, the Emperor charges me to give you the order to direct your army corps on Chatelet where you will cross the Sambre and will march in advance, while following the Fleurus road, the direction that the Emperor takes at this time with a part of the army, with the object of attacking an enemy corps which stopped there at the head of the woods of Jambusart. If this corps still holds after you will have crossed the Sambre, you will also attack it. Report your positions to me, and inform me if the 14th Cavalry Division is following you; in this case you will have it advance also.

Soult to Delort

Charleroi, June 15, 1815.

Order to Général Delort to take a position behind the city.

D'Erlon to Soult at 4:30 pm

Marchienne-au-Pont, June 15, 1815 at 4:30 in the evening

Your Highness,

I received the two letters that your Excellency has done me the honor of writing to me today. The first was given to me in Montigny-le-Tigneux and I just received another at Marchienne. Under yesterday's general order I left a brigade of cavalry in Solre and Bienne-sous-Thuin, and my infantry division at Thuin, Lobbes, and Aulnes abbey.
My other troops begin to arrive at Marchienne, as soon as the last units of the 2nd Corps has filed past, I will have them cross the Sambre, I will place a brigade on the Mons road, another brigade will remain ahead of Marchienne and with the two other infantry divisions I will march on Gosselies.

I saw the position of Thuin; it is very strong as it is, but given what the localities are, we cannot establish a bridge head there.

I ask Your Excellency to let me know if I should still leave troops at Thuin, Solre, and surroundings.

Deign, Your Highness, to accept my deep respect,

Lieutenant-General Commander in Chief of the 1st Corps Count d'Erlon

Lobau to Soult at 8 pm

To the headquarters on the plateau one league behind Charleroi between Jamignon and the woods of Prince de Liège on June 15, 1815 at 8 o'clock in the evening.

Marshal

The 6th Corps, according to the general order of movement received last night, have taken up arms this morning at 3:30 and began to march at four o'clock.

I have quickly joined the left of the 3rd Corps, where I halted until seven o'clock because it was not until six o'clock that this army corps began its movement. I let the engineer park and a party of pontoon bridge trains pass before me. I followed the direction of the 3rd Corps, and I passed by Clermont, by Donstienne, Marbais, Ham sur Eure, the Hayes de Nalines.

Our march has been very slow, because of the passes and the bad roads. It is eight o'clock and I arrive just on the plateau that I occupy, though I made at most only six leagues in the course of the day.

The troops are very tired, but the artillery horses even more. Not receiving instructions, I took it on myself to make my camp, and to await your orders.

I do not have news of the army corps' supplies. I think that they will join us tomorrow; ....I saw others in front of me. I have the honor to be of Your Excellency, the very humble and very obeying servant, the Lieutenant General Aide-de-Camp of the Emperor, commanding the 6th Corps,

Cte. Lobau

P.S. Herein is the sketch of my position made by Mr. Guibert. My Chief of Staff sent a position to you on the 11th, of Capelle, he [..] you this night.

D'Erlon to Soult around 8 pm

Jumay, June 15, 1815

Your Highness,

In accordance with the Order of Y.E. as of today, 3 pm, I was directed to Gosselies. I found the 2nd corps established there; consequently I placed my fourth division behind this village, and my second in front of Jumay, the cavalry brigade is in the latter place. The 3rd Division remained in Marchienne and the 1st in Thuin, my other cavalry brigade is in Solre and Biel-sous-Thuin, which disperses my troops very much; I pray Y.E. to kindly let me know if I must recall those I left behind. The reconnaissance party that I sent to Fontaine-l'Eveque learned that 1500 Prussians, who were there this morning with three pieces of artillery, left at noon heading on Marchele-le-Chateau; they took with them a lot of cattle. I await the order for tomorrow which will be carried by the officer who will have the honor to give this letter to Y.E. I ask acceptance of my deep respect.

(Signed) Count d'Erlon

D'Erlon to Ney after 8 pm

In his 11 pm correspondence to Soult, Ney indicated he had received d'Erlon's dispositions.

Appendix XII – Translated Select Correspondence

Lefebvre-Desnouettes to Ney at 9 pm

Frasnes, June 15, 9 o'clock in the evening

Your Highness,

Arriving at Frasnes following your orders, we found it occupied by a regiment of Nassau infantry of approximately 1500 men and 8 pieces of artillery. As they observed that we were maneuvering to turn them, they left the village; there we would have effectively surrounded them by our squadrons. General Colbert was even within musket shot of Quatre Bras on the main road; but as the terrain was difficult and the enemy fixed at the Bossu woods and he struck very sharp fire with his 8 pieces of cannon, it was impossible for us to carry it.

This troops that we found in Frasnes have not advanced this morning and were not engaged at Gosselies; they are under the orders of Lord Wellington and seem to be retiring towards Nivelles; they lit a lantern at Quatre Bras and fired their cannons heavily. None of the troops who fought this morning at Gosselies passed by here; they marched towards Fleurus.

The peasants cannot give me information about a large gatherings of troops in these surroundings, just that there is an artillery park at Tubise made up of 100 caissons and 12 pieces of artillery. they say that the Belgian Army is in the environs of Mons and that the headquarters of young Prince Frederic of Orange is at Braine-le-Comte. We took fifteen prisoners and we had ten men killed or wounded.

Tomorrow at the break of day I will send a reconnaissance to Quatre Bras that will occupy it if possible, because I think that the Nassau troops have gone.

A battalion of infantry has just arrived, and I placed it in front of the village. My artillery has not joined me, so I have sent the order for them to bivouac with the Bachelu Division; they will join me tomorrow morning. I have not written to the Emperor as I having nothing more important to report to him than I am telling your Excellency.

I have the honor to be, with respect, Your Highness, your very humble and very devoted servant,

Lefebvre Desnouettes

I send to you a sergeant who will receive the orders of Your Excellence. I have the honor to remark to Your Excellence that the enemy did not reveal cavalry in front of us, but the artillery is light artillery.

Reille to Soult at 9 pm

Gosselie June 15, 1815 at 9 o'clock in the evening

His Excellency Marshal Duke of Dalmatia Major General,

Marshal,

According to the order of the army I received at Lair Fauster with the 2nd Corps at three o'clock in the morning, I met in front of Thuin an enemy advance guard of cavalry and infantry and in this village about 800 men; after some cannon fire and rather sharp musketry fire, we drove them out of this position, which is very difficult to access. The enemy left some people; wounded men and some prisoners, among them two officers. The bridges of Lobbes, Thuin, and Aulne remained in good condition. We met the enemy again in Bois de Montigny le Tigneux; engaged in very sharp musketry fire; we drove them out of the village and they then sought to retreat on Marchienne; but being hard pressed by our infantry, I had Generals Piré and Hubert debouch with the 1st Chaussers who vigorously charged them; a hundred were sabered and more than 200 prisoners taken.

After crossing the Marchienne bridge I directed the cavalry to leave to the left the Bois de Monceaux and I crossed it with the infantry column; arriving close to Jumay, General Bachelu fell on the enemy column, who had forced the 1st Chasseurs to retreat; he killed some men and took some prisoners. The 2nd Corps then marched ahead and took a position; the 5th and 9th Infantry Divisions as well as the cavalry on the right and left of Gosselies and the 6th Division behind the Bois de Lombuc. The 7th, which was second in line from the 6th, received the order according to His Majesty, one hour before nightfall, to take the Jumay road to Fleurus and to send skirmishers to this village.

The 2nd Light Infantry, who all day held the lead of the column, showed the greatest force, it had approximately 80 men killed or wounded, the 1st Chasseurs had 20 to 25; the number of the prisoners sent to the General Staff is 255 and 5 officers.

I ask Your Excellency to accept my respect,

Commanding General of the 2nd Corps Count Reille

Gérard to Soult, late evening

Armée de la Moselle
To the Headquarters at Chatelet, June 15, 1815

To his Excellency, Major General at Charleroy

Your Highness,

I have already passed the hedges at Nalinnes in the direction of Charleroy, when I received the order from Your Excellency to direct to <u>Chatelet</u> and to cross the Sambre there.

Three infantry divisions with their artillery arrived at Chatelet, the Fourteenth Infantry Division, commanded by Maréchal-de-Camp Hulot, crossed the Sambre and occupied Chatelineau.

Two other infantry divisions are in Chatelet. I have had some reconnaissance sent to the two banks of the Sambre and observe the communications towards Namur and Dinant.

The Sixth Cavalry Division commanded by Lieutenant-Général Maurin could only make it to Bouflieu.

General Delort's Cuirassiers Division is still behind on the Philippeville road; I sent three officers to him in succession, to have him take the Chatelet direction.

Everyplace that the Army of the Moselle passed today, the Belgian inhabitants welcomed them with acclamations of "Vive l'Empereur".

The officer carrying this dispatch is, at the same time, charged to escort to your Excellency, a captain of the 28th Régt. of the Prussian infantry, named Neuhaus, who was taken prisoner today by the Dragoons.

I ask Your Excellence to accept my respect,

General in Chief,
Peer of France
Cte. Gérard

Vandamme to Napoleon around 10 pm

At the farm of Fontenelle, June 15, 1815 10 o'clock in the evening

Sire,

I have the honor to report to Your Majesty that Lieutenant Generals Burth and Cardinal command what is before us. I think that the enemy has only 12 to 15,000 men. Marshal Grouchy believes that there are 30,000 men.

The enemy revealed only 10 to 12 cannons.

The enemy is now behind Fleurus, completely in retreat. They left only some light cavalry posts in Fleurus. I am entirely assembled; the right in front of Winage to the right of the Namur road. It is the 8th Division.

I have my headquarters at the Fontenelle farm. From this farm on the right side of Namur is the 3rd Light Cavalry Division which has its posts in Lambusart.

The 10th Division is to be found from the right of the Farm to the Fleurus road.

The 11th Division is at Camp d'Andois.

Part of my artillery reserve is arriving here right now.

I have the honor to be, Sire, of your Imperial Majesty, the very humble and very obedient servant and faithful subject,

Appendix XII – Translated Select Correspondence

Vandamme

Grouchy to Napoleon around 10 pm

The village of Campinaire, June 15 at 10 o'clock in the evening

    Sire, I have the honor to report to Your Majesty that General Exelmans' Corps, intended to outflank the position which the enemy occupied beyond the village of Gilly, having crossed the ravine which separated it from the village, charged in the plain above Chatelineau; pushed the enemy until a step beyond Ronchamps, and having driven off its cavalry a distance, fell on the squares of infantry; broke them and took more than 400 prisoners.

    The enemy, trying to take a position in the woods, was again in a position to debouch under the protection of its infantry fire, several companies of Dragoons dismounted, contained this Prussian infantry by their fire and gave time for General Vandamme's Infantry to arrive.

    This group, marching on the road that crosses the woods, was again supported by the Dragoons who pursued the Prussians until beyond the village of Lambusart where General Chastel still chased them. It is impossible to show more intrepidity than did General Exelmans' Corps and especially General Vincent's Brigade, composed of the 15th and 20th Dragoon Regiments. Major Guibourg, of the 15th Regiment, attacked a square and took 300 prisoners. I respect the kindness of Your Majesty. General Pajol, at the head of the 1st Corps, chased the enemy from the road straight from Gilly to Fleurus, took several hundred prisoners and no less distinguished himself than General Exelmans, of whom I cannot praise enough to Your Majesty. It is constantly to the shouts of "Vive l'Empereur" and with enthusiasm, difficult to describe that the troops everywhere confronted the enemy.

Respectfully, Sire,

Signed, Marshal Grouchy

Ney to d'Erlon before 11 pm

In his 11 pm correspondence to Soult, Ney indicates he has just send orders to d'Erlon.

Ney to Soult around 11 pm

Gosselies, June 15, 11 o'clock in the evening

Marshal,
    I have the honor to report to Your Excellency that, in accordance with the Emperor's orders, I went this afternoon to Gosselies to dislodge the enemy with General Piré's Cavalry and General Bachelu's Infantry. The enemy made only a slight resistance; we exchanged 25 to 30 cannon shots; he withdrew through Heppignies on Fleurus.
    We took 5 to 600 Prussian prisoners from General Zieten's Corps.
    Here is the position of the troops:
    General Lefebvre Desnouettes with the Lancers and the Chassuers of the Guard at Frasnes.
    General Bachelu with the 5th Division at Mellet.
    General Foy with the 9th Division at Gosselies.
    General Piré's Light Cavalry at Heppignies.
    I do not know where to find General in Chief Reille.
    General Count d'Erlon informs me that he is in Jumet with the greater part of his Army Corps. I have just transmitted the arrangements to him, prescribed by the letter from Your Excellency, dated today.
    I am enclosing in my letter a report from General Lefebvre-Desnouettes.
    Accept, Marshal, the assurances of my highest regards,

Marshal Prince de la Moskowa, Ney

Soult to d'Erlon before midnight, or 9:30 pm

Documents inédits, pages 25-26

Appendix XII – Translated Select Correspondence

Note how this particular order so revealing on the status of the left wing during the evening of the 15th of June was *not* copied into the order book. or not shared by Grouchy.

> *To Count d'Erlon, Commander of the 1st Corps*
> *Charleroi, June 15, 1815*
>
> *Count, the intention of the Emperor is that you rally your corps on left bank of the Sambre, to join the 2nd Corps at Gosselies, according to the orders Marshal Prince de la Moskowa will give you on this subject.*
>
> *Thus, you will recall the troops that you left in Thuin, Sobre, and surroundings; you must however always have many parties on your left to scout the Mons road.*
>
> *Marshal of the Empire, Major General,*
> *Duke of Dalmatia*

Army Bulletin

> *Charleroi, June 15, 1815, in the evening.*
>
> *On the 14th, the army was placed in the following manner:*
> *The Imperial Headquarters at Beaumont.*
> *The 1st Corps, commanded by General d'Erlon, was at Solre, on the Sambre.*
> *The 2nd Corps, commanded by General Reille, was at Ham-sur-Heure.*
> *The 3rd Corps, commanded by General Vandamme, was to the right of Beaumont.*
> *The 4th Corps, commanded by General Gérard, arrived at Philippeville.*
> *On the 15th, at three o'clock in the morning, General Reille attacked the enemy and marched on Marchienne-au-Pont, he had different engagements in which his cavalry charged a Prussian battalion and took 300 prisoners.*

At one o'clock in the morning, the Emperor was at Jamioulx-sur-Heure.

General Domon's Light Cavalry Division sabred two Prussian battalions and took 400 prisoners.

General Pajol entered Charleroi at midday. The Sappers and the Marines of the Guard were in the spearhead to repair the bridges; fighting as skirmishers, they were first to enter the town, Général Reille with the 1st Hussars marched on Gosselies on the Brussels road, and Général Pajol on Gilly on the Namur road.

At three o'clock in the afternoon, General Vandamme debouched with his Corps on Gilly.

Marshal Grouchy arrived with General Exelmans' Cavalry.

The enemy occupied the left of the Fleurus location. At five o'clock in the afternoon, the Emperor ordered the attack. The position was turned and dislodged. The four Service Squadrons of the Guard, commanded by General Letort, Aide-de-Camp of the Emperor, fell on three squares: the 26th, 27th, and 28th Prussian regiments were routed. Our squadrons sabred 400 or 500 men and took 1,500 prisoners.

During this time, General Reille crossed the Sambre at Marchienne-au-Pont, to march on Gosselies with Prince Jérôme and General Bachelu's divisions, attacked the enemy, took 250 prisoners and continued on the Brussels road.

Thus we became masters of the entire Fleurus position.

At eight o'clock in the evening, the Emperor returned to his headquarters in Charleroi.

This day cost the enemy five pieces of cannon and 2,000 men, including 1,000 prisoners. Our loss is 10 killed men and 80 wounded, the majority of these were from the service squadrons, who charged home, and of the three squadrons of 20th Dragoons, who also charged a square with the greatest intrepidity. Our loss, light in numbers, was sensitive to the Emperor, with the serious wound received by General Letort, his Aide-de-Camp, while charging at the head of the Service Squadrons. This officer has the greatest distinction. He was struck by a ball in the stomach, and the surgeon fears that his wound is mortal.

We found some magazines in Charleroi. The Belgian's joy can not be described. There are villages that, at the sight of their liberators, began dancing, and everywhere there is spirit from the heart.

In the report to the General Staff, we will include the names of the officers and soldiers who distinguished themselves.

The Emperor gave the command of the left to the Prince de la Moskowa, who had, in the evening, his headquarters at Quatre Bras on the Brussels road.

The Duke of Treviso, to whom the Emperor had given the command of the Young Guard, remained in Beaumont, suffering from a sciatica that forced him to bed.

The 4th Corps, commanded by General Gérard, arrives this evening at Châtelet. General Gérard reported that Lieutenant General Bourmont, Colonel Clouet, and Major Villoutreys went over to the enemy. A Lieutenant of the 11th Chasseurs also passed to the enemy. The Major General ordered that these deserters be judged immediately in accordance with the laws.

Nothing can portray the good spirit and fervor of the army. We regard this as a happy event, the desertion of this small number of traitors, who reveal themselves this way.

June 16, 1815

Soult to Napoleon

Charleroi, June 16, 1815.

SIRE,

The service that General Staff Officers have to actively fulfill each day requires a great number of horses, that most cannot afford, for lack of pecuniary means.

I have, therefore, the honor to propose to Your Majesty to grant as extraordinary gratification to the Adjutants, Commandants, and General Staff Officers listed in the attached statement, the sum of eight hundred francs for the Adjudant-Commandants and that of six hundred francs for the Staff Officers.

I request Your Majesty to inform me of your decision on this subject,

*Major General
Duke of Dalmatia*

D'Arsonval to General Nogues at 3am

Quartier Général at Marchienne-au-Pont,

According to the intention of the General in Chief, the Lieutenant General charges me to invite you to make your brigade leave immediately, it has to be at six o'clock in the morning, and earlier if it is possible, at Gosselies.

Adjudant Commandant, Chief of Staff,.
Ch. d'Arsonval.

P. S. The 2nd Brigade remains here until the arrival of the First Division, to go together to the same destination.

Napoleon to Joseph

Charleroi, June 16, 1815

My Brother, the bulletin will inform you of what has occurred. I bring my headquarters to Fleurus. We are in a great movement. I regret deeply the loss of Général Letort. The losses of yesterday are not considerable and are almost all limited to the four service squadrons.
The confiscation of goods from the traitors who gather in Ghent is necessary.

Napoléon

Appendix XII – Translated Select Correspondence

Grouchy to Soult at 5 am

Campinaire, June 16, 1815 at 5 o'clock in the morning

Marshal,

The four Cavalry Corps are arranged in the following way:
The 1st has one of its divisions at Lambusart, and the Second on the road from Gilly to Fleurus in front of the Capinaire junction. The 2nd Corps has one of its Divisions at Lambusart and the other behind the defile of Ronchamp.
The 4th Corps rallied its Second Division and is at the village of St. Francois and surrounding hamlets.
The 3rd Corps must be found between Charleroi and the point where we charged the Prussian infantry squares. General Kellerman did not contact me from Charleroi, his position; but he is on this side.
I still do not have the report of the losses, just those of the 1st and 2nd Corps today. I have requested – and will forward – it when I've received it. The copy that I addressed to the Emperor yesterday is enclosed.
The total prisoners taken by the cavalry yesterday is eight to nine hundred men.

Receive, Marshal, the assurances of my highest regards,

The Marshal Commander of the Cavalry
Count Grouchy

P.S. The First Hussars that left the 1st Corps was detached by Your Orders, and I wish that you would have them join Soult's Division, if it will be possible

Soult to the Army

Charleroi, June 16, 1815.
Order to not deliver the honors to the Emperor when he is found at the outposts.

Soult to Ney around 5 am

Charleroi, June 16, 1815.

Marshal, Emperor has just ordered the Count of Valmy, commander of the 3rd Cavalry Corps, to assemble and lead it to Gosselies where it will be available. The intention of his Majesty is that his Guard Cavalry that was placed on the road to Brussels, remain behind and join the rest of the Imperial Guard; but so that it does not make a retrograde movement, it can, after being substituted on the line, remain slightly to the rear, where orders will be sent in the movement of the day; for this General Lefebvre-Desnouettes will send an officer to take the orders.

Please inform me whether the First Corps has made its move, and what is this morning the exact position of the 1st and 2nd Corps, and of the two attached cavalry divisions, while noting what is in front of you and what you learned.

Ney to Soult at 7 am
Houssaye, pages 344 and 346

Houssaye apparently saw the 7 am report, and quoted from it to confirm the undiscovered report of Ney to Soult from the previous evening.

Soult to Comte de Valmy

Charleroi, June 16, 1815.

Order Count of Valmy to assemble and direct the 3rd Cavalry Corps to Gosselies where it will be under the command of Marshal Ney.

Soult to Lobau before 8 am

Carried by M. Poirau.

Charleroi, June 16, 1815

Count, the Emperor orders that you march the 6th Corps to have them take a position halfway from Charleroi to Fleurus, and at the same time you'll guard Charleroi where you will name a provisional commander. I ordered that all the prisoners as well as all of the enemy and French wounded be directed to Avesnes. I ask that you be sure that this order is executed.

Soult to Drouot before 8 am

Charleroi, June 16, 1815

M. Comte, the Emperor orders that the Imperial Guard, Infantry, Cavalry, and Artillery immediately march for Fleurus; please give them orders accordingly; Général Lefebvre-Desnouettes' Division, being detached, will receive them directly.

Soult to Gérard before 8 am

Carried by M. Crava.

Same date.

Count, the Emperor orders that you have the 4th Army Corps march and that you direct it on Sombreffe, while keeping Fleurus to the left, in order to avoid congestion.

I advise you that the intention of His Majesty is that you take orders from Marshal Grouchy as Wing Commander, therefore will instruct you of your movement. You will send an officer to him at once and ask him for orders, without however delaying your march. Marshal Grouchy must, at this moment, be around Fleurus. You will receive direct orders only from the Emperor when H.M. is present; but you will continue to address your reports and records to me as established.

Soult to Vandamme before 8 am

Carried by M. Guyardin.

Charleroi, June 16, 1815

General, the Emperor orders that you march with the 3rd Corps, directed to Sombreffe where the 4th Corps and the Reserve Cavalry Corps will also go. H.M. also orders that you take orders from Marshal Grouchy as commander of an army wing. Thus he will instruct you in your movement and you will send an officer to him at once to ask him his orders, without however delaying your march. Count Grouchy must be at this time on the outskirts of Fleurus, you will receive direct orders from the Emperor when H.M. is present; but you will continue to address your reports and records to me as established.

Soult to Grouchy around 8 am

Carried by M. Lion.

Same date.

Marshal, the Emperor orders that you march with the 1st, 2nd and 4th Cavalry Corps, and that you will direct them on Sombreffe where you will take position. I give similar orders to M. Lieutenant-General Vandamme for the 3rd Infantry Corps, and to M. Lieutenant-General Gérard for the 4th Corps, and I advise these two Generals that they are under your command and that they must immediately send to you officers to inform you of their march and to take your instructions. I tell them however that when H.M. is present, they will be able to receive direct orders from him, and that they must continue to send to me service reports and records that they normally provide.

I advise also General Gérard that in his movement on Sombreffe he must have the town of Fleurus on the left, in order to avoid congestion; thus you will direct him so that he marches otherwise well organized and within reach of the 3rd Corps, and is able to contribute to the attack on Sombreffe if the enemy puts up resistance.

You will also give instructions, consequently, to M. General Count Vandamme.

I have the honor to advise you that Count of Valmy received orders to go to Gosselies, with the 3rd Cavalry Corps, where he will be at Marhsal Ney's disposal.

The 1st Hussars Regiment will return to the 1st Cavalry Corps during the day, I will include this subject in the Emperor's orders.

I have the honor to advise you that Marshal Ney receives the order to march with the 1st and 2nd Infantry Corps and 3rd Cavalry Corps, at the intersection of the roads called the Trois Bras, *on the Brussels road, and that he will detach a full corps to* Marbais *to link with you at Sombref and to assist with your operational needs.*

After you have taken Sombreffe, you'll immediately send an advanced guard to Gembloux *and scout all of the directions that lead to Sombref, particularly the main Namur road, at the same time you will establish your communications with Marshal Ney.*

The Imperial Guard directs to Fleurus.

Soult to Ney before 8 am

Carried by M. Leroux

Charleroi, June 16, 1815

Marshal, the Emperor orders that you have the 2nd and 1st Army Corps, as well as the 3rd Cavalry Corps that was placed at your disposal and direct them to the intersection of the roads known as the Trois-Bras *(Brussels road), where they will take their position. At the same time you will send a reconnaissance, as forward as possible on the road to Brussels and Nivelles, where the enemy has probably retreated. H.M. wishes that, if there is no harm, you establish a division with cavalry at Genappe, and orders that you march another division in the direction of Marbais to cover the space between Sombreffe and Trois Bras. You will place, close to this division, the cavalry division of the Imperial Guard commanded by General Lefebvre-Desnouettes, as well as the 1st Hussars Regiment which was detached yesterday towards Gosselies.*

The Corps that will be at Marbais *will also plan to support the movements of Marshal Grouchy on Sombreffe, and support you at the position at the Trois Bras, if that becomes necessary. You will recommend to the General who will be at Marbais, to scout well in all directions, particularly those of Gembloux and Wavre.*

If, however, General Lefebvre-Desnouettes' Division is too engaged on the Brussels road, you will leave it there and replace it at Marbais by the 3rd Cavalry Corps, that will be under command of the Count of Valmy, and by the 1st Hussars Regiment.

I have the honor to advise you that the Emperor will march on Sombreffe, where, according to the orders of H.M., Marshal Grouchy must move with the 3rd and 4th Infantry Corps, and the 1st, 2nd and 4th Cavalry Corps. Marshal Grouchy will occupy Gembloux.

Please report to me as well as to the Emperor about your arrangments, to execute the order that I send to you as well as all that you will have learned about the enemy.

H.M. desires me to tell you to prescribe to the Generals commanding the army corps to keep their troops united, and send isolated men back to their units, to maintiain perfect order in the troops and rally all the artillery carts and ambulances that have been left behind.

Napoleon to Ney before 9 am

Charleroi, June 16, 1815.

My cousin, I send my Aide-de-Camp General Flahaut to you, who brings you this letter. The Major General should have given you orders but you will receive mine first because my officers move faster than his. You will receive the day's movement orders, but I want to write to you in detail, because it is of the highest importance.

I am sending Marshal Grouchy with the 3rd and 4th Infantry Corps to Sombreffe; I am taking my Guard to Fleurus, and I will be there in person before midday, I will attack the enemy if I find them there, and I will clear the roads as far as Gembloux. There, according to what will happen, I shall come to a decision, perhaps at three o'clock in the afternoon, perhaps this evening. My intention is that, immediately after I have made up my mind, you will be ready to march on Brussels. I will support you with my Guard who will be at Fleurus or Sombreffe, and I wish to arrive at Brussels

Appendix XII – Translated Select Correspondence

tomorrow morning. You will march this evening; if I make up my mind at an early hour then you will be informed of it during the day and then this evening will go three or four leagues and reach Brussels tomorrow by seven o'clock in the morning.

You can arrange your troops in the following way:

The first division, two leagues in front of Quatre Bras, if there is no harm; six divisions of infantry around Quatre Bras, and a division at Marbais, so that I can draw it to me at Sombreffe, if I need; it would not otherwise delay your march;

Count of Valmy's Corps, who has 3,000 Elite Cuirassiers, will be placed at the intersection of Roman and Brussels roads, so that I can draw it to me if needed. As soon as I take my course of action, you will send him the order to come join you.

I will want to have the Guard Division with me, commanded by General Lefebvre-Desnoëttes, and I am sending you two divisions of Count of Valmy's Corps to replace it. But, in my current endeavor, I prefer to place Count of Valmy so as to recall if I need him, and I do not wish to cause General Lefebvre-Desnoëttes to make unnecessary marches, since it is likely that I will decide this evening to march on Brussels with the Guard. However, cover Lefebvre's division with d'Erlon and Reille's Divisions of Cavalry, in order to save the Guard: if there was a skirmish with the English, it is preferable that it is on the Cavalry of the line rather than on the Guard.

I have adopted as a general principle, during this campaign, to divide my army into two wings and a reserve. Your wing will consist of four divisions of the 1st Corps, four divisions of the 2nd Corps, two divisions of Light Cavalry, and two divisions of the Count of Valmy's Corps. That should be roughly 45 to 50,000 men.

Marshal Grouchy will have about the same force and will command the right wing.

The Guard will form the reserve, and I will move to one or the other wing, according to circumstances. The Major General gives the most precise orders so that there is no difficulty in obeying such orders that you receive; the corps commanders will take my orders directly when I am present.

According to circumstances, I will diminish one wing or the other, to strengthen my reserve.

You understand the considerable importance in taking Brussels. This may also lead to incidents, because such a swift and abrupt movement will isolate the English army from Mons, Ostend, etc. I want your arrangements to be well made, so that at the first order your eight divisions can go quickly and without obstacles to Brussels.

Napoléon

Napoleon to Grouchy before 9 am

Charleroi, June 16, 1815

My Cousin, I send to you Labédoyère, my Aide-de-Camp, to bring you this letter. The Major-Général should have informed you of my intentions; but, as he has poorly mounted officers, my Aide-de-Camp will arrive perhaps earlier.

My intention is that, as commander the right wing, you take command of the 3rd Corps commanded by General Vandamme, of the 4th Corps commanded by General Gérard, the Cavalry Corps commanded by Generals Pajol, Milhaud, and Exelmans; this should make roughly 50,000 men. Converge with this right wing at Sombreffe. Have the Corps of Generals Pajol, Milhaud, Exelmans, and Vandamme march off in succession, and, without stopping, continue your movement on Sombreffe. The 4th Corps, which is in Châtelet, received the order directly to go to Sombreffe without passing by Fleurus. This observation is important because I am moving my headquarters to Fleurus and obstructions should be avoided. Send an officer immediately to General Gérard to inform him of your movement so that he executes his march at once.

My intention is that all of the Generals take your orders directly; they will take mine only when I am present. I will be in Fleurus between ten and eleven o'clock; I will go to Sombreffe leaving my Guard, Infantry and Cavalry, in Fleurus. I will bring them to Sombreffe only if it is necessary. If the enemy is in Sombreffe, I will attack them; I want to attack them in Gembloux as well, and also to seize this position, my intention being, after gaining these two positions, to leave this night, and to engage the English with my

Appendix XII – Translated Select Correspondence

left wing, commanded by Marshal Ney. So do not lose a moment, because the sooner I will depart, better that it will help the success of my operations. I presume that you are in Fleurus. Keep in constant communication with Général Gérard, so that he can help you attack Sombreffe, if it is necessary.

Girard's division is within reach of Fleurus; do not use them unless absolutely necessary, because it will have to march all night. Also leave my Young Guard and all of their artillery in Fleurus.

Count of Valmy, with his two divisions of Cuirassiers, marches on the Brussels road to unite with Marshal Ney, to contribute to this evening's operation on the left wing.

As I have said to you, I will be in Fleurus at ten to eleven o'clock. Send me reports on all that you learn. Be sure that the Fleurus route is free. All the information I have suggests that the Prussians cannot oppose us with more than 40,000 men.

Napoléon

Sout to Ney before 10 am

Carried by M. Waleski

Charleroi, June 16, 1815

Marshal, a Lancer officer has just told the Emperor that the enemy is present en mass at Quatre Bras; assemble the Corps of Counts Reille and d'Erlon and that of Count of Valmy who is at this moment en route to join you; with these forces you must attack and destroy all the enemy corps that present themselves; Blücher was in Namur yesterday and it is not credible that he moved troops towards Quatre Bras, thus you are opposed by only what comes from Brussels.

Marshal Grouchy will execute the movement on Sombreffe that I announced to you, and the Emperor will go to Fleurus; it is there that you will address your new reports to H.M.

Reille to Ney at 10 am

Gosselies, June 16, 1815, 10:15 in the morning

Marshal,

I have the honor to inform Your Excellency of the report from Général Girard given to me verbally by one of his officers.

The enemy continues to occupy Fleurus with light cavalry and in front troops in vedette duty; we see two enemy masses coming by the Namur road whose head has reached Saint-Amand. They were formed gradually, and gained some ground as they were reinforced; one could hardly judge their force because of the distance, however this general thinks that each one could be six battalions in column by battalion. We noticed troop movements at the rear.

Lieutenant-General Flahaut told me of the orders carried to Your Excellency; I advised Count d' Erlon, so that he can follow my movement. I would have begun mine on Frasnes at soon as the divisions would have been under arms; but according to the report of General Girard, I will keep the troops ready to march while waiting for the orders of Your Excellency, and as they can reach me very quickly, very little time will have been wasted.

I sent the officer to the Emperor who submitted the report to me from General Girard.

I renew with Your Excellence the assurances of my respectful devotion.

The General in Chief of the 2th Corps
Count Reille

Reille to d'Erlon

Per above, Reille communicated the intentions of Flahaut to d'Erlon, possibly verbally.

Note however, due to report of Girard of massing Prussians, Reille did not commence execution until hearing from Ney. This extenuates the delays.

Appendix XII – Translated Select Correspondence

Ney to d'Erlon before 11 am

There is no record of this, but d'Erlon and staff from his divisions write that they received orders to march anywhere from 10 am to noon. As II Corps was in the way still, there was a delay in execution.

Ney to Reille at 11 am

To M. Comte Reille,
Commanding the 2nd Corps d'Armée.

Frasnes, June 16, 1815.

MOVEMENT ORDERS

In accordance with the Emperor's instructions, the 2nd Corps will begin to march at once to take a position, the Fifth Division behind Genappes, *on the heights which dominate this town, the left supported by the main road. A battalion or two will cover all the debouches ahead on the Brussels road. The reserve and supplies park for this division will remain with the second line.*
   The Ninth Division will follow the movement of the Fifth, and will come to take a position in the second line on the heights on the right and to the left of the village of Banterlet.
   The Sixth and the Seventh Divisions will be located at the Quatre Bras junction, where your headquarters will be. The three First Divisions of Count d'Erlon will take a position at Frasnes; *the division on the right will be established at* Marbais *with General Piré's Second Division of Light Cavalry; the 1st covering your march, and will scout towards Brussels and your two flanks. My quarters at* Frasnes.

For the Marshal Prince de la Moskowa,
Colonel, first Aide-de-Camp,
HEYMÈS

Count of Valmy's two divisions will be established at Frasnes *and at* Liberchies.

The Guard Divisions of General Lefebvre Desnouettes and Colbert will remain in their current position at Frasnes.

True copy:
Comte Reille

Ney to Soult at 11 am

Frasnes, June 16, 1815 at 11 o'clock in the morning.

To His Excellency Marsal Duke of Dalmatia Major General,

I receive at this moment your instructions for the movement of the 1st and 2nd Infantry Corps, and for General Piré's Light Cavalry Division and the two Cavalry Divisions of the 3rd Corps.

Those of the Emperor have already reached me. Here are the placements that I have just ordered:

The 2nd Corps, General Reille, will have a division behind Genappe, another at Bauterlet, and the two others at Quatre Bras.

A Light Cavalry division of General Piré will cover the 2nd Corps' march.

The 1st Corps will set up as follows: a division at Marbais, two others in Frasne, a Light Cavalry Division at Marbais, two divisions of Comte de Valmy at Frasne and Liberchies.

The two Divisions of Light Cavalry of the Guard will remain in Frasne where I establish my headquarters.

All of the information reveals that there are about 3000 enemy infantrymen at Quatre Bras and very few cavalry. I think that the arrangements of the Emperor for the subsequent march on Brussels will be carried out without great obstacles.

Marshal Prince de la Moskowa,

Ney

Appendix XII – Translated Select Correspondence

Delcambre, Chief of Staff of I Corps to Donzelot after Noon

At Headquarters, June 16 1815

My General,

I ask you to give the order to your division to take up arms at once. The army is going to march.
The Emperor does not want to be honored when he is at the outposts because it may reveal that H.M. is there and that can be a risk.
Please give your orders accordingly.

Maréchal de Camp,
Chief of Staff of the 1st Corps,
Bon DELCAMBRE.

Lobau to Napoleon around 1 pm

Sire,

In accordance with Your Majesty's orders, I sent Adjudant-Commandant Jeanin to the corps commanded by Marshal Ney. This officer found these troops positioned from the surroundings of Gosselies to beyond the village of Frasnes. He has a lot of experience in war and thinks that the enemy is not in very great force; but it is difficult, because of the forests, to judge precisely.
The previously mentioned Colonel talked with several superior officers, and he finally interrogated deserters, and none of the individuals questioned brought the number of the enemy beyond 20,000 men; when this officer left the site, there were only skirmishers engaged, these in a rather small number.
I am still positioned in front of Charleroi where I will remain until given new orders. It would be good if Your Majesty wanted to replace the battalion that I have in town for police and the large numbers of baggage; to protect the wounded etc; this position cannot, it seems to me, remain completely devoid of troops.

Charleroi, June 16, 1815

Lieutenant General, Aide-de-Camp of the Emperor, Commander in Chief of the 6th Corps

Lobau

P.S. Colonel Jeanin reports that Colonel Tancarville, Chief of Staff of Cte of Valmy, said to him that the emissaries who came to Cte D'Erlon reportedly said to him that the enemy was marching today from Mons to Charleroi. Your Majesty will surely be able to fully appreciate the value of this information.

D'Erlon to Soult between 1 pm and 3 pm

Houssaye, page 117 and Footnote 41 on page 362

There [Gosselies] d'Erlon halted his troops, until the return of a strong reconnaissance which he had sent from Jumet, in the direction of Chapelle-Herlaymont. A false account given by the peasants led him to believe he would find a corps of Anglo-Belgians threatening his left at the latter village.[41] ... Be this as it may, it was three o'clock when he started on his march again.

41. Letter from d'Erlon to Soult, Gosselies, 16th June (without any reference to time, between one and three o'clock), (General G.'s papers).

Soult to Ney at 2 pm

Before Fleurus, June 16, at two o'clock.

Marshal, the Emperor desires me to inform you that the enemy has assembled a corps of troops between Sombreffe and Bry, and at 2:30 pm Marshal Grouchy will attack the enemy position with the 3rd and 4th Corps. The intention of His Majesty is that you attack what is before you, and that after having vigorously pressed them, you will turn back on us so as to envelop the enemy corps that I just mentioned. If this corps is overthrown first, then His Majesty will manoeuver in your direction, to hasten your operations as well.

Inform the Emperor of your dispositions and what occurs on your front.

Soult to Ney at 3:15 pm

Before Fleurus, on the 16th at 3:15 and 3:30

Marshal, I wrote to you, an hour ago, that the Emperor would attack the enemy at 2:30 pm, in the position that it took between the village of St. Amand and Bry, at this moment the action is in full swing. H.M. charged me to say to you that you must maneuver immediately, so as to envelop the enemy line and strike his rear. This army is lost if you act aggressively. The fate of France is in your hands; thus do not hesitate a moment to carry out the movement that the Emperor orders and is aimed at the heights of St. Amand and Bry to contribute to a possible decisive victory, the enemy has been caught in the act, at the moment when they look to join the English.

Major General, Duke of Dalmatia

Soult to Ney at 3:30 pm

(Duplicate of 3:15 order)

Soult to Lobau to 3:30 pm

Before Fleurus, June 16, at three thirty.

Am Count Lobau,
Order Count Lobau to go to Fleurus; he will leave a battalion at Charleroi to maintain the place and to protect the park.

Ney to Soult at 10 pm

Frasnes, June 16, 1815, 10 o'clock in the evening.

Marshal! The attack that I directed against the English on the Quatre Bras position was with the greatest vigor; a misunderstanding on the part of Count d'Erlon deprived me of a beautiful victory because at the time General Reille's 5th and 9th Division had all overwhelmed everything in the front of them, the 1st Corps marched to Saint Amand, to support the left of H.M., but what was fatal, was that this corps then counter-marched to join me, thus it could not be useful to anyone. The Division of Prince Jerome fought with great valor. His Royal Highness was slightly wounded. There was therefore only three infantry divisions and a brigade of Cuirassiers and General Piré's Cavalry actually engaged. The Count of Valmy made a beautiful charge. Everyone fulfilled their duty except the 1st Corps. The enemy lost many soldiers; we took some cannons and a flag. We have lost only about two thousand men killed and four thousand wounded. I asked for reports from Générals Reille and d'Erlon and I will send them to Your Excellency.

Receive, Marshal, the assurances of my highest regards,

Marshal Prince de la Moskowa,

Ney

June 17, 1815

Soult to Ney at 8 am

Marshal,

General Flahaut, who arrived at this moment, discloses that you are uncertain about yesterday's results. I believe however you were already acquainted with the victory that the Emperor has won. The Prussian army was routed. General Pajol is in pursuit on the Namur and Liege roads. We have already taken several thousand prisoners and 30 cannons. Our troops performed well. A charge of six battalions of the Guard and some Service Squadrons, and General Delort's Division, pierced the enemy line, brought the greatest disorder in its ranks, and cleared the position.

The Emperor travels to the Bry Mill where the main road leads from Namur to Quatre Bras, it is therefore possible that the English Army can take action to engage you; if that were so, the Emperor would go directly by the Quatre Bras route, while you would attack in the front with your divisions which must be assembled by now, and this army in an instant would be destroyed; thus, inform H.M. of the exact position of the divisions and all that occurs in front of you.

The Emperor has seen with regret that you did not succeed yesterday: the divisions acted separately; so you have experienced losses. If Counts d'Erlon and Reille's Corps had been together, not a man of the English corps that attacked you would have survived; if Count d'Erlon had carried out the movement on Saint-Amand that the Emperor ordered, the Prussian Army would be completely destroyed and we would have taken perhaps 30 thousand prisoners. General Vandamme and Gérard's Corps and the Imperial Guard were always together; we expose ourselves to reverses when detachments are made.

The Emperor hopes and wishes that your seven infantry divisions and the cavalry are together, and that they do not occupy more than a league of ground, to have them well in hand and ready to employ them as needed.

The intention of H.M. is that you take a position at Quatre Bras, as you were ordered; but if it is not possible, immediately report the details and the Emperor will go there as I have told you; if on the contrary there is only a rear-guard, attack it and take the position.

Today it is necessary to finish this operation and to fill the munitions, to rally the isolated soldiers, and to return the detachments. Give orders accordingly and assure that all casualties are bandaged and directed to the rear. Some have complained that the ambulances have not performed as they should.

The famous partisan Lützow, who was taken prisoner, said that the Prussian Army was lost and that Blücher had exposed the Prussian Monarchy for a second time.

Soult to Davout before 10 am

Fleurus, June 17.

From the battlefield of Ligny, I announced yesterday to H.I.H. Prince Joseph, the noteworthy victory that the Emperor had won: I returned with H.M. at 11 o'clock in the evening, and the night should have been spent looking after the wounded, because the ambulances are so badly organized and are lacking so much either of personnel or other essential items that we cannot count on them.

The Emperor rides on horseback to oversee the success of the Battle of Ligny; we fought relentlessly and with the greatest enthusiasm by the troops; we were one against three. At eight o'clock in the evening the Emperor marched with his Guard; six battalions of the Old Guard, Dragoons, and Grenadiers à Cheval, and the Cuirassiers of Général Delort debouched by Ligny, and executed a charge that divided the enemy line. Lord Wellington and Blücher could hardly save themselves, it had a theatrical effect, in a moment fire ceased and the enemy was routed in all directions. We have already taken several thousand prisoners and 40 guns. The 6th and the 1st Corps did not contribute, Count d'Erlon had false directions; because if he had carried out the movement order that the Emperor had prescribed the Prussian army was entirely lost.

The left wing fought against the English Army and took guns and flags.

Tomorrow night I will give you more details, because at every moment prisoners are announced.

Our losses do not appear enormous, since without knowing it precisely, I do not estimate it at more than 3000 men; but it is time to send us troops and increase the levy of 200,000 men. I have just given orders to ten battalions of the 16th Military Division to assemble on the field at Avesnes, to be used to escort the prisoners, or to place them.

I ask you to give orders to speed their assembly, and to prescribe that we choose those who are the most complete and in the best condition, it will be necessary to put in command Generals and senior officers there. If these are encouraged, all will want to march, already

Appendix XII – Translated Select Correspondence

the Emperor received several requests for this; we must gain from this enthusiasm. In France, it is always the moment that we must choose; furthermore this increase of military means will prevail and will ensure new success.

P.S. The army has formed on the main road from Namur to Brussels where the Emperor travels at this moment. The last report from General Pajol is marked from Mazi, and the left in the direction of the Trois Bras.

Soult to Ney, Noon

To Marshal Prince de la Moskowa
4th Corps d'Armée, at Gosselies

In front of Ligny, the 17th at midday.

Marshal, the Emperor has just taken a position in front of Marbais, with a corps of Infantry and the Imperial Guard; H.M. desires me to tell you that his intention is that you attack the enemies at Quatre Bras, to drive them out of their position, and that the corps that is in Marbais will assist your operations; H.M. will go to Marbais, and waits impatiently for your reports.

Marshal of the Empire, Major General,
Duke of Dalmatia

Napoleon to Ney, after 1pm

Prince de la Moskowa,

I am surprised at your long delay in carrying out my orders. There is no more time to lose; attack with the greatest impetuosity all that is before you. The fate of the country is in your hands.

1 o'clock after noon

Napoleon

Napoleon to Grouchy after 11:30 am and before 2 pm

Ligny, June 17, 1815, 11:30 am.
Dictated to Bertrand, in the absence of Soult.

Order General Domon to go to Marbais immediately. He will be there under the orders of Count Lobau. He will direct detachments to the Quatre Bras, Brussels road, and will assemble by the left with the troops of the 1st and 2nd Corps, that this morning occupy the village of Frasne and who must also go to the Quatre Bras where the English are supposed to be.
Order General Milhaud to go to Marbais. He will have before him General Domon's Light Cavalry. He will find Count Lobau's Corps and Guard there.

Napoleon to Grouchy after 11:45 am and before 2 pm

Ligny, June 17, 1815, 11:45.
Dictated to Bertrand, in the absence of Soult.

Go to Gembloux with General Pajol's Cavalry Corps, the Light Cavalry of the 4th Corps, General Exelmans' Cavalry Corps, General Teste's Division , because it is detached from its Army Corps, pay particular attention to it, and the 3rd and 4th Infantry Corps. You will scout in the direction of Namur and Maestricht, and you will pursue the enemy. Scout his march and inform me of his movements so that I can perceive what he will do.
I bring my headquarters to the Quatre Bras where the English remained this morning. Our communication will therefore be direct, along the paved Namur road. If the enemy has evacuated Namur, write to the commanding General of the 2nd Military Division at Charlemont to occupy Namur with some National Guard battalions and a battery of artillery which he will form in Charlemont. He will give this command to a Maréchal de Camp.

Appendix XII – Translated Select Correspondence

It is important to perceive what the enemy wants to do. Either it separates from the English, or they want to assemble again to cover Brussels and Liege, while tempting fate with a new battle. In any case, always keep your two Infantry Corps gathered together in one league of ground and every evening occupy a good military position, having several debouches for retreat. Position detachments of intermediary cavalry to communicate with the headquarters.

D'Erlon to Soult after 8 pm

At bivouac, before Frasne, June 17, 1815 (morning).

Marshal, according to the orders from His Majesty, the 1ˢᵗ Corps holds the first line on both sides of the Brussels road; the 1ˢᵗ Cavalry Division flanks the Corps and covers their front.

I have the honor to inform Your Excellency, that the 1ˢᵗ Cavalry Division, made several successful charges and they captured some wagons and some prisoners.

Deign to accept the homage of my respect,
Lieutenant General, Commander in Chief of the 1ˢᵗ Corps,
Count d'Erlon

Grouchy to Napoleon at 10 pm

Gembloux, June 17, 1815, at ten o'clock in the evening

SIRE,

I have the honor to report to you that I occupy Gembloux where the Fourth Corps begins to arrive; the Third is in front of this town, and part of my Cavalry is in Sauvenière.
The Prussian Corps, about thirty thousand men in strength, who were still here this morning, carried out his retreat movement toward Sauvenières. According to various reports, he appears to have arrived at Sauvenières, part of the Prussian Army would be divided: a column would have marched to Pervès-le-Marchez,

another would have taken the Wavre road, while passing by Sart-à-Walhain. Perhaps we can infer that some Prussian Corps are going to join Wellington, and that others would be withdrawing to Liege.

A Prussian column with artillery, has taken, in leaving the battlefield of Fleurus, the Namur road. The enemy abandoned for us at Gembloux, a park of four hundred cattle, magazines, and baggage.

General Exelmans has ordered to drive, this evening, six squadrons on Sart-à-Walhain, and three squadrons on Perwez.

If I learn by reports that, I hope, will reach me during the night, that strong Prussian forces march on Wavre, I will follow them in this direction and will attack them as soon as I meet them.

Generals Thielmann and Borstell are part of the army that Your Majesty fought yesterday: they were still here this morning, admitting that twenty thousand of their men had been casualties. They requested, while leaving, the distances of Wavre and Perwez.

Blücher was slightly wounded in the arm, on the 16th, which did not prevent him from continuing to command, after being bandaged. He did not continue to Gembloux.

I am, etc, etc.

Marshal Grouchy

Napoleon to Army around 10 pm

[Order by which the Emperor indicates to everyone their position for battle].

Napoleon to Grouchy at 10 pm

Napoleon's Memoirs, Page 517-518

At ten o'clock in the evening, I sent an officer to Marshal Grouchy whom I supposed to be at Wavres, in order to let him know that there would be a big battle next day; that the Anglo-Dutch army was in position in front of the forest of Soignes, with its left resting on the village of La Haye; that I ordered him to detach from his camp at Wavres a division of 7,000 men of all arms and sixteen guns, before daylight, to go to Saint-Lambert to join the right of the Grand Army and co-operate with it; that as soon as he was satisfied that Marshal Blücher had evacuated Wavres, whether to continue his retreat on Brussels or to go in any other direction, he was to march with the bulk of his troops to support the detachment which he had sent to Saint-Lambert.

June 18, 1815

Grouchy to Napoleon at 3 am

Gembloux, June 18, 1815, three o'clock in the morning.

Sire,

All my reports and information confirm that the enemy withdraws to Brussels, concentrating there, to give battle there, after having joined Wellington.

Namur is evacuated, indicated to me by General Pajol.

Blücher's First and Second Army Corps appear to direct, the First on Corbais, and the Second on Chaumont. They must have left yesterday evening, at 8:30, from Toürrines and marched through the night; fortunately it was so bad, that they would not be able to go very far.

I leave at this time for Sart-à-Valliain, from where I will march to Corbaix and Wavres. I will have the honor to write to you from one and another of these towns.

I am, etc, etc.

Marshal Grouchy

P. S. According to your orders, I write to the General Commandant of the 2nd Militaire in Charlemont, to occupy Namur with several National Guard Battaillons and some artillery batteries that he will form in Charlemont.

> *I leave twenty-five horses here to ensure correspondence with Your Majesty.*
>
> *The Infantry and Cavalry Corps that I have with me have only one provisionment and a half, so that in the event of a major event it seems necessary to me that Your Majesty will want to draw on the munitions reserves, or indicate to me the places where artillery could go to find supplies.*

Napoleon to Grouchy at 4 am

Napoleon's Memoirs, page 518

> *A second officer was sent to him at four o'clock in the morning to repeat the order which had been sent to him at ten in the evening.*

Soult to Army at 5 am

> *The emperor orders that the army be positioned to attack the enemy at 9 o'clock in the morning; General Officers commanding Army Corps will rally their troops, will have their arms ready, and will allow the soldiers to make soup; they will also have the soldiers eat so that at precisely 9 am everyone is ready with artillery and ambulances, in the battle position that the Emperor indicated by his overnight order.*
>
> *The Lieutenant-Generals, commanding both the Infantry and Cavalry Corps will immediately send officers to the Major General to indicate their position and bring back future orders.*
>
> *Given at the Imperial Headquarters, June 18, 1815.*
> *Marshal of the Empire, Major General,*
> *Duke of Dalmatia*

Soult to Grouchy at 10 am

> *By the Adjutant Count Lenowich.*

Appendix XII – Translated Select Correspondence

In front of the Ferme du Caillou, on June 18, at 10 o'clock in the morning.

Marshal, the Emperor received your last report dated from Gembloux, you spoke to His Majesty only about the two Prussian columns that went to Sauvenières *and* Sart à Walhain. *However reports say that a third column which was rather strong went to* Géry *and* Gentinnes *directing to* Wavre.

The Emperor charges me to advise you that at this moment His Majesty will attack the English army which has taken a position at Waterloo close to the Forest of Soignes; thus His Majesty wishes that you direct your movements on Wavre, *in order to bring you closer to us, to report operations, and to maintain communications about the Prussian Army Corps pushing before you those which took this direction, and which have stopped at* Wavre *where you must arrive as soon as possible.*

You will follow the enemy columns which are on your right with some light troops in order to observe their movements and to pick up their stragglers.

Immediately inform me of your arrangements and your march as well as the news that you have about the enemy, and do not neglect to maintain your communications with us; the Emperor wishes to have your news rather often.

Soult to Ney at 11 am

Once the entire army is arranged for battle, at about 1 o'clock in the afternoon, the Emperor will give the order to Marshal Ney, and the attack will begin to capture the village of Mont Saint Jean at the intersection of the roads. For this result, the 12-pdr. batteries of the 2nd Corps and those of the 6th will mass with those of the 1st Corps. These 24 guns will fire on the troops at Mont Saint Jean, and Count d'Erlon will begin the attack by marching his left division forward and supporting it, according to the circumstances, with the 1st Corps Divisions.

The 2nd Corps will advance to the extent to maintain progress with Count d'Erlon.

The company of Engineers belonging to the 1st Corps will prepare to barricade at once in Mont Saint Jean.

(Written in pencil from Maréchal Ney.)

Added by M. Maréchal Ney:

Count d'Erlon understands that it is by the left that the attack will begin, instead of the right.
Communicate this new provision with General in Chief Reille.
(On the back) Orders dictated by the Emperor, on the battle field of Mount-St-Jean, on the 18th, around eleven o'clock in the morning, and written by Marshal Duke of Dalmatia, Major General.
Paris, June 21, 1815.

Maréchal Prince de LA MOSKOWA,
Peer of France, NEY

Grouchy to Napoleon at 11 am

Sart-à-Valhain, on June 18, 1815 at eleven o'clock in the morning

Sire,

I do not lose a moment in transmitting the information that I collect here; I regard it as authentic, and so that Your Majesty receives it as quickly as possible, I dispatch it by Major Lafresnaye, your former page; he has a good mount and is a good rider.
Blücher's First, Second, and Third Corps march in the direction of Brussels. Two of these corps marched through Sart-à-Walhain; or at a short distance to the right; they filed in three columns, marching at about the same level. Their passage lasted six hours, without interruption. Of those who marched within view of Sart-à-Valhain can be estimated at 30,000 men at least, and had in materiel, 50 to 60 cannons.
A corps from Liege joined with those who fought in Fleurus (Enclosed is a requisition which proves it.) Some of the Prussians

Appendix XII – Translated Select Correspondence

that are in front of me are directed towards the Chyse plain, located near the Louvain road, and two and half leagues from this city.

It seems that they intend to mass there or lead the troops into battle to their pursuers, or ultimately to unite with Wellington, a plan announced by their officers, who, in their ordinary conversation, claim to have only left the battle field, on the 16th, in order to ensure their joining the English Army, at Brussels.

This evening, I am going to be massed in Wavre, and to be between Wellington, whom I suppose is in retreat before Your Majesty, and the Prussian army.

I need final instructions for what Your Majesty orders that I do. The country between Wavre and the plain of Chyse is difficult, cut, and somewhat marshy.

By the Vilvorde road, I will easily arrive at Brussels before all who will stop in Chyse, if the Prussians halt there.

Deign, Lord, to transmit your orders to me; I can then receive them before beginning my movement tomorrow.

I am, etc, etc.
Marshal Grouchy

Ney to Lobau

http://www.russborough.com/omnium_g/manuscripts/ney-waterloo-dispatch.html

The English are amassed on Mont-Saint-Jean, that is in front of the forest of Soignes. If the Prussians retreat behind the forest of Soignes you must send a thousand cavalry behind them, and come with your troops to join us. If one finds they intend to come in front of the forest at Mont Saint-Jean, then make a screen and bar the route. Ney

Soult to Grouchy around 1 pm

Marshal, you wrote to the emperor this morning at 3 am that you will march on Sart Walhain, therefore your plan was to march to Corbaix and Wavre. This movement is consistent with the provisions that

His Majesty has provided to you. However the Emperor commands me to tell you that you should always maneuver in our direction and look to draw the army closer, so that you can contact us before any Corps can come between us. I do not tell you direction, it is for you to see where we are, to adjust yourself accordingly and link to our communications and as to always be capable of falling on some enemy troops who would seek to disturb our right, and crush them.

18 this afternoon at 1 pm

Signed Marshal Duke of Dalmatia

P.S. A letter that has just been intercepted reveals that General Bülow is about to attack our right flank; we believe we see this corps on the heights of St.Lambert. Thus, do not lose one instant to approach and join us, and to crush Bülow, whom you will catch in the very act.

Soult to Davout at 2:30 pm

Bivouac before Caillou, June 18, at 1:15

Marshal, we are fighting at this moment, the enemy is in position in front of the Forest of Soignes, his center at Waterloo.

We will use much ammunition; we have already used a great quantity at the battle of Ligny. The Emperor orders that you direct ammunition to the northern towns, on Avesnes, in an accelerated way. These munitions will be escorted from Avesnes by the battalions that we ordered to establish there to escort prisoners; the direction that you must have them take is from Beaumont on Charleroi to join the army.

You will sense, M. Marshal, how important it is that the Emperor's orders are carried out promptly. I ask you to inform me of those that you will give in this respect.

P.S. It is two thirty, the cannonade is engaged on the entire line; the English are at the center, the Dutchmen and Belgians at the right of the German troops, the Prussians are at the left, the battle is general; 400 firing muzzles thunder at this moment.

Soult to Girard in evening

June 18, in front of Caillou

Order to Maréchal-de-Camp Remond to take command of Girard's Division and march to Quatre Bras to take a position there.

BIBLIOGRAPHY

ARCHIVES, EYEWITNESS ACCOUNTS, AND HISTORIES WRITTEN BY COMBATTANTS

Baudus , M.É.G.(de) *Etudes sur Napoléon*. Debécourt, 1841. <https://books.google.com/books?id=0LhBAAAAcAAJ>.

Blocqueville, L.A.E. (de)*Le maréchal Davout, prince d'Eckmühl: Un dernier commandement, l'exil et la mort*. Didier et cie, 1880. <http://books.google.com/books?id=Mn1KAAAAYAAJ>.

Bonaparte, Napoleon. *Correspondance de Napoléon Ier*, 28: publiée par ordre de l'empereur Napoléon III. Plon, 1869. <http://books.google.com/books?id=7BZi24-JtyQC>.

Castlereagh, V.R.S. and C.W.V. Londonderry. *Memoirs and correspondence of Viscount Castlereagh, second Marquess of Londonderry*. H. Colburn, 1853. <http://books.google.com/books?id=OysMAAAAYAAJ>.

Chuquet, A. *Ordres et apostilles de Napoléon: 1799 - 1815*. Champion, 1911. <http://books.google.com/books?id=wGlitwAACAAJ>.

Chuquet, Arthur. *Inédits napoléoniens*. Ed. E. de Boccard. Vol. 2. Paris : Fontemoing : [puis] E. de Boccard, 1914-1919. <http://gallica.bnf.fr/ark:/12148/bpt6k2015354>.

—. *Inédits napoléoniens*. Ed. E. de Boccard. Vol. 1. Paris : Fontemoing : [puis] E. de Boccard, 1913. <http://gallica.bnf.fr/ark:/12148/bpt6k201534r>.

Clausewitz, C. (von), *La campagne de 1815 [i.e. dix-huit cent quinze] en France*. R. Chapelot, 1900. <https://books.google.com/books?id=rhcbAAAAYAAJ>.

Clouet, A.L.A. *Quelques notes sur la conduite de m. le comte de Bourmont en 1815*. G. A. Dentu, 1832. <https://books.google.com/books?id=uh5BAAAAYAAJ>.

Coignet, Jean-Roch. *The Narrative of Captain Coignet.* Ed. Lorédan Larchey. Thomas Y. Crowell \& Co., 1890. <https://archive.org/details/narrativeofcaptaoocoig>.

Damitz, K.(von) and C.W. Grolman (von). *Geschichte des Feldzugs von 1815 in den Niederlanden und Frankreich: Als Beitrag zur Kriegsgeschichte der neueren Kriege: Mit drei illuminirten Plänen.* Mittler, 1837. <https://books.google.com/books?id=s2BDAAAAcAAJ>.

Davout, L.N. and C. de Mazade-Percin. *Correspondance, ses commandements, son ministère, 1801-1815.* E. Plon, Nourrit, 1885. <http://books.google.com/books?id=sik3AQAAMAAJ>.

De Chair, S. *Napoleon's Memoirs.* Faber \& Faber, 1948. <https://books.google.com/books?id=qt8onQEACAAJ>.

Despots de Zenowicz (de), G. *Waterloo, déposition sur les quatre journées de la campagne de 1815, par G. Zenowicz,...* Ledoyen, 1848. <http://books.google.com/books?id=KUhCygAACAAJ>.

Dupuy, Victor (Commandant). *Souvenirs militaires de Victor Dupuy, chef d'escadrons de Hussards : 1794-1816 / publiés, avec une préface, par le général Thoumas.* 1892. <http://gallica.bnf.fr/ark:/12148/bpt6k6365518j>.

Gamot, M. *Réfutation, en ce qui concerne le maréchal Ney, de l'ouvrage ayant pour titre, 'Campagne de 1815 ... Par le général Gourgaud'.* 1818. <https://books.google.com/books?id=aiVcAAAAQAAJ>.

Gérard, É.M. *Quelques Documens sur la Bataille de Waterloo, propres à éclairer la question portée devant le public par ... le Marquis de Grouchy.* 1829. <https://books.google.com/books?id=erS9mgEACAAJ>.

Grouchy, E. and G. (de). *Mémoires du maréchal de Grouchy.* E. Dentu, 1874. <https://books.google.com/books?id=zQlBAAAAYAAJ>.

Grouchy, E. (de) *Fragments historiques relatifs a la campagne de 1815 et a la bataille de Waterloo: lettre a messieurs Méry et Barthélemy.* Firmin Didot, 1829. <https://books.google.com/books?id=pBYbAAAAYAAJ>.

—. *Observations sur la relation de la campagne de 1815, publiée par le général Gourgaud: et réfutation de quelques-unes des assertions d'autres écrits relatifs à la bataille de Waterloo.* Mogimel, 1819. <https://books.google.com/books?id=MGVIAAAAYAAJ>.

—. *Publications de Mm. les généraux Grouchy et Gérard sur la campagne de Waterloo.* publisher not identified, 1830. <https://books.google.com/books?id=bmShuAAACAAJ>.

—. *Relation succincte de la campagne de 1815 en Belgique: et notamment des mouvements, combats et opérations des troupes sous les ordres du Maréchal Grouchy, suivie de l'exposition de quelquesunes des causes de la perte de la bataille de Waterloo*. E. B. Delanchy, 1843. <http://books.google.com/books?id=aowUAAAAYAAJ>.

Gourgaud, G. *Campagne de 1815: opérations militaires en France et en Belgique.* 1818. <https://books.google.com/books?id=M9aoOB8PupUC>.

—. *La campagne de 1815: ou Relation des opérations militaires qui ont eu lieu en France et en Belgique, pendant les cent jours*. Imprimé pour J. Ridgway, 1818. <http://books.google.com/books?id=mHRJAAAAMAAJ>.

Hulot, E. "Un Chapitre Inédit sur Ligny-Waterloo-Paris." *Le Spectateur Militaire* 24 (1884). <http://babel.hathitrust.org/cgi/pt?view=plaintext;size=100;id=hvd.hw27gs;page=root;seq=127;num=121>.

Himly, P. "Observations Sur La Bataille de Waterloo (1815)." *Journal des sciences militaires* (1840): 465-486. <http://books.google.com/books?id=BrKroPY8UqoC>.

Janin, E.F. *Campagne de Waterloo: Ou Remarques Critiques Et Historiques (1820)*. Kessinger Publishing, 2010. <https://books.google.com/books?id=TmpdewAACAAJ>.

Las Cases, E.A.D. (de) *Memorial de Sainte Hélène: Journal of the Private Life & Conversations of the Emperor Napoleon at Saint Helena*. Bliss, 1823. <https://books.google.com/books?id=nGhIAAAAYAAJ>.

Levavasseur, O.R.L. *Souvenirs militaires d'Octave Levavasseur: officer d'artillerie, aide de camp du Maréchal Ney (1802-1815) : publiés par le commandant Beslay, son arrière-petit-fils*. Plon-Nourrit, 1914. <https://books.google.com/books?id=H5XPZaSXwWcC>.

MacMahon, E.P.M(de). and G. de Miribel. *Mémoires du maréchal de Mac Mahon: duc de Magenta. Souvenirs d'Algérie*. Plon, 1932. <https://books.google.com/books?id=bHkcAAAAMAAJ>.

Malet, M. Albert. *Louis XVIII et les Cent-Joursà Gand: recueil de documents inédits*. Ed. Romberg. Picard, 1902. <http://books.google.com/books?id=Facf9oBJHqYC>.

Marbot, Marcellin de. *Mémoires du général baron de Marbot. Polotsk-La Bérésina-Leipzig-Waterloo*. Plon-Nourrit (Paris), 1891. <http://gallica.bnf.fr/ark:/12148/bpt6k202274g.r=.langEN>.

Mauduit, Hippolyte de. *Histoire des derniers jours de la Grande armée.* 2. Vol. 1. Dion-Lambert (Paris), 1854. <http://gallica.bnf.fr/ark:/12148/bpt6k6527927w>.

—. *Histoire des derniers jours de la Grande armée.* 2. Vol. 2. Dion-Lambert (Paris), 1854. <http://gallica.bnf.fr/ark:/12148/bpt6k8529086/f9.image>.

Moniteur universel (le). Houdin, 1815. <http://books.google.com/books?id=DTxHAAAAcAAJ>.

Ney, Michel Louis Felix. *Documents inédits sur la campagne de 1815.* 1840. <http://books.google.com/books?id=noQFAAAAIAAJ>.

O'Meara, B.E. *Napoleon at St. Helena.* Scribner and Welford, 1889. <http://books.google.com/books?id=sHAuAAAAMAAJ>.

PhilologicalSociety. *The European Magazine, and London Review. Philological Society of London, 1815.* <http://books.google.com/books?id=sygoAAAAYAAJ>.

Picard, E., et al. *Unpublished Correspondence of Napoleon I: Preserved in the War Archives.* Duffield, 1913. <http://books.google.com/books?id=Fes-AAAAYAAJ>.

Pontécoulant, G. *Souvenirs militaires: Napoléon à Waterloo; ou, Précis rectifié de la campagne de 1815, avec des documents nouveaux et des pièces inédites.* J. Dumaine, 1866. <http://books.google.com/books?id=MU1BAAAAIAAJ>.

Rumigny, Marie Thédore de Gueilly. *Souvenirs du Général Comte de Rumigny.* 4th. Émile-Paul frères, n.d. <https://archive.org/details/souvenirsdugnoorumi>.

Sarrans, B. *Lafayette, Louis-Philippe, and the revolution of 1830; or, History of the events and men of July.* Tr. 1832. <http://books.google.com/books?id=4ibWlqU_N4EC>.

Siborne, H.T. *Waterloo Letters: A Selection from Original and Hitherto Unpublished Letters Bearing on the Operations of the 16th, 17th, and 18th June, 1815, by Officers who Served in the Campaign.* Cassell & Company, 1891. <https://books.google.com/books?id=zVMwAQAAMAAJ>.

Siborne, W. *The Waterloo Campaign, 1815.* A. Constable, 1900. <https://books.google.com/books?id=-8hCAAAAYAAJ>.

Rilliet de Constant . "Les Cent Jours en Belgique." Bibliothèque universelle de Genève. Nouvelle série 35 (1857): 352-354. <http://books.google.com/books?id=tZ9CAAAAcAAJ>.

Saint-Chamans, A.A.R. (de)*Mémoires du général Cte de Saint-Chamans: ancien aide de camp du Maréchal Soult, 1802-1832* ... E. Plon, Nourrit et cie, 1896. <http://books.google.com/books?id=ZVVBAAAAIAAJ>.

MILITARY AND POLITICAL HISTORY

Austin, P.B. *1815: The Return of Napoleon*. Greenhill Books, 2002. <http://books.google.com/books?id=4wYiAQAAIAAJ>.

Becke, A.F. *Napoleon and Waterloo,...: By Captain A. F. Becke,...* Kegan Paul, Trench, Trübner and Company, 1914. <http://books.google.com/books?id=gmwwQwAACAAJ>.

Bernard, H. *La Campagne de 1815 en Belgique, ou la Faillite de la liaison et des transmissions*. [With maps.]. 1954. <https://books.google.com/books?id=lkH6MgEACAAJ>.

Bonnal de Ganges, E. *Les royalistes contre l'armée (1815-1820): d'après les archives du ministère de la guerre*. R. Chapelot et cie, 1906. <http://books.google.com/books?id=qBtBAAAAYAAJ>.

Bustelli, G. *L'Enigma di Ligny e di Waterloo (15-18 Giugno 1815)*. Vignuzzi, 1896. <https://books.google.com/books?id=pJ8UAAAAYAAJ>.

Callatay Phillipe (de); English Translation John Hussey, Philippe. "The Concentration of the French Army for the Campaign of June 1815." First Empire 102 (2008).

Chalfont, Artur Gwynne Jones, Lord, editor, *Waterloo : Battle of Three Armies*, London: Sidgwick and Jackson, 1979, < https://books.google.com/books?id=qNJnAAAAMAAJ&dq>

Charras, J.B.A. *Histoire de la campagne de 1815: Waterloo*. Lacroix, Verboeckhoven etce, 1863. <http://books.google.com/books?id=oBUgAAAAMAAJ>.

Chesney, C.C. *Waterloo Lectures: A Study of the Campaign of 1815*. Longmans, Green, 1907. <https://books.google.com/books?id=-NZCAAAAYAAJ>.

Cole, H. *Fouché: the Unprincipled Patriot*. McCall Publishing Company, 1971. <http://books.google.com/books?id=1hqfAAAAMAAJ>.

Cronin, V. *Napoleon*. HarperCollins, 2009. <http://books.google.com/books?id=jQOq8Cb6h8wC>.

Cubberly, R.E. and University of Wisconsin-Madison. Dept. of History. *The role of Fouché during the Hundred Days*. State Historical Society of

Wisconsin for the Dept. of History, University of Wisconsin, 1969. <https://books.google.com/books?id=LpwfAAAAMAAJ>.

Cyr, P. *Waterloo : origines et enjeux*. Editions L'Harmattan, 2011. <https://books.google.com/books?id=CMIUHlzUXJkC>.

Dunn-Pattison, R. P. *Napoleon's Marshals*. Methuen & Co., London, 1909. <http://www.gutenberg.org/files/34400/34400-h/34400-h.htm>.

Elting, J.R. *Swords Around a Throne*. Da Capo Press, Incorporated, 2009. <http://books.google.com/books?id=Xv5v4qDln_UC>.

Franklin, J. and G. Embleton. *Waterloo 1815 (1): Quatre Bras*. Osprey Publishing, Limited, 2014. <https://books.google.com/books?id=voSOBAAAQBAJ>.

—. *Waterloo 1815 (2): Ligny*. Osprey Publishing Limited, 2015. <https://books.google.com/books?id=YHSWBQAAQBAJ>.

Goldstein, R.J. *Censorship of Political Caricature in Nineteenth-century France*. Kent State University Press, 1989. <http://books.google.com/books?id=vIA1F2QmoWgC>.

Green, Jonathon and N.J. Karolides. *Encyclopedia of Censorship*. Facts On File, Incorporated, 2009. <http://books.google.com/books?id=bunHURgi7FcC>.

Hall, J.R. *The Bourbon Restoration*. A. Rivers, Limited, 1909. <http://books.google.com/books?id=Aj1BAAAAIAAJ>.

Hamilton-Williams, D. *The fall of Napoleon: the final betrayal*. Wiley, 1994. <https://books.google.com/books?id=OIYOAQAAMAAJ>.

—. *Waterloo: New Perspectives: The Great Battle Reappraised*. Wiley, 1996. <https://books.google.com/books?id=Ar8NAAAACAAJ>.

Hayman, P. *Soult: Napoleon's Maligned Marshal*. Arms and Armour, 1990. <http://books.google.com/books?id=OYpiQgAACAAJ>.

Hofschröer, P. *1815, the Waterloo Campaign : the German Victory: From Waterloo to the Fall of Napoleon*. Greenhill Books, 1999. <https://books.google.com/books?id=C46fAAAAMAAJ>.

—. *1815, the Waterloo Campaign: Wellington and his German allies and the battles of Ligny and Quatre Bras*. Greenhill Books, 1998. <https://books.google.com/books?id=qs9nAAAAMAAJ>.

Houssaye, H. *1815 : La Premiére Restauration*. Perrin, 1892. <http://books.google.com/books?id=9ZMXQHG5tooC>,

- *Waterloo*, Perrin, 1899.

Houssaye, H., A.E. Mann and A.E. Smith. *1815, Waterloo*. Black, 1900. <http://books.google.com/books?id=xWBAAAAAYAAJ>.

Lachouque, H. and A.S.K. Brown. *The Anatomy of Glory: Napoleon and His Guard : a Study in Leadership*. Greenhill Books, 1997. <https://books.google.com/books?id=f8avQgAACAAJ>.

Lachouque, H. *Le secret de Waterloo*. Amiot-Dumont, 1952. <https://books.google.com/books?id=mFCmQAAACAAJ>.

Lamartine, A.(de), *The History of the Restoration of Monarchy in France...* George Bell \& sons, 1882. <http://books.google.com/books?id=hAVeaCHfr_AC>.

Largeaud, J.M. *Napoléon et Waterloo: la défaite glorieuse de 1815 à nos jours*. Boutique de l'histoire, 2006. <https://books.google.com/books?id=4gJoAAAAMAAJ>.

Le Gallo, Emile. *Les Cent-Jours : essai sur l'histoire intérieure de la France depuis le retour de l'île d'Elbe jusqu'à la nouvelle de Waterloo*. Ed. F. Alcan. Librairie Félis Alcan, 1923. <http://gallica.bnf.fr/ark:/12148/bpt6k5427468n>.

Lentz, T. *Waterloo, 1815*. EDI8, n.d. <https://books.google.com/books?id=UbwrBgAAQBAJ>.

Lettow-Vorbeck, O (von), *Napoleons Untergang 1815*. E. S. Mittler und Sohn, 1904. <http://books.google.com/books?id=D_Y8AQAAIAAJ>.

Logie, J. *Waterloo: la campagne de 1815*. Racine, 2003. <https://books.google.com/books?id=MlHPhDReBX4C>.

Margerit, R. *Waterloo: 18 juin 1815*. Gallimard, 1964. <https://books.google.com/books?id=CeAZnQEACAAJ>.

Ollech, K.R. (von) *Geschichte des Feldzuges von 1815 nach archivalischen Quellen*. E. S. Mittler und Sohn, 1876. <https://books.google.com/books?id=TyoAAAAAQAAJ>.

Piérart, Z.J. *Le drame de Waterloo: grande restitution historique : rectifications, justifications, réfutations, souvenirs, éclaircissements, rapprochements, enseignements, faits inédits et jugements nouveaux sur la campagne de 1815*. Bureau de la revue spiritualiste, 1868. <https://books.google.com/books?id=fRpCAAAAcAAJ>.

Pingaud, L. *Bourmont et Fouché*. Impr. P. Brodard, 1912. <http://books.google.com/books?id=pSQpnQEACAAJ>.

Pollio, A. and F.L.A. Goiran. *Waterloo (1815): avec de nouveaux documents*. H. Charles-Lavauzelle, 1908. <http://books.google.com/books?id=mgJyAAAAIAAJ>.

Polowetzky, M. *A Bond Never Broken: The Relations Between Napoleon and the Authors of France*. Fairleigh Dickinson University Press, 1993. <http://books.google.com/books?id=XrdFJV1iVBsC>.

Price, M. *The Perilous Crown: France Between Revolutions, 1814-1848*. Pan Macmillan, 2010. <http://books.google.com/books?id=CQowmIj8D4sC>.

Quintin, D. and B. Quintin. *Dictionnaire des colonels de Napoléon: Kronos N° 22*. SPM, 2013. <https://books.google.com/books?id=kt-MP75BW_sC>.

Regnault, J.C.L. *La campagne de 1815: mobilisation et concentration*. L. Fournier, 1935. <https://books.google.com/books?id=lKkOAQAAMAAJ>.

Roberts, A. *Napoleon: A Life*. Penguin Publishing Group, 2014. <https://books.google.com/books?id=rjVBAwAAQBAJ>.

Ropes, J.C. *The Campaign of Waterloo: A Military History*. C. Scribner's sons, 1892. <http://books.google.com/books?id=6F9AAAAAYAAJ>.

Spitzer, A.B. *Old Hatreds and Young Hopes: The French Carbonari Against the Bourbon Restoration*. Harvard University Press, 1971. <https://books.google.com/books?id=Teo7Ek6iHY0C>.

Taylor, G.V. and W.H. Hoyt. *Scholarship and Legend: William Henry Hoyt's Research on the Ney Controversy*. North Carolina, 1960. <https://books.google.com/books?id=KSjRAAAAMAAJ>.

Thiers, A., D.F. Campbell and H.W. Herbert. *History of the Consulate and the Empire of France Under Napoleon*. J. B. Lippincott \& Company, 1863. <http://books.google.com/books?id=dLlOAQAAIAAJ>.

Tulard, J.F. and T. J. *Dictionnaire Napoleon*. French \& European Publications, Incorporated, 1989. <https://books.google.com/books?id=XktEPQAACAAJ>.

Uffindell, A. and A. Roberts. *The Eagle's Last Triumph: Napoleon's Victory at Ligny, June 1815*. Greenhill, 2006. <https://books.google.com/books?id=ZaSBCl4JDMwC>.

Vachée, Colonel, *Napoleon at Work*, translated by G. Frederic Lees, London, 1914. < https://archive.org/details/napoleonatworkoovachuoft>

Vaulabelle, A. (de) *1815, Ligny-Waterloo*. Perrotin, 1866. <https://books.google.com/books?id=qxVdPvxXNjEC>.

Wilkes, J. *Encyclopaedia Londinensis*, or, *Universal dictionary of arts, sciences, and literature*. 1821. <http://books.google.com/books?id=0F0MAQAAMAAJ>.

About The Author

The son of a U.S. army major and Vietnam veteran, Stephen was raised in an ever-changing backdrop of military bases. His father, one of the largest military board game collectors in the U.S., kept the table clothed in game maps, recreating the battles of the eras. These strategy-based games cemented a foundation for future constructs.

A fascination with 19th Century military history developed after seeing the movies Zulu and Waterloo as a child, and Stephen became a fan of "The Thin Red Line."

Though initially biased against Napoleon, while doing a school report, he soon realized that the wars named for Napoleon were not an attempt to conquer Europe, as so often portrayed, but were Napoleon's efforts to defend France and its people's choice of government against the combined nobility of Europe, dedicated to destroying the French Revolution and reasserting the legitimacy of a royal family.

He began recreating Napoleon's battles, which allowed him to witness the leader's rare brilliance in real-time detail. In effort to share this with others, he began developing grand tactical military simulation computer games.

A game he co-created, *Napoleon in Russia: Borodino 1812*, won the Charles S. Roberts award for best pre-20th Century Computer Wargame (1987). Stephen followed this endeavor with an even more comprehensive game: *Napoleon vs. The Evil Monarchies: Austerlitz 1805* (1989).

The experience from computer games was eventually parlayed into a successful enterprise software career as a serial entrepreneur and technical visionary for companies such as Witness Systems, Inc., Cliffstone Corporation, and his current endeavor as Chief Scientist for OpenSpan, Inc.

Stephen lives in Canton Georgia with his wife Lorrie and his two kids, Alissa and Spencer.

Those wishing to discuss or debate the content of this book may contact the author directly at: stephen.beckett@mapleflowerhouse.com

About The Translator

Robert Curran

Certified in French to English translation by Words Language Services of Dublin, Ireland.

Member of American Translators Association, Delaware Valley Translators Association, Delaware Translator Information Network.

MA with a concentration in European History from West Chester University.

BA in Social Studies including French language study.
Teaching Certification in Social Studies.

Also translates: general, business, technical, and medical translations.

Email: rcurran1851@yahoo.com
Phone: 610-513-7808

Jean-Marc Largeaud also assisted with the translations, specifically contemporary rhetoric, idioms, and military terms.

www.ingramcontent.com/pod-product-compliance
Lightning Source LLC
Chambersburg PA
CBHW071358160426
42811CB00111B/2227/J